GOBI   6/20...   28 -

FRAGMENTARY
REPUBLICAN LATIN
V

LCL 542

FRAGMENTARY REPUBLICAN LATIN

ORATORY

PART 3

EDITED AND TRANSLATED BY

GESINE MANUWALD

HARVARD UNIVERSITY PRESS
CAMBRIDGE, MASSACHUSETTS
LONDON, ENGLAND
2019

First published 2019

LOEB CLASSICAL LIBRARY® is a registered trademark
of the President and Fellows of Harvard College

Library of Congress Control Number 2018962593
CIP data available from the Library of Congress

ISBN 978-0-674-99725-7

Composed in ZephGreek and ZephText by
Technologies 'N Typography, Merrimac, Massachusetts.
Printed on acid-free paper and bound by
Maple Press, York, Pennsylvania

CONTENTS

CONTENTS

CONTENTS

CONTENTS

CONTENTS

CONTENTS

CONTENTS

CONTENTS

ORATORY
PART 3

126 M. PORCIUS CATO MINOR

M. Porcius Cato minor (95–46 BC; praet. 54 BC; RE Porcius 16) killed himself in Utica during the African war against C. Iulius Caesar (121) and therefore was nicknamed Uticensis, also to distinguish him from his great-grandfather M. Porcius Cato Censorius (8). Cato served as military tribune, quaestor, Tribune of the People, and provincial governor and was an active member of the Senate. He was well known for his modesty, moral uprightness, and exemplary conduct in office, which led to clashes with other politicians (on his career and oratory see van der Blom 2016, 204–47, on his speeches pp. 315–22).

T 1 Cic. *Brut.* 118–19

tum BRUTUS: "quam hoc idem in nostris contingere intellego quod in Graecis, ut omnes fere Stoici prudentissimi in disserendo sint et id arte faciant sintque architecti paene verborum, idem traducti a disputando ad dicendum inopes reperiantur. unum excipio Catonem, in quo perfectissimo Stoico summam eloquentiam non desiderem . . ." [119] et ego [CICERO]: ". . ." inquam, ". . . tuus autem avunculus, quem ad modum scis, habet a Stoicis id quod ab illis petendum fuit; sed dicere didicit a dicendi magistris eorumque more se exercuit. . . ."

126 M. PORCIUS CATO MINOR

In Cicero it is noted that the oratory of Cato, though a Stoic, was not affected by the common defects of adherents of this philosophical school and that he even managed to include elements of Stoic doctrine successfully in public speeches; he was able to employ brevity or long speeches as the situation required (T 1–3). Cato's eloquence was appreciated (T 4–5), and he was said to practice effective public speaking (T 6).

A letter from Cato to Cicero is extant (Cic. Fam. 15.5).

T 1 Cicero, *Brutus*

Thereupon BRUTUS [said]: "Remarkable: I see the same thing applies to our countrymen as to the Greeks, that practically all Stoics are very able in precise exposition, and they do it skillfully and are almost architects of words; but when the same people are transferred from debating to speaking, they are found to be deficient. One exception I make for Cato, in whom, though a most accomplished Stoic, I feel no desire for the most perfect eloquence . . ." [119] And I [CICERO] said: ". . . And your uncle [Cato], as you know, has acquired from the Stoics what was to be sought from them, but he learned to speak from masters of speaking and trained himself in their methods. . . ."

T 2 Cic. *Parad. prooem.* 1–3

animadverti, Brute, saepe Catonem avunculum tuum,
cum in senatu sententiam diceret, locos graves ex philosophia tractare abhorrentes ab hoc usu forensi et publico,
sed dicendo consequi tamen ut illa etiam populo probabi-
lia viderentur. [2] quod eo maius est illi quam tibi aut
nobis, quia nos ea philosophia plus utimur quae peperit
dicendi copiam et in qua dicuntur ea quae non multum
discrepent ab opinione populari; Cato autem, perfectus
mea sententia Stoicus, et ea sentit quae non sane proban-
tur in vulgus, et in ea est haeresi quae nullum sequitur
florem orationis neque dilatat argumentum; minutis inter-
rogatiunculis quasi punctis quod proposuit efficit. [3] sed
nihil est tam incredibile quod non dicendo fiat probabile,
nihil tam horridum, tam incultum, quod non splendescat
oratione et tamquam excolatur. . . . Cato enim dumtaxat
de magnitudine animi, de continentia, de morte, de omni
laude virtutis, de diis immortalibus, de caritate patriae
Stoice solet oratoriis ornamentis adhibitis dicere . . .

T 3 Cic. *Leg.* 3.40

[M.:] nam brevitas non modo senatoris sed etiam oratoris
magna laus est in ‹dicenda› sententia,[1] nec est umquam

---

[1] ‹dicenda› sententia *Dyck* (sententia ‹dicenda› *Moser*)

T 2 Cicero, *Paradoxa Stoicorum*

I have often noticed, Brutus, that when your uncle Cato made a speech in the Senate, he dealt with weighty arguments drawn from philosophy that do not conform to our usual practice in the law courts and politics, but nevertheless achieved by his speaking that such things seemed acceptable even to the general public. [2] This is a greater achievement for him than it would be for you or us, because we make more use of that system of philosophy that is the parent of oratorical fluency and in which matters are put forward that do not greatly differ from popular opinion. But Cato, a perfect Stoic in my view, both holds opinions of a kind that are not at all accepted by the multitude, and belongs to a school of thought that does not aim at any oratorical ornament or employ a copious mode of exposition; it achieves what it has proposed by means of tiny questions like pinpricks. [3] But nothing is so impossible to believe that it cannot be made plausible by speaking, nothing so rough, so uncultured that it does not gain brilliance from eloquence and is ennobled, as it were. . . . For Cato at any rate usually speaks about grandeur of mind, about self-control, about death, about every glory of virtue, about the immortal gods, about the love for one's country in the Stoic way, while applying all oratorical ornaments . . .

T 3 Cicero, *On the Laws*

[M.:] For brevity in ⟨expressing⟩ an opinion is a great virtue on the part not only of a senator, but also of an ora-

longa oratione utendum, <quod fit ambitione saepis-
sime>,[2] nisi aut[3] <cum>[4] peccante senatu, nullo magistratu
adiuvante, tolli diem utile est, aut cum tanta causa est ut
opus sit oratoris copia vel ad hortandum vel ad docendum;
quorum generum in utroque magnus noster Cato est.

[2] quod fit ambitione saepissime *huc transposuit Bake, post*
peccante senatu *codd.*   [3] nisi aut *ed. Ald.*: nisi ut *codd.*
    [4] cum *hic add. Powell* (*ante* nullo magistratu *Ursinus ex cod.*)

T 4 Sall. *Cat.* 54.1

= **121** T 3.

T 5 Quint. *Inst.* 11.1.36

= **111** T 4.

T 6 Plut. *Cat. min.* 4.3–4

ἤσκει δὲ καὶ τὸν ὀργανικὸν εἰς πλήθη λόγον, ἀξιῶν
ὥσπερ ἐν πόλει μεγάλῃ τῇ πολιτικῇ φιλοσοφίᾳ καὶ
μάχιμον εἶναί τι παρατρεφόμενον. [4] οὐ μέντοι μεθ᾽
ἑτέρων ἐποιεῖτο τὰς μελέτας, οὐδ᾽ ἠκροάσατο λέγοντος οὐδείς, ἀλλὰ καὶ πρός τινα τῶν ἑταίρων εἰπόντα
"μέμφονταί σου Κάτων οἱ ἄνθρωποι τὴν σιωπήν,"
"μόνον" ἔφη "μὴ τὸν βίον. ἄρξομαι δὲ λέγειν, ὅταν
μὴ μέλλω λέγειν ἄξια σιωπῆς."

T 7 Quint. *Inst.* 12.7.3–4

... ideoque principes in re publica viri non detrectaverunt

6

tor. And a long speech ⟨which very often happens out of ambition⟩ should never be used unless either ⟨when⟩ the Senate is making a mistake and no magistrate is taking steps to prevent it, and it is therefore useful to use up the whole day, or when the matter is so important that copiousness of the orator is necessary to urge or to inform. Our Cato is great at both these types.

T 4 Sallust, *The War with Catiline*

= **121** T 3.

T 5 Quintilian, *The Orator's Education*

= **111** T 4.

T 6 Plutarch, *Life of Cato the Younger*

He [Cato] practiced also the kind of speaking effective with the multitude, deeming it right that in political philosophy, as in a great city, a certain warlike element should also be maintained. [4] He did not, however, perform his exercises in company with others, nor did anyone ever hear him rehearsing a speech. Indeed, to one of his companions, who said, "Men find fault with you, Cato, because of your silence," he replied: "Only [let them] not [blame] my life. I will begin to speak when I am not going to say what was worthy of silence."

T 7 Quintilian, *The Orator's Education*

. . . and leading men in the Republic have therefore not refused this field of duty [i.e., acting as prosecutors], and

hanc officii partem, creditique sunt etiam clari iuvenes
opsidem rei publicae dare malorum civium accusationem,
quia nec odisse improbos nec simultates provocare nisi
ex fiducia bonae mentis videbantur: [4] idque cum ab
Hortensio, Lucullis, Sulpicio, Cicerone, Caesare, plurimis
aliis, tum ab utroque Catone factum est: quorum alter
appellatus est sapiens, alter nisi creditur fuisse vix scio cui
reliquerit huius nominis locum . . .

On the Basilica Porcia in the Forum (F 8)

*Cato's first recorded appearance as an orator is his oppo-
sition to alterations (requested by the Tribunes of the
People) to the Basilica Porcia, built by his great-grandfather*

F 8 Plut. *Cat. min.* 5.1–5

ἡ δὲ καλουμένη Πορκία βασιλικὴ τιμητικὸν ἦν ἀνά-
θημα τοῦ παλαιοῦ Κάτωνος. εἰωθότες οὖν ἐκεῖ χρημα-
τίζειν οἱ δήμαρχοι, καὶ κίονος τοῖς δίφροις ἐμποδὼν
εἶναι δοκοῦντος, ἔγνωσαν ὑφελεῖν αὐτὸν ἢ μεταστῆ-
σαι. [2] τοῦτο Κάτωνα πρῶτον εἰς ἀγορὰν ἄκοντα
προήγαγεν· ἀντέστη γὰρ αὐτοῖς, καὶ πεῖραν ἅμα τοῦ
λόγου καὶ τοῦ φρονήματος δούς, ἐθαυμάσθη. [3] καὶ
γὰρ ὁ λόγος νεαρὸν μὲν οὐδὲν οὐδὲ κομψὸν εἶχεν,

even distinguished young men have been held to give a pledge to the Republic through the prosecution of bad citizens, because they would not hate evil men or provoke hostile encounters, it would seem, if not out of confidence in their own rectitude. [4] And this was done by Hortensius [Q. Hortensius Hortalus (**92**)], the Luculli [L. Licinius Lucullus (**90**) and M. Licinius Lucullus (**91**)], Sulpicius [P. Sulpicius Rufus (**76**)], Cicero, Caesar [C. Iulius Caesar Strabo (**73**) or C. Iulius Caesar (**121**)], and many others, particularly by each of the Catos, of whom one [M. Porcius Cato (**8**)] was called the wise, and as for the other, if he is not thought to have been [wise], I can hardly imagine to whom he could have surrendered the place for this title . . .

On the Basilica Porcia in the Forum (F 8)

*M. Porcius Cato (**8**). This seems to have been a single, impressive appearance before he entered public life and intervened more frequently later.*

F 8 Plutarch, *Life of Cato the Younger*

The so-called Basilica Porcia had been dedicated by the elder Cato [M. Porcius Cato (**8**)] when he was censor [184 BC]. Here, then, the Tribunes of the People were accustomed to transact business; and as a pillar was thought to be in the way of their seats, they determined to take it down or move it to another place. [2] This brought Cato for the first time, and against his wishes, into the Forum; for he opposed them, and he was admired for giving proof of both eloquence and high character. [3] For his speech

9

ἀλλ' ἦν ὄρθιος καὶ περιπαθὴς[1] καὶ τραχύς. οὐ μὴν
ἀλλὰ καὶ χάρις ἀγωγὸς ἀκοῆς ἐπέτρεχε τῇ τραχύτητι
τῶν νοημάτων, καὶ τὸ ἦθος αὐτοῦ καταμειγνύμενον
ἡδονήν τινα καὶ μειδίαμα τῷ σεμνῷ παρεῖχεν οὐκ
ἀπάνθρωπον. [4] ἡ δὲ φωνὴ μεγέθει μὲν ⟨ἦν⟩[2] ἀπο-
χρῶσα καὶ διαρκὴς εἰς τοσοῦτον ἐξικέσθαι δῆμον,
ἰσχὺν δὲ καὶ τόνον ἄρρηκτον εἶχε καὶ ἄτρυτον· ἡμέραν γὰρ ὅλην εἰπὼν πολλάκις οὐκ ἀπηγόρευσε. [5]
τότε δ' οὖν κρατήσας τῆς δίκης, πάλιν ἑαυτὸν εἰς τὴν
σιωπὴν καὶ τὴν ἄσκησιν συνέστειλε.

1 περιπαθὴς Cobet: περιπληθὴς codd.   2 add. Schaefer

In Support of Friends (F 9)

F 9 Plut. *Cat. min.* 16.1

ἐπανελθὼν δ' εἰς Ῥώμην, τὸν μὲν ἄλλον χρόνον κατ'
οἶκον Ἀθηνοδώρῳ ⟨συσχολάζων⟩[1] ἢ κατ' ἀγορὰν τοῖς
φίλοις παριστάμενος διετέλεσεν.

1 add. Emperius: συνών add. Sintenis

Against Q. Lutatius Catulus and His Client (F 9A)

When Cato was quaestor probably in 64 BC (MRR II 163
with n. 5), he made an effort to ensure good practices
among the clerks. One of them was taken to court because

had nothing that was juvenile or affected; instead, it was straightforward, full of matter, and harsh. Indeed, a charm attractive to the ear ran through the harshness of his sentiments, and the mingling of his character with them gave their austerity a kind of smiling graciousness that won men's hearts. [4] His voice <was> sufficiently loud and penetrating to reach the ears of so large a multitude, and it had a strength and tension that could not be broken or worn out; for he often spoke all day and did not get tired. [5] At this time, then, after winning his case, he went back again to his silence and his discipline.

In Support of Friends (F 9)

After his return to Rome from his military tribunate (67/66 BC), Cato is said to have assisted friends in court cases.

F 9 Plutarch, *Life of Cato the Younger*

After his return to Rome, he [Cato] spent most of his time at home <in the company of> Athenodorus [of Cordylium, Stoic philosopher] or in the Forum assisting his friends.

Against Q. Lutatius Catulus and His Client (F 9A)

of fraud, and Cato clashed with Q. Lutatius Catulus (96), who defended the clerk.

11

F 9A Plut. *Cat. min.* 16.5–10

. . . τὸν μὲν πρῶτον αὐτὸς[1] καταγνοὺς περὶ πίστιν ἐν κληρονομίᾳ γεγονέναι πονηρόν, ἀπήλασε τοῦ ταμιείου, δευτέρῳ δέ τινι ῥᾳδιουργίας προὔθηκε κρίσιν. [6] ᾧ Κάτλος Λουτάτιος ὁ τιμητὴς ἀνέβη βοηθήσων, ἀνὴρ μέγα τὸ τῆς ἀρχῆς ἔχων ἀξίωμα, τὸ δὲ τῆς ἀρετῆς {ἔχων}[2] μέγιστον, ὡς πάντων δικαιοσύνῃ καὶ σωφροσύνῃ Ῥωμαίων διαφέρων· ἦν δὲ καὶ τοῦ Κάτωνος ἐπαινέτης καὶ συνήθης διὰ τὸν βίον. [7] ὡς οὖν ἡττώμενος τοῖς δικαίοις ἐξῃτεῖτο φανερῶς τὸν ἄνθρωπον, οὐκ εἴα ταῦτα ποιεῖν αὐτὸν ὁ Κάτων· ἔτι δὲ μᾶλλον προσλιπαροῦντος, "αἰσχρόν" εἶπεν, "ὦ Κάτλε, σὲ τὸν τιμητὴν καὶ τοὺς ἡμετέρους βίους ὀφείλοντα δοκιμάζειν ὑπὸ τῶν ἡμετέρων ὑπηρετῶν ἐκβάλλεσθαι." [8] ταύτην τὴν φωνὴν ἀφέντος τοῦ Κάτωνος, ὁ Κάτλος προσέβλεψε μὲν αὐτὸν ὡς ἀμειψόμενος, εἶπε δ᾽ οὐδέν, ἀλλ᾽ εἴθ᾽ ὑπ᾽ ὀργῆς εἴθ᾽ ὑπ᾽ αἰσχύνης ἀπῆλθε σιωπῇ διηπορημένος. οὐ μὴν ἥλω γ᾽ ὁ ἄνθρωπος, [9] ἀλλ᾽ ἐπεὶ μιᾷ ψήφῳ τὰς ἀφιείσας ὑπερέβαλλον αἱ καθαιροῦσαι, καὶ Λόλλιος Μᾶρκος εἷς συνάρχων τοῦ Κάτωνος ὑπ᾽ ἀσθενείας ἀπελέλειπτο τῆς δίκης, πέμπει πρὸς τοῦτον ὁ Κάτλος, δεόμενος βοηθῆσαι τῷ ἀνθρώπῳ, κἀκεῖνος ἐν φορείῳ ⟨μετα⟩κομισθεὶς ⟨εἰς⟩ {μετὰ}[3] τὴν δίκην, ἔθετο τὴν ἀπολύουσαν. [10] οὐ μὴν ἐχρήσατό γε τῷ γραμματεῖ {ὁ}[4] Κάτων, οὐδὲ τὸν μισθὸν ἀπέδωκεν, οὐδ᾽ ὅλως ἐνάριθμον τοῦ Λολλίου τὴν ψῆφον ἔσχεν.

[1] αὐτὸς Ziegler: αὐτὸν vel αὐτῶν codd.

F 9A Plutarch, *Life of Cato the Younger*

. . . he [Cato] himself expelled from the treasury the chief
[of the clerks], whom he found guilty of a breach of trust
in the matter of an inheritance, and he brought a second
one to trial for fraud. [6] This person Catulus Lutatius [Q.
Lutatius Catulus (**96**)], the censor [in 65 BC], came forward to support, having great authority because of his
office, but the greatest because of his virtue, being thought
to surpass all Romans in justice and discretion; he was a
eulogist of Cato and was intimate with him on account of
his way of life. [7] Accordingly, when he [Catulus] had lost
the case on its merits and began to beg openly for the
acquittal of the man, Cato tried not to allow him to do this.
When he [Catulus] was even more importunate, he [Cato]
said: "It would be shameful, Catulus, if you who are censor
and should scrutinize our lives were thrown out of court
by our bailiffs." [8] When Cato had uttered these words,
Catulus fixed his eyes upon him as if he would make reply,
but he said nothing; instead, either from anger or from
shame, he went off in silence, much perplexed. However,
the man was not convicted, [9] but when the votes for
condemnation exceeded those for acquittal by a single
vote, and one Marcus Lollius [quaest. 64 BC], a colleague
of Cato, missed the trial because of illness, Catulus sent to
him, begging him to help the man. And he [Lollius], having been brought in a litter to the trial, cast the vote that
won acquittal. [10] Nevertheless, Cato did not employ the
clerk, or give him his pay, or in any way take Lollius' vote
into his reckoning.

---

² *del. Coraes*   ³ εἰς *add. et* μετὰ *transp. Ziegler*
⁴ *del. Sintenis*

On Bribery to the People (F 10)

F 10 Plut. *Cat. min.* 21.3

ἀποδειχθεὶς δὲ δήμαρχος σὺν ἑτέροις καὶ τῷ Με-
τέλλῳ, τὰς ὑπατικὰς ἀρχαιρεσίας ὁρῶν ὠνίους οὔσας,
ἐπετίμησε τῷ δήμῳ, καὶ καταπαύων τὸν λόγον ἐπώ-
μοσε τοῦ δόντος ἀργύριον ὅστις ἂν ᾖ κατηγορήσειν,
ἕνα Σιλανὸν ὑπεξελόμενος δι᾽ οἰκειότητα· Σερβιλίαν
γὰρ ἀδελφὴν Κάτωνος ὁ Σιλανὸς εἶχε.

Against L. Licinius Murena (F 11–12)

*In 63 BC Cato, along with Ser. Sulpicius Rufus (**118** F 6)
and two other supporters, prosecuted L. Licinius Murena
(cos. 62 BC) for ambitus in the election campaign. Murena
was defended by Q. Hortensius Hortalus (**92** F 36–37), M.*

F 11 Plut. *Cat. min.* 21.4–8

διὸ τοῦτον μὲν παρῆκε, Λεύκιον δὲ Μουρρήναν ἐδίω-
κεν, ἀργυρίῳ διαπραξάμενον ἄρχοντα μετὰ τοῦ Σιλα-
νοῦ γενέσθαι. . . . [7] τῆς δὲ δίκης λεγομένης ὁ Κικέ-
ρων, ὕπατος ὢν τότε καὶ τῷ Μουρρήνᾳ συνδικῶν,
πολλὰ διὰ τὸν Κάτωνα τοὺς Στωϊκοὺς φιλοσόφους
καὶ ταῦτα δὴ τὰ παράδοξα καλούμενα δόγματα χλευ-

On Bribery to the People (F 10)

As Tribune designate in 63 BC, Cato spoke before the People about bribery in that year's election campaign for the consulship (CCMR, App. A: 265).

F 10 Plutarch, *Life of Cato the Younger*

After he [Cato] was declared Tribune [for 62 BC] with others and with Metellus [Q. Caecilius Metellus Nepos (**120**)], seeing that the consular elections were affected by bribery, he rebuked the People; and, in concluding his speech, he swore that he would prosecute the briber, whoever he might be, making an exception only of Silanus [D. Iunius Silanus, cos. 62 BC] because of their familial relationship: for Silanus had Servilia, Cato's sister, as his wife. [continued by F 11]

Against L. Licinius Murena (F 11–12)

*Licinius Crassus Dives (**102** F 8–9), and Cicero (Cic. Mur.), who discussed alleged utterances of the opponents in his speech (TLRR 224; Plut. Cic. 35.4).*

F 11 Plutarch, *Life of Cato the Younger*

For this reason [continued from F 10] he [Cato] let him [D. Iunius Silanus] alone, but prosecuted Lucius Murena on the charge of having secured his becoming consul [for 62 BC] with Silanus by bribery. . . . [7] When the trial was held [63 BC], Cicero, who was consul at that time and one of Murena's advocates, railed and jested a lot at Cato's

15

ἄζων καὶ παρασκώπτων, γέλωτα παρεῖχε τοῖς δι-
κασταῖς. [8] τὸν οὖν Κάτωνά φασι διαμειδιάσαντα
πρὸς τοὺς παρόντας εἰπεῖν· "ὦ ἄνδρες, ὡς γελοῖον
ὕπατον ἔχομεν."

F 12 Cic. *Mur.* 3, 6, 11, 13, 31, 54, 56, 58, 66, 67, 68, 70,
72, 74, 78

negat fuisse rectum Cato me et consulem et legis ambitus
latorem et tam severe gesto consulatu causam L. Murenae
attingere. . . . [6] negat esse eiusdem severitatis Catilinam
exitium rei publicae intra moenia molientem verbis et
paene imperio ex urbe expulisse et nunc pro L. Murena
dicere. . . . [11] intellego, iudices, tris totius accusationis
partis fuisse, et earum unam in reprehensione vitae, alte-
ram in contentione dignitatis, tertiam in criminibus ambitus esse versatam. atque harum trium partium prima illa
quae gravissima debebat esse ita fuit infirma et levis ut
illos lex magis quaedam accusatoria quam vera male dicendi facultas de vita L. Murenae dicere aliquid coegerit.
obiecta est enim Asia . . . [13] saltatorem appellat L. Mure-
nam Cato. maledictum est, si vere obicitur, vehementis
accusatoris, sin falso, maledici conviciatoris. . . . [31] verum haec Cato nimium nos nostris verbis magna facere
demonstrat et oblitos esse bellum illud omne Mithridaticum cum mulierculis esse gestum. . . . [54] nunc mihi

expense about the Stoic philosophers and their so-called paradoxes; thus he made the judges laugh. [8] Then Cato, they say, said with a smile to the bystanders: "Gentlemen, what an amusing consul we have!"

F 12 Cicero, *Pro Murena*

Cato says that it was not right for me to accept L. Murena's case, as I am a consul [63 BC], have carried a law against bribery [*Lex Tullia de ambitu*: LPPR, p. 379], and have carried out my consulship in such severe fashion. . . . [6] He says that I am not showing the same severity in speaking now on behalf of L. Murena that I used in expelling Catiline from the city [of Rome] through my words [cf. Cic. *Cat.* 1] and virtually through my magisterial power when he was contriving the destruction of the Republic inside the city walls. . . . [11] I see, judges, that there were three parts of the prosecution as a whole, and that one of these focused on an attack upon his private life, another on disputing his fitness for office, and the third on charges of bribery. And of these three parts, that first one, which should have been the most serious, was so feeble and trivial that a sort of convention of accusers rather than any true opportunity for abuse compelled them to say something about L. Murena's private life. For Asia was laid to his charge . . . [13] Cato calls L. Murena a dancer. This is a reproach, if the criticism is true, from a forceful prosecutor; if it is false, from an abusive slanderer. . . . [31] Cato, however, shows that we are making too much of this [Murena's military achievements] in our speech and have forgotten that that entire war against Mithridates [king of Pontus] was fought against some little women. . . . [54]

tertius ille locus est relictus orationis, de ambitus criminibus, perpurgatus ab eis qui ante me dixerunt, a me, quoniam ita Murena voluit, retractandus; quo in loco . . . M.
Catoni, homini in omni virtute excellenti, de ipsius accusatione, de senatus consulto, de re publica respondebo. . . .
[56] . . . accusat M. Cato qui cum a Murena nulla re umquam alienus fuit, tum ea condicione nobis erat in hac
civitate natus ut eius opes, ut ingenium praesidio multis
etiam alienis, exitio vix cuiquam inimico esse deberet. . . .
[58] venio nunc ad M. Catonem, quod est fundamentum
ac robur totius accusationis; qui tamen ita gravis est accusator et vehemens ut multo magis eius auctoritatem quam
criminationem pertimescam. in quo ego accusatore, iudices, primum illud deprecabor ne quid L. Murenae dignitas illius, ne quid exspectatio tribunatus, ne quid totius
vitae splendor et gravitas noceat, denique ne ea soli huic
obsint bona M. Catonis quae ille adeptus est ut multis
prodesse possit. . . . [66] . . . quemquamne existimas Catone, proavo tuo, commodiorem, communiorem, modera-
tiorem fuisse ad omnem rationem humanitatis? de cuius
praestanti virtute cum vere graviterque diceres, domesti-
cum te habere dixisti exemplum ad imitandum. . . . [67]
. . . quid accusas, Cato, quid adfers ad iudicium, quid arguis? ambitum accusas; non defendo. me reprehendis,
quod idem defendam quod lege punierim. punivi ambi-

Now that third item of the speech remains for me, about the charges of bribery; it has been fully dealt with by those who have spoken before me [the other advocates for the defense]; it must be examined again by me since this is what Murena wished. In this context . . . I will reply to M. Cato, a man outstanding in every virtue, on his charge, on the decree of the Senate, on the state of the Republic. . . . [56] . . . A prosecutor is M. Cato, who was never estranged from Murena in any matter, who, moreover, was born in this community for us into such a position that his resources and talent should offer protection to many, even strangers, destruction rarely, even to an enemy. . . . [58] I come now to M. Cato, who is the root and core of the whole prosecution; he is, indeed, so authoritative and forceful a prosecutor that I fear his prestige far more than his charges. In the case of this prosecutor, judges, I shall first offer this prayer, that his authority, that his expectation of the Tribunate [62 BC], that the luster and dignity of his whole life may not do any harm to L. Murena; secondly, that he may not be the only man to be harmed by those resources that M. Cato has acquired so that he could help many. . . . [66] . . . Can you think of anyone more affable, more sociable, more inclined to every consideration of humanity than Cato, your great-grandfather [M. Porcius Cato (8)]? When you spoke of his outstanding virtue truthfully and seriously, you said that you had an example to imitate in your own family. . . . [67] . . . What accusation do you make, Cato, what allegation do you bring to court, what is your charge? You make an accusation of bribery; I do not defend it. You censure me for defending the very offense that I have punished by my law. I punished bribery, not innocence. I shall certainly pros-

19

tum, non innocentiam; ambitum vero ipsum vel tecum accusabo, si voles. dixisti senatus consultum me referente esse factum, si mercede[1] obviam candidatis issent, si conducti sectarentur, si gladiatoribus volgo locus tributim et item prandia si volgo essent data, contra legem Calpurniam factum videri. . . . [68] . . . "multi obviam prodierunt de provincia decedenti." consulatum petenti solet fieri; eccui[2] autem non proditur revertenti? "quae fuit ista multitudo?" . . . [70] "at sectabantur multi." . . . "quid opus est" inquit "sectatoribus?" . . . [72] "at spectacula sunt tributim data et ad prandium volgo vocati." . . . [74] at enim agit mecum austere et Stoice Cato, negat verum esse adlici benivolentiam cibo, negat iudicium hominum in magistratibus mandandis corrumpi voluptatibus oportere. ergo, ad cenam petitionis causa si quis vocat, condemnetur? "quippe" inquit "tu mihi summum imperium, ‹tu›[3] summam auctoritatem, tu gubernacula rei publicae petas fovendis hominum sensibus et deleniendis animis et adhibendis voluptatibus? utrum lenocinium" inquit "a grege delicatae iuventutis, an orbis terrarum imperium a populo Romano petebas?" horribilis oratio; sed eam usus, vita, mores, civitas ipsa respuit. . . . [78] at enim te ad accusandum res publica adduxit. credo, Cato, te isto animo atque ea opinione venisse; sed tu imprudentia laberis.

---

[1] conducti *add. nonnulli codd.*: corrupti *add. codd. cet.*: *del. Garatoni*   [2] eccui *ed. Ascensiana 1511*: et cui *codd.*
[3] *add. Lambinus*

ecute even with you a true case of bribery, if you wish. You said that on my proposal a decree of the Senate was passed that it be deemed a contravention of the *Lex Calpurnia* [*Lex [Acilia] Calpurnia de ambitu*, 67 BC: *LPPR*, p. 374] if men went to meet candidates for payment, if their companions were hired, if places were given tribe by tribe randomly at the gladiatorial games and if likewise dinners were given at random. . . . [68] . . . "Crowds went out to meet him coming back from the province [after Murena's provincial governorship in Gallia Transalpina in 64 BC]." [alleged point of opponent] That is the normal practice in the case of a consular candidate. And for whom do people not go out to meet them on their return home? "Who formed that large crowd?" . . . [70] "But a large crowd accompanied him." . . . "What need is there," he says, "of this retinue?" . . . [72] "But shows were given tribe by tribe and invitations to dinner were given at random." . . . [74] Cato, however, deals sternly with me and like a true Stoic: he says that it is wrong to attract goodwill with food; he says that one ought not to seduce men's judgment by means of pleasure in an election of magistrates. Thus, if anyone issues an invitation to dinner because of his candidacy, will he be condemned? "Indeed," he says, "would you seek supreme power, supreme authority, the government of the Republic by pandering to men's senses, bewitching their minds, and providing pleasures? Were you seeking," he says, "a job as a pimp from a gang of spoiled youths or world dominion from the Roman People?" A horrible speech; but convention, way of life, customs, the community itself reject it. . . . [78] But [concern for] the Republic prompted you to prosecute. I believe, Cato, that you have come with such a mind and such an opinion; but you slip up through lack of consideration.

21

FRL V: ORATORY, PART 3

On the Catilinarian Conspirators (F 13–16A)

In the discussion about the fate of the Catilinarian conspirators at the end of 63 BC, Cato supported severe punishment, in contrast to C. Iulius Caesar's (**121** F 32–36A)
milder view; the Senate adopted Cato's position (Suet. Iul.
14.2; App. B Civ. 2.6.21; Plut. Caes. 8.1–2; Cic. 21.4). A

F 13 Plut. Cat. min. 23.1–5

γενομένης δὲ τοιαύτης τῆς τροπῆς, καὶ ἁπάντων ἐπὶ
τὸ πρᾳότερον ῥυέντων καὶ φιλανθρωπότερον, ὁ Κάτων
πρὸς τὴν γνώμην ἀναστὰς εὐθὺς ἵετο τῷ λόγῳ μετ᾽
ὀργῆς καὶ πάθους, τόν τε Σιλανὸν κακίζων τῆς μετα-
βολῆς, καὶ καθαπτόμενος τοῦ Καίσαρος ὡς σχήματι
δημοτικῷ καὶ λόγῳ φιλανθρώπῳ τὴν πόλιν ἀνα-
τρέποντος, καὶ δεδιττομένου τὴν βουλὴν ἐφ᾽ οἷς αὐτὸν
ἔδει δεδιέναι καὶ ἀγαπᾶν εἰ τῶν γεγονότων ἀθῷος
ἀπαλλάξει[1] καὶ ἀνύποπτος, [2] οὕτως περιφανῶς καὶ
ἰταμῶς τοὺς κοινοὺς ἐξαρπάζων πολεμίους καὶ τὴν
παρ᾽ οὐδὲν ἐλθοῦσαν ἀπολέσθαι πατρίδα τοιαύτην
καὶ τοσαύτην ὁμολογῶν μὴ ἐλεεῖν, ἀλλ᾽ οὓς ἔδει
μὴ γενέσθαι μηδὲ φῦναι δακρύων καὶ ἀνακαλιόμενος,
εἰ φόβων[2] μεγάλων καὶ κινδύνων ἀπαλλάξουσι τὴν
πόλιν ἀποθανόντες. [3] τοῦτον μόνον ὧν Κάτων εἶπε
διασῴζεσθαί φασι τὸν λόγον, Κικέρωνος τοῦ ὑπάτου
τοὺς διαφέροντας ὀξύτητι τῶν γραφέων σημεῖα προ-

---

[1] ἀπαλλάξει Emperius: ἀπαλλάξειε duo codd.: ἀπαλλάξαι
codd. cet.   [2] φόβων Naber: φόνων codd. (φόνων καὶ
μεγάλων Reiske, μεγ. φ. καὶ Sintenis)

22

On the Catilinarian Conspirators (F 13–16A)

version of the speech is presented by Sallust (F 16A; cf.
121 *F 36A). According to Plutarch (F 13), this was the*
only speech of Cato's to be preserved, because Cicero made
arrangements for it to be recorded.

F 13 Plutarch, *Life of Cato the Younger*

After such a change had been made and all had rushed to
the milder and more humane option [suggested by C. Iulius Caesar (**121**), F 32–36A], Cato rose to give his opinion
and launched at once into a speech full of passion and
anger, abusing Silanus [D. Iunius Silanus, cos. 62 BC] for
his change of mind [since he had originally proposed the
death penalty] and assailing Caesar: he, under a popular
pretext and with humane words, was trying to subvert the
state and was seeking to frighten the Senate in a case
where he himself had to be afraid and should be pleased
if he came off guiltless of what had been done and free
from suspicion, [2] since he was so openly and recklessly
trying to rescue their common enemies, while for his
country, which had been on the brink of ruin, and was so
good and great, he confessed that he had no pity; yet for
men who ought not to have lived or been born even, he
was shedding tears and lamenting, when by their deaths
they would free the community from great fears and per-
ils. [3] This speech only of those that Cato delivered has
been preserved, they say: Cicero the consul [63 BC] had
previously given to those clerks who excelled in rapid writing instruction in the use of signs, which, in small and

διδάξαντος, ἐν μικροῖς καὶ βραχέσι τύποις πολλῶν
γραμμάτων ἔχοντα δύναμιν, εἶτ᾽ ἄλλον ἀλλαχόσε τοῦ
βουλευτηρίου σποράδην ἐμβαλόντος. [4] οὔπω γὰρ
ἤσκουν οὐδ᾽ ἐκέκτηντο τοὺς καλουμένους σημειογρά-
φους, ἀλλὰ τότε πρῶτον εἰς ἴχνος τι καταστῆναι λέ-
γουσιν. [5] ἐκράτησε δ᾽ οὖν ὁ Κάτων καὶ μετέστησε
τὰς γνώμας, ὥστε θάνατον καταψηφίσασθαι τῶν ἀν-
δρῶν.

F 14 Cic. *Sest.* 61

consule me cum esset designatus tribunus plebis, obtulit
in discrimen vitam suam; dixit eam sententiam cuius invidiam capitis periculo sibi praestandam videbat; dixit vehementer, egit acriter; ea quae sensit prae se tulit; dux, auctor, actor rerum illarum fuit, non quo periculum suum non
videret, sed in tanta rei publicae tempestate nihil sibi nisi
de patriae periculis cogitandum putabat.

F 15 Cic. *Att.* 12.21.1

legi Bruti epistulam eamque tibi remisi, sane non pruden-
ter rescriptum ad ea quae requisieras. sed ipse viderit.
quamquam illud turpiter ignorat: Catonem primum sententiam putat de animadversione dixisse, quam omnes
ante dixerant praeter Caesarem, et, cum ipsius Caesaris

short figures, comprised the force of many letters; these clerks he had then distributed in various parts all over the Senate house. [4] For up to that time the Romans did not employ or even possess so-called shorthand writers, but then for the first time, they say, some steps toward the practice were taken. [5] At any rate Cato carried the day and changed their minds, so that they decreed the men's' death.

F 14 Cicero, *Pro Sestio*

During my consulship [63 BC], when he [Cato] was Tribune of the People designate, he exposed his life to danger; he expressed such an opinion in the Senate, for the unpopularity of which he saw that he would have to be responsible at the risk of his life; he spoke vehemently, he argued energetically; he openly expressed what he felt; he was the leader, the instigator, the authority for those measures; not that he did not see the danger to himself, but he thought that, amid such a storm in the Republic, he should think of nothing except the dangers to his country.

F 15 Cicero, *Letters to Atticus*

I have read Brutus' [M. Iunius Brutus (**158**)] letter and am returning it to you, not a very sagacious answer to what you had inquired about [concerning Brutus' work on Cato; cf. **158** F 27–28]. But he shall see to that himself. Yet, disgracefully, he [Brutus] is ignorant of that matter: he thinks [as transpires from his piece] that Cato was the first to put forward the proposal for punishment (which all previous speakers had advocated except Caesar), and although the statement by Caesar himself [C. Iulius Caesar

tam severa fuerit qui tum praetorio loco dixerit, consularium putat leniores fuisse, Catuli, Servili, Lucullorum, Curionis, Torquati, Lepidi, Gelli, Vulcati, Figuli, Cottae, L. Caesaris, C. Pisonis, M'. Glabrionis, etiam[1] Silani, Murenae, designatorum consulum. cur ergo in sententiam Catonis? quia verbis luculentioribus et pluribus rem eandem comprehenderat. me autem hic laudat quod rettulerim, non quod patefecerim, cohortatus[2] sim, quod denique ante quam consulerem ipse iudicaverim. quae omnia quia Cato laudibus extulerat in caelum perscribendaque censuerat, idcirco in eius sententiam est facta discessio. hic autem se etiam tribuere multum mi putat quod scripserit "optimum consulem."

[1] *transp. Boot*: etiam *ante* M'. Glabrionis *codd.*   [2] quod *ante* cohortatus *add. Victorius*

F 16 Vell. Pat. 2.35.3–4

hic tribunus plebis designatus et adhuc admodum adules-

(**121**), F 32–36A], who then spoke in the praetorian position [praet. 62 BC], was so severe, he [Brutus] thinks that
those of the ex-consuls were more lenient [cf. Cic. *Phil.*
2.12]: those of Catulus [Q. Lutatius Catulus, cos. 78 BC],
Servilius [P. Servilius Vatia Isauricus, cos. 79 BC], the
Luculli [L. Licinius Lucullus (**90**), cos. 74 BC; M. Licinius
Lucullus (**91**), cos. 73 BC], Curio [C. Scribonius Curio
(**86**), cos. 76 BC], Torquatus [L. Manlius Torquatus (**109**),
cos. 65 BC], Lepidus [M'. Aemilius Lepidus, cos. 66 BC],
Gellius [L. Gellius Poplicola (**101**), cos. 72 BC], Vulcatius
[L. Volcatius Tullus, cos. 66 BC], Figulus [C. Marcius
Figulus, cos. 64 BC], Cotta [L. Aurelius Cotta, cos. 65
BC], L. Caesar [L. Iulius Caesar, cos. 64 BC], C. Piso [C.
Calpurnius Piso (**108**), cos. 67 BC], M'. Glabrio [M'.
Acilius Glabrio, cos. 67 BC], even Silanus [D. Iunius Sila-
nus] and Murena [L. Licinius Murena], the consuls designate [for 62 BC]. Why then on Cato's motion? Because it
had comprised the same substance in more impressive
and ample wording. And this man here [Brutus] praises
me for bringing the question before the Senate, not for
exposing the plot, for urging them on, finally for passing
my own judgment before I asked their opinion. Because
Cato had praised all this to the skies and asked for it to be
officially recorded, therefore the vote was called on his
motion. And this man here [Brutus] thinks he is even giving me a fine tribute because he has written "an excellent
consul."

F 16 Velleius Paterculus, *Compendium of Roman History*

As Tribune of the People designate and still quite a young
man, while others [C. Iulius Caesar (**121**), F 32–36A]

cens, cum alii suaderent, ut per municipia Lentulus con-
iuratique custodirentur, paene inter ultimos interrogatus
sententiam, tanta vi animi atque ingenii invectus est in
coniurationem, eo ardore oris orationem omnium lenita-
tem suadentium societate consilii suspectam fecit, [4] sic
inpendentia ex ruinis incendiisque urbis et commutatione
status publici pericula exposuit, ita consulis virtutem am-
plificavit, ut universus senatus in eius sententiam transiret
animadvertendumque in eos, quos praediximus, censeret
maiorque pars ordinis eius Ciceronem prosequerentur
domum.

F 16A Sall. *Cat.* 52.1–53.1

*After C. Iulius Caesar presented his view [**121** F 36A],
Cato is said to have made a speech along the following
lines: Cato points out that it is not a question of prosecuting offenses committed, but of taking precautions. To encourage the audience, he appeals to their concern for their
possessions; he adds that he has often deplored the ex-
travagance and greed of current citizens, but public prosperity has enabled this careless attitude. Now, however, it
is no longer a question of morals or greatness; what is at
issue is who will control the Republic. In these circumstances Caesar's advice is worthless and suggests fear on
his part. Cato reminds the senators that they are passing
a decree concerning Catiline's army and all the conspira-*

were urging that Lentulus [P. Cornelius Lentulus Sura (**100**)] and the conspirators should be placed in custody in Italian towns, he [Cato], though practically among the last to be asked for his opinion, inveighed against the conspiracy with such great vigor of spirit and intellect; with such earnestness of expression he made the speeches of all those who urged leniency suspect of complicity in the plot; [4] such a picture did he present of the impending dangers from the destruction and burning of the city [of Rome] and the subversion of the political situation; in such a way did he extol the consul's virtue, that the entire Senate passed over to the support of his motion and voted to impose the death penalty upon those whom we have mentioned earlier, and the majority of the senators escorted Cicero to his home.

F 16A Sallust, *The War with Catiline*

tors; the more vigorously this is done, the weaker will be the opponents' courage. He recalls that the ancestors have made the Republic great not by arms, but by high moral values, now lost. Then he questions whether the senators are hesitating what to do with foes seized within the walls; this is not the place for compassion, and there should be no doubt about what to decree with regard to the most ruthless traitors. There is need of haste, with the Republic in the greatest peril; therefore, only punishment after the manner of the forefathers is appropriate. The Senate praises this proposal, and a corresponding decree is passed.

Against Consul M. Pupius Piso Frugi
Calpurnianus Before the People (F 17)

*In 61 BC Cato spoke against the consul M. Pupius Piso Frugi Calpurnianus (**104**), who had put forward a bill concerning an investigation into P. Clodius Pulcher (**137**),*

F 17 Cic. *Att.* 1.14.5

nam cum dies venisset rogationi ex senatus consulto ferendae . . . Piso autem consul, lator rogationis, idem erat dissuasor. operae Clodianae pontis occuparant, tabellae ministrabantur ita ut nulla daretur "uti rogas." hic tibi ‹in›[1] rostra Cato advolat, commulcium Pisoni consuli mirificum facit, si id est commulcium, vox plena gravitatis, plena auctoritatis, plena denique salutis. accedit eodem etiam noster Hortensius, multi praeterea boni; insignis vero opera Favoni[2] fuit.

[1] in *add. Boot*: ad *add. A. Klotz*   [2] favoni *duo codd.*: avoni *codd. plerique*

On the Tax Collectors in the Senate (F 18–20)

Against Consul M. Pupius Piso Frugi
Calpurnianus Before the People (F 17)

for having disturbed the Bona Dea cult celebrations (Lex
Pupia Valeria de incestu Clodii: LPPR, *p. 385*).

F 17 Cicero, *Letters to Atticus*

When the day had come for the bill to be put forward [to
the meeting of the People] according to the decree of the
Senate . . . But the consul Piso [M. Pupius Piso Frugi
Calpurnianus (**104**)], the proposer of the bill, also spoke
against it. Clodius' [P. Clodius Pulcher (**137**)] roughs had
taken possession of the gangways [leading to the voting
compartments]; the voting tablets were being distributed
in such a way that none saying "aye" were given out. At
this point Cato rushes <to> the Rostra, he gives consul Piso
a spectacular dressing-down, if a speech full of dignity, full
of authority, indeed full of salvation is a dressing-down.
Our friend Hortensius [Q. Hortensius Hortalus (**92**)] also
joined him, many honest men besides; Favonius' effort
[M. Favonius (**166**), F 2] in fact was especially notable.

On the Tax Collectors in the Senate (F 18–20)

In 61–60 BC Cato opposed arrangements for the benefit
of the tax collectors, delivering at least one long speech in
the Senate.

31

F 18 Schol. Bob. ad Cic. *Planc.* 31 (p. 157.24–31 Stangl)

quod autem de patre dicit, illud est: cum princeps esset publicanorum Cn. Plancii pater et societas eadem in exercendis vectigalibus gravissimo damno videretur adfecta, desideratum est in senatu nomine publicanorum ut cum iis ratio putaretur lege Sempronia et remissionis tantum fieret de summa pecuniae quantum aequitas postularet, pro quantitate damnorum quibus fuerant hostili incursione vexati. adfuit igitur Caesar causae publicanorum eorumque desideriis:[1] contradixit pro vigore duritiae suae M. Cato et diem totum prolixitate orationis suae occupavit, ut senatus decernendi spatium non haberet.

[1] *em. Leo Ziegler*: Ad | it igitur Caesar causae | publicanorum eorū | quib. fuerant hostili᾽ | incursione uexati Ad | fuit igitur Caesar᾽ que | desideriis *cod.*

F 19 Cic. *Att.* 1.18.7

unus est qui curet, constantia magis et integritate quam, ut mihi videtur, consilio aut ingenio, Cato; qui miseros publicanos, quos habuit amantissimos sui, tertium iam mensem vexat neque iis a senatu responsum dari patitur.

F 20 Cic. *Att.* 2.1.8

nam Catonem nostrum non tu amas plus quam ego; sed tamen ille optimo animo utens et summa fide nocet interdum rei publicae; dicit enim tamquam in Platonis πολι-

F 18 Scholia Bobiensia to Cicero, *Pro Plancio*

And what he [Cicero] says about the father is this: When Cn. Plancius' father was the leader of the tax collectors, and that very society seemed to be afflicted with very great financial loss in carrying out the tax business, it was requested in the Senate, in the name of the tax collectors, that accounts be made up with them under the *Lex Sempronia* [*Lex Sempronia de novis portoriis*: *LPPR*, p. 311] and so much of a reduction incurred from the sum of money as fairness demanded, in proportion to the extent of the financial losses by which they had been affected through the inroads made by the enemy. Therefore Caesar [C. Iulius Caesar (**121**)] supported the case of the tax collectors and their demands: M. Cato spoke against in line with the vigor of his austerity and used up the entire day by the prolixity of his speech, so that the Senate did not have time to decide.

F 19 Cicero, *Letters to Atticus*

There is one man who cares for that, with more resolution and integrity than, it seems to me, judgment or intelligence, Cato: he is tormenting the unfortunate tax collectors, whom he had as his most devoted friends, for the third month now, and he does not grant them to be given an answer from the Senate.

F 20 Cicero, *Letters to Atticus*

For, as for our friend Cato, you do not love him more than I do. Still, despite having the best intentions and the greatest integrity, he sometimes does damage to the Republic; for he gives his opinion in the Senate as though in Plato's

33

τεία, non tamquam in Romuli faece, sententiam. . . . quid
impudentius publicanis renuntiantibus? fuit tamen reti-
nendi ordinis causa facienda iactura. restitit et pervicit
Cato.

On C. Iulius Caesar in the Senate (F 21)

*When C. Iulius Caesar (121) returned from Hispania in
60 BC and asked both for a triumph and to stand as a
candidate for the consulship from outside the city of Rome,*

F 21 Plut. *Cat. min.* 31.3–6

ὁ γὰρ Καῖσαρ ἀπὸ τῆς ἐν Ἰβηρίᾳ στρατηγίας ἐπανή-
κων, ἅμα μὲν ὑπατείαν ἐβούλετο παραγγέλλειν, ἅμα
δ᾽ ᾔτει θρίαμβον. [4] ἐπεὶ δὲ κατὰ νόμον ἔδει τοὺς μὲν
ἀρχὴν μετιόντας παρεῖναι, τοὺς δὲ μέλλοντας εἰσ-
ελαύνειν θρίαμβον ἔξω τείχους ὑπομένειν, [5] ἠξίου
παρὰ τῆς βουλῆς αὐτῷ δοθῆναι δι᾽ ἑτέρων αἰτεῖσθαι
τὴν ἀρχήν. βουλομένων δὲ πολλῶν, ἀντέλεγεν ὁ Κά-
των· ὡς δ᾽ ᾔσθετο χαριζομένους τῷ Καίσαρι, λέγων
ὅλην κατανάλωσε τὴν ἡμέραν, καὶ τὴν βουλὴν οὕτως
ἐξέκρουσε. [6] χαίρειν οὖν ἐάσας τὸν θρίαμβον ὁ Καῖσαρ εἰσελθὼν εὐθὺς εἴχετο Πομπηΐου καὶ τῆς ὑπα-
τείας·. . .

Republic, not in Romulus' cesspool. . . . What could be more shameless than tax collectors repudiating their contract? All the same, the loss was worth incurring to keep this group on our side. Cato opposed them and carried his point.

On C. Iulius Caesar in the Senate (F 21)

Cato opposed this request (cf. Plut. Caes. 13.1–2; Cass. Dio 37.54.2).

F 21 Plutarch, *Life of Cato the Younger*

For Caesar [C. Iulius Caesar (**121**)], on returning from his praetorship in Hispania [61 BC], wanted to be a candidate for the consulship and at the same time asked for a triumph. [4] But since by law candidates for a magistracy must be present, while those about to celebrate a triumph must remain outside the walls, [5] he asked permission from the Senate through others to stand for the office. While many were willing, Cato opposed it; when he noticed that they were ready to appease Caesar, he consumed the whole day in speaking and thus adjourned the Senate. [6] Accordingly, Caesar gave up his triumph, entered the city, and at once attached himself to Pompey [Cn. Pompeius Magnus (**111**), with whom Caesar became allied in 60 BC] and the consulship [for 59 BC]. . . . [continued by F 22]

FRL V: ORATORY, PART 3

On C. Iulius Caesar's Agrarian Law (F 22–23)

F 22 Plut. *Cat. min.* 31.6–33.4

. . . ἀποδειχθεὶς δὲ ὕπατος, τήν τε Ἰουλίαν ἐνεγγύη-
σεν αὐτῷ, καὶ συστάντες ἤδη μετ᾽ ἀλλήλων ἐπὶ τὴν
πόλιν, ὁ μὲν εἰσέφερε νόμους, τοῖς πένησι κληρου-
χίαν καὶ νομὴν χώρας διδόντας, ὁ δὲ παρῆν τοῖς
νόμοις βοηθῶν. [7] οἱ δὲ περὶ Λεύκολλον καὶ Κικέρωνα
Βύβλῳ τῷ ἑτέρῳ τῶν ὑπάτων συντάξαντες ἑαυτοὺς
ἀντέπραττον, μάλιστα δὲ Κάτων, ἤδη μὲν ὑφορώμε-
νος τὴν Καίσαρος καὶ Πομπηΐου φιλίαν καὶ σύστα-
σιν ἐπ᾽ οὐδενὶ δικαίῳ γεγενημένην, φοβεῖσθαι δὲ φά-
σκων οὐ τὴν νομὴν τῆς χώρας, ἀλλ᾽ ὃν ἀντὶ ταύτης
ἀπαιτήσουσι μισθὸν οἱ χαριζόμενοι καὶ δελεάζοντες
τὸ πλῆθος. [32.1] ὡς δὲ ταῦτα λέγων τήν τε βουλὴν
ὁμόψηφον εἶχε καὶ τῶν ἐκτὸς ἀνθρώπων οὐκ ὀλίγοι
παρίσταντο δυσχεραίνοντες τὴν ἀτοπίαν τοῦ Καίσαρος— [2] . . . [33.1] ἐπαρθεὶς οὖν ὁ Καῖσαρ ἄλλον εἰσέφερε νόμον, τὴν Καμπανίαν σχεδὸν ὅλην προσκατα-
νέμοντα τοῖς ἀπόροις καὶ πένησιν· ἀντέλεγε δ᾽ οὐδεὶς
πλὴν τοῦ Κάτωνος, [2] καὶ τοῦτον ἀπὸ τοῦ βήματος ὁ

On C. Iulius Caesar's Agrarian Law (F 22–23)

*After C. Iulius Caesar (**121**) had become consul (59 BC),*
Cato spoke against his proposals for an agrarian law (Lex
Iulia agraria: LPPR, *pp. 387–88; cf. Plut.* Caes. *14.11;*
Suet. Iul. *20.7;* Val. Max. *2.10.7;* Cass. Dio *38.3).*

F 22 Plutarch, *Life of Cato the Younger*

. . . [continued from F 21] After he [C. Iulius Caesar
(**121**)] had been elected consul, he joined Julia [Caesar's
daughter] to him [Cn. Pompeius Magnus (**111**)] in marriage, and now that the two were united with one another
against the city, the one would bring in laws offering allot-
ment and distribution of land to the poor, the other would
be there supporting the laws. [7] But the party of Lucullus
[L. Licinius Lucullus (**90**)] and Cicero, attaching themselves to Bibulus [M. Calpurnius Bibulus (**122**)], the other
consul [59 BC], worked against the measures, above all
Cato, who now suspected that the friendly alliance between Caesar and Pompey had been made for no just
purpose and declared that he was afraid, not of the distribution of land, but of the reward that would be demanded
in return for this by those who were gratifying and enticing
the multitude. [32.1] By saying such things, he made the
Senate unanimous, and not a few of the men outside the
Senate supported him, unhappy with the strange conduct
of Caesar— [2] . . . [33.1] Elated, then, Caesar introduced
another law, which provided that almost the whole of
Campania be divided among the poor and needy [*Lex
Iulia agraria campana* (?): *LPPR*, pp. 387–88]. No one
spoke against the law except Cato, [2] and him Caesar

Καῖσαρ εἷλκεν εἰς τὸ δεσμωτήριον, οὐδέν τι μᾶλλον
ὑφιέμενον τῆς παρρησίας, ἀλλ' ἐν τῷ βαδίζειν ἅμα
περὶ τοῦ νόμου διαλεγόμενον καὶ παραινοῦντα παύ-
σασθαι τοιαῦτα πολιτευομένους. [3] ἐπηκολούθει δ' ἡ
βουλὴ μετὰ κατηφείας καὶ τοῦ δήμου τὸ βέλτιστον
ἀγανακτοῦν σιωπῇ καὶ ἀχθόμενον, ὥστε τὸν Καίσαρα μὴ λανθάνειν βαρέως φέροντας, ἀλλὰ φιλονι-
κῶν καὶ περιμένων ὑπὸ τοῦ Κάτωνος ἐπίκλησιν γενέσθαι καὶ δέησιν, προῆγεν. [4] ἐπεὶ δ' ἐκεῖνος ἦν δῆλος
οὐδὲ μέλλων <τούτων> τι ποιήσειν,[1] ἡττηθεὶς ὑπ' αἰσχύνης καὶ ἀδοξίας ὁ Καῖσαρ αὐτός τινα τῶν δημάρχων ὑφῆκε, πείσας ἐξελέσθαι τὸν Κάτωνα.

[1] μέλλων <τούτων> τι ποιήσειν *Reiske*: μελλήσων τι ποιεῖν
codd.

F 23 Gell. *NA* 4.10.8

in eodem libro Capitonis id quoque scriptum est [C.
Ateius Capito, F 18 Huschke / Seckel / Kübler]: "C." inquit "Caesar consul M. Catonem sententiam rogavit. Cato
rem, quae consulebatur, quoniam non e republica videbatur, perfici nolebat. eius rei ducendae gratia longa oratione
utebatur eximebatque dicendo diem. erat enim ius sena-
tori, ut sententiam rogatus diceret ante quicquid vellet
aliae rei et quoad vellet. Caesar consul viatorem vocavit
eumque, cum finem non faceret, prendi loquentem et in
carcerem duci iussit. senatus consurrexit et prosequebatur

ordered to be dragged from the Rostra to prison: he [Cato] did not any the more rein in his bold utterances, but, as he walked along, at the same time he discoursed about the law and advised the citizens to put a stop to such matters. [3] Moreover, the Senate followed him with downcast looks, as well as the best part of the People, in silence, though annoyed and troubled, so that it was not hidden from Caesar that they were displeased; but being obstinate and expecting that appeal or entreaty would come from Cato, he had him led along. [4] When, however, it was clear that he [Cato] did not even think of doing anything ⟨of that sort⟩, Caesar, overcome by shame and infamy, himself secretly approached one of the Tribunes of the People, persuading him to rescue Cato.

F 23 Gellius, *Attic Nights*

In the same book [*De officio senatorio*] of Capito [C. Ateius Capito, F 18 Huschke / Seckel / Kübler] this too is written: "The consul C. Caesar [C. Iulius Caesar (**121**), cos. 59 BC]," he says, "called upon M. Cato for his opinion. Cato did not wish to have the matter that was being debated concluded, since it did not seem to be in the interest of the Republic. So as to draw out proceedings, he presented a long speech and used up the whole day in talking. For it was a senator's right, when asked for his opinion, to speak beforehand on any other subject he wished and for as long as he wished. Caesar, the consul, summoned an attendant and ordered him, since he would not stop, to be arrested while speaking and taken to prison. The Senate

Catonem in carcerem. hac" inquit "invidia facta Caesar destitit et mitti Catonem iussit."

On Pompey and Crassus to the People (F 24)

In the elections for the praetorship of 55 BC, Cato was defeated by a candidate supported by Cn. Pompeius Magnus (111) and M. Licinius Crassus Dives (102) through

F 24 Plut. *Cat. min.* 42.5–6

αὖθις δὲ πολλῷ χρησάμενοι τῷ δεκασμῷ, ⟨καὶ⟩[1] τοὺς βελτίστους ὤσαντες ἐκ τοῦ πεδίου βίᾳ, διεπράξαντο Βατίνιον ἀντὶ Κάτωνος αἱρεθῆναι στρατηγόν. [6] ἔνθα δὴ λέγεται τοὺς μὲν οὕτω παρανόμως καὶ ἀδίκως θεμένους τὴν ψῆφον εὐθὺς ὥσπερ ἀποδράντας οἴχεσθαι, τοῖς δ' ἄλλοις συνισταμένοις καὶ ἀγανακτοῦσι δημάρχου τινὸς αὐτόθι παρασχόντος ἐκκλησίαν, καταστάντα τὸν Κάτωνα, ἅπαντα μὲν ὥσπερ ἐκ θεῶν ἐπίπνουν τὰ μέλλοντα τῇ πόλει προειπεῖν, παρορμῆσαι δὲ τοὺς πολίτας ἐπὶ Πομπήιον καὶ Κράσσον, ὡς τοιαῦτα συνειδότας αὐτοῖς καὶ τοιαύτης ἁπτομένους πολιτείας, δι' ἣν ἔδεισαν Κάτωνα μὴ στρατηγῶν αὐτῶν περιγένηται.

[1] add. Ziegler

arose in a body and accompanied Cato to the prison. With such indignation aroused," he says, "Caesar yielded and ordered Cato to be released."[1]

[1] This passage does not mention the agrarian law, but it refers to a measure during Caesar's consulship, and the description of the incident is similar to F 22, where it is connected with the agrarian law.

On Pompey and Crassus to the People (F 24)

bribery, influence on associates, and changes to laws. Thereupon, Cato, in a speech to the People, criticized the procedures and the men involved (CCMR, App. A: 319).

F 24 Plutarch, *Life of Cato the Younger*

Then they [Cn. Pompeius Magnus (**111**) and M. Licinius Crassus Dives (**102**)], resorting again to extensive bribery ⟨and⟩ ejecting the best citizens from the Campus [Martius] by force, got Vatinius [P. Vatinius] elected praetor [for 55 BC] instead of Cato. [6] Then, indeed, it is said, those who had thus illegally and wrongfully cast their votes went off at once like runaways, while the others, who were banding together and expressing their indignation, when a Tribune had formed an assembly there, were addressed by Cato: as if inspired by gods, he foretold all that would happen to the city [of Rome] and tried to set the citizens against Pompey and Crassus, who, he said, were privy to such plans and engaged in such a policy as a result of which they were afraid of Cato, lest as praetor he should get the better of them.

41

On Lex Trebonia de provinciis consularibus (*F 25*)

F 25 Plut. *Cat. min.* 43.1–8

Γαΐου δὲ Τρεβωνίου γράψαντος νόμον ὑπὲρ νομῆς
ἐπαρχιῶν τοῖς ὑπάτοις, ὥστε τὸν μὲν Ἰβηρίαν ἔχοντα
καὶ Λιβύην ὑφ᾽ αὑτῷ,[1] τὸν δὲ Συρίαν καὶ Αἴγυπτον,
οἷς βούλοιντο πολεμεῖν καὶ καταστρέφεσθαι ναυτι-
καῖς καὶ πεζικαῖς δυνάμεσιν ἐπιόντας, [2] οἱ μὲν ἄλλοι
τὴν ἀντίπραξιν καὶ κώλυσιν ἀπεγνωκότες, ἐξέλιπον
καὶ τὸ ἀντειπεῖν, Κάτωνι δ᾽ ἀναβάντι πρὸ τῆς ψηφο-
φορίας ἐπὶ τὸ βῆμα καὶ βουλομένῳ λέγειν μόλις
ὡρῶν δυεῖν λόγον ἔδωκαν. [3] ὡς δὲ πολλὰ λέγων καὶ
διδάσκων καὶ προθεσπίζων κατανάλωσε τὸν χρόνον,
οὐκέτι λέγειν αὐτὸν εἴων, ἀλλ᾽ ἐπιμένοντα κατέσπα-
σεν ὑπηρέτης προσελθών. [4] ὡς δὲ καὶ κάτωθεν ἱστά-
μενος ἐβόα καὶ τοὺς ἀκούοντας καὶ συναγανακτοῦν-
τας εἶχε, πάλιν ὁ ὑπηρέτης ἐπιλαβόμενος καὶ ἀγαγὼν
αὐτὸν ἔξω τῆς ἀγορᾶς κατέστησε. [5] καὶ οὐκ ἔφθη
πρῶτον ἀφεθείς, καὶ πάλιν ἀναστρέψας ἵετο πρὸς τὸ
βῆμα, μετὰ κραυγῆς ἐγκελευόμενος τοῖς πολίταις
ἀμύνειν. [6] πολλάκις δὲ τούτου γενομένου, περιπαθῶν
ὁ Τρεβώνιος ἐκέλευσεν αὐτὸν εἰς τὸ δεσμωτήριον
ἄγεσθαι, καὶ πλῆθος ἐπηκολούθει, λέγοντος ἅμα
{σὺν}[2] τῷ βαδίζειν ἀκροώμενον, ὥστε δείσαντα τὸν

---

[1] ὑφ᾽ αὑτῷ *Coraes*: ὑπ᾽ αὐτῷ *codd. plerique*: ὑπ᾽ αὐτὸν *codd.*
duo   [2] *del.* Ziegler

On Lex Trebonia de provinciis consularibus *(F 25)*

*In 55 BC, when C. Trebonius, a Tribune of the People,
proposed a law on the consular provinces* (Lex Trebonia
de provinciis consularibus: LPPR, p. 408), *Cato opposed
it (cf. Cass. Dio 39.33–34:* **166** *F 5; Liv.* Epit. 105).

F 25 Plutarch, *Life of Cato the Younger*

Now Gaius Trebonius [tr. pl. 55 BC] had proposed a law
for the assignment of provinces to the consuls [Cn. Pompeius Magnus (**111**) and M. Licinius Crassus Dives (**102**)],
so that one of them was to have Hispania and Africa under
him, the other Syria and Egypt, and both were to wage war
on whom they pleased and subdue them, attacking them
with land and sea forces. [2] The others, weary of resis-
tance and prevention, abandoned even speaking against it;
but to Cato, climbing the Rostra before the vote and wishing to speak, they allowed a speech of just two hours. [3]
After he had used up the time, saying a lot, explaining and
making predictions, they did not let him speak any longer,
but an official went up to him as he continued and pulled
him down [from the Rostra]. [4] When, standing below,
he kept shouting and had men listen to him and share his
indignation, the official once more laid hands on him, led
him away, and put him out of the Forum. [5] And immediately, as soon as he was released, he turned back again
and moved toward the Rostra, amid shouting, commanding the citizens to defend him. [6] After this had happened
several times, Trebonius in a passion ordered him to be
led to prison; and a crowd followed, listening to him as he
spoke at the same time while he went along, so that Tre-

Τρεβώνιον ἀφεῖναι. [7] κἀκείνην μὲν οὕτω τὴν ἡμέραν
ὁ Κάτων κατανάλωσε· ταῖς δ᾽ ἐφεξῆς οὓς μὲν δεδιξά-
μενοι τῶν πολιτῶν, οὓς δὲ συσκευασάμενοι χάρισι
καὶ δωροδοκίαις, ἕνα δὲ τῶν δημάρχων Ἀκύλλιον
ὅπλοις εἴρξαντες ἐκ τοῦ βουλευτηρίου προελθεῖν, αὐτὸν δὲ τὸν Κάτωνα βροντὴν γεγονέναι βοῶντα τῆς
ἀγορᾶς ἐκβαλόντες, οὐκ ὀλίγους δὲ τρώσαντες, ἐνίων
δὲ καὶ πεσόντων, βίᾳ τὸν νόμον ἐκύρωσαν, ὥστε πολλοὺς συστραφέντας ὀργῇ τοὺς Πομπηΐου βάλλειν
ἀνδριάντας. [8] ἀλλὰ τοῦτο μὲν ἐπελθὼν ὁ Κάτων δι-
εκώλυσε . . .

On Behalf of T. Annius Milo (F 26)

F 26 Asc. in Cic. *Mil.*, *arg.* (p. 30 KS = 34.15–21 C.)
= **92** F 49.

On Caesar's Candidacy in the Senate (F 27)

F 27 Caes. *BCiv.* 1.32.2–3
= **121** F 41A.

bonius became afraid and let him go. [7] In this manner
Cato used up that day; and during the days that followed
they [Cato's opponents] intimidated some of the citizens,
won over others by bribes and favors, prevented one of the
Tribunes, Aquillius [P. Aquillius Gallus, tr. pl. 55 BC], with
arms from leaving the Senate house, cast Cato himself out
of the Forum when he cried out that there had been thun-
der, wounded not a few, while some had actually been
slain, and thus accomplished the passage of the law by
force. Consequently, many banded together and pelted
the statues of Pompey in anger. [8] But Cato came up and
stopped this. . . .

On Behalf of T. Annius Milo (F 26)

In 52 BC Cato was among the advocates defending T. An-
nius Milo (138) in one of the trials of that year (TLRR
306).

F 26 Asconius on Cicero, *Pro Milone*

= **92** F 49.

On Caesar's Candidacy in the Senate (F 27)

In 52 BC Cato spoke against a bill, proposed by the Tri-
bunes of the People, that would allow C. Iulius Caesar's
(121) candidacy for office in his absence (Plebiscitum de
petitione Caesaris: LPPR, p. 412; cf. Liv. Epit. 107).

F 27 Caesar, *Civil War*

= **121** F 41A.

Further Political Speeches (F 27A)

Further speeches by Cato in the Senate and before the
People are mentioned (Cic. Att. 1.14.5; Fam. 15.5.1; Sest.
60; Caes. BCiv. 4.1: **154** F 3; Plut. Cat. min. 26.1, 26.4–5,
30.2, 31.1–2, 33.5, 40.2–3, 44.5–6, 47, 48, 51.3–7, 52.2–3,
54.8–9; Cic. 23.5–6); there are more political occasions on
which Cato must have spoken even if orations are not
explicitly attested. An address to Cn. Pompeius Magnus

F 27A Plut. Cat. min. 45.2–46.1

. . . καὶ καταβοῶν τοῦ Κάτωνος, ὡς πολλὰ μὲν ἐκ
Κύπρου χρήματα νοσφισαμένου, Πομπηΐῳ δὲ πολε-
μοῦντος ἀπαξιώσαντι γάμον αὐτοῦ θυγατρός. [3] ὁ δὲ
Κάτων ἔλεγεν, ὅτι χρήματα μὲν ἐκ Κύπρου τοσαῦτα
τῇ πόλει συναγάγοι μήθ᾽ ἵππον ἕνα μήτε στρατιώτην
λαβών, ὅσα Πομπήϊος ἐκ πολέμων τοσούτων καὶ θρι-
άμβων τὴν οἰκουμένην κυκήσας οὐκ ἀνήνεγκε· [4]
κηδεστὴν δὲ μηδέποτε προελέσθαι Πομπήϊον, οὐκ
ἀνάξιον ἡγούμενος, ἀλλ᾽ ὁρῶν τὴν ἐν τῇ πολιτείᾳ
διαφοράν. [5] "αὐτὸς μὲν γὰρ" ἔφη "διδομένης μοι
μετὰ τὴν στρατηγίαν ἐπαρχίας ἀπέστην, οὗτος δὲ
τὰς μὲν ἔχει λαβών, τὰς δὲ δίδωσιν ἑτέροις· [6] νυνὶ
δὲ καὶ τέλος, ἑξακισχιλίων ὁπλιτῶν δύναμιν,[1] Καίσαρι κέχρηκεν εἰς Γαλατίαν· ἣν[2] οὔτ᾽ ἐκεῖνος ᾔτησε
παρ᾽ ὑμῶν, οὔθ᾽ οὗτος ἔδωκε μεθ᾽ ὑμῶν, ἀλλὰ δυνά-
μεις τηλικαῦται καὶ ὅπλα καὶ ἵπποι χάριτές εἰσιν ἰδι-

---

[1] ἑξακισχιλίων ὁπλιτῶν δύναμιν del. Schaefer: δύναμιν del.
Reiske: τέλος del. Cobet   [2] ἣν Coraes: ἃ codd. (ὁ Reiske)

Further Political Speeches (F 27A)

(**111**) *individually, rather than the People, is referred to* (*Plut.* Cat. min. *43.8–9*).

Plutarch provides an example of such a political speech, including "verbatim" quotations, in which Cato defends his own conduct while confronting P. Clodius Pulcher (**137**)*, Cn. Pompeius Magnus* (**111**)*, and C. Iulius Caesar* (**121**)*.*

F 27A Plutarch, *Life of Cato the Younger*

. . . and he [P. Clodius Pulcher (**137**), instigated by Cn. Pompeius Magnus (**111**)] loudly denounced Cato for having appropriated much money from Cyprus, and for being hostile to Pompey, who had declined marriage with his daughter. [3] But Cato said that, without taking a single horse or soldier, he had accumulated from Cyprus more money for the city than Pompey had brought back from all his wars and triumphs after stirring up the habitable world; [4] that he never chose Pompey for a marriage connection, not because he thought him unworthy, but because he saw the difference in their policies. [5] "I, for my part," he said, "when a province was offered to me after my praetorship, declined it, but this man took provinces, some of which he holds himself and some of which he offers to others; [6] now he has actually lent Caesar [C. Iulius Caesar (**121**)] an army, a force of six thousand legionaries, for use in Gaul. Neither did he [Caesar] ask for this force from you, nor did the other [Pompey] give it with your consent, but such enormous forces and arms and

ωτῶν καὶ ἀντιδόσεις. [7] καλούμενος δὲ αὐτοκράτωρ
καὶ στρατηγὸς, ἄλλοις τὰ στρατεύματα καὶ τὰς ἐπαρχίας παραδέδωκεν, αὐτὸς δὲ τῇ πόλει παρακάθηται
στάσεις ἀγωνοθετῶν ἐν ταῖς παραγγελίαις καὶ θορύ-
βους μηχανώμενος, ἐξ ὧν οὐ λέληθε δι᾽ ἀναρχίας
μοναρχίαν ἑαυτῷ μνηστευόμενος." [46.1] οὕτως μὲν
ἠμύνατο τὸν Πομπήϊον.

127 L. CALPURNIUS PISO CAESONINUS

*L. Calpurnius Piso Caesoninus (cos. 58, censor 50 BC; RE
Calpurnius 90) was provincial governor in Macedonia after his consulship, while his colleague A. Gabinius administered Syria (on Piso's career and oratory see van der
Blom 2013; 2016, 181–203, on his speeches pp. 313–14).
Cicero argued for measures that would effectively recall
the two men from their provinces in the speech* De provinciis consularibus *(56 BC). After his return to Rome, Piso
delivered an invective against Cicero in the Senate (F 1);*

To the People (F 1A)

*The main reason for Cicero's invectives against Piso is his
view that there was some responsibility on Piso's part for
Cicero having had to go into exile and not being recalled*

F 1A Cic. *Pis.* 14

idem illo fere biduo productus in contionem ab eo cui si-

horses are now the mutual gifts of private persons. [7] And
though called imperator and general, he has handed over
to others his armies and his provinces, while he himself
takes up his post near the city [of Rome], managing factions at the elections as though he were directing games
and contriving disturbances, from which it is clear that by
way of anarchy, he is seeking to win for himself a monar-
chy." [46.1] With such words did Cato fend off Pompey.

127 L. CALPURNIUS PISO CAESONINUS

Cicero responded with the speech In Pisonem *(55 BC),
whereupon Piso replied with another oration against Cicero, which seems to have existed in writing (F 2).*

*As consul in 58 BC, Piso is attested to have spoken at a
meeting of the People (F 1A; CCMR, App. A: 296) and to
have appeared in public on other occasions (Cic.* Red. sen.
17*; Sest. 33; Cass. Dio 38.16.5–6). Earlier, the involvement
of Piso as a prosecutor in a trial is recorded (TLRR 174;
Cic.* Div. Caec. 64*).*

To the People (F 1A)

*during Piso's consulship (58 BC). In this context Cicero
refers to a speech Piso delivered at a meeting of the People
that included criticism of Cicero's consulship (63 BC).*

F 1A Cicero, *Against Piso*

Then, about two days later you [Piso] were brought before
a public meeting by the man [P. Clodius Pulcher (**137**), tr.

cam quandam[1] praebebas consulatum tuum, cum esses
interrogatus quid sentires de consulatu meo, gravis auctor,
Calatinus credo aliquis aut Africanus aut Maximus et non
Caesoninus Semiplacentinus Calventius, respondes altero
ad frontem sublato, altero ad mentum depresso supercilio
crudelitatem tibi non placere.

[1] sicam quandam *Clark*: sic aequatum *codd.*: quasi addictum
Halm: emancipatum *Kayser*: inlaqueatum *Müller*

Against M. Tullius Cicero in the Senate (F 1)

F 1 Asc. in Cic. *Pis.*, *arg.* (p. 2 KS = 2.4–10 C.)

nam cum revocati essent ex provinciis Piso et Gabinius
sententia Ciceronis quam dixerat de provinciis consularibus Lentulo et Philippo consulibus, reversus in civitatem Piso de insectatione Ciceronis in senatu conquestus
est et in eum invectus, fiducia maxime Caesaris generi qui
tum Gallias obtinebat.

Cf. Cic. *Pis.*, esp. *Pis.* 2, 18, 31, 34, 39, 47, 56, 60, 62, 64, 72–75,
78, 82, 92, 94.

127 L. CALPURNIUS PISO CAESONINUS

pl. 58 BC] to whom you offered your consulship like a kind of dagger; when you were asked what you thought about my consulship [63 BC], you, like a serious speaker—some Calatinus [A. Atilius Calatinus, cos. 258, 254, cens. 247 BC], I believe, or an Africanus [P. Cornelius Scipio Africanus (4)] or a Maximus [Q. Fabius Maximus Verrucosus Cunctator (3)], and not a Caesoninus Semiplacentinus Calventius[1]—answer, with one eyebrow raised to your forehead, the other tucked down to the chin, that cruelty was not approved by you.

[1] Cf. F 2 n. 1.

Against M. Tullius Cicero in the Senate (F 1)

F 1 Asconius on Cicero, *Against Piso*

For when Piso and Gabinius [cos. 58 BC] had been recalled from their provinces, in accordance with Cicero's view that he had expressed [in the speech] on the consular provinces, in the consulship [56 BC] of Lentulus [Cn. Cornelius Lentulus Marcellinus (**128**)] and Philippus [L. Marcius Philippus], Piso, returning to the community, complained about Cicero's hostile attack in the Senate and inveighed against him, trusting particularly in his son-in-law Caesar [C. Iulius Caesar (**121**), married to Piso's daughter Calpurnia], who then held the Gallic provinces.

Again Against M. Tullius Cicero (F 2)

F 2 Cic. *Q Fr.* 3.1.11

alterum est de Calventi Mari oratione: quod scribis tibi placere me ad eam rescribere, miror,[1] praesertim cum illam nemo lecturus sit si ego nihil rescripsero, meam in illum pueri omnes tamquam dictata perdiscant.

[1] miror *transp. Shackleton Bailey: post* scribis *codd.*

Against Marc Antony in the Senate (F 2A)

F 2A Cic. *Phil.* 1.10–15

exque eo primum cognovi quae Kalendis Sextilibus in senatu fuisset L. Pisonis oratio: qui quamquam parum erat—id enim ipsum a Bruto audieram—a quibus debuerat adiutus, tamen et Bruti testimonio—quo quid potest

Again Against M. Tullius Cicero (F 2)

F 2 Cicero, *Letters to Quintus*

The second point concerns Calventius Marius'[1] speech: I
am surprised that you write that in your view I should
write a rejoinder to that, especially as nobody will read
that [speech of Piso] if I write nothing in reply, whereas
all the boys learn mine against him [Cic. *Pis.*] by heart as
though it was part of their lessons.

[1] Cicero ironically refers to Piso as Calventius Marius: Piso's
maternal grandfather, described by Cicero as an Insubrian Gaul
and involved in lowly trades, was called Calventius (Cic. *Pis.* F 9,
13; cf. Cic. *Pis.* 14: F 1A; *Prov. cons.* 7; *Red. sen.* 13). Piso is
compared with C. Marius (seven-time consul) and his supporter
L. Appuleius Saturninus (**64A**), who prompted Q. Caecilius Metellus Numidicus (**58**) to go into exile.

Against Marc Antony in the Senate (F 2A)

In 44 BC Piso was among the first to oppose M. Antonius,
(159) by delivering a courageous speech in the Senate on
August 1, 44 BC (Cic. Phil. *1.28, 5.19: 159 F 15, 12.14;*
Att. *16.7.5, 16.7.7;* Fam. *12.2.1).*

F 2A Cicero, *Philippics*

And from him [M. Iunius Brutus (**158**)] I first learned of
L. Piso's speech in the Senate on the Kalends of Sextilis
[August 1, 44 BC]; although he [Piso] received too little
support from those from whom he ought to—that very fact
too I had heard from Brutus—nevertheless, both on Brutus' testimony—what can be weightier than that?—and on

esse gravius?—et omnium praedicatione quos postea vidi, magnam mihi videbatur gloriam consecutus. . . . [14] . . . atque utinam, patres conscripti, Kalendis Sextilibus adesse potuissem! non quo profici potuerit aliquid, sed ne unus modo consularis, quod tum accidit, dignus illo honore, dignus re publica inveniretur. qua quidem ex re magnum accipio dolorem, homines amplissimis populi Romani beneficiis usos L. Pisonem ducem optimae sententiae non secutos. . . . non modo voce nemo L. Pisoni consularis sed ne voltu quidem adsensus est. [15] . . . qua re primum maximas gratias et ago et habeo Pisoni, qui non quid efficere posset in re publica cogitavit, sed quid facere ipse deberet.

In Support of Marc Antony in the Senate (F 2B)

F 2B App. *B Civ.* 3.54.221–61.249

*Piso is made to claim that Cicero has accused M. Antonius [**159**] in his absence and he therefore has come forward on Antony's behalf to show that these charges are false. By going through the events of the recent past in detail, outlining what Cicero and Antony have done or have not done, Piso argues that Cicero's behavior has been inconsistent and has not taken sufficient account of the views of the People, whereas Antony has acted in line with the laws and*

the laudatory report of all whom I saw later, he [Piso] seemed to me to have earned great glory. . . . [14] . . . And I only wish, Members of the Senate, that I could have been present on the Kalends of Sextilis! Not because anything could have been accomplished, but to prevent what then happened, that only a single consular was found worthy of that rank, worthy of the Republic. Indeed, that matter grieves me to the heart that men who have enjoyed the highest gifts of the Roman People did not follow the lead given by L. Piso in his most admirable motion. . . . Not only did no consular support L. Piso by word but not even by look. [15] . . . Thus, in the first place, I both express and feel the greatest gratitude to Piso, who did not think about what he could achieve in the Republic, but what he ought to do.

In Support of Marc Antony in the Senate (F 2B)

In 43 BC, Piso was among those who proposed peace with M. Antonius (159) (Cic. Phil. 12.1–3) and defended him in the Senate (App. B Civ. 3.50.205); a long speech in support of Antony is put into Piso's mouth by Appian.

F 2B Appian, *Civil Wars*

initiated beneficial political actions when he had the opportunity. Piso claims thereby to have demonstrated Antony's defense and Cicero's fickleness. The speech ends with the proposal to allow Antony to have Gaul, to call back D. Iunius Brutus with his three legions and then send him to Macedonia, and to summon to the city the two legions that had deserted from Antony to Octavian. Then, according to Piso, they might be able to pass good decrees as they would

be fully in power, not depending on anybody else's favor;
moreover, they should have regard for the People, who had
been pursuing Caesar's murderers not long ago. Thereby
Piso defends Antony and reproaches his enemies; he thus

128 CN. CORNELIUS LENTULUS MARCELLINUS

Cn. Cornelius Lentulus Marcellinus (cos. 56 BC; RE Cor-
nelius 228) is described in Cicero as an eloquent speaker,
not lacking words or ideas, and showing wit (T 1).
   As consul designate in the second half of 57 BC, Lentu-

T 1 Cic. *Brut.* 247

[CICERO:] Cn.[1] autem Lentulus Marcellinus nec umquam
indisertus et in consulatu pereloquens visus est, non tar-
dus sententiis, non inops verbis, voce canora, facetus satis.

   [1] Cn. *Manutius*: C. *codd.*

In Support of the Sicilians (F 2–3)

Lentulus was present at the trial of C. Verres in 70 BC
(TLRR 177) and provided a witness statement (cf. Cic.
Verr. 2.4.53: Cn. Lentulus Marcellinus dissuasit, sicut ip-

F 2 Cic. *Div. Caec.* 13

scit is qui est in consilio, C. Marcellus, scit is quem adesse
video, Cn. Lentulus Marcellinus; quorum fide atque prae-

*alarms the senators and induces them not to vote Antony
an enemy; he does not succeed, however, in securing for
Antony the governorship of Gaul.*

128 CN. CORNELIUS LENTULUS
MARCELLINUS

*lus was the first to be asked in the Senate for his views
during the discussion about the restoration of Cicero's
house upon the latter's return from exile (Cic. Att. 4.2.4;
Har. resp. 13).*

T 1 Cicero, *Brutus*

[CICERO:] But Cn. Lentulus Marcellinus was never seen
as lacking eloquence, and in his consulship [he was seen]
as very eloquent, not slow in thought, not deficient in
language, with a sonorous voice, fairly witty.

In Support of the Sicilians (F 2–3)

sum dicere audistis. recita. ARCHAGATHI ET LENTULI
TESTIMONIUM.).

F 2 Cicero, *Against Caecilius*

He who is here as a member of the court, C. Marcellus [C.
Claudius Marcellus, praet. 80 BC, proconsul in Sicilia],
knows it [i.e., that the Sicilians have requested Cicero's
support]; he who I see is present, Cn. Lentulus Marcelli-

sidio Siculi maxime nituntur,[1] quod omnino Marcellorum nomini tota illa provincia adiuncta est.

[1] nituntur *Manutius*: utuntur *codd.*

F 3 Cic. *Verr.* 2.2.103

qua de re Cn. Lentulum, patronum Siciliae, clarissimum adulescentem, dicere audistis, Siculos, cum se causam quae sibi in senatu pro his agenda esset docerent, de Stheni calamitate questos esse, propterque hanc iniuriam quae Sthenio facta esset eos statuisse ut hoc quod dico postularetur.

On Campanian Land and Issues of Trials in the Senate (F 4)

At a meeting of the Senate in December 57 BC Lentulus, as consul designate, intervened on the issue of the distribution of the Campanian land and was the first to be con-

nus, knows it: in their honor and protection the Sicilians put particular trust, since that entire province is altogether attached to the name of the Marcelli.[1]

[1] See Ps.-Asc. *ad loc.* (p. 190.22–24 St.): *Marcellus et Marcellinus inter se gentiles sunt: qua re reddidit rationem cur isti Siculorum patroni sint, scilicet quia a M. Marcello originem ducant, qui Syracusas cepit nec tamen delevit* ("Marcellus and Marcellinus are members of the same family: thereby he [Cicero] has provided a reason why these men are patrons of the Sicilians, obviously because they derive their descent from M. Marcellus, who conquered Syracuse and still did not destroy it.").

F 3 Cicero, *Verrine Orations*

You have heard Cn. Lentulus, a patron of Sicily, a very distinguished young man, say on that subject that, when the Sicilians were putting before him the issue on which he was to support their interests in the Senate, they complained about the misfortune of Sthenius [of Thermae], and that because of this wrong that had been done to Sthenius [by C. Verres; cf. Cic. *Verr.* 2.2.83–99] they had resolved to present the petition I speak of.

On Campanian Land and Issues of Trials in the Senate (F 4)

sulted on the question of procedures for trials concerning P. Clodius Pulcher (**137**).

F 4 Cic. *Q Fr.* 2.1.1–2

senatus fuit frequentior quam putabamus esse posse
mense Decembri sub dies festos. . . . fuimus omnino ad
CC. commorat exspectationem Lupus; egit causam agri
Campani sane accurate, auditus est magno silentio. materiam rei non ignoras. nihil ex nostris actionibus prae-
termisit; fuerunt non nulli aculei in Caesarem, contume-
liae in Gellium, expostulationes cum absente Pompeio.
causa sero perorata sententias se rogaturum negavit, ne
quod onus simultatis nobis imponeret; ex superiorum
temporum conviciis et ex praesenti silentio quid senatus
sentiret se intellegere dixit. senatum[1] coepit dimittere.[2]
tum Marcellinus "noli" inquit "ex taciturnitate nostra,
Lupe, quid aut probemus hoc tempore aut improbemus,
iudicare. ego, quod ad me attinet, itemque arbitror ceteros, idcirco taceo quod non existimo, cum Pompeius absit,
causam agri Campani agi convenire." [2] tum ille se senatum negavit tenere. Racilius surrexit et de iudiciis referre
coepit; Marcellinum quidem primum rogavit. is cum gra-
viter de Clodianis incendiis, trucidationibus, lapidationi-

---

[1] senatum *Watt*: senatus *vel om. codd.*

[2] *ordinem in manuscriptis correxit Mommsen, denique pauca emendavit Sternkopf*

F 4 Cicero, *Letters to Quintus*

The Senate was better attended than we had thought could be the case in the month of December just before the holiday [Saturnalia]. . . . We were indeed numerous, almost two hundred. Lupus [P. Rutilius Lupus (**129**), F 1] had aroused expectation [having just come into office as tr. pl. for 56 BC]: he dealt with the issue of the Campanian land in a rather detailed manner; he was heard in great silence. You are well aware of the matter. He omitted nothing from my own contributions [apparently Cicero's earlier comments on agrarian laws since 63 BC]. There were some barbs against Caesar [C. Iulius Caesar (**121**)], some insults against Gellius [follower of P. Clodius Pulcher (**137**), perhaps brother of L. Gellius Poplicola (**101**)], some complaints against Pompey [Cn. Pompeius Magnus (**111**)], who was absent. After he [Lupus] had brought his case to a conclusion rather late, he said he would not ask for a debate since he did not wish to put any pressure on us to make ourselves enemies: he said that from the angry clamor of the past and the present silence he understood what the Senate felt. He began to dismiss the Senate. Then Marcellinus said: "You should not, Lupus, infer from our silence what we now approve or disapprove of. So far as I myself am concerned, and I imagine the same applies to others, I am silent for the reason that I do not think the issue of the Campanian land can properly be handled while Pompey is absent." [2] He [Marcellinus] then said that he would not detain the House. Racilius [another new tr. pl. for 56 BC] rose and began to bring forward the matter of trials; he asked Marcellinus for his opinion first. After he [Marcellinus] had strongly criticized Clodius' [P.

bus questus esset, sententiam dixit ut ipse iudices {per} praetor{em} urbanus[3] sortiretur, iudicum sortitione facta comitia haberentur; qui iudicia impedisset, eum contra rem publicam esse facturum. approbata valde sententia C. Cato contra dixit et Cassius maxima acclamatione senatus, cum comitia iudiciis anteferre<n>t.[4]

[3] {per} praetor{em} urbanus (*i.e.*, pr. urb.) *Manutius*: per praetorem urbanum *codd.*: per se praetor urbanus *Sternkopf*   [4] anteferre<n>t *Orelli*: anteferret *codd.*

On Cn. Pompeius Magnus to the People (F 5)

*As consul in 56 BC, Lentulus questioned and spoke against the excessive powers pursued by M. Licinius Crassus Dives (**102**) and Cn. Pompeius Magnus (**111**) (Cass. Dio.*

F 5 Val. Max. 6.2.6

Cn. Lentulus Marcellinus consul, cum in contione de Magni Pompei nimia potentia quereretur, adsensusque ei clara voce universus populus esset, "acclamate" inquit, "acclamate, Quirites, dum licet: iam enim vobis impune facere non licebit."

129 P. RUTILIUS LUPUS

Clodius Pulcher's (**137**)] arsons, killings, and stonings, he gave his opinion that the city praetor should personally appoint judges by lot and that, when judges had been appointed by lot, elections should be held; any person obstructing the trials would be acting contrary to the Republic. This proposal was warmly approved; C. Cato [C. Porcius Cato (**136**), another new tr. pl. for 56 BC] spoke against it, as did Cassius [identity uncertain], amid very loud cries of protest from the Senate, since they put the elections before the trials.

On Cn. Pompeius Magnus to the People (F 5)

39.27.3, 39.28.5, 39.30.1–2; Plut. Pomp. *51.6–8;* Crass. *15.2–3;* Apophth. Pomp. *12).*

F 5 Valerius Maximus, *Memorable Doings and Sayings*

When Cn. Lentulus Marcellinus, the consul [56 BC], was complaining at a public meeting of Pompey the Great's [Cn. Pompeius Magnus (**111**)] excessive power, and the entire People loudly agreed with him, he said: "Applaud, Romans, applaud while you may; for soon you will not be allowed to do it with impunity."

129 P. RUTILIUS LUPUS

*P. Rutilius Lupus (praet. 49 BC; RE Rutilius 27) favored Cn. Pompeius Magnus (**111**) and opposed C. Iulius Caesar (**121**) after being elected Tribune of the People for 56 BC.*

On Campanian Land in the Senate (F 1)

F 1 Cic. *Q Fr.* 2.1.1–2
= **128** F 4.

130 AP. CLAUDIUS PULCHER

*Ap. Claudius Pulcher (cos. 54, censor 50 BC; RE Claudius
297), a brother of P. Clodius Pulcher (**137**), governed the
province of Cilicia after his consulship and was awarded
the title of* imperator *after defeating the Parthians. He was
Cicero's predecessor in Cilicia (and did not administer the
province well); all letters in the third book of Cicero's* Ad
familiares *are addressed to him. Pulcher wrote a work on
the augural discipline, dedicated to Cicero (T 2, 3; Cic.
Fam. 3.4.1, 3.9.3; GRF, pp. 426–27). In Cicero, Pulcher is
described as a learned man and a well-versed orator (T 1).*

*Speeches at public meetings during Pulcher's praetor-
ship (57 BC) are mentioned (Cic. Att. 4.3.4 [CCMR, App.
A: 311]; Cic. Sest. 126 [CCMR, App. A: 306]).*

T 1 Cic. *Brut.* 267

[CICERO:] . . . Appius Claudius socer tuus, conlega et
familiaris meus: hic iam et satis studiosus et valde cum
doctus tum etiam exercitatus orator et cum auguralis tum
omnis publici iuris antiquitatisque nostrae bene peritus
fuit.

On Campanian Land in the Senate (F 1)

Just after he had come into office as Tribune of the People in December 57 BC, Rutilius spoke in the Senate on issues concerning the Campanian land.

F 1 Cicero, *Letters to Quintus*
= **128** F 4.

130 AP. CLAUDIUS PULCHER

*In 50 BC Pulcher was prosecuted by P. Cornelius Dolabella (**173**) for* maiestas *and* ambitus, *but was acquitted, defended by Q. Hortensius Hortalus (**92** F 53–54) and M. Iunius Brutus (**158** F 22) presumably on the latter charge (TLRR 344, 345; Sumner 1973, 122–23; Cic. Fam. 3.11.1–3, 3.12.1, 8.6.1; Vir. ill. 82.4). In the same year, when he was censor, Pulcher spoke on his own behalf when accused by M. Caelius Rufus (**162**) under the* Lex Scantinia *(or* Scatinia) de nefanda venere *(LPPR, p. 293; Elster 2003, 422–24) and because of a* sacellum *in his house (TLRR 348, 351; Cic. Fam. 8.12.1–3; Brut. 230, 324).*

T 1 Cicero, *Brutus*

[CICERO:] . . . Appius Claudius, your father-in-law [of M. Iunius Brutus (**158**)], my colleague [as augur] and friend: he was rather fond of studying, an orator greatly learned and also highly experienced, and thoroughly versed in augural and also all public law, and our past history.

T 2 Cic. *Fam.* 3.11.4 [ad Appium Pulchrum]

. . . tuumque simul promptum animum et alacrem per-
spexi ad defendendam rem publicam. . . . nam auguralis
libros ad commune utriusque nostrum otium serva. ego
enim a te cum tua promissa per litteras flagitabam, ad
urbem te otiosissimum esse arbitrabar. nunc tamen, ut
ipse polliceris, pro auguralibus libris orationes tuas con-
fectas omnis exspectabo.

T 3 Cic. *Fam.* 2.13.2 [ad Caelium Rufum]

ego Appium, ut saepe tecum locutus sum, valde diligo
meque ab eo diligi statim coeptum esse ut simultatem
deposuimus sensi. nam et honorificus in me consul fuit et
suavis amicus et studiosus studiorum etiam meorum. mea
vero officia ei non defuisse tu es testis . . . quid est causae
cur mihi non in optatis sit complecti hominem florentem
aetate, opibus, honoribus, ingenio, liberis, propinquis,
adfinibus, amicis, collegam meum praesertim et in ipsa
collegi laude et scientia studiosum mei? . . . genus institu-
torum et rationum mearum dissimilitudinem non nullam
habet cum illius administratione provinciae. ex eo quidam
suspicati fortasse sunt animorum contentione, non opinio-
num dissensione, me ab eo discrepare. nihil autem feci
umquam neque dixi quod contra illius existimationem
esse vellem; post hoc negotium autem et temeritatem nostri Dolabellae deprecatorem me pro illius periculo prae-
beo.

T 2 Cicero, *Letters to Friends* [to Appius Pulcher]

. . . and at the same time I have noticed your ready and eager spirit in the defense of the Republic. . . . So keep the books on augury until both of us have time to spare. For when I demanded from you the fulfillment of your pledge in a letter, I imagined you near the city [of Rome] with lots of time to spare. But now I will expect, as you yourself promise, the edition of your complete speeches instead of the books on augury.

T 3 Cicero, *Letters to Friends* [to Caelius Rufus]

I have a real regard for Appius, as I have often told you, and I perceived that I began to be respected by him as soon as we buried our hatchet. For as consul [54 BC] he was conferring honors upon me, a pleasant friend, and even keen on my literary pursuits. In fact, that friendliness toward him on my side was not wanting you can testify . . . What reason is there that it should not be desirable for me to embrace a man flourishing in the prime of life, wealth, offices, ability, children, connections of blood and marriage, friends, in particular a colleague of mine [as augur] and [showing himself] devoted to me precisely by the learned praise of our college? . . . The character of my ordinances and principles has some dissimilarity to his administration of the province [Cilicia]. Hence perhaps some have suspected that I differ from him out of personal animus, not from theoretical disagreement. But I have never said or done anything out of a desire to injure his reputation; and after this recent trouble and our friend Dolabella's precipitate behavior [P. Cornelius Dolabella (**173**), prosecuting Pulcher *de maiestate*], I am ready with my intercession on his behalf in the hour of danger.

Against Terentius Varro (F 4)

F 4 Ps.-Asc. in Cic. *Div. Caec.* 24 (pp. 193.29–94.1 Stangl)
= **92** F 22.

131 L. DOMITIUS AHENOBARBUS

L. Domitius Ahenobarbus (cos. 54 BC; RE Domitius 27),
a son of Cn. Domitius Ahenobarbus (69), was an opponent
of C. Iulius Caesar (121); he died in the battle of Pharsa-
lus, described poetically in Lucan (7.599–616).

T 1 Cic. *Brut.* 267

[Cicero:] L. Domitius nulla ille quidem arte, sed Latine
tamen et multa cum libertate dicebat.

On the Lands of Amphiaraus in the Senate (F 2A)

In 73 BC Domitius made an intervention in the Senate
concerning the question of whether the lands of Amphi-
araus were exempt from being assigned to tax collectors.
The Oropians were of the opinion that this was the case as
a result of L. Cornelius Sulla's arrangements for sacred
areas (SIG II³ 747.20–23). Domitius supported the tax

Against Terentius Varro (F 4)

*In 74 BC Pulcher prosecuted Terentius Varro for extortion; the accused was defended by Q. Hortensius Hortalus (**92** F 21–22) (TLRR 158).*

F 4 Pseudo-Asconius on Cicero, *Against Caecilius*
= **92** F 22.

131 L. DOMITIUS AHENOBARBUS

In Cicero it is noted that Domitius spoke without much theoretical training, but used pure Latin and exercised great liberty (T 1).

T 1 Cicero, *Brutus*
[Cicero:] L. Domitius spoke without any theoretical knowledge, but still in pure Latin and with great liberty.

On the Lands of Amphiaraus in the Senate (F 2A)

collectors with the argument that Sulla's rules did not apply since Amphiaraus was not a god. The so-called senatus consultum de Amphiarai Oropii agris, *epigraphically preserved, records an excerpt from Domitius' comments (and confirms the decision that the lands are to be exempt). The controversy is alluded to by Cicero (Cic. Nat. D. 3.49).*

F 2A *SIG* II³ 747.24–29

καὶ περὶ ὧν Λεύκιος Δομέτιος Αἰνόβαλβος ὑπὲρ δη-
μοσιωνῶν εἶπεν, | ἐπεὶ ἐν τῶι τῆς μισθώσεως νόμωι
αὗται αἱ χῶραι ὑπεξειρημέναι εἰσίν, | ἃς Λεύκιος
Σύλλας θεῶν ἀθανάτων ἱερῶν τεμενῶν φυλακῆς ἕνε-
κεν | συνεχώρησεν, οὔτε¹ ὁ Ἀμφιάραος, ὧι αὗται αἱ
χῶραι συνκεχωρημέναι | λέγονται, θεός ἐστιν, ὅπως
ταύτας τὰς χῶρας καρπίζεσθαι ἐξῇ | τοὺς δημοσιώ-
νας . . .

¹ Cf. *SIG* II³ 747 n. 32: "Soloece Latinum *neque* expressit,
cum deberet οὐδὲ scribere."

On C. Iulius Caesar (F 2–3)

*Having come into office as praetor (for 58 BC), Ahenobar-
bus and his colleague C. Memmius (**125** F 7–10) questioned some of C. Iulius Caesar's (**121**) activities during*

F 2 Suet. *Iul.* 23.1

= **121** F 38.

F 3 Suet. *Nero* 2.2

huius filius praetor C. Caesarem abeuntem consulatu,
quem adversus auspicia legesque gessisse existimabatur,
ad disquisitionem senatus vocavit . . .

F 2A An inscription

And about that [the issue under discussion] Lucius Domitius Ainobalbus [i.e., Ahenobarbus][1] said on behalf of the
tax collectors: Since in the law on farming out by contract,
these lands have been exempted, those that Lucius Sulla
[L. Cornelius Sulla] gave up because of the protection of
the sacred precincts of the immortal gods, but Amphiaraus, to whom these lands are said to have been granted,
is not a god, so that it may be allowed for the tax collectors
to enjoy the fruits of these lands . . .

[1] Cf. *SIG* II³ 732 n. 2.

On C. Iulius Caesar (F 2–3)

*his (first) consulship in the previous year (59 BC), which
triggered replies by Caesar (**121** F 38–41).*

F 2 Suetonius, *Life of Caesar*
= **121** F 38.

F 3 Suetonius, *Life of Nero*

His [Cn. Domitius Ahenobarbus (**69**)] son, as praetor [58
BC], summoned C. Caesar [C. Iulius Caesar (**121**), F 38–
41] at the close of his consulship [59 BC] to an investigation before the Senate, because it was thought that he had
acted against the auspices and the laws . . .

132 C. MANILIUS

*C. Manilius (tr. pl. 66 BC; RE Manilius 10) as Tribune of
the People put forward several bills, including the proposal (F 1–2; CCMR, App. A: 251) to transfer the command in the Mithridatic War to Cn. Pompeius Magnus
(**111**) (Vell. Pat. 2.33.1; Cic. Phil. 11.18; Plut. Pomp. 30;
Cass. Dio 36.42.4–43.2), which Cicero supported in the*

On Lex Manilia de imperio Cn. Pompei *(F 1–2)*

F 1 Liv. *Epit.* 100.1–2

C. Manilius[1] tr. pl. magna indignatione nobilitatis legem
tulit, ut Pompeio Mithridaticum bellum mandaretur. [2]
contio[2] eius bona.

    [1] c. *vel* gn. *vel* t. *vel* cum *vel om. codd.*   Manilius *ed.
princ.*: manlius *codd.*   [2] *lac. ante* contio *indicavit Jal, sua-
dente Rossbachio*

F 2 Cic. *Leg. Man.* 69

. . . C. Manili, primum istam tuam et legem et voluntatem
et sententiam laudo vehementissimeque comprobo . . .

133 T. LABIENUS

*T. Labienus (tr. pl. 63 BC; RE Labienus 6) was a legatus
pro praetore for C. Iulius Caesar (**121**) during the Gallic
War (58–49 BC); in the ensuing civil war he switched his*

132 C. MANILIUS

speech Pro lege Manilia (Lex Manilia de imperio Cn. Pompei: LPPR, *pp. 375–76*).

After his time in office, Manilius was first charged with extortion, but the trial was not completed (TLRR 205); then he was accused of treason and found guilty in his absence (TLRR 210; Schol. Bob. ad Cic. Mil. 22 [p. 119.14–19 St.]; Asc. in Cic. Corn. [p. 60.9–12 C.]).

On Lex Manilia de imperio Cn. Pompei *(F 1–2)*

F 1 Livy, *Epitome*

C. Manilius, a Tribune of the People, proposed a law, to the great indignation of the nobility, that the Mithridatic War should be handed over to Pompey [Cn. Pompeius Magnus (**111**)]. [2] His speech before the People [was] good.

F 2 Cicero, *Pro Lege Manilia*

. . . C. Manilius, first of all I praise and very strongly approve of this your law, intention, and presentation of your proposal . . .

133 T. LABIENUS

*allegiance to Cn. Pompeius Magnus (**111**) and fell in the battle at Munda in 45 BC.*

Against C. Rabirius (F 1–2)

As Tribune of the People in 63 BC, Labienus prosecuted
C. Rabirius, who was defended by Q. Hortensius Hortalus
(**92** F 34–35) and Cicero (Cic. Rab. perd.). Rabirius was
accused of involvement in the killing of L. Appuleius

F 1 Cic. Rab. perd. 6–8, 10, 12–13, 18, 22, 28–29

nunc quoniam, T. Labiene, diligentiae meae temporis
angustiis obstitisti meque ex comparato et constituto spa-
tio defensionis in semihorae articulum coegisti, parebitur
et, quod iniquissimum est, accusatoris condicioni et, quod
miserrimum, inimici potestati. quamquam in hac prae-
scriptione semihorae patroni mihi partis reliquisti, consulis ademisti, propterea quod ad defendendum prope
modum satis erit hoc mihi temporis, ad conquerendum
vero parum. [7] nisi forte de locis religiosis ac de lucis quos
ab hoc violatos esse dixisti pluribus verbis tibi respondendum putas; quo in crimine nihil est umquam abs te dictum, nisi a C. Macro obiectum esse crimen id C. Rabirio.
in quo ego demiror meminisse te quid obiecerit C. Rabirio
Macer inimicus, oblitum esse quid aequi et iurati iudices
iudicarint. [8] an de peculatu facto aut de tabulario in-
censo longa oratio est expromenda?[1] . . . an de sororis filio
diligentius respondendum est? quem ab hoc necatum esse

---

[1] expromenda *Manutius*: exprimenda *codd.*

Against C. Rabirius (F 1–2)

*Saturninus (**64A**) in 100 BC under the ancient charge of*
perduellio; *the proceedings took place before the People.*
In his speech Cicero comments on the arguments allegedly
*put forward by Labienus (*TLRR 220, 221*).*

F 1 Cicero, *Pro Rabirio Perduellionis Reo*

Now, T. Labienus, since you have impeded my thorough-
ness by limit of time and have reduced the standard and
customary period for the defense to the narrow limits of
half an hour, one must submit both to the terms of the
prosecutor, which is extremely unjust, and the power of
the enemy, which is extremely wretched. Still, by this lim-
iting regulation of half an hour, you have left me the part
of an advocate, but have robbed me of that of a consul [in
63 BC], for the reason that this time will be almost sufficient for me for defense, but for protest too little. [7] Or
perhaps you believe that I should reply at some length to
you concerning the holy places and groves that you have
said had been violated by this man here [Rabirius]; regarding this charge nothing has ever been said by you,
except that this charge was brought against C. Rabirius by
C. Macer [C. Licinius Macer (**110**), F 4]. With respect to
this, I am amazed that you remembered what Macer, his
enemy, charged C. Rabirius with, but forgot what impar-
tial judges decided upon oath. [8] Or should a long speech
be produced upon the charge of embezzlement or of the
burning of public records [of which a relative of Rabirius
had been acquitted and which does not apply to Rabirius]?
. . . Or should one reply rather carefully about his sister's

dixisti, cum ad iudici moram familiaris funeris excusatio quaereretur. . . . an de servis alienis contra legem Fabiam retentis, aut de civibus Romanis contra legem Porciam verberatis aut necatis plura dicenda sunt, cum tanto studio C. Rabirius totius Apuliae, singulari voluntate Campaniae ornetur, cumque ad eius propulsandum periculum non modo homines sed prope regiones ipsae convenerint, aliquanto etiam latius excitatae quam ipsius vicinitatis nomen ac termini postulabant? nam quid ego ad id longam orationem comparem quod est in eadem multae inrogatione praescriptum, hunc nec suae nec alienae pudicitiae pepercisse? . . . [10] nam de perduellionis iudicio, quod a me sublatum esse criminari soles, meum crimen est, non Rabiri. . . . [12] popularis vero tribunus pl. custos defensorque iuris et libertatis! Porcia lex virgas ab omnium civium Romanorum corpore amovit, hic misericors flagella rettulit; Porcia lex libertatem civium lictori eripuit, Labienus, homo popularis, carnifici tradidit; C. Gracchus legem

son? You said that he was killed by this man here, since the excuse of the death of a member of the family was sought for delaying the trial. . . . Or is there more to say about his having detained another man's slaves against the *Lex Fabia* [*Lex Fabia de plagiariis*: *LPPR*, pp. 258–59; dated to 209? BC] or having scourged or killed Roman citizens against the *Lex Porcia* [*Leges Porciae de provocatione / de tergo civium*: *LPPR*, pp. 268–69; Elster 2003, 296–301; dated to 195? BC], when C. Rabirius is honored by the great enthusiasm of all Apulia and the remarkable goodwill of Campania, and when, to avert his peril, not only individuals but almost whole districts have assembled, roused even over a substantially larger area than what the name and closeness of neighborhood itself provoked? For why should I prepare a long speech on the charge that was entered in the same demand for a fine, namely that he had respected neither his own chastity nor that of others? . . . [10] Now as regards the procedure for high treason that you constantly allege was abolished by me, that is a charge against me, not against Rabirius. . . . [12] A friend of the People certainly this Tribune of the People, a guardian and defender of its rights and liberty! The *Lex Porcia* removed the rod from the body of any Roman citizen: this merciful man has brought back the lash. The *Lex Porcia* wrested the liberty of the citizens from the lictor: Labienus, the friend of the People, has handed it over to the executioner. C. Gracchus [C. Sempronius Gracchus (**48**)] carried a law forbidding sentence to be passed on the life of a Roman citizen without your orders [*Lex Sempronia de capite civis Romani*, 123 BC: *LPPR*, pp. 309–10]: this friend of the People has forced

tulit ne de capite civium Romanorum iniussu vestro iudicaretur, hic popularis a IIviris iniussu vestro non iudicari de cive Romano sed indicta causa civem Romanum capitis condemnari coegit. [13] tu mihi etiam legis Porciae, tu C. Gracchi, tu horum libertatis, tu cuiusquam denique hominis popularis mentionem facis, qui non modo suppliciis invisitatis[2] sed etiam verborum crudelitate inaudita violare libertatem huius populi, temptare mansuetudinem, commutare disciplinam conatus es? namque haec tua, quae te, hominem clementem popularemque, delectant, "i, lictor, conliga manus," {quae}[3] non modo huius libertatis mansuetudinisque non sunt sed ne Romuli quidem aut Numae Pompili; Tarquini, superbissimi atque crudelissimi regis, ista sunt cruciatus carmina quae tu, homo lenis ac popularis, libentissime commemoras: "caput obnubito, arbori infelici suspendito," quae verba, Quirites, iam pridem in hac re publica non solum tenebris vetustatis verum etiam luce libertatis oppressa sunt. . . . [18] . . . arguis occisum esse a C. Rabirio L. Saturninum. . . . [22] . . . "patruus," inquit, "meus cum Saturnino fuit." . . . [28] etenim si C. Rabirio, quod iit ad arma, crucem T. Labienus in campo Martio defigendam putavit, quod tandem excogitabitur in eum supplicium qui vocavit? ac si fides Saturnino data est, quod abs te saepissime dicitur, non eam C. Rabirius sed C. Marius dedit, idemque violavit, si in

---

[2] invisitatis *Kayser*: inusitatis *codd.*   [3] *del. Angelius*

through, not indeed that sentence is passed on a Roman
citizen by the *duumviri* without your orders, but that he
is condemned to death without the case being heard. [13]
Are you really making mention to me of the *Lex Porcia*, of
C. Gracchus, of the liberty of these men here [the People],
finally of some friend of the People, you who have attempted not merely by the use of novel punishments but
also by the unparalleled cruelty of your language to violate
the liberty of the People here, to put their clemency to the
test, to alter their traditions? For those phrases of yours
that delight you, a merciful man and a friend of the People, such as "go, lictor, bind his hands," {which} are foreign
not only to the present liberty and clemency, but even to
Romulus or Numa Pompilius; from the torture chamber
of Tarquinius, the haughtiest and most cruel king, come
those mottoes that you, a gentle person and the People's
friend, very gladly record, such as "veil his head, hang him
on the tree of shame."[1] Such phrases, Romans, have long
since been vanquished in this Republic, not only by the
shadows of antiquity, but also by the light of liberty. . . .
[18] . . . You maintain that L. Saturninus [L. Appuleius
Saturninus (**64A**)] was killed by C. Rabirius. . . . [22] . . .
"My uncle," he says, "was with Saturninus." . . . [28] Indeed, if T. Labienus believed that a cross should be
erected in the Campus Martius for C. Rabirius because he
took up arms, what punishment will then be devised for
the man who summoned him? And if a promise of safety
was given to Saturninus, as is asserted by you very frequently, it was not C. Rabirius, but C. Marius who gave it;

[1] A formula from the traditional *perduellio* proceedings (Liv.
1.26.6–7).

fide non stetit. quae fides, Labiene, qui potuit sine senatus consulto dari? adeone hospes es huiusce urbis, adeone ignarus disciplinae consuetudinisque nostrae ut haec nescias, ut peregrinari in aliena civitate, non in tua magistratum gerere videare? [29] "quid iam ista C. Mario," inquit, "nocere possunt, quoniam sensu et vita caret?"

F 2 Quint. *Inst.* 5.13.20

. . . eaque non modo in propositionibus aut rationibus, sed in toto genere actionis intuenda: an sit crudelis, ut Labieni in Rabirium lege perduellionis . . .

134 L. NOVIUS

As Tribune on the Political Situation (F 1)

F 1 Asc. in Cic. *Mil.* 37 (pp. 41 KS = 46.21–47.9 C.)

Pisone et Gabinio coss. pulso Cicerone in exilium, cum III Idus Sextiles Pompeius in senatum venit, dicitur servo P. Clodi sica excidisse, eaque ad Gabinium consulem delata

and the same person broke it if it was not kept. This promise, Labienus, how could it be given without a decree of the Senate? Are you such a stranger to this city, so ignorant of our traditions and our custom as not to know this, so that you seem to be visiting in a foreign country, not holding a magistracy in your own? [29] "What harm," he says, "can this do to C. Marius now, since he is without life and feeling?"

F 2 Quintilian, *The Orator's Education*

. . . and those points [general principles of defining cases] are to be considered in connection not only with the statements of a case or the reasons given, but with the whole tenor of the pleading: whether it is cruel, as in Labienus' prosecution of Rabirius under the law of treason . . . [**175** F 5] . . .

134 L. NOVIUS

L. Novius (tr. pl. 58 BC; RE Novius 7) was a Tribune of the People in 58 BC and, when appealed to, made a statement about political behavior and procedures in the heated atmosphere of the period (CCMR, App. A: 299).

As Tribune on the Political Situation (F 1)

F 1 Asconius on Cicero, *Pro Milone*

When Piso [L. Calpurnius Piso Caesoninus (**127**)] and Gabinius [A. Gabinius] were consuls [58 BC] and Cicero had been driven into exile, when on the third day before the Ides of Sextilis [August 11] Pompey [Cn. Pompeius Magnus (**111**)] came into the Senate, a dagger is said to

dictum est servo imperatum a P. Clodio ut Pompeius occideretur. Pompeius statim domum rediit ⟨et⟩ ex eo domi ⟨se⟩ tenuit.[1] obsessus est etiam a liberto Clodi Damione, ut ex Actis eius ⟨anni⟩[2] cognovi, in quibus XV kal. Sept. L. Novius tribunus plebis, collega Clodi, cum Damio adversum ⟨L.⟩[3] Flavium praetorem appellaret tribunos et tribuni de appellatione cognoscerent, ita sententiam dixit: "et[4] hoc apparitore P. Clodi vulneratus sum[5] et hominibus armatis praesidiis dispositis a re publica remotus {sum}[6] Cn. Pompeius obsessus[7] est. cum appeller, non utar eius exemplo quem vitupero et iudicium tollam," et reliqua de intercessione.

[1] rediit ⟨et⟩ ex eo domi ⟨se⟩ tenuit *Rinkes*: rediit ex eodem tenuis *codd.*: rediit ex eo domi tenus *Poggius*   [2] *add. Baiter*: temporis *add. Manutius*   [3] *add. KS*   [4] et *codd.*: et ⟨si ab⟩ *KS*: ab *Pighius*   [5] sum *codd., an delendum?*   [6] *del. KS*   [7] obsessus *codd.*: obsessus⟨que⟩ *KS*

135 P. SESTIUS

P. Sestius (praet. 54/50 BC; RE Sestius 6) served in various political offices up to the praetorship. He supported Cicero during the latter's exile (Cic. Q Fr. 1.4.2; Att. 3.20.3).

have slipped out of the hands of a slave of P. Clodius [P. Clodius Pulcher (**137**)], and when it was brought to the consul Gabinius, it was said that the slave had been ordered by P. Clodius to kill Pompey. Pompey immediately returned home ⟨and⟩ from then onward stayed at home. He was even besieged by a freedman of Clodius, Damio, as I have discovered from the records of that ⟨year⟩, in which, on the fifteenth day before the Kalends of September [August 16], L. Novius, a Tribune of the People, a colleague of Clodius, made the following statement, when Damio appealed to the Tribunes against the praetor ⟨L.⟩ Flavius [tr. pl. 60, praet. 58 BC], and the Tribunes were investigating the appeal: "Both I was hurt by this attendant of P. Clodius, and Cn. Pompeius, after armed men had been stationed as guards, has been removed from public life and besieged.[1] When I am appealed to, I will not follow the example of the man whom I criticize and annul the verdict,"[2] and further matters about intercession.

[1] This is what the transmitted reading says (on the text see Sumner 1965, 135–36). Since, according to Asconius, the issue concerns Pompey, and there is no mention of an attack on Novius, there may be confusion in the text, and Pompey might be the subject of the first half of this sentence too.   [2] Perhaps the Tribune P. Clodius Pulcher was inclined to accept the appeal, and therefore Novius announced that he would not do the same.

135 P. SESTIUS

*When Sestius was Tribune of the People in 57 BC, he was badly handled by P. Clodius Pulcher's (**137**) gangs (Cic. Sest. 79–83, 85, 90; Red. sen. 7; Mil. 38; Q Fr. 2.3.6).*

In the following year he was accused under the Lex Plautia de vi *by P. Albinovanus, who was instigated by P. Clodius Pulcher (**137**) to bring the charge (Cic. Vat. 41; Schol. Bob. ad Cic. Sest. [p. 125.15–18 St.]). Defended by many, including Q. Hortensius Hortalus (**92** F 43–45), M. Licinius Crassus Dives (**102** F 11), C. Licinius Macer Calvus (**165** F 29), and Cicero (Cic. Sest.), Sestius was acquitted*

T 1 Cic. *Att.* 7.17.2
= **111** T 10.

Against Antius (F 2)

Catullus mentions a speech by Sestius against someone described as Antius petitor. *The identity and role of Antius (*petitor: *"candidate" or "plaintiff") are uncertain; the con-*

F 2 Catull. 44.10–21

nam, Sestianus dum volo esse conviva, / orationem in Antium[1] petitorem / plenam veneni et pestilentiae legi. / hic me gravedo frigida et frequens tussis / quassavit . . . / . . . / [18] nec deprecor iam, si nefaria scripta / Sesti recepso, quin gravedinem et tussim / [20] non mi, sed ipsi Sestio ferat frigus, / qui tunc vocat me, cum malum librum legi.

[1] orationem in Antium *Statius*: oratione (*vel* -nem) minantium *codd.*

135 P. SESTIUS

(Cic. Q Fr. 2.4.1) (TLRR 271). In the same year Sestius
was charged with ambitus (TLRR 270; *Cic.* Q Fr. 2.3.5),
and again in 52 BC, when he was also defended by Cicero
(TLRR 323; *Cic.* Pro P. Sestio [de ambitu]: *Crawford*
1984, 222–24).

Cicero does not speak very highly of Sestius' style (T 1).

T 1 Cicero, *Letters to Atticus*
= **111** T 10.

Against Antius (F 2)

text and the usage of the word petitor *(cf.* **21** F 30; *Hor.*
Carm. 3.1.11) *suggest that Antius was a candidate for of-*
fice. Sestius might have tried to eliminate him.

F 2 Catullus

For, as I wanted to be Sestius' dining companion, I read
his speech against the candidate Antius, full of poison and
plague. Thereupon a shivering cold and a constant cough
battered me . . . [18] Nor do I now complain, if I should
ever take up Sestius' abominable writings again, if a chill
brings cold and cough [20] not upon me, but upon Sestius
himself, who only invites me when I have read a nasty
book.

136 C. PORCIUS CATO

C. Porcius Cato (tr. pl. 56 BC; RE Porcius 6) is described by Fenestella as an unruly and audacious young man, but a ready speaker (T 1).

In 54 BC Cato was prosecuted by C. Asinius Pollio (174

T 1 Fenestella 22, *FRHist* 70 F 2 (ap. Non., p. 385.6–12 M. = 615 L.)

= F 4.

As a Young Man on Cn. Pompeius Magnus (F 2)

At his earliest recorded public appearance, in 59 BC, Cato called Cn. Pompeius Magnus (111) a "private dictator" when Cato attempted to charge A. Gabinius (cos. 58 BC)

F 2 Cic. *Q Fr.* 1.2.15

rem publicam funditus amisimus, adeo ut ⟨C.⟩[1] Cato, adulescens nullius consilii, sed tamen civis Romanus et Cato, vix vivus effugerit[2] quod, cum Gabinium de ambitu vellet postulare neque praetores diebus aliquot adiri possent vel potestatem sui facerent, in contionem ascendit et Pompeium privatum[3] dictatorem appellavit.

[1] *add. Orelli*   [2] effugerit *Lambinus*: effugeret *codd.*
[3] privatum *nonnulli codd.*: privatus *codd. plerique*

136 C. PORCIUS CATO

F 15–18) for his activities as Tribune of the People; he was defended by M. Aemilius Scaurus (139 F 4) and acquitted (TLRR 283, 286; Cic. Att. 4.15.4, 4.16.5; on the role of C. Licinius Macer Calvus, see 165 F 30).

T 1 Fenestella (quoted by Nonius Marcellus)
= F 4.

As a Young Man on Cn. Pompeius Magnus (F 2)

with bribery and was unable to approach the praetors (CCMR, App. A: 290).

F 2 Cicero, *Letters to Quintus*

We have completely lost the Republic, so much so that <C.> Cato, a young man of no plan, but still a Roman citizen and a Cato, had a narrow escape with his life: when he wanted to charge Gabinius [A. Gabinius, cos. 58 BC] with bribery and for several days the praetors would not let themselves be approached or make themselves available, he [Cato] mounted the platform at a public meeting and called Pompey [Cn. Pompeius Magnus (111)] a private dictator.

*As Tribune of the People for 56 BC, Cato spoke against Cn.
Pompeius Magnus (**111**) in the Senate (F 3–3A; cf. Cic.
Fam. 1.5b.1) and proposed the abrogation of the impe-
rium of P. Cornelius Lentulus Spinther (cos. 57 BC) (Cic.
Q Fr. 2.3.1); he delivered speeches to the People, including*

Against Cn. Pompeius Magnus in the Senate
(F 3–3A)

F 3 Cic. *Q Fr.* 2.3.3

a. d. V[1] Id. Febr. senatus ad Apollinis. . . . eo die Cato
vehementer est in Pompeium invectus et eum oratione
perpetua tamquam reum accusavit; de me multa me invito
cum mea summa laude dixit, cum illius in me perfidiam
increparet. auditus est magno silentio malevolorum.

[1] V *Tunstall*: VI *vel* III *codd.*

F 3A Cic. *Fam.* 1.5b.1 [ad P. Cornelium Lentulum Spin-
therem]

= **111** F 22A.

As Tribune to the People (F 4–5)

F 4 Fenestella 22, *FRHist* 70 F 2 (ap. Non., p. 385.6–12
M. = 615 L.)

Fenestella Annalium lib. XXII: "itaque ut magistratum
tribuni inierunt, C. Cato, turbulentus adulescens et audax
nec imparatus ad deicendum, contionibus adsiduis invi-

criticism of the consuls and of political procedures (F 4–5;
CCMR, App. A: 312); and he spoke on the respective im-
portance of elections and the selection of judges in a debate
*in the Senate in December 57 BC (**128** F 4).*

Against Cn. Pompeius Magnus in the Senate
(F 3–3A)

F 3 Cicero, *Letters to Quintus*

On the fifth day before the Ides of February [February 9,
56 BC] Senate in Temple of Apollo. . . . That day Cato
inveighed against Pompey [Cn. Pompeius Magnus (**111**),
F 24] with great force and prosecuted him in a set speech
like a defendant; he said many things about me with the
greatest praise, against my will, while he denounced that
man's treachery toward me. He was heard in rapt silence
by the ill-disposed.

F 3A Cicero, *Letters to Friends* [to P. Cornelius Lentulus
Spinther]

= **111** F 22A.

As Tribune to the People (F 4–5)

F 4 Fenestella (quoted by Nonius Marcellus)

Fenestella, *Annals*, Book 22: "Therefore, as soon as the
Tribunes had entered office [in Dec. 57 BC], C. Cato, an
unruly and audacious young man and not ill-equipped for
speaking, began, with constant speeches to the People, to
plan hostility, indeed with approving clamor of the People,

89

diam et Ptolomaeo simul, qui iam profectus ex urbe erat, et Publio Lentulo consuli, paranti iam iter, cogitare secundo quidem populi rumore coepit."

F 5 Cic. *Q Fr.* 2.5.4 = 2.4.6

C. Cato contionatus est comitia haberi non siturum si sibi cum populo dies agendi essent exempti.

137 P. CLODIUS PULCHER

P. Clodius Pulcher (tr. pl. 58 BC; RE Clodius 48) was a brother of Ap. Claudius Pulcher (130) and thus a member of the patrician gens Claudia. In 59 BC he transferred to the plebs by adoption, so that he could become a Tribune of the People; presumably from then onward he used the name Clodius instead of Claudius (on his career, see Tatum 1999; on his policies, see Benner 1987). Clodius was recognized as an eloquent speaker (Cic. Att. 4.15.4; Vell. Pat. 2.45.1; Plut. Caes. 9.2).

As a young man, Clodius prosecuted L. Sergius Catilina (112) on a charge of extortion in 65 BC, but Catiline was acquitted (TLRR 212; Cic. Pis. 23; Asc. in Cic. Pis. 23 [p. 9.17–18 C.], in Cic. Tog. cand. [pp. 85.10–20, 89.9–12, 92.8–10 C.]).

During the night of December 4, 62 BC, Clodius, in disguise, entered Bona Dea cult celebrations, which were being held at C. Iulius Caesar's (121) house and were open only to women. When caught, he was brought to trial be-

at the same time against both Ptolomaeus [Ptolemy XII], who had already set off from the city [of Rome], and Publius Lentulus, the consul [P. Cornelius Lentulus Spinther, cos. 57 BC], who was just preparing his departure."

F 5 Cicero, *Letters to Quintus*

C. Cato declared in a public meeting that he would not allow elections to be held if the days for interacting with the People in the assembly were taken away from him.

137 P. CLODIUS PULCHER

fore a special court but acquitted, probably owing to bribery (TLRR 236; Cic. Att. 1.16; Clod. et Cur. [Crawford 1994, 227–63]; Schol. Bob. ad Cic. Clod. et Cur. [p. 85.16–34 St.]; Val. Max. 8.5.5). In early 52 BC Clodius was attacked and killed by T. Annius Milo (138) and some of his followers on the Via Appia.

As Tribune of the People in 58 BC, Clodius proposed many laws. The best known is the Lex Clodia de capite civis Romani (LPPR, *pp. 394–95), according to which anyone who killed a Roman citizen without trial was to be exiled; this measure was aimed at Cicero, who had arranged for the execution of the captured Catilinarian conspirators at the end of his consular year in 63 BC (CCMR, App. A: 296); the* Lex Clodia de exilio Ciceronis (LPPR, *pp. 395–96) confirmed Cicero's exile. Further speeches to the People by Clodius in 57 BC are mentioned (Cic.* Att. *4.3.4; CCMR, App. A: 311).*

As Quaestor to the People (F 1–2)

F 1 Cic. *Att.* 1.14.5

Clodius contiones miseras habebat, in quibus Lucullum,
Hortensium, C. Pisonem, Messallam consulem contume-
liose laedebat; me tantum comperisse omnia criminabatur.

F 2 Schol. Bob. ad Cic. *Clod. et Cur.*, *arg.* (pp. 85.34–86.4
Stangl)

inde igitur kapitalis inimicus in M. Tullium coepit efferri[1]
et, cum illo anno potestate quaestoria fungeretur, aput
populum creberrimis eum contionibus lacessebat; minas
quin immo praetendens ad familiam se plebeiam trans-
iturum, ut tribunus pl. fieret, denuntiabat.

[1] e . . erri *cod.*: efferari *Schuetz*

Altercation with Cicero in the Senate (F 3)

137 P. CLODIUS PULCHER

As Quaestor to the People (F 1–2)

As quaestor in 61 BC, Clodius delivered speeches against his political opponents, including Cicero, before the People (Cic. Att. 1.16.1; CCMR, App. A: 279).

F 1 Cicero, *Letters to Atticus*

Clodius was delivering pitiful public speeches, in which he made abusive attacks on Lucullus [L. Licinius Lucullus (**90**)], Hortensius [Q. Hortensius Hortalus (**92**)], C. Piso [C. Calpurnius Piso (**108**)], and Messalla, the consul [M. Valerius Messalla Niger (**124**), cos. 61 BC]; me he merely accused of having fully informed myself.

F 2 Scholia Bobiensia to Cicero, *Against Clodius and Curio*

Thus, from then onward, he [Clodius] began to be carried away as a deadly enemy of M. Tullius [Cicero] and, since he was holding the office of quaestor in that year [61 BC], harangued him with very frequent speeches before the People; he declared threats, even alleging that he would make the transition to a plebeian family, so that he could become Tribune of the People.

Altercation with Cicero in the Senate (F 3)

In his year as quaestor (61 BC) Clodius confronted his opponents, including Cicero, in the Senate. The altercation Cicero reports seems to have been a dialogue rather than a sequence of set speeches.

F 3 Cic. *Att.* 1.16.10

redeo ad altercationem. surgit pulchellus puer, obicit mihi
me ad Baias fuisse. falsum, sed tamen. "quid? hoc simile
est" inquam "quasi in operto dicas fuisse?" "quid" inquit,
"homini Arpinati cum aquis calidis?" "narra" inquam
"patrono tuo, qui Arpinatis aquas concupivit" (nosti enim
Marianas).[1] "quousque" inquit "hunc regem feremus?"
"regem appellas" inquam "cum Rex tui mentionem nullam
fecerit?"—ille autem Regis hereditatem spe devorarat.
"domum" inquit "emisti." "putes" inquam "dicere 'iudices
emisti.'" "iuranti" inquit "tibi non crediderunt." "mihi
vero" inquam "XXV iudices crediderunt, XXXI, quoniam
nummos ante acceperunt, tibi nihil crediderunt." magnis
clamoribus adflictus conticuit et concidit.

[1] Marianas *codd. det. vel edd. vet.*: marinas *codd.*

Cf. Plut. *Cic.* 29.8.

On Cicero's House in the Senate (F 4)

*In 57 BC Clodius gave a speech in the Senate against the
plan to restore Cicero's house to him, after Clodius had
appropriated it and turned part of the property into a
shrine during Cicero's exile. On the same subject, with*

F 3 Cicero, *Letters to Atticus*

I return to our altercation. The beautiful little boy [Clodius] gets to his feet; he accuses me of having been at Baiae. False, but still. "Well," I say, "is that like saying I have been in a secret place?" "What business," he says, "has a man from Arpinum with the warm springs?" "Tell that to your counsel,"[1] I say, "who was keen to get an Arpinum man's waters" (you know Marius' place, of course). "How long," he says, "are we going to put up with this king [*rex*]?" "You talk about a king," I say, "when Rex made no mention of you?" (he had devoured Rex' inheritance in anticipation).[2] "You have bought a house," he says. "You might think," I say, "he is saying: 'you have bought judges.'" "They did not credit you on oath," he says. "On the contrary," I say, "twenty-five judges gave me credit, and thirty-one gave you none, as they received money in advance." Affected by roars of applause, he fell silent and collapsed.

[1] Clodius' advocate C. Scribonius Curio (**86** F 8) at the trial after the Bona Dea scandal (*TLRR* 236). In the proscriptions, Curio had acquired a villa near Baiae that used to belong to C. Marius, who, like Cicero, came from Arpinum (Schol. Bob. ad Cic. *Clod. et Cur.* [p. 89.4–5 St.]).   [2] Clodius' brother-in-law Q. Marcius Rex (cos. 68 BC) had left him no inheritance.

On Cicero's House in the Senate (F 4)

emphasis on its religious dimension, Clodius spoke to the People (Cic. Har. resp. 8–9; Att. 4.2.3; CCMR, App. A: 310; cf. also Corbeill 2018).

F 4 Cic. *Att.* 4.2.4

. . . Kal. Oct. habetur senatus frequens. adhibentur omnes pontifices qui erant senatores. . . . itaque suo quisque horum loco sententiam rogatus multa secundum causam nostram disputavit. cum ad Clodium ventum est, cupiit diem consumere, neque ei finis est factus; sed tamen, cum horas tris fere dixisset, odio et strepitu senatus coactus est aliquando perorare.

In Response to L. Racilius in the Senate (F 5)

F 5 Cic. *Q Fr.* 2.1.3

tum Clodius rogatus diem dicendo eximere coepit. furebat a Racilio se contumaciter urbaneque vexatum.

Against T. Annius Milo (F 6–7)

In 57 BC Clodius was prosecuted under the Lex Plautia de vi *by T. Annius Milo (138) (TLRR 261, 262). In 56 BC, in turn, Clodius (as aedile) prosecuted T. Annius Milo for*

F 6 Schol. Bob. ad Cic. *Mil.* 40 (p. 122.33–34 Stangl)

id tempus et hic significatur quo Miloni diem dixit P. Clodius, quod gladiatores adhibuisset, ut rogationem posset de Cicerone perferre.

F 4 Cicero, *Letters to Atticus*

. . . on the Kalends of October [October 1, 57 BC] there was a meeting of the Senate, well attended. All the pontiffs who were senators were called in. . . . Accordingly, each of them, as they were called upon for their view in their turn, spoke at length in favor of my case. When Clodius' turn came, he intended to use up the entire day, and there was no putting a stop to him. But still, after he had spoken for something like three hours, he was finally forced to conclude his speech by annoyed noises from the Senate.

In Response to L. Racilius in the Senate (F 5)

At the end of 57 BC Clodius responded to an attack from L. Racilius (tr. pl. 56 BC) in the Senate.

F 5 Cicero, *Letters to Quintus*

Then Clodius was called and began to use up the entire day by his speaking. He was furious that he had been attacked insultingly and wittily by Racilius.

Against T. Annius Milo (F 6–7)

violence, apparently in a trial before the People (TLRR 266; cf. Cic. Sest. 95; Cass. Dio 39.19.1–2).

F 6 Scholia Bobiensia to Cicero, *Pro Milone*

That point of time is indicated here too at which P. Clodius took Milo [T. Annius Milo (**138**)] to court on the grounds that he had called in gladiators, so that he could carry through a motion regarding Cicero.

F 7   Cic. *Q Fr.* 2.3.2

a. d. VII[1] Id. Febr. Milo adfuit. dixit Pompeius . . . sed ut
peroravit, surrexit Clodius. ei tantus clamor a nostris (pla-
cuerat enim referre gratiam) ut neque mente nec lingua
neque ore consisteret. ea res acta est, cum hora sexta vix
Pompeius perorasset, usque ad horam octavam, cum omnia maledicta, versus denique obscenissimi in Clodium et
Clodiam dicerentur. ille furens et exsanguis interrogabat
suos in clamore ipso quis esset qui plebem fame necaret:
respondebant operae "Pompeius." quis Alexandriam ire
cuperet: respondebant "Pompeius." quem ire vellent: respondebant "Crassum" (is aderat tum,[2] Miloni animo non
amico). hora fere nona quasi signo dato Clodiani nostros
consputare coeperunt. exarsit dolor. urgere illi ut loco nos
moverent. factus est a nostris impetus. fuga operarum,
eiectus de rostris Clodius. ac nos quoque tum fugimus, ne
quid in turba. . . . Clodius in Quirinalia prodixit diem.

[1] VII *vel* IIII *codd.*: VIII *Manutius*   [2] *dist. post* tum
edd.: *post* Miloni *Shackleton Bailey*

Against Procilius (F 8)

*In 54 BC Clodius successfully prosecuted Procilius, appar-
ently for murder of a* pater familias *(which may be linked
to the disturbances in 56 BC); Q. Hortensius Hortalus (***92**

F 7 Cicero, *Letters to Quintus*

On the seventh day before the Ides of February [February 7, 56 BC] Milo [T. Annius Milo (**138**)] appeared. Pompey [Cn. Pompeius Magnus (**111**)] spoke [in support of Milo] . . . but when he came to the end, Clodius rose: he received such a clamor from our side (for it had been decided to repay the compliment), that he did not retain control of his thoughts, tongue, and countenance. That situation, with Pompey having finished just at the sixth hour, lasted until the eighth hour, when all manner of insults and, at the end, highly scabrous verses were uttered against Clodius and Clodia. That man, furious and pale, started to ask his followers, in the middle of the shouting, who it was who was starving the commons to death. The gang answered: "Pompey." Who wanted to go to Alexandria. They answered: "Pompey." Whom they wanted to go. They answered: "Crassus" [M. Licinius Crassus Dives (**102**)] (he was present at the time, not with a friendly mind toward Milo). At around the ninth hour the Clodians started spitting at our men, as though on a signal. Resentment flared up. They made a push to dislodge us from our place. There was a countercharge from our side. The flight of the gang; Clodius hurled from the Rostra. And we too then fled, fearing that something [might happen] in the mêlée. . . . Clodius had the trial postponed to the Quirinalia [February 17].

Against Procilius (F 8)

F 47) *defended the accused* (TLRR 284; *cf.* Cic. Att. 4.16.5).

F 8 Cic. *Att.* 4.15.4

= **92** F 47.

On Behalf of M. Aemilius Scaurus (F 9)

F 9 Asc. in Cic. *Scaur.*, *arg.* (p. 18 KS = 20.13–18 C.)

= **92** F 48.

On Behalf of Lentulus (F 9A)

F 9A Val. Max. 4.2.5

Ciceronis autem factum adeo visum est probabile ut imitari id ne inimicissimus quidem illi P. Pulcher dubitaverit.
qui, incesti crimine a tribus Lentulis accusatus, unum ex
his ambitus reum patrocinio suo protexit, atque in animum
induxit et iudices et praetorem et Vestae aedem intuens
amicum Lentulo agere, inter quae ille, salutem eius foedo
crimine obruere cupiens, hostili voce peroraverat.

F 8 Cicero, *Letters to Atticus*

= **92** F 47.

On Behalf of M. Aemilius Scaurus (F 9)

*Also in 54 BC, Clodius spoke on behalf of M. Aemilius Scaurus (**139**), who was accused of extortion by P. Valerius Triarius (**148** F 1–2) and defended by several advocates (TLRR 295; cf. **148**).*

F 9 Asconius on Cicero, *Pro Scauro*

= **92** F 48.

On Behalf of Lentulus (F 9A)

*Clodius spoke on behalf of one of the Lentuli (cf. **157** F 3–4), who had previously prosecuted him in the Bona Dea scandal and was now charged with bribery (TLRR 237).*

F 9A Valerius Maximus, *Memorable Doings and Sayings*

And Cicero's action [to defend individuals who had previously acted against him] seemed so deserving of approval that even his greatest enemy, P. Pulcher, did not hesitate to imitate it. Accused on a charge of sexual impurity by three Lentuli, he protected one of them, accused of bribery, with his advocacy and brought himself to act as Lentulus' friend, looking at the judges and the praetor and the Temple of Vesta, among which that man [Lentulus] had argued the case to the end with a hostile voice, seeking to overwhelm his safety with a foul charge.

138 T. ANNIUS MILO

*T. Annius Milo (tr. pl. 57 BC; RE Annius 67) prosecuted
P. Clodius Pulcher (137) in 57 BC (TLRR 261, 262); in 56
BC he was charged by P. Clodius Pulcher (137 F 6–7)
(TLRR 266); in 52 BC Milo had P. Clodius Pulcher killed.
Milo spoke about this incident to the People or at least to*

On P. Clodius Pulcher to the People (F 1–2)

F 1 Asc. in Cic. *Mil.*, *arg.* (p. 29 KS = 33.21–24 C.)

contionem ei post aliquot dies dedit M. Caelius tribunus
plebis atque ipse etiam causam egit[1] ad populum. dicebant uterque Miloni a Clodio factas esse insidias.

[1] atque *Madvig:* ac ci *vel* acci *vel* aci *codd.:* ac Cicero *coni. in*
codd. rec.   egit *Madvig:* etiam *vel* et *codd.:* eius egit *Halm*

F 2 App. *B Civ.* 2.22.80–82

καὶ αὐτὸν ὁ Καίλιος εὐθὺς ἐσιόντα εἷλκεν ἐς τὴν
ἀγορὰν ἐπὶ τοὺς παρ᾿ αὐτοῦ δεδωροδοκηκότας ὥσπερ
ἐπ᾿ ἐκκλησίαν, ὑποκρινόμενος μὲν ἀγανακτεῖν καὶ οὐ
διδόναι τῆς δίκης ἀναβολήν, ἐλπίζων δέ, εἰ αὐτὸν οἱ
παρόντες μεθεῖεν, ἐκλύσειν τὴν δίκην τὴν ἀληθε-
στέραν. [81] καὶ Μίλων μὲν οὐ βουλεῦσαι τὸ ἔργον
εἰπών (οὐ γὰρ ἂν μετὰ σκευῆς καὶ γυναικὸς ἐπὶ ταῦτα
ὁρμῆσαι), τὸν λοιπὸν λόγον κατὰ τοῦ Κλωδίου διε-
τίθετο ὡς θρασυτάτου δὴ καὶ φίλου θρασυτάτων, οἳ

138 T. ANNIUS MILO

a group of them (F 1–2; CCMR, App. A: 329). At the trial Milo was found guilty of the murder despite Cicero's defense (Cic. Mil.; cf. Cic. Sest. 86–89; Off. 2.58) and went into exile (TLRR 309). In the same year Milo was subject to multiple charges (TLRR 306, 310, 311, 312).

On P. Clodius Pulcher to the People (F 1–2)

F 1 Asconius on Cicero, *Pro Milone*

A few days later M. Caelius, a Tribune of the People [M. Caelius Rufus (**162**), tr. pl. 52 BC, F 29–30], granted him [Milo] an appearance before a public meeting, and he [Caelius] himself even presented the case before the People. Both said that an ambush for Milo had been set by Clodius [P. Clodius Pulcher (**137**)].

F 2 Appian, *Civil Wars*

And immediately as he [Milo] entered [the city of Rome], Caelius [M. Caelius Rufus (**162**), tr. pl. 52 BC] dragged him to the Forum to those whom he had bribed, as though to a meeting of the People, pretending to be very indignant and not willing to grant any delay to the trial, but hoping that, if those present should acquit him [Milo], he would escape a more regular trial. [81] And Milo said that the deed was not premeditated (for one would not set out for that with luggage and a wife); he directed the remainder of his speech against Clodius [P. Clodius Pulcher (**137**)] as an extremely rash man and a friend of extremely rash men, who had even set fire to the Senate house [Cu-

103

καὶ τὸ βουλευτήριον ἐπικατέπρησαν αὐτῷ· [82] ἔτι δ᾽
αὐτοῦ λέγοντος οἵ τε λοιποὶ δήμαρχοι καὶ τοῦ δήμου
τὸ ἀδιάφθορον ὁπλισάμενοι ἐνέβαλον ἐς τὴν ἀγοράν.

139 M. AEMILIUS SCAURUS FILIUS

*M. Aemilius Scaurus (praet. 56 BC; RE Aemilius 141), a
son of M. Aemilius Scaurus (43), administered the province of Sardinia after his praetorship. Upon his return he
was prosecuted for extortion by P. Valerius Triarius (148
F 1–2); defended by six advocates, including Cicero (Cic.
Scaur.) as well as himself (F 5), he was acquitted (TLRR*

Against Cn. Cornelius Dolabella (F 1–3)

F 1   Cic. *Verr.* 2.1.97

itaque M. Scaurus, qui Cn. Dolabellam accusavit, istum in
sua potestate ac dicione tenuit. homo adulescens cum istius in inquirendo multa furta ac flagitia cognosset, fecit
perite et callide; volumen eius rerum gestarum maximum
isti ostendit; ab homine quae voluit in Dolabellam abstulit;
istum testem produxit; dixit iste quae velle accusatorem
putavit.

ria Hostilia] over his body [52 BC]. [82] While he was still
speaking, the other Tribunes, with the unbribed portion
of the People, burst into the Forum, armed.

139 M. AEMILIUS SCAURUS FILIUS

*295; cf. 148; Gruen 1974, 333–37). Later, Scaurus was
prosecuted for* ambitus *by the same accuser; this time,
though again defended by Cicero (Cic.* Pro M. Aemilio
Scauro [de ambitu]: *Crawford 1984, 198–201), he was
sent into exile in 52 BC (TLRR 300, 319).*

Against Cn. Cornelius Dolabella (F 1–3)

*Scaurus successfully prosecuted Cn. Cornelius Dolabella
(praet. 81 BC) when the latter returned from the governorship of Cilicia (80–79 BC), where C. Verres had been
among his staff (TLRR 135).*

F 1 Cicero, *Verrine Orations*

Therefore M. Scaurus, who prosecuted Cn. Dolabella,
kept that man [C. Verres] in his power and under his control. Being a young man, when in the course of his inquir-
ies he had discovered that man's numerous thefts and evil
deeds, he acted ingeniously and skillfully: he showed him
a very large book full of his exploits; he extracted from the
man what he wanted against Dolabella; he called him as a
witness; that man [Verres] said what he supposed the prosecutor wished.

F 2 Asc. in Cic. *Scaur.* II.45 (p. 23 KS = 26.13–18 C.)
= **121** F 20.

F 3 Ps.-Asc. in Cic. *Div. Caec.* 24 (p. 194.6–8 Stangl)
= **92** F 19.

On Behalf of C. Porcius Cato (F 4)

*After C. Porcius Cato (**136**) had been Tribune of the People in 56 BC, he was prosecuted in 54 BC by C. Asinius Pollio (**174** F 15–18) for his activities in that office; Scau-*

F 4 Asc. in Cic. *Scaur.*, arg. (p. 16 KS = 18.15–17 C.)

erat tamen aliquando inter patronos causarum {s}et,[1] postquam ex provincia redierat, dixerat pro C. Catone, isque erat absolutus a. d. IIII[2] Non. Quint.

[1] {s}et *Madvig*: sed *codd.*: scilicet *Baiter*   [2] a. d. IIII *Beier*: ad IIII *vel* ad III *codd.*

On His Own Behalf (F 5)

F 5 Asc. in Cic. *Scaur.*, arg. (p. 18 KS = 20.18–21 C.)

ipse quoque Scaurus dixit pro se ac magnopere iudices movit et squalore et lacrimis et aedilitatis effusae memoria

F 2 Asconius on Cicero, *Pro Scauro*
= **121** F 20.

F 3 Pseudo-Asconius on Cicero, *Against Caecilius*
= **92** F 19.

On Behalf of C. Porcius Cato (F 4)

*rus defended him successfully in what seems to have been
a second trial* (TLRR 286; Cic. Att. 4.15.4: **92** F 47; 4.16.5;
on the role of C. Licinius Macer Calvus, see **165** F 30).

F 4 Asconius on Cicero, *Pro Scauro*

Still he [Scaurus] sometimes appeared among the pleaders of cases and, after he had returned from the province
[from his propraetorship in Sardinia], he had spoken on
behalf of C. Cato [C. Porcius Cato (**136**)], and the latter
was acquitted on the fourth day before the Nones of Quintilis [July 4].

On His Own Behalf (F 5)

*When Scaurus was prosecuted for extortion by P. Valerius
Triarius* (**148** F 1–2), *he was defended by six advocates,
including Cicero (Cic. Scaur.) as well as himself, and was
acquitted* (TLRR 295).

F 5 Asconius on Cicero, *Pro Scauro*

Scaurus himself also spoke on his own behalf and greatly
moved the judges, by filthy appearance, by tears, and by

ac favore populari ac praecipue paternae auctoritatis recordatione.

140 M. CALIDIUS

*M. Calidius (praet. 57 BC; RE Calidius 4) supported Cic-
ero's recall from exile in 57 BC (Cic. Red. sen. 22). Later,
he unsuccessfully stood for the consulship twice (Cic. Fam.
8.4.1; Att. 5.19.3, 6.8.3). In the civil war he followed C.
Iulius Caesar (121) and was given the administration of
the province of Gallia Cisalpina; he died at Placentia in
48/47 BC.*

*Calidius studied oratory with the Greek rhetorician
Apollodorus of Pergamon (Hieron. Ab Abr. 1953 = 64 BC
[p. 154a Helm]) and was one of the older Atticists in Rome.*

T 1 Cic. *Brut.* 274–76

[CICERO:] sed de M. Calidio dicamus aliquid, qui non fuit
orator unus e multis, potius inter multos prope singularis
fuit: ita reconditas exquisitasque sententias mollis et per-
lucens vestiebat oratio. nihil tam tenerum quam illius
comprehensio verborum, nihil tam flexibile, nihil quod
magis ipsius arbitrio fingeretur, ut nullius oratoris aeque
in potestate fuerit: quae primum ita pura erat ut nihil li-
quidius, ita libere fluebat ut nusquam adhaeresceret; nullum nisi loco positum et tamquam in vermiculato emble-
mate, ut ait Lucilius [Lucil. 84 Marx], structum verbum
videres; nec vero {n}ullum[1] aut durum aut insolens aut

---

[1] {n}ullum *edd.*: nullum *codd.*

the memory of his lavish aedileship [58 BC; cf. Cic. *Off.* 2.57], as well as by his popularity with the People and particularly by the recollection of his father's authority [M. Aemilius Scaurus (**43**)].

140 M. CALIDIUS

In Cicero, Calidius is described as an outstanding orator, because of his elegant and pure diction, the appropriate choice and careful positioning of words, the use of figures, and a precise arrangement of material; the only aspect he is said to have lacked is a forceful presentation moving the listeners (T 1; cf. T 2; Quint. Inst. *12.10.39; Vell. Pat. 2.36.2).*

In 54 BC Calidius made an attempt to speak on behalf of A. Gabinius (cos. 58 BC) (Cic. Q Fr. *3.2.1; TLRR 303).*

T 1 Cicero, *Brutus*

[CICERO:] But let us say something about M. Calidius, who was not just one orator out of the many, but rather among the many almost unique: to such an extent did he always clothe recondite and carefully chosen thoughts in a flexible and translucent diction. Nothing as smooth as his arrangement of words, nothing as flexible, nothing that could not be fashioned more according to his own will, so that no orator had the power in the same way: first of all, his language was so pure that nothing was clearer; it flowed so clearly that it stuck nowhere; you would only see words placed in their proper position and arranged as if in a mosaic design, as Lucilius says [Lucil. 84 Marx]; and none was harsh, unusual, trivial, or far-fetched; and not only

humile aut {in}[2] longius ductum; ac non propria verba rerum sed pleraque translata, sic tamen ut ea non inruisse in alienum locum sed immigrasse in suum diceres; nec vero haec soluta nec diffluentia sed astricta numeris, non aperte nec eodem modo semper sed varie dissimulanterque conclusis. [275] erant autem et verborum et sententiarum illa lumina quae vocant Graeci σχήματα, quibus tamquam insignibus in ornatu distinguebatur omnis oratio. qua de re agitur autem illud quod multis locis in iuris consultorum includitur formulis, id[3] ubi esset videbat. [276] accedebat ordo rerum plenus artis, actio liberalis totumque dicendi placidum et sanum genus. quod si est optimum suaviter dicere, nihil est quod melius hoc quaerendum putes. sed cum a nobis paulo ante dictum sit tria videri esse quae orator efficere deberet, ut doceret, ut delectaret, ut moveret, duo summe tenuit, ut et rem illustraret disserendo et animos eorum qui audirent devinciret voluptate; aberat tertia illa laus, qua permoveret atque incitaret animos, quam plurimum pollere diximus; nec erat ulla vis atque contentio: sive consilio, quod eos, quorum altior oratio actioque esset ardentior, furere atque bacchari arbitraretur, sive quod natura non esset ita factus sive quod non consuesset sive quod non nosset.[4] hoc unum illi, si nihil utilitatis habebat, afuit; si opus erat, defuit.

[2] *del. edd.*
[3] id *Corradus*: et *codd.*
[4] nosset *Friedrich*: posset *codd.*

words in their proper meanings, but also many in a meta-
phorical sense, yet in such a way that you would say, not
that they had usurped an alien place, but rather that they
had moved into their own; furthermore, these [words]
were not left loose and disjointed, but were bound together by rhythms, constructed not obviously and not in
always the same manner, but rather in varied and dis-
guised ways. [275] There were also those highlights of
words and ideas that the Greeks call *schemata* ["figures"],
with which, like decorations on a garment, his entire
speech was embellished. Moreover, he saw clearly "the
point at issue," that [phrase] that is included in the formu-
lae of legal experts in many places. [276] In addition there
was an arrangement of subject matter full of technical
skill, a gentlemanlike delivery, and, overall, a quiet and
sincere manner of speaking. If then it is best to speak with
charm, you should think that there is nothing better that
needs to be sought than him. But since it was said by us a
little while ago that there seem to be three things that the
orator must effect, to teach, to please, and to move, two
of these he mastered to the highest degree, so that he
lucidly explained a matter in exposition and bound the
minds of those who listened by charm. That third merit
was absent, that by which one moves and arouses emo-
tions, which we have described as being most powerful;
there was no force and vigor: be it due to deliberate
choice, since he believed that those whose language was
more elevated and whose delivery was more vehement
were in frenzy and delirium, or because he was not pre-
disposed to this by nature, or because he was not used to
it, or because he did not have the knowledge. The absence
of this one quality for him was, if it was of no use, a lack,
if it was essential, a defect. [continued by F 3]

T 2 Quint. *Inst.* 12.10.11

tum deinde efflorescat non multum inter se distantium tempore oratorum ingens proventus. hic vim Caesaris, indolem Caeli, subtilitatem Calidi, diligentiam Pollionis, dignitatem Messalae, sanctitatem Calvi, gravitatem Bruti, acumen Sulpici, acerbitatem Cassi reperiemus . . .

Against Q. Gallius (F 3–6)

In the mid 60s BC Calidius prosecuted Q. Gallius (aed. pl. 67, praet. 65 BC) for ambitus *during his campaign for the praetorship (Asc. in Cic.* Tog. cand. *[p. 88.5–9 C.]) and*

F 3 Cic. *Brut.* 277–78

[Cicero:] quin etiam memini, cum in accusatione sua Q. Gallio crimini[1] dedisset sibi eum venenum paravisse idque a se esse deprensum seseque chirographa testificationes indicia quaestiones manifestam rem deferre diceret deque eo crimine accurate et exquisite disputavisset, me in respondendo, cum essem argumentatus, quantum res ferebat, hoc ipsum etiam posuisse pro argumento, quod ille, cum pestem capitis sui, cum indicia mortis se comperisse manifesto et manu tenere diceret, tam solute egisset, tam

---

[1] crimini *edd.*: crimine *codd.*

T 2 Quintilian, *The Orator's Education*

Then let the great crop of orators who were not much distant from each other in time flourish. Here we will find the vigor of Caesar [C. Iulius Caesar (**121**)], the talent of Caelius [M. Caelius Rufus (**162**)], the subtlety of Calidius, the accuracy of Pollio [C. Asinius Pollio (**174**)], the dignity of Messalla [M. Valerius Messalla Corvinus (**176**)], the scrupulousness of Calvus [C. Licinius Macer Calvus (**165**)], the gravity of Brutus [M. Iunius Brutus (**158**)], the acumen of Sulpicius [Ser. Sulpicius Rufus (**118**)], and the asperity of Cassius [Cassius Severus] . . .

Against Q. Gallius (F 3–6)

added a charge of attempted poisoning at the trial; the defendant was supported by Cicero (Cic. Pro Q. Gallio: Crawford 1994, 149–62) and acquitted (TLRR 214).

F 3 Cicero, *Brutus*

[CICERO:] [continued from T 1] Indeed I recall the following: in his prosecution he [Calidius] had charged that Q. Gallius had attempted to poison him, and he said that he had discovered that himself and that he was bringing autographs, proofs, circumstantial evidence, confessions under torture, clear evidence, and he had talked about this charge with attention to detail and meticulous care. In my reply, then, after presenting such arguments as the case afforded, I put as an argument also this very point: that, although he said that he had obtained and held in hand proofs of the [planned] destruction of his own life, indications of his being killed, he had presented his case so

leniter, tam oscitanter. [278] "tu istuc, M. Calidi, nisi fingeres, sic ageres? praesertim cum ista eloquentia alienorum hominum pericula defendere acerrime sole‹a›s,[2] tuum neglegeres? ubi dolor, ubi ardor animi, qui etiam ex infantium ingeniis elicere voces et querelas solet? nulla perturbatio animi, nulla corporis, frons non[3] percussa, non femur; pedis, quod minimum est, nulla supplosio. itaque tantum afuit[4] ut inflammares nostros animos, somnum isto loco vix tenebamus." sic nos summi oratoris vel sanitate vel vitio pro argumento ad diluendum crimen usi sumus.

[2] sole‹a›s *edd.*: soles *codd.*   [3] frons non *codd.*: non frons *Quint. Inst. 11.3.123*   [4] afuit *codd.*: abest *Quint.*

Cf. Val. Max. 8.10.3; Quint. *Inst.* 11.3.123, 11.3.155.

F 4 Caelius ap. Cic. *Fam.* 8.9.5

Calidius in defensione sua fuit disertissimus, in accusatione satis frigidus.

F 5 Fest., p. 404.29–35 L.

SUFES dict‹us Poenorum ma›|gistratus, ut Oscor‹um meddix tuticus.› | Calidius in oration‹e in Q. Gal›|lium:[1] "nonne vobis i[2] [– – –] | et fumus[3] prosequ‹i›[4] [– – –] | videtur? senatus cens ⌊uit referentibus⌋ | sufetis."

[1] *suppl. Müller (post Scaligerum)*   [2] i‹udices› *Müller*
[3] *an* funus? *Lindsay*   [4] ‹i› *cod. teste Ursino*

Cf. Paul. *Fest.*, p. 405.6–7 L.: sufes consul lingua Poenorum. Calidius: "senatus," inquit, | "censuit referentibus sufetis."

languidly, so calmly, so listlessly: [278] "Would you, M.
Calidius, present your case in that way if you were not
inventing? Particularly since with that eloquence of yours
you are in the habit of warding off the dangers of other
men very vigorously, would you neglect your own? Where
is the distress, where the burning indignation that tends
to bring out outbursts and complaints even from the intel-
lects of those who are not eloquent? But no hint of agita-
tion, neither of mind nor of body; no striking of the forehead, not of the thigh; no stamping of the foot, which is
the least. Therefore, you were so far from igniting our
feelings; we could scarcely refrain from going to sleep
then and there." In such fashion we used this great orator's
manner of speaking, whether it is wise restraint or a defect, as an argument for breaking down his accusation.

F 4 Caelius in Cicero, *Letters to Friends*

In his own defense Calidius was very eloquent, in the
prosecution rather without energy.[1]

[1] Since the prosecution of Q. Gallius is the only one known
for Calidius, the remark has been referred to this speech. It has
also been connected with the only known occasion when Calidius
was prosecuted (F 11–12).

F 5 Festus

sufes is the na<me for a ma>gistrate <among the Cartha-
ginians>, as among the Os<cans *meddix tuticus*.> Calidius
in the speech <against Q. Gal>lius: "Does it not seem to
you . . . and smoke accompany [him] [?]? The Senate has
issued a decree on the motion of the Carthaginian magistrates."

F 6 Non., p. 208.27–30 M. = 307 L.

HORREA genere neutro, ut saepe. feminino Calidius oratione in Quintum Gallium: "quarum iacent muri, navalia
horreae curiaque et tabulariae publicae." eiusdem generis
tabularias quo et horreas dixit.

On Cicero's House (F 7)

F 7 Quint. *Inst.* 10.1.23
= **158** F 19.

On Behalf of the People of Tenedos (F 8)

F 8 Cic. *Q Fr.* 2.10(9).2
= **122** F 7.

F 6 Nonius Marcellus

horrea ["granaries"], of neuter gender, as commonly. Of feminine gender, Calidius in the oration against Quintus Gallius: "their walls, shipyards, granaries, meeting house, and public archives lie in ruins." According to the same principle by which he also said *horreae*, he said *tabulariae* ["archives"; fem. pl.].

On Cicero's House (F 7)

As praetor in 57 BC, Calidius spoke on the issue of the restoration of Cicero's house to him after his return from exile, like Cicero himself (Cic. Dom.).

F 7 Quintilian, *The Orator's Education*
= **158** F 19.

On Behalf of the People of Tenedos (F 8)

In 54 BC, along with others, Calidius spoke on behalf of the liberty of the people of Tenedos.

F 8 Cicero, *Letters to Quintus*
= **122** F 7.

On Behalf of M. Aemilius Scaurus (F 9)

F 9 Asc. in Cic. *Scaur.*, *arg.* (p. 18 KS = 20.13–18 C.)
= **92** F 48.

On Behalf of T. Annius Milo (F 10)

F 10 Asc. in Cic. *Mil.*, *arg.* (p. 30 KS = 34.15–21 C.)
= **92** F 49.

On His Own Behalf (F 11–12)

F 11 Caelius ap. Cic. *Fam.* 8.4.1

invideo tibi. tam multa cottidie quae mireris[1] istoc perferuntur. primum illud, absolutum Messalam, deinde eun-
dem condemnatum; C. Marcellum consulem factum, M.
Calidium[2] ab repulsa postulatum a Galli‹i›s[3] duobus . . .

[1] mireris *codd. det. vel edd. vet.*: mirer *codd.*: mirere *Rutilius*   [2] Cal(l)idium *Corradus*: claudium *codd.*   [3] Galli‹i›s
Corradus: gallis *codd.*

118

On Behalf of M. Aemilius Scaurus (F 9)

Also in 54 BC, Calidius was one of the advocates who defended M. Aemilius Scaurus (*139*) (TLRR 295; cf. *148*).

F 9 Asconius on Cicero, *Pro Scauro*

= **92** F 48.

On Behalf of T. Annius Milo (F 10)

In 52 BC Calidius contributed to the defense of T. Annius Milo (*138*) at one of his trials (TLRR 306).

F 10 Asconius on Cicero, *Pro Milone*

= **92** F 49.

On His Own Behalf (F 11–12)

In 51 BC Calidius was prosecuted for misconduct in that year's election campaign for the consulship by two Gallii, who may have been the sons of Q. Gallius (cf. F 3–6), and seems to have defended himself (TLRR 330).

F 11 Caelius in Cicero, *Letters to Friends*

I envy you. So much that you must be surprised at is conveyed in your direction every day: first this, that Messalla [M. Valerius Messalla Rufus, cos. 53 BC] was acquitted; then, that the same person was convicted; that C. Marcellus [C. Claudius Marcellus, cos. 50 BC] was elected consul; that M. Calidius, after his electoral defeat, was prosecuted by the two Gallii . . .

F 12 Caelius ap. Cic. *Fam.* 8.9.5

= F 4.

On Cn. Pompeius Magnus in the Senate (F 12A)

F 12A Caes. *BCiv.* 1.2.3–5

dixerat aliquis leniorem sententiam, ut . . . M. Calidius, qui censebat ut Pompeius in suas provincias proficisceretur ne quae esset armorum causa; timere Caesarem correptis ab eo duabus legionibus ne ad eius periculum reservare et retinere eas ad urbem Pompeius videretur. ut M. Rufus, qui sententiam Calidi paucis fere mutatis rebus sequebatur. [4] hi omnes convicio L. Lentuli consulis correpti exagitabantur. [5] Lentulus sententiam Calidi pronuntiaturum se omnino negavit.

141 C. SICINIUS

C. Sicinius (quaest. ca. 70 BC; RE Sicinius 7) died after holding the office of quaestor. According to Cicero, at that point C. Sicinius was already a promising orator and a recognized speaker in the law courts; he was influenced by

F 12 Caelius in Cicero, *Letters to Friends*
= F 4.

On Cn. Pompeius Magnus in the Senate (F 12A)

In 49 BC Calidius put forward a motion concerning Cn.
Pompeius Magnus (111) at a meeting of the Senate.

F 12A Caesar, *Civil War*

Some had made milder proposals [than Q. Caecilius Metellus Pius Scipio Nasica (**154**)], such as . . . M. Calidius,
who proposed that Pompey [Cn. Pompeius Magnus (**111**)]
leave for his provinces so that there should not be any
cause for fighting; Caesar [C. Iulius Caesar (**121**)] was
afraid, he said, after two of his legions had been snatched
away by him, that Pompey might seem to be holding them
in reserve and keeping them near the city [of Rome] as a
threat against him. Or such as M. Rufus [M. Caelius Rufus
(**162**)], who supported Calidius' proposal with just a few
amendments. [4] All these men, rebuked with abuse from
L. Lentulus, the consul [L. Cornelius Lentulus Crus
(**157**), F 5], had strong feelings aroused. [5] Lentulus refused outright to ask for a vote on Calidius' proposal.

141 C. SICINIUS

the school of the Greek rhetorician Hermagoras and relied
on discipline and preparation, along with a good com-
mand of language (T 1).

T 1 Cic. *Brut.* 263

[CICERO:] C. Sicinius[1] igitur Q. Pompei illius, qui censor fuit, ex filia nepos, quaestorius mortuus est; probabilis orator, iam vero etiam probatus, ex hac inopi ad ornandum, sed ad inveniendum expedita Hermagorae disciplina. ea dat rationes certas et praecepta dicendi, quae si minorem habent apparatum—sunt enim exilia—tamen habent ordinem et quasdam errare in dicendo non patientis vias. has ille tenens et paratus ad causas veniens, verborum non egens, ipsa illa comparatione disciplinaque dicendi iam in patronorum numerum pervenerat.

1 Sicinius *edd.*: Sinicius *vel* sinucius *codd.*

142 C. VISELLIUS VARRO

C. Visellius Varro (tr. mil. 80–79 BC; RE Visellius 3) was a cousin of Cicero (T 1; Cic. De or. 2.2; Prov. cons. 40). He reached the office of curule aedile (precise date uncertain) and died afterward while in charge of a court (T 1; TLRR 254).

Cicero reports that the public did not regard Varro's oratory very highly; he agrees that his manner of speaking was abrupt and fast, and thus obscure, but notes his learning, appropriateness of diction, and frequent use of sententiae (T 1).

T 1 Cicero, *Brutus*

[CICERO:] C. Sicinius, then, a grandson of that Q. Pompeius, who was censor [Q. Pompeius (**30**), censor 131 BC], by his daughter, died after having been quaestor; an orator deserving of recognition, indeed even already recognized; from that school of Hermagoras [rhetorician from Temnos], meager in embellishment, but handy for invention [cf. **145** T 1]. It furnishes precise principles and rules of speaking, which, though they give rather little embellishment—they are in fact barren—still provide order and certain lines that do not permit one to stray in speaking. Keeping close to them and coming to his cases well prepared, not lacking in words, with that equipment and schooling in speaking, he [Sicinius] had already come to be included in the ranks of pleaders. [continued by **142** T 1]

142 C. VISELLIUS VARRO

Varro seems to have appeared as a witness in the trial of C. Verres in 70 BC (Cic. Verr. 2.1.71). In 58 BC Varro produced a draft bill on Cicero's recall from exile for the Tribune of the People T. Fadius (Cic. Att. 3.23.4). A charge advanced by Otacilia, Laterensis' wife, with whom Varro was allegedly having an affair, was dismissed by the presiding magistrate (TLRR 391; Val. Max. 8.2.2).

T 1 Cic. *Brut.* 264

[CICERO:] erat etiam vir doctus in primis C. Visellius Varro, consobrinus meus, qui fuit cum Sicinio aetate coniunctus. is, cum post curulem aedilitatem iudex quaestionis esset, est mortuus; in quo fateor vulgi iudicium a iudicio meo dissensisse. nam populo non erat satis vendibilis: praeceps quaedam et cum idcirco obscura quia peracuta, tum rapida et celeritate caecata oratio; sed neque verbis aptiorem cito alium dixerim neque sententiis crebriorem. praeterea perfectus in litteris iurisque civilis iam a patre Aculeone traditam tenuit disciplinam.

142A C. CALPURNIUS PISO FRUGI

C. Calpurnius Piso Frugi (quaest. 58 BC; RE Calpurnius 93) was married to Cicero's daughter Tullia from 67 BC (Cic. Att. 1.3.3). Piso supported Cicero during the latter's exile in 58 BC (e.g., Cic. Red. sen. 17, 38; Red. pop. 7; Sest.

T 1 Cic. *Brut.* 272

[CICERO:] studio autem neminem nec industria maiore cognovi, quamquam ne ingenio quidem qui praestiterit facile dixerim C. Pisoni genero meo. nullum tempus illi umquam vacabat aut a forensi dictione aut a commentatione domestica aut a scribendo aut a cogitando. itaque tantos processus efficiebat ut evolare, non excurrere vide-

T 1 Cicero, *Brutus*

[CICERO:] There was also a man of conspicuous learning, C. Visellius Varro, my cousin, who was similar in age to Sicinius [C. Sicinius (**141**)]. When he, after his curule aedileship, was serving as chair of a court, he passed away. In his case I confess that the judgment of the multitude differed from my judgment. For his oratory found no ready sale with the People: his oratory was abrupt to some extent and obscure because very clever, and also fast and unclear because of speed. Yet I could not easily name anyone superior in appropriateness of diction or in frequent use of well-expressed thoughts. Moreover, he was thoroughly trained in literature, and he had mastery of civil law already passed on to him from his father Aculeo [C. Aculeo, husband of Cicero's aunt Helvia].

142A C. CALPURNIUS PISO FRUGI

54, 68; Fam. 14.2.2); he died in 57 BC before Cicero's return to Rome (Cic. Sest. 68). In Cicero, Piso is presented as a serious and excellent speaker (T 1).

T 1 Cicero, *Brutus*

[CICERO:] But I have not known anyone with greater zeal and industry; to be sure, I would not easily say that even in talent anyone surpassed C. Piso, my son-in-law. For him no space of time was ever free from pleading in the forum or from rehearsal at home or from writing or from planning. Accordingly, he achieved so much progress that he seemed to fly, not to run; and his words were carefully

retur; eratque verborum et dilectus elegans et apta et quasi rotunda constructio; cumque argumenta excogitabantur ab eo multa et firma ad probandum tum concinnae acutaeque sententiae; gestusque natura ita venustus ut ars etiam, quae non erat, et e disciplina motus quidam videretur accedere. vereor ne amore videar plura quam fuerint in illo dicere; quod non ita est; alia enim de illo maiora dici possunt. nam nec continentia nec pietate nec ullo genere virtutis quemquam eiusdem aetatis cum illo conferendum puto.

143 + 144 P. ET L. COMINII

About the brothers P. and L. Cominius (RE Cominius 4, 8, 11) and their style of speaking nothing more is known than what emerges from the references to their oratorical appearances (F 1, 3); an extant speech is mentioned by Asconius (F 2). Cicero names the brothers P. and L. Co-

Against C. Aelius Paetus Staienus (F 1)

F 1 Cic. *Clu.* 99–102

quid quod Staienus est condemnatus? non dico hoc tempore, iudices, id quod nescio an dici oporteat, illum maiestatis esse condemnatum; non recito testimonia hominum

chosen, his sentences compact and periodic; and the arguments devised by him were varied and strong in order to convince; above all, his ideas shrewd and neatly put; and the movement of his body was so graceful by nature that art and some movement based on training seemed to be there, as well, which was not the case. I am afraid lest out of affection I seem to mention more than there was in him. This is not the case; for other and greater qualities could be mentioned for him. For to be sure, for self-control, for devotion, or indeed for any other kind of virtue I do not think that anyone of the same period could be compared with him.

143 + 144 P. ET L. COMINII

minius (F 1), while Asconius talks of Publius and Gaius Cominius (F 2): one of these references must be a mistake. Unless there is an error in the manuscripts, it is more likely that the contemporary Cicero is correct (Badian 1955, 220).

Against C. Aelius Paetus Staienus (F 1)

*Soon after 74 BC, the brothers prosecuted C. Aelius Paetus Staienus (**107A**) for treason because of his behavior as quaestor in 77 BC (TLRR 159).*

F 1 Cicero, *Pro Cluentio*

What of the fact that Staienus was condemned? I do not mention at this point, judges, what should perhaps be mentioned, that he was condemned for treason. I do not read out the evidence of very trustworthy people that was

honestissimorum quae in Staienum sunt dicta ab eis qui Mam. Aemilio,[1] clarissimo viro, legati et praefecti et tribuni militares fuerunt; quorum testimoniis planum factum est maxime eius opera, cum quaestor esset, in exercitu seditionem esse conflatam; ne illa quidem testimonia recito quae dicta sunt de HS D̄C̄ quae ille, cum accepisset nomine iudicii Safiniani, sicut in Oppianici iudicio postea, reticuit atque suppressit. [100] omitto et haec et alia permulta quae illo iudicio in Staienum dicta sunt; hoc dico, eandem tum fuisse P. et L. Cominiis, equitibus Romanis, honestis hominibus et disertis, controversiam cum Staieno quem accusabant quae nunc mihi est cum Attio. Cominii dicebant idem quod ego dico, Staienum ab Oppianico pecuniam accepisse ut iudicium corrumperet; Staienus conciliandae gratiae causa accepisse dicebat. [101] inridebatur haec illius reconciliatio et persona viri boni suscepta, sicut in statuis inauratis quas posuit ad Iuturnae, quibus subscripsit reges ab se in gratiam esse reductos. exagitabantur omnes eius fraudes atque fallaciae, tota vita in eius modi ratione versata aperiebatur, egestas domestica, quaestus forensis in medium proferebatur, nummarius interpres pacis et concordiae non probabatur. itaque tum Staienus cum idem defenderet quod Attius condemnatus est; [102] Cominii cum hoc agerent quod nos in tota causa egimus probaverunt.

---

[1] Mam. Aemilio *Manutius*: M. Aemilio *codd.*

provided against Staienus by those who served under
Mam. Aemilius [Mam. Aemilius Lepidus Livianus, cos. 77
BC], a very distinguished man, as generals, prefects, and
military tribunes; by their evidence it was made obvious
that it was chiefly through his [Staienus'] activity, when he
was quaestor [77 BC], that mutiny was stirred up in the
army. I do not even read out the evidence that was given
about the 600,000 sesterces that he had accepted on behalf of Safinius' trial [76 BC; cf. Cic. *Clu.* 68; *TLRR* 142]
and then, as afterward at Oppianicus' trial [74 BC; *TLRR*
149], kept secret and concealed. [100] I pass over this and
very many other things that were said against Staienus at
that trial. I say this, that P. and L. Cominius, Roman
knights, honorable and eloquent men, then had the same
quarrel with Staienus, whom they were accusing, that I
now have with Attius [T. Accius Pisaurensis (**145**), the
prosecutor]. The Cominii said the same that I say, that
Staienus took money from Oppianicus to bribe the court;
Staienus said that he took it to effect a reconciliation. [101]
There was laughter at this reconciliation of his and his
assuming the role of an honest man, as he had done in the
matter of the gilt statues that he erected in the Temple of
Iuturna [in Rome] and to which he added an inscription
at the foot, recording the kings whom he had restored to
friendship [with Rome]. Then all his dishonest practices
and impostures were driven out; a whole lifetime spent in
pursuits of that kind was disclosed; his personal poverty
and his source of income from the courts were brought to
light; his pose as the paid agent of peace and goodwill did
not win approval. Thus at the time Staienus, when answer-
ing the same charge as Attius is now, was found guilty.
[102] The Cominii, doing what I have been doing all
through the case, proved their point.

Against C. Cornelius (F 2–6)

The brothers, Publius in particular, prosecuted C. Corne-
lius (tr. pl. 67 BC) for treason in 66 BC (case abandoned)
and in 65 BC, when several eminent men provided witness

F 2 Asc. in Cic. *Corn.*, *arg.* (pp. 52–54 KS = 59.15–62.2
C.)

sequenti deinde anno M'. Lepido L. Volcacio coss., quo
anno praetor Cicero fuit, reum Cornelium duo fratres
Cominii lege Cornelia de maiestate fecerunt. detulit nomen Publius, subscripsit Gaius. et cum P. Cassius praetor
decimo die, ut mos est, adesse iussisset, eoque die ipse
non adfuisset seu avocatus propter publici frumenti curam
seu gratificans reo, circumventi sunt ante tribunal eius
accusatores a notis operarum ducibus ita ut mors intenta-
retur, si mox non desisterent. quam perniciem vix effuge-
runt interventu consulum qui advocati reo descenderant.
et cum scalas quasdam Cominii fugissent, clausi in noctem
ibi se occultaverunt, deinde per tecta vicinarum aedium
profugerunt ex urbe. postero die, cum P. Cassius adsedis-
set et citati accusatores non adessent, exemptum nomen
est de reis Corneli; Cominii autem magna infamia flagra-
verunt vendidisse silentium magna pecunia. sequente de-

1–2 Asconius is likely to have made a mistake with the *prae-*
nomen, and this is probably L. Cassius Longinus (praet. 66 BC).

Against C. Cornelius (F 2–6)

statements (*cf.* **92** *F 31–32) and Cicero spoke on behalf of
the defendant (Cic.* Pro C. Cornelio I *and* II*: Crawford
1994, 65–144), who was acquitted (TLRR 203, 209).*

F 2 Asconius on Cicero, *Pro Cornelio*

Then, in the following year, in the consulship of M'. Lepidus [M'. Aemilius Lepidus] and L. Volcacius [L. Volcatius
Tullus], in the year in which Cicero was praetor [66 BC],
the two brothers Cominii took Cornelius to court under
the *Lex Cornelia* on treason [*Lex Cornelia de maiestate*,
81 BC: *LPPR*, p. 360]. Publius raised the accusation; Gaius
seconded. And when P. Cassius,[1] the praetor, had ordered
them to be there on the tenth day, as is customary, and on
that day he himself [the praetor] had been absent, whether
called away because of his responsibility for the public
grain supply or obliging the defendant, his prosecutors
were surrounded in front of the tribunal by well-known
leaders of gangs so that death was threatened if they did
not stop soon. They just avoided such destruction by the
intervention of the consuls, who had come down as advocates for the defendant. And when the Cominii had fled
along some flights of steps, locked in, they hid there until
nightfall; then they fled over the roofs of adjoining houses
out of the city [of Rome]. On the following day, when P.
Cassius[2] had taken his seat and the prosecutors, when
summoned, were not present, the name of Cornelius was
removed from the defendants; the Cominii, on their part,
suffered from great defamation, to the effect that they had
sold their silence for a large sum. Then, in the following

inde anno L. Cotta L. Torquato coss., quo haec oratio a
Cicerone praetura nuper peracta[1] dicta est, cum primum
apparuisset Manilius[2] qui iudicium per operarum duces
turbaverat, deinde quod ex S. C. ambo consules <. . .>
praesidebant[3] ei iudicio, non respondisset atque[4] esset
damnatus, recreavit se Cominius, ut infamiam acceptae
pecuniae tolleret, ac repetiit Cornelium[5] lege maiestatis.
res acta est magna exspectatione. paucos autem comites[6]
Cornelius perterritus Manili exitu <. . .>[7] in iudicium adhi-
buit, ut ne clamor quidem ullus ab advocatis eius orire-
tur. . . . res acta est magno conventu, magnaque exspectatione quis eventus iudicii futurus esset. <. . .> a summis
viris dici testimonia[8] et id quod ei dicerent confiteri reum[9]
animadvertebant. exstat oratio Comini[10] accusatoris quam
sumere in manus est aliquod operae pretium, non solum
propter Ciceronis orationes quas pro Cornelio habemus
sed etiam propter semet ipsam.

[1] praetura nuper peracta *KS*: pretura pretore *vel* praetura . . .
praetore *vel* . . . pretore *codd.*: praetorio *Sigonius*
[2] *suppl. Sigonius*: cum prima pars . . . Manilius *vel* pars M.
Manilius *codd.*   [3] ambo *Popma*: anno *codd.*   cons.
(*vel* cos.) . . . praesidebant *vel* consules praesidebant *codd.*: *fort.*
praesentes erant et *supplendum coni. Clark*
[4] ei *KS*: et *codd.*   *corr. man. rec. in cod. un.*: respondi
(*vel* -is) . . . que *vel* respondi atque *codd.*
[5] *suppl. KS*: recreavisset . . . (*lac. om. unus cod.*) iam accepta
pecunia tollere ait (*vel* et) . . . Cornelium *codd.*   [6] autem
comites *Clark*: ante (*vel* añ) me go . . . *codd.*: autem homines *KS*:
ante menses. ergo *Madvig*   [7] exitu . . . *codd.*: <recenti>
suppl. KS   [8] *Manutius*: dicit extimo . . . (*om. lac. unus cod.*)
codd.   [9] *suppl. Manutius*: confiteri . . . (*om. lac. unus cod.*)
codd.   [10] Comini *Gronovius*: hominis *codd.*

132

year, in the consulship [65 BC] of L. Cotta [L. Aurelius
Cotta] and L. Torquatus [L. Manlius Torquatus (**109**)],
when this speech was delivered by Cicero, after he had
recently completed his praetorship [66 BC], when Manilius [tr. pl. 66 BC], who had disturbed the trial through
the leaders of gangs, had first appeared, then, since according to a decree of the Senate both consuls ‹. . .› were
overseeing that trial, had not answered and had been convicted [in absence], Cominius recovered himself, so that
he removed the defamation of having accepted money,
and charged Cornelius again under the law of treason. The
proceedings were carried out amid great expectation. Cornelius brought few companions to court, terrified by the
outcome for Manilius ‹. . .›, so that not even a shout arose
from his advocates. . . . The matter was carried out amid
a large mass of people and great expectation as to what the
result of the trial would be. ‹. . .› They noted that testi-
monies were given by the most distinguished men and that
the defendant admitted what they said. The speech of the
prosecutor Cominius is extant; and it is worth taking into
one's hands, not only because of Cicero's orations that we
have on behalf of Cornelius, but also for its own sake.

F 3 Cic. *Brut.* 271

[CICERO:] itaque ne hos quidem equites Romanos amicos nostros, qui nuper mortui sunt, ⟨omittam⟩[1] P. Cominium Spoletinum, quo accusante defendi C. Cornelium, in quo et compositum dicendi genus et acre et expeditum fuit . . .

[1] *add. Kayser*

F 4 Cic. *Corn.* I, F 7 Puccioni = 6 Crawford, ap. Quint. *Inst.* 4.4.8

est et nuda propositio, qualis fere in coniecturalibus: "caedis ago," "furtum obicio," e{s}t[1] ratione subiecta, ut: "maiestatem minuit C. Cornelius; nam codicem tribunus plebis ipse pro contione legit."

[1] e{s}t *Meister*: est *codd.*

= Iul. Vict., *RLM*, p. 417.17–19.

F 5 Cic. *Corn.* I, F 29 Puccioni = Crawford, ap. Quint. *Inst.* 5.13.25

quod autem posui, referre quo quidque accusator modo dixerit, huc pertinet ut, si est minus efficaciter elocutus, ipsa eius verba ponantur, si acri et vehementi fuerit usus oratione, eandem rem nostris verbis mitioribus proferamus, ut Cicero de Cornelio: "codicem attigit" . . .

F 3 Cicero, *Brutus*

[CICERO:] For this reason, not even these Roman knights, our friends, who have died recently, ⟨shall I pass over⟩: P. Cominius of Spoletum [modern Spoleto in Umbria], against whose prosecution I defended C. Cornelius; he had a well-ordered style of speaking, vigorous, and fluent . . . [cf. **145** T 1]

F 4 Cicero, *Pro Cornelio* (quoted by Quintilian)

There are both propositions on their own, as usually in conjectural cases ("I prosecute for murder," "I charge with theft"), and those accompanied by a reason, such as: "C. Cornelius committed an act of treason: for as Tribune of the People he read out a document in person before a public meeting."[1]

[1] Apparently, an alleged statement of the prosecutor. For the offense see **92** F 31.

F 5 Cicero, *Pro Cornelio* (quoted by Quintilian)

And the point I have made, that the manner in which the prosecutor has presented each point is important, applies to the following issue: if he has spoken less effectively, his actual words should be quoted; if he has used energetic and vigorous language, we should present the same matter in our own milder terms, like Cicero about Cornelius: "he touched the document" [avoiding talking of "reading"] . . .

F 6 Cic. *Corn.* I, F 10 Puccioni = 14 Crawford, ap. Asc. in Cic. *Corn.* I (pp. 56–57 KS = 64.11–16 C.)

"legem," inquit, "de libertinorum suffragiis Cornelius C. Manilio dedit." quid est hoc "dedit"? attulit? an rogavit? an hortatus est? attulisse[1] ridiculum est, quasi legem aliquam aut ad scribendum difficilem aut ad excogitandum reconditam: quae lex paucis his annis non modo scripta sed etiam lata esset.

[1] attulisse *Madvig*: an tulisse *codd.*

145 T. ACCIUS PISAURENSIS

T 1 Cic. *Brut.* 271

[CICERO:] itaque ne hos quidem equites Romanos, amicos nostros, qui nuper mortui sunt, ⟨omittam⟩[1] . . . T. Accium Pisaurensem, cuius accusationi respondi pro A. Cluentio, qui et accurate dicebat et satis copiose, eratque praeterea doctus Hermagorae praeceptis, quibus etsi ornamenta non satis opima dicendi, tamen, ut hastae velitibus amentatae, sic apta quaedam et parata singulis causarum generibus argumenta traduntur.

[1] *add. Kayser*

F 6 Cicero, *Pro Cornelio* (quoted by Asconius)

"Cornelius," he says, "gave the law about the voting rights of freedmen to C. Manilius [tr. pl. 66 BC]."[1] What does this "gave" mean? He brought it with him? Or he asked for approval? Or he urged the passage? That he brought it with him [as a draft] is ridiculous, as if it were some law either difficult to compose or obscure to think out: for the last few years this law had not only been written down, but also been passed.

[1] Apparently, Cicero's speech included this alleged quotation of what the prosecutor said.

145 T. ACCIUS PISAURENSIS

T. Accius (RE Accius 1a) of Pisaurum (modern Pesaro on the Adriatic), a Roman knight, is described in Cicero as an accurate and reasonably eloquent speaker, familiar with the principles of the Greek rhetorician Hermagoras (T 1).

T 1 Cicero, *Brutus*

[CICERO:] For this reason not even these Roman knights, our friends, who have died recently, ⟨shall I pass over⟩: ... [cf. **143** + **144** F 3] ... T. Accius of Pisaurum, in reply to whose prosecution I acted on behalf of A. Cluentius [Habitus]; he spoke both painstakingly and with tolerable eloquence; and he was trained, moreover, in the rules of Hermagoras, which, though they do not supply sufficiently the richest embellishments of oratory, yet, like spears fitted with throwing straps for the light-armed, thus furnish some outlines of argument ready for use and available for every single type of case [cf. **141** T 1].

Against A. Cluentius Habitus (F 2)

*When Accius prosecuted A. Cluentius Habitus in 66 BC
(Alexander 2002, 173–88), who was charged with having
poisoned his stepfather Oppianicus, the accused was defended by Cicero (Cic. Clu.; T 1; TLRR 198). Both speak-*

F 2 Cic. *Clu.* 62, 65, 84, 156, 160

quaero enim de te, T. Atti,[1] relictis iam ceteris argumentis
omnibus, num Fabricios quoque innocentis condemnatos
existimes, num etiam illa iudicia pecunia corrupta esse
dicas, quibus in iudiciis alter a Staieno solo absolutus est,
alter etiam ipse se condemnavit. . . . [65] . . . te, Oppianice,
appello, te, T. Atti, quorum alter eloquentia damnationem
illam, alter tacita pietate deplorat; audete negare ab Oppianico Staieno iudici pecuniam datam, negate, negate,[2]
inquam, meo loco. quid tacetis? an negare non potestis
quod repetistis, quod confessi estis, quod abstulistis? quo
tandem igitur ore mentionem corrupti iudicii facitis, cum
ab ista parte iudici pecuniam ante iudicium datam, post
iudicium ereptam esse fateamini? . . . [84] at enim pecuniam Staieno dedit Oppianicus non ad corrumpendum
iudicium sed ad conciliationem gratiae. tene hoc, Atti,

---

[1] Atti *vel* Acci *codd.*   [2] negate *semel hab. nonnulli codd.*

Against A. Cluentius Habitus (F 2)

ers made reference to the earlier trial, in 74 BC, when Cluentius prosecuted Oppianicus for having attempted to poison him (TLRR 149). Cicero engages with the arguments of the opponent in his own speech.

F 2 Cicero, *Pro Cluentio*

Now putting aside all other arguments [proving that the accuser would not have used bribery at the earlier trial], I ask you, T. Attius [Accius], whether you think that the Fabricii [accomplices of Oppianicus], too, were convicted when innocent, whether you say that at their trials also the court was bribed with money, trials in which the one was acquitted by Staienus [C. Aelius Paetus Staienus (**107A**), allegedly bribed judge] alone [cf. **143 + 144** F 1], and the other [of the Fabricii] even convicted himself.... [65] ... I challenge you, Oppianicus [Statius Albius Oppianicus, the son], and you, T. Attius, who both deplore that conviction [of Oppianicus, the father], one with eloquence, the other with mute dutifulness. Deny if you dare that money was given by Oppianicus to Staienus, the judge, deny it, deny it, I say, in my place. Why are you silent? Or are you not able to deny what you sought to recover, what you acknowledged, what you carried off? With what kind of face then are you making mention of a corrupt court when it was from your side, as you acknowledge, that money was given to a judge before the trial and wrested from him after the trial? ... [84] But Oppianicus gave Staienus the money, not to bribe the court, but to effect a reconciliation [alleged statement of prosecutor]. To think that you, At-

dicere, tali prudentia, etiam usu atque exercitatione prae-
ditum! . . . [156] agit enim sic causam T. Attius, adulescens
bonus et disertus, omnis civis legibus teneri omnibus . . .
[160] haec si T. Attius aut cognovisset aut cogitasset, profecto ne conatus quidem esset dicere, id quod multis verbis egit, iudicem quod ei videatur statuere et non devinc-
tum legibus esse oportere.

146 L. MANLIUS TORQUATUS FILIUS

*L. Manlius Torquatus (praet. 49 BC; RE Manlius 80), a
son of L. Manlius Torquatus (109), was killed in Africa in
the civil war (BAfr. 96).*

*In Cicero, Torquatus is described as an able speaker,
with extensive knowledge of literature, refined language,*

T 1 Cic. *Brut.* 265–66

[CICERO:] "reliqui sunt, qui mortui sint, L. Torquatus,
quem tu non tam cito rhetorem dixisses, etsi non deerat
oratio, quam, ut Graeci dicunt, πολιτικόν. erant in eo
plurimae litterae nec eae vulgares, sed interiores quaedam
et reconditae, divina memoria, summa verborum et gravitas et elegantia; atque haec omnia vitae decorabat gravitas
et integritas. . . ." [266] tum BRUTUS Torquati et Triari
mentione commotus—utrumque enim eorum admodum
dilexerat—"ne ego, inquit, ut omittam cetera quae sunt

tius, should say such a thing, you who are endowed with such sagacity, also practice and experience! . . . [156] For this is how T. Attius, an upright and eloquent young man, is conducting the case: on the assumption that all citizens are bound by all laws . . . [160] Had T. Attius either realized these things or reflected upon them, he would indeed not even have attempted to say what he has set out in many words; namely, that a judge ought to decide as he thinks best and not be bound by laws.

146 L. MANLIUS TORQUATUS FILIUS

*and outstanding memory (T 1; Cic. Fin. 1.13–14: **147** T 1). Torquatus is made to outline Epicurean philosophy in Cicero's treatise* De finibus *(Cic. Fin. 1.13–14). Torquatus was interested in poetry (Cic. Fin. 1.25, 2.107) and composed some himself (Plin. Ep. 5.3.5).*

T 1 Cicero, *Brutus*

[CICERO:] "There remain of those who are dead: L. Torquatus, whom you would not have called a technically trained orator so easily, though the ability to speak was not lacking, as, like the Greeks say, a *politikos* ['statesman']. He had very wide knowledge of literature, and that not of the ordinary, but of some more uncommon and recondite kind, a superhuman memory, the greatest dignity and refinement of language; and all this was adorned by the dignity and uprightness of his life. . . ." [266] Thereupon BRUTUS said, moved by the mention of Torquatus and Triarius [C. Valerius Triarius (**147**), T 2]—for he had greatly liked both of these men—"Ah, so as to pass over

innumerabilia, de istis duobus cum cogito, doleo nihil tuam perpetuam auctoritatem de pace valuisse! nam nec istos excellentis viros nec multos alios praestantis civis res publica perdidisset."

Against P. Cornelius Sulla (F 2–2A)

*In 62 BC, after the Catilinarian Conspiracy, Torquatus prosecuted (Alexander 2002, 189–205) P. Cornelius Sulla (a relative of the dictator Sulla), defended by Q. Hortensius Hortalus (**92** F 38–39) and Cicero (Cic. Sull.), under the Lex Plautia de vi (TLRR 234; cf. Schol. Bob. ad Cic. Sull. [pp. 77–84 St.]). P. Cornelius Sulla (like P. Autronius Paetus; TLRR 200) had been prosecuted by Torquatus*

F 2 Gell. *NA* 1.5.3

= **92** F 39.

F 2A Cic. *Sull.* 2, 3, 10–11, 21, 22, 25, 30, 35–36, 38, 39–40, 48, 54, 60, 62, 63, 67, 68, 78, 81, 82

et quoniam L. Torquatus, meus familiaris ac necessarius, iudices, existimavit, si nostram in accusatione sua necessitudinem familiaritatemque violasset, aliquid se de auctoritate meae defensionis posse detrahere, cum huius periculi propulsatione coniungam defensionem offici mei. . . . [3] ac primum abs te illud, L. Torquate, quaero, cur me a ceteris clarissimis viris ac principibus civitatis in hoc officio atque in defensionis iure secernas. quid enim est quam ob rem abs te Q. Hortensi factum, clarissimi viri atque

other matters that are countless, when I think about those two men, how I grieve that your persistent advocacy of peace was without avail! For then the Republic would have lost neither those excellent men nor many other outstanding citizens."

Against P. Cornelius Sulla (F 2–2A)

(Cic.), who may have been a subsidiary prosecutor, or his father (Asc.), for bribery in the consular elections for 65 BC; the successful conviction had enabled the elder L. Manlius Torquatus (109) to assume the consulship for that year (TLRR 201; cf. 86 F 12; Cic. Sull. 49–50, 90; Fin. 2.62; Asc. in Cic. Corn. [p. 75.7–9 C.]; Sall. Cat. 18.2; Suet. Iul. 9.1; Cass. Dio 36.44.3).

F 2 Gellius, *Attic Nights*

= **92** F 39.

F 2A Cicero, *Pro Sulla*

And since L. Torquatus, my close and intimate friend, judges, thought that if he had violated our intimacy and friendship in his speech for the prosecution, he might in some way diminish the authority of my speech for the defense, I will combine a defense of my role with repelling the danger to this man [Sulla]. . . . [3] And first I ask you this, L. Torquatus, why you are setting me apart from other very distinguished figures and leading men in the community over this obligation and over the right to appear for the defense. For why is it that the action of Q. Hortensius [Q. Hortensius Hortalus (92)], a most distin-

ornatissimi, non reprehendatur, reprehendatur meum? nam, si est initum a P. Sulla consilium inflammandae huius urbis,[1] exstinguendi imperi, delendae civitatis, mihi maiorem hae res dolorem quam Q. Hortensio, mihi maius odium adferre debent, meum denique gravius esse iudicium, qui adiuvandus in his causis, qui oppugnandus, qui defendendus, qui deserendus esse videatur? "ita," inquit; "tu enim investigasti, tu patefecisti coniurationem." [4] ... [10] "in Autronium testimonium dixisti," inquit; "Sullam defendis." . . . videor enim iam non solum studium ad defendendas causas verum etiam opinionis aliquid et auctoritatis adferre; qua ego et moderate utar, iudices, et omnino non uterer, si ille me non coegisset. [11] duae coniurationes abs te, Torquate, constituuntur, una quae Lepido et Volcacio consulibus patre tuo consule designato facta esse dicitur, altera quae me consule; harum in utraque Sullam dicis fuisse. . . . [21] hic ait se ille, iudices, regnum meum ferre non posse. quod tandem, Torquate, regnum? consulatus, credo, mei . . . an tum in tanto imperio, tanta potestate non dicis me fuisse regem, nunc privatum regnare dicis? quo tandem nomine? "quod, in quos testimonia dixisti," inquit, "damnati sunt; quem defendis, sperat se absolutum iri." . . . [22] "nisi tu," inquit, "causam recepisses, numquam mihi restitisset, sed indicta causa profugisset." . . . at hic etiam, id quod tibi necesse minime

---

[1] huius urbis *Halm*: huius urbis huius *vel* huius civitatis *vel* civitatis huius *codd.*

guished and illustrious man, is not attacked by you, but
mine is attacked? For, if a plan was made by P. Sulla to
burn this city, to annihilate the empire, to destroy the
community, ought these acts to inspire greater anguish,
greater hatred in me than in Q. Hortensius? In short,
ought my judgment to be more serious as to who ought to
be supported in these cases, who attacked, who defended,
who abandoned? "Yes," he says; "for you investigated, you
exposed the conspiracy." [4] . . . [10] "You gave evidence
against Autronius [P. Autronius Paetus]," he says; "you are
defending Sulla." . . . I feel that I now bring to the defense
of cases not only enthusiasm, but also some reputation and
prestige; this I shall use in moderation, judges, and I
would not use it at all if that man [Torquatus] had not
forced me to. [11] Two conspiracies are posited by you,
Torquatus: one that is said to have been formed in the
consulship of Lepidus and Volcacius [66 BC], when your
father [L. Manlius Torquatus (**109**)] was consul designate,
the other during my consulship [63 BC]; you say that Sulla
was involved in both of them. . . . [21] At this point [when
Cicero describes his attitude and his reasons for taking on
the current case] that man says, judges, that he cannot
bear my kingly rule. What kingly rule is that, then, Torquatus? My consulship, I suppose . . . Or are you not saying that I was a king when I had so much control, so much
power, but are saying that I rule as a king now being a private citizen? On what account then? "Because," he says,
"those against whom you gave evidence have been condemned; the man whom you defend hopes to be acquitted." . . . [22] "If you had not accepted the case," he says,
"he would never have opposed me, but would have gone
into exile without standing trial." . . . But at this point

145

fuit, facetus esse voluisti, cum Tarquinium et Numam et
me tertium peregrinum regem esse dixisti. mitto iam de
rege quaerere; illud quaero peregrinum cur me esse dixeris. nam si ita sum, non tam est admirandum regem esse
me, quoniam, ut tu ais, duo iam[2] peregrini reges Romae
fuerunt, quam consulem Romae fuisse peregrinum. "hoc
dico," inquit, "te esse ex municipio." [23] . . . [25] ac si,
iudices, ceteris patriciis me et vos peregrinos videri oporteret, a Torquato tamen hoc vitium sileretur . . . qua re
neque tu me peregrinum posthac dixeris, ne gravius refu-
tere, neque regem, ne derideare. . . . [30] at vero quid ego
mirer, si quid ab improbis de me improbe dicitur, cum L.
Torquatus primum ipse his fundamentis adulescentiae
iactis, ea spe proposita amplissimae dignitatis, deinde L.
Torquati, fortissimi consulis, constantissimi senatoris,
semper optimi civis filius, interdum efferatur immodera-
tione verborum? qui cum suppressa voce de scelere P.
Lentuli, de audacia coniuratorum omnium dixisset, tantum modo ut vos qui ea probatis exaudire possetis, de
supplicio, de carcere magna et queribunda voce dicebat.
[31] . . . [35] . . . sed iam redeo ad causam atque hoc vos,
iudices, testor: mihi de memet ipso tam multa dicendi
necessitas quaedam imposita est ab illo. nam si Torquatus
Sullam solum accusasset, ego quoque hoc tempore nihil
aliud agerem nisi eum qui accusatus esset defenderem;

---

[2] duo iam *Clark*: etiam *codd.*: iam *Müller*

[when Cicero suggests that in fact Torquatus is a "tyrant"] too you wanted to be funny, which was absolutely unnecessary for you, when you said that there were Tarquin, Numa, and myself as the third foreign king. I am now leaving aside asking about "king"; I do ask why you said that I was a foreigner. For if I am such a one, it is not so astonishing that I am a king, since, as you say, there have already been two foreign kings in Rome, than that I was a foreign consul in Rome. "I mean," he says, "that you come from a municipal town." [23] . . . [25] And if, judges, it was appropriate that I and you appeared to other patricians to be foreigners, this defect should still be passed over in silence by Torquatus . . . Therefore do not say again either that I am a foreigner, lest you should be refuted more conclusively, or that I am a tyrant, lest you should be ridiculed. . . . [30] Yet why should I be surprised if evil men speak evil of me, when even L. Torquatus who, firstly, laid such good foundations in his youth and has such hope of the highest office before him, secondly, is the son of L. Torquatus, a most valiant consul, a most steadfast senator, always a most loyal citizen, is sometimes carried away by a lack of restraint in his language? When he had spoken in a low voice of the crime of P. Lentulus [P. Cornelius Lentulus Sura (**100**)], of the recklessness of all the conspirators, just so that you could hear, you who approve these things, he then began to speak of punishment and of prison in a loud and indignant voice. [31] . . . [35] . . . But now I return to the case and I call you, judges, to witness this fact: a certain necessity to say so much about myself was imposed upon me by that man. For, if Torquatus had only accused Sulla, I too would not be doing anything else at this time other than defending the accused; but since

147

sed cum ille tota illa oratione in me esset invectus et cum, ut initio dixi, defensionem meam spoliare auctoritate voluisset, etiam si dolor me meus respondere non cogeret, tamen ipsa causa hanc a me orationem flagitavisset. [36] ab Allobrogibus nominatum Sullam esse dicis. . . . [38] . . . sed tamen quid respondit de Sulla Cassius? se nescire certum. "non purgat," inquit. . . . [39] . . . etenim cum se negat scire Cassius, utrum sublevat Sullam an satis probat se nescire? "sublevat apud Gallos." quid ita? "ne indicent." quid? si periculum esse putasset ne illi umquam indicarent, de se ipse confessus esset? "nesciit videlicet." . . . sed iam non quaero purgetne Cassius Sullam; illud mihi tantum satis est contra Sullam nihil esse in indicio. [40] exclusus hac criminatione Torquatus rursus in me inruit, me accusat; ait me aliter ac dictum sit in tabulas publicas rettulisse. . . . [48] neque vero quid mihi irascare intellegere possum. si, quod eum defendo quem tu accusas, cur tibi ego non suscenseo, quod accusas eum quem ego defendo? "inimicum ego," inquis, "accuso meum." et amicum ego defendo meum. "non debes tu quemquam in coniurationis quaestione defendere." immo nemo magis eum de quo nihil umquam est suspicatus quam is qui de aliis multa cognovit. "cur dixisti testimonium in alios?" quia coactus sum. "cur damnati sunt?" quia creditum est. "regnum est

throughout that entire speech that man had attacked me and since, as I said at the beginning, he wished to rob my defense of its authority, even if my distress did not compel me to respond, the case alone would still have demanded of me this speech. [36] You say that Sulla was named by the Allobroges. . . . [38] . . . But what did Cassius [L. Cassius Longinus, praet. 66 BC] reply about Sulla? That he did not know for certain. "He does not clear him," he says. . . . [39] . . . Indeed, when Cassius says that he does not know, is he clearing Sulla or is he demonstrating sufficiently that he does not know? "He is clearing him with the Gauls." Why is that? "So that they do not inform on him." What? If he had thought that there was a danger that they might ever plant information, would he have confessed about his own part? "He evidently did not know." . . . But I am not inquiring now whether Cassius clears Sulla; it is quite sufficient for me that there is nothing against Sulla in the information. [40] Thwarted on this charge, Torquatus attacks me again, makes another accusation against me; he says that I entered in the public records something other than what was said. . . . [48] Moreover, I cannot understand why you are angry with me. If it is because I am defending a man whom you are accusing, why am I not angry with you because you accuse the man whom I am defending? "I am accusing my enemy," you say. And I am defending my friend. "You should not defend anyone in a judicial investigation about a conspiracy." On the contrary, nobody should be more [ready to defend] one whom he has never suspected of anything than a man who has known much about others. "Why did you give evidence against others?" Because I was forced. "Why were they convicted?" Because the evidence was

dicere in quem velis et defendere quem velis." . . . [54]
quid ergo indicat aut quid adfert aut ipse Cornelius aut vos
qui haec ab illo mandata defertis? gladiatores emptos esse
Fausti simulatione ad caedem ac tumultum? "ita prorsus;
interpositi sunt gladiatores." quos testamento patris de-
beri videmus. "adrepta est familia." quae si esset praetermissa, posset alia familia Fausti munus praebere. utinam quidem haec ipsa non modo iniquorum invidiae sed[3]
aequorum exspectationi satis facere posset! "properatum
vehementer est, cum longe tempus muneris abesset."
quasi vero tempus dandi muneris non valde appropinqua-
ret. "nec opinante Fausto, cum is neque sciret neque vellet, familia est comparata." [55] . . . [60] iam vero quod
obiecit Pompeianos esse a Sulla impulsos ut ad istam coniurationem atque ad hoc nefarium facinus accederent, id
cuius modi sit intellegere non possum. an tibi Pompeiani
coniurasse videntur? quis hoc dixit umquam, aut quae fuit
istius rei vel minima suspicio? "diiunxit," inquit, "eos a
colonis ut hoc discidio ac dissensione facta oppidum in sua
potestate posset per Pompeianos habere." . . . [62] . . . "at
enim et gladiatores et omnis ista vis rogationis Caeciliae
causa comparabatur." atque hoc loco in L. Caecilium,
pudentissimum atque ornatissimum virum, vehementer

---

[3] invidiae sed *Lambinus*: invidiae esset *codd.*

accepted. "It is tyranny to attack whom you wish and defend whom you wish." . . . [54] What information, then, or what charge is being laid either by Cornelius himself [second prosecutor] or by you who convey the instructions from him? That gladiators were bought on a pretext furnished by Faustus [Faustus Cornelius Sulla (**156**)] for murder and riot? "Yes, indeed; gladiators were introduced." We see that they were required by his father's will. "The company was engaged in a hurry." If this company had been missed, another would be able to put on Faustus' games. If only this very company could satisfy not only the ill will of his enemies, but the expectation of his friends! "There was great haste although the date of the games was a long way off." As if the date for giving the games was not in fact getting very close. "The company was acquired with Faustus being unaware, when he neither knew of it nor wanted it." [55] . . . [60] Furthermore, I cannot understand what is the nature of his [Torquatus'] charge that the inhabitants of Pompeii were instigated by Sulla to join that conspiracy and set their hand to this nefarious crime. Do the inhabitants of Pompeii seem to you to have joined the conspiracy? Who ever said this, or what suspicion was there of that matter, even the slightest? "He set them at odds," he says, "with the colonists, so that by causing this division and dissension he could get the town under his control with the aid of the inhabitants of Pompeii." . . . [62] . . . "But both the gladiators and all that display of force were mustered for the sake of Caecilius' bill [L. Caecilius Rufus, tr. pl. 63 BC, half brother of defendant, proposed bill to restore civil rights to Autronius and Sulla]." And at this point he inveighed violently against L. Caecilius, a man of the greatest integrity and highest

invectus est. . . . [63] atque in ea re per L. Caecilium Sulla accusatur in qua re est uterque laudandus. primum Caecilius—qui‹d›?[4] "id promulgavit in quo res iudicatas videbatur voluisse rescindere, ut restitueretur Sulla." recte reprehendis . . . [67] hic tu epistulam meam saepe recitas quam ego ad Cn. Pompeium de meis rebus gestis et de summa re publica misi, et ex ea crimen aliquod in P. Sullam quaeris et, si furorem incredibilem biennio ante conceptum erupisse in meo consulatu scripsi, me hoc demonstrasse dicis, Sullam in illa fuisse superiore coniuratione. . . . [68] de quo etiam si quis dubitasset antea an[5] id quod tu arguis cogitasset, ut interfecto patre tuo consul{e}[6] descenderet Kalendis Ianuariis cum lictoribus, sustulisti hanc suspicionem, cum dixisti hunc, ut Catilinam consulem efficeret, contra patrem tuum operas et manum comparasse. . . . [78] quaestiones nobis servorum accusator et tormenta minitatur. . . . [81] accusati sunt uno nomine ‹omnes›[7] consulares, ut iam videatur honoris amplissimi nomen plus invidiae quam dignitatis adferre. "adfuerunt," inquit, "Catilinae illumque laudarunt." . . . quin etiam parens tuus, Torquate, consul reo de pecuniis repetundis Catilinae fuit advocatus, improbo homini, at supplici, fortasse audaci, at aliquando amico. . . . "at idem non adfuit alio in iudicio, cum adessent ceteri." . . .

---

[4] qui‹d› *Clark*: qui *codd.*: qui si *Halm*   [5] an *Eberhard*: num *codd.*   [6] consul{e} *ed. R., Müller*: consule *codd.*
[7] *add. Clark* (*ante* uno *Lambinus*)

146 L. MANLIUS TORQUATUS FILIUS

distinction. . . . [63] And in a matter in which both men
deserve praise Sulla is attacked via L. Caecilius. Firstly,
Caecilius—what? "introduced such a bill that gave the
impression that he wanted to reverse the decision of the
court in order to reestablish Sulla." You condemn this
rightly . . . [67] At this point you repeatedly quote from
my letter that I sent to Pompey [Cn. Pompeius Magnus
(**111**)] about my achievements and the general situation
of the Republic. And in it you look for some charge against
P. Sulla, and you say that, if I wrote that the incredible folly
conceived two years previously had erupted in my consulship, I showed that Sulla had been in that earlier conspiracy. . . . [68] Even if anyone had previously been in
doubt about him [Sulla] whether he had in mind what you
allege, namely that, after having murdered your father, he
would enter the Forum as consul with lictors on the Kalends of January [January 1], you removed such a suspicion when you said that he had collected a force of thugs
against your father in order to make Catiline [L. Sergius
Catilina (**112**)] consul. . . . [78] The prosecutor threatens
us with the examination of slaves under torture. . . . [81]
‹All› the ex-consuls were charged under a single heading,
so that the title of the highest magistracy now seems to
attract more odium than respect. "They supported Catiline in court," he says, "and were character witnesses for
him [at trial for extortion in 65 BC: *TLRR* 212]." . . . Furthermore, your father, Torquatus, when he was consul,
defended Catiline—an immoderate man, but a suppliant;
reckless perhaps, but once a friend—against a charge of
extorting money. [**109** F 2]. . . . "But he did not support
him in court in another trial [in 64 BC for activities in
connection with the Sullan proscriptions: *TLRR* 217],

[82] "at idem eis qui ante hunc causam de coniuratione dixerunt non adfuerunt."

147 C. VALERIUS TRIARIUS

C. Valerius Triarius (RE *Valerius* 365), *a brother of P. Valerius Triarius (148), supported Cn. Pompeius Magnus (111) in the civil war and may have fallen in the battle of Pharsalus (Caes.* BCiv. *3.5, 3.92).*

T 1 Cic. *Fin.* 1.13–14

[Cicero:] accurate autem quondam a L. Torquato, homine omni doctrina erudito, defensa est Epicuri sententia de voluptate, a meque ei responsum, cum C. Triarius, in primis gravis et doctus adulescens, ei disputationi interesset. [14] nam cum ad me in Cumanum salutandi causa uterque venisset, pauca primo inter nos de litteris, quarum summum erat in utroque studium, deinde Torquatus, "quoniam nacti te," inquit, "sumus aliquando otiosum, certe audiam quid sit quod Epicurum nostrum non tu quidem oderis, ut fere faciunt qui ab eo dissentiunt, sed certe non probes, eum quem ego arbitror unum vidisse verum maximisque erroribus animos hominum liberavisse et omnia tradidisse quae pertinerent ad bene beateque vivendum. sed existimo te, sicut nostrum Triarium, minus ab eo delectari quod ista Platonis, Aristoteli, Theophrasti

when others did." . . . [82] "But the same men did not support those who were on trial for the conspiracy before him [Sulla]."

147 C. VALERIUS TRIARIUS

C. Triarius is present at the dialogues recorded in Cicero's De finibus 1 and 2 (e.g., T 1).

In Cicero the mature, learned, and earnest oratory of C. Triarius is mentioned favorably (T 2).

T 1 Cicero, *On Ends*

[CICERO:] And Epicurus' views on pleasure were once defended meticulously by L. Torquatus [L. Manlius Torquatus (**146**)], a man well versed in all kinds of learning; a reply to him was given by me, while C. Triarius, a particularly serious and learned young man, took part in that discussion. [14] When both of them had come to pay me their respects at my place at Cumae, there were first a few remarks among us about literature, of which both were enthusiastic students. Then Torquatus said: "As we have for once found you at leisure, I am resolved to hear the reason why it is that you regard our Epicurus, not indeed with hatred, as those who disagree with him mostly do, but certainly with disapproval: I myself consider him as the one person who has discerned the truth and who has delivered the minds of men from the gravest errors and imparted to them everything that concerns living well and happily. But I believe that you, like our friend Triarius, are less pleased by him because he has neglected those ornaments of speech found in Plato, Aristotle, and Theophras-

orationis ornamenta neglexerit. nam illud quidem adduci
vix possum, ut ea quae senserit ille tibi non vera videantur."

T 2   Cic. *Brut.* 265

[CICERO:] reliqui sunt, qui mortui sint, L. Torquatus . . .
me quidem admodum delectabat etiam Triari in illa aetate
plena litteratae senectutis oratio. quanta severitas in vultu!
quantum pondus in verbis! quam nihil non consideratum
exibat ex ore!

148 P. VALERIUS TRIARIUS

P. Valerius Triarius (RE *Valerius* 367), *a brother of C.
Valerius Triarius* (*147*), *prosecuted* (F 1–2) M. *Aemilius
Scaurus* (*139*) *for extortion in 54 BC* (*Alexander 2002,
98–109*). *Scaurus was defended by the six advocates P.
Clodius Pulcher* (*137* F 9), *M. Claudius Marcellus* (*155*
F 5), *M. Calidius* (*140* F 9), *M. Valerius Messalla Niger*
(*124* F 4), *Q. Hortensius Hortalus* (*92* F 48), *and Cicero*
(*Cic.* Scaur.), *as well as by himself* (*139* F 5), *and he was*

Against M. Aemilius Scaurus (F 1–2)

F 1   Asc. in Cic. *Scaur.*, *arg.* (pp. 16 KS = 18.18–19.6 C.)

ipse cum ad consulatus petitionem a. d. III Kal. Quint.
Romam redisset, querentibus de eo Sardis, a P. Valerio

tus. For I can scarcely bring myself to believe that his opinions do not seem true to you."

T 2 Cicero, *Brutus*

[CICERO:] There remain of those who are dead: L. Torquatus [L. Manlius Torquatus (**146**), T 1] . . . On my part, what also pleased me greatly was the speaking of Triarius, at that [young] age full of learned maturity. What earnestness of expression in his face! What weight in his words! How nothing ill-considered came out of his mouth!

148 P. VALERIUS TRIARIUS

acquitted (TLRR 295; cf. Cic. Att. 4.15.9, 4.16.6, 4.17.4; Q Fr. 2.16.3, 3.1.11, 3.1.16).

*Later in the same year, P. Triarius accused M. Aemilius Scaurus (**139**) again, this time of bribery in the election campaign; the proceedings were completed in 52 BC. On this occasion Scaurus was found guilty, although Cicero (Cic. Pro M. Aemilio Scauro [de ambitu]: Crawford 1984, 198–201) defended him again (TLRR 300, 319; Cic. Q Fr. 3.2.3; Quint. Inst. 4.1.69; App. B Civ. 2.24.91).*

Against M. Aemilius Scaurus (F 1–2)

F 1 Asconius on Cicero, *Pro Scauro*

When, so as to stand as a candidate for the consulship, he [Scaurus] had returned to Rome [from his propraetorship in Sardinia] on the third day before the Kalends of Quintilis [June 28, 54 BC], and the Sardinians complained

Triario, adulescente parato ad dicendum et notae indus-
triae—filio eius qui in Sardinia contra M. Lepidum arma
tulerat et post in Asia legatus Pontoque L. Luculli fuerat,
cum is bellum contra Mithridatem gereret—postulatus
⟨est⟩[1] apud M. Catonem praetorem repetundarum, ut in
Actis scriptum est, pridie Nonas Quintil. post diem tertium quam C. Cato erat absolutus.

[1] *add. Baiter*

F 2 Val. Max. 8.1.abs.10

M. quoque Aemilius Scaurus, repetundarum reus, adeo
perditam et comploratam defensionem in iudicium attulit
ut, cum accusator diceret lege sibi centum atque viginti
hominibus denuntiare testimonium licere, seque non re-
cusare quominus absolveretur, si totidem nominasset quibus in provincia nihil abstulisset, tam bona condicione uti
non potuerit. tamen propter vetustissimam nobilitatem et
recentem memoriam patris absolutus est.

149 L. MUNATIUS PLANCUS

L. Munatius Plancus (cos. 42, censor 22 BC; RE Munatius
*30), a brother of T. Munatius Plancus Bursa (**150**) (T 3),*
was a pupil and friend of Cicero (T 4; Cic. Fam. 10.3.2,
13.29.1; Hieron. Ab Abr. 1992 = 25 BC [p. 164h Helm]).

about him, he was taken to court by P. Valerius Triarius, a
young man ready to speak and of known industry—the
son of the man [C. Valerius Triarius; *RE* Valerius 363] who
had taken up arms against M. Lepidus [M. Aemilius Lepidus (**95**)] in Sardinia and later in Asia and Pontus had
been legate of L. Lucullus [L. Licinius Lucullus (**90**)],
when the latter waged war against Mithridates—before
M. Cato, the praetor in charge of the extortion court [M.
Porcius Cato (**126**), praet. 54 BC], as is written in the records, on the day before the Nones of Quintilis [July 6], on
the third day after C. Cato [C. Porcius Cato (**136**)] had
been acquitted.

F 2 Valerius Maximus, *Memorable Doings and Sayings*

M. Aemilius Scaurus, too, prosecuted for extortion,
brought a hopeless and lamentable defense into court, so
much so that, when the prosecutor said that under the law
he was permitted to call one hundred and twenty witnesses and that he would not object to his acquittal if he
[Scaurus] had named that number of persons from whom
he had taken nothing in the province, he [Scaurus] was
unable to take advantage of so fair an offer. All the same,
because of his age-old nobility and the recent memory of
his father [M. Aemilius Scaurus (**43**)], he was acquitted.

149 L. MUNATIUS PLANCUS

*Plancus was also on good terms with C. Iulius Caesar
(**121**): he was his legate from 54 BC and served under him
during the civil war. In 46 BC he became city prefect; after
Caesar's death Plancus was provincial governor in Gallia*

(as appointed by Caesar). In the subsequent political struggles, Plancus first cooperated with D. Iunius Brutus, then supported M. Antonius (159), and finally Octavian.

A poem by Horace is addressed to Plancus (Hor. Carm. 1.7). A letter by him to the Senate, the magistrates, and the People of Rome (Cic. Fam. 10.8) and a letter by him and D. Iunius Brutus to the Senate (Cic. Fam. 11.13a) are

T 1 Cic. *Fam.* 10.3.3 [ad Plancum]

consul es designatus, optima aetate, summa eloquentia, maxima orbitate rei publicae virorum talium. incumbe, per deos immortalis, in eam curam et cogitationem quae tibi summam dignitatem et gloriam adferat; unus autem est, hoc praesertim tempore, per tot annos re publica divexata,[1] rei publicae bene gerendae cursus ad gloriam.

[1] divexata *Lambinus*: devexata *vel* de vexata *codd.*

T 2 Plin. *HN* 7.55

e diverso L. Plancus orator histrioni Rubrio cognomen inposuit . . .

Cf. Solin. 1.81: oratorem L. Plancum Rubrius histrio sic implevit, ut et ipse Plancus a populo vocaretur.

T 3 Asc. in Cic. *Mil.*, *arg.* (p. 28 KS = 32.26 C.)

. . . ⟨T.⟩[1] Munatius Plancus, frater L. Planci oratoris . . .

[1] *add. Manutius*

*extant, as is correspondence between him and Cicero (esp.
Cic. Fam. 10.1–24).*

*Ancient authorities praise Plancus as a great orator,
while they note his political fickleness and disloyalty (T 1,
4; Vell. Pat. 2.63.3, 2.83, 2.95.3; Hieron. Ab Abr. 1992 = 25
BC [p. 164h Helm]). Plancus made a poignant remark
when C. Asinius Pollio (174 F 39) was preparing speeches
against him to be published after his death.*

T 1 Cicero, *Letters to Friends* [to Plancus]

You are consul elect, in the prime of life and with the
greatest eloquence, while the Republic is very much be-
reft of such men. By the immortal gods, devote yourself
to that concern and to thought that will bring you the
highest honor and glory. There is only one path to glory,
especially at this time, when the Republic has been torn
asunder for so many years: running the Republic well.

T 2 Pliny the Elder, *Natural History*

Vice versa [rather than actors giving their names to men
in public life], L. Plancus, an orator, gave his surname to
the actor Rubrius . . .

Cf. Solinus: The actor Rubrius embodied the orator L. Plancus
to such an extent that he himself was also called Plancus by the
People.

T 3 Asconius on Cicero, *Pro Milone*

. . . ⟨T.⟩ Munatius Plancus [T. Munatius Plancus Bursa
(**150**), F 1], a brother of the orator L. Plancus . . .

T 4 Suet. *De oratoribus* 7 (p. 84.1–3 Reifferscheid)

Munatius Plancus, Ciceronis discipulus, orator habetur insignis; qui, cum Galliam comatam regeret, Lugdunum condidit.

On Caesar's Assassins in the Senate (F 5)

F 5 Plut. *Brut.* 19.1

οὐ μὴν ἀλλὰ τῇ ὑστεραίᾳ τῆς βουλῆς συνελθούσης εἰς τὸ τῆς Γῆς ἱερόν, Ἀντωνίου δὲ καὶ Πλάγκου καὶ Κικέρωνος εἰπόντων περὶ ἀμνηστίας καὶ ὁμονοίας, ἔδοξε μὴ μόνον ἄδειαν εἶναι τοῖς ἀνδράσιν, ἀλλὰ καὶ γνώμην ὑπὲρ τιμῶν προθεῖναι τοὺς ὑπάτους.

On the Title Augustus in the Senate (F 6)

F 6 Suet. *Aug.* 7.2

postea Gai Caesaris et deinde Augusti cognomen assumpsit, alterum testamento maioris avunculi, alterum Munati Planci sententia, cum quibusdam censentibus Romulum

149 L. MUNATIUS PLANCUS

T 4 Suetonius, *Lives of Illustrious Men. Orators*

Munatius Plancus, a disciple of Cicero, was regarded as an outstanding orator; when he was in charge of the province Gallia Comata, he founded Lugdunum [modern Lyon].

On Caesar's Assassins in the Senate (F 5)

After the assassination of C. Iulius Caesar (121) on the Ides of March 44 BC, Plancus was one of those who spoke in the Senate in favor of an amnesty for the assassins.

F 5 Plutarch, *Life of Brutus*

On the following day [March 17, 44 BC], however, the Senate met in the temple of Tellus, and Antony [M. Antonius (159)], Plancus, and Cicero spoke in favor of amnesty and concord. It was then voted not only that there should be immunity for the men [the assassins], but also that the consuls should put forward a proposal for honors.

On the Title Augustus in the Senate (F 6)

In 27 BC Plancus successfully put forward the motion in the Senate that Octavian should adopt the title Augustus (cf. Censorinus, DN 21.8; Liv. Epit. 134; Cass. Dio 53.16.6; Oros. 6.20.2; Aug. Res gest. 34.2).

F 6 Suetonius, *Life of Augustus*

Later he [Octavian] took the surname of Gaius Caesar and then of Augustus, the former by the will of his great-uncle, the latter on the motion of Munatius Plancus. For, when some expressed the opinion that he ought to be called

appellari oportere quasi et ipsum conditorem urbis, prae-valuisset, ut Augustus potius vocaretur, non tantum novo sed etiam ampliore cognomine, quod loca quoque religiosa et in quibus augurato quid consecratur augusta dicantur, ab auctu vel ab avium gestu gustuve . . .

150 T. MUNATIUS PLANCUS BURSA

T. Munatius Plancus Bursa (tr. pl. 52 BC; RE Munatius 32), a brother of L. Munatius Plancus (149), was a sympathizer of Cn. Pompeius Magnus (111); he supported P. Clodius Pulcher (137) against T. Annius Milo (138), when he was Tribune of the People in 52 BC and contributed to triggering the burning of the Senate house (Curia Hostilia) when Clodius' body was cremated. After his term of office, Plancus was prosecuted under the Lex Pompeia de vi *by*

As Tribune to the People (F 1–7)

When Tribune of the People in 52 BC, Plancus, along with colleagues, delivered several speeches before the People (CCMR, App. A: 333) against T. Annius Milo (138) and in vindication of P. Clodius Pulcher (137) (Asc. in Cic. Mil. *3 [p. 42.9–11 C.]; in Cic.* Mil. *71 [p. 52.11–15 C.]; Cass.*

F 1 Asc. in Cic. *Mil.*, arg. (pp. 28–29 KS = 32.24–33.5 C.)

erat domus Clodi ante paucos menses empta de M. Scauro

Romulus as if he too was a founder of the city, he [Plancus] had carried the proposal that he should rather be named Augustus, not merely by a new, but also by a more honorable name, since sacred places too and those in which anything is consecrated after due observance of auguries are called "august" [*augusta*], from the increase [*auctus*] in dignity, or from the movement or feeding of birds [*avium gestus gustusve*] . . .

150 T. MUNATIUS PLANCUS BURSA

*Cicero (Cic. In T. Munatium Plancum Bursam: Crawford 1984, 230–34) and had to go into exile (TLRR 327; Cic. Fam. 7.2.2–3; Phil. 6.10, 13.27). He was recalled by C. Iulius Caesar (**121**) in 49 BC (Cic. Phil. 6.10, 10.22, 11.14, 13.27) and was later a legate of M. Antonius (**159**) in the fighting at Mutina in 43 BC. Cicero seems to suggest that Plancus had little learning (Cic. Fam. 9.10.2).*

As Tribune to the People (F 1–7)

Dio 40.49.1–2). In that year Milo was charged with having killed Clodius, was found guilty despite Cicero's defense (Cic. Mil.; cf. Cic. Sest. 86–89; Off. 2.58), and went into exile (TLRR 309).

F 1 Asconius on Cicero, *Pro Milone*

Clodius' [P. Clodius Pulcher (**137**)] house, bought a few months earlier from M. Scaurus [M. Aemilius Scaurus

in Palatio: eodem ⟨T.⟩[1] Munatius Plancus, frater L. Planci oratoris, et Q. Pompeius Rufus, Sullae dictatoris ex filia nepos, tribuni plebis accurrerunt: eisque hortantibus vulgus imperitum corpus nudum ac calcatum,[2] sicut in lecto erat positum, ut vulnera videri possent in forum detulit et in rostris posuit. ibi pro contione Plancus et Pompeius qui competitoribus Milonis studebant invidiam Miloni fecerunt.

[1] *add. Manutius*   [2] ac calcatum *Daniel*: caldatum *codd.*: calciatum *Manutius*

F 2 Asc. in Cic. *Mil.*, *arg.* (pp. 33 KS = 37.18–38.3 C.)

inter primos et Q. Pompeius et C. Sallustius et T. Munatius Plancus tribuni plebis inimicissimas contiones de Milone habebant, invidiosas etiam de Cicerone, quod Milonem tanto studio defenderet. eratque maxima pars multitudinis infensa non solum Miloni sed etiam propter invisum patrocinium Ciceroni. postea Pompeius et Sallustius in suspicione fuerunt redisse in gratiam cum Milone ac Cicerone; Plancus autem infestissime perstitit, atque in Ciceronem quoque multitudinem instigavit. Pompeio autem suspectum faciebat Milonem, ad perniciem eius comparari vim vociferatus . . .

(**139**)], was on the Palatine: to that place <T.> Munatius Plancus, a brother of the orator L. Plancus [L. Munatius Plancus (**149**)], and Q. Pompeius Rufus [Q. Pompeius Rufus (**153**)], a grandson of the dictator Sulla by his daughter, Tribunes of the People [52 BC], came running. And at their urging, the ignorant mob brought the naked and bruised body [of Clodius], as it had been put on the bier, so that the wounds could be seen, into the Forum and put it on the Rostra. There, before a meeting of the People, Plancus and Pompeius, who favored the rivals of Milo [T. Annius Milo (**138**)], aroused resentment against Milo.

F 2 Asconius on Cicero, *Pro Milone*

Among the first, Q. Pompeius [Q. Pompeius Rufus (**153**)], C. Sallustius [C. Sallustius Crispus (**152**)], and T. Munatius Plancus, Tribunes of the People [52 BC], delivered very hostile speeches about Milo [T. Annius Milo (**138**)] at public meetings, and also hateful ones about Cicero since he defended Milo with such eagerness. And a very great part of the masses was hostile not only to Milo, but also to Cicero because of his hated advocacy. Later Pompeius and Sallustius were suspected of having become reconciled with Milo and Cicero; Plancus, however, persisted in very hostile fashion and set the masses also against Cicero. And he made Milo suspect to Pompey [Cn. Pompeius Magnus (**111**)], having cried out that violent action was being prepared for the latter's destruction . . .

F 3 Cic. *Mil.* 12

quando enim frequentissimo senatu quattuor aut summum quinque sunt inventi qui Milonis causam non
probarent? declarant huius ambusti tribuni plebis illae
intermortuae contiones quibus cotidie meam potentiam
invidiose criminabatur, cum diceret senatum non quod
sentiret sed quod ego vellem decernere.

F 4 Asc. in Cic. *Mil.* 12 (p. 37 KS = 42.16–25 C.)

T. Munatius Plancus et Q. Pompeius Rufus tribuni pl., de
quibus ⟨in⟩[1] argumento huius orationis diximus, cum contra Milonem Scipioni et Hypsaeo studerent, contionati
sunt eo ipso tempore plebemque in Milonem accenderunt
quo propter Clodi corpus curia incensa est, nec prius des-
titerunt quam flamma eius incendii fugati sunt e contione.
erant enim tunc rostra non eo loco quo nunc sunt sed ad
comitium, prope iuncta curiae. ob hoc T. Munatium "am-
bustum tribunum" appellat; fuit autem paratus ad dicendum.

[1] *add. Manutius*

F 5 Asc. in Cic. *Mil.* 67 (p. 45 KS = 51.8–14 C.)
= **111** F 28.

F 3 Cicero, *Pro Milone*

Indeed, when at the Senate's most crowded meetings have there been found four, or at most five, men who did not approve of Milo's [T. Annius Milo (**138**)] case? That is made manifest by those moribund public speeches of this half-burnt Tribune of the People [cf. F 4], in which he daily and maliciously inveighed against my power, when he said that the Senate decreed not what it felt, but what I wished.

F 4 Asconius on Cicero, *Pro Milone*

T. Munatius Plancus and Q. Pompeius Rufus [**153**], Tribunes of the People [52 BC], about whom we spoke ‹in› the summary of this speech, as they supported Scipio [Q. Caecilius Metellus Pius Scipio Nasica (**154**), consular candidate in 53 BC] and Hypsaeus [P. Plautius Hypsaeus, consular candidate in 53 BC] against Milo [T. Annius Milo (**138**)], delivered speeches at public meetings and ignited the mob against Milo at this very time when, because of Clodius' [P. Clodius Pulcher (**137**)] corpse, the Senate house [Curia Hostilia] was set on fire [52 BC], and they did not stop until they were put to flight from the popular meeting by the flames of that fire. For at that time the Rostra was not in the spot where it is now, but by the *comitium*, closely adjoining the Senate house. For this reason he [Cicero] calls T. Munatius "a half-burnt Tribune" [F 3]; and he was well equipped for speaking.

F 5 Asconius on Cicero, *Pro Milone*

= **111** F 28.

F 6 Asc. in Cic. *Mil.* 14 (pp. 39 KS = 44.8–45.4 C.)

sed ego, ut curiosius aetati vestrae satisfaciam, Acta etiam
totius illius temporis persecutus sum; in quibus cognovi
pridie Kal. Mart. S.C.[1] esse factum, P. Clodi caedem et
incendium curiae et oppugnationem aedium M. Lepidi
contra rem p. factam; ultra relatum in[2] Actis illo die nihil;
postero die, id est Kal. Mart., ⟨T.⟩[3] Munatium in contione
exposuisse populo quae pridie acta erant in senatu: in qua
contione haec dixit ad verbum: "Q.[4] Hortensium dixisse[5]
ut extra ordinem quaereretur apud quaesitorem;[6] existimare[7] ⟨f⟩ut⟨u⟩rum[8] ut, cum pusillum dedisset dulcedinis,
largiter acerbitatis devorarent: adversus hominem inge-
niosum nostro[9] ingenio usi sumus; invenimus Fufium, qui
diceret 'divide{ret}';[10] reliquae parti sententiae ego et Sallustius intercessimus." haec contio, ut puto, explicat et
quid senatus decernere voluerit, et quis divisionem postu-
laverit, et quis intercesserit et cur.

---

[1] S.C. *Manutius*: sic *codd.*
om. codd. rel.   [3] *add.* KS
codd.: quod Q. *Baiter*: cum KS
Hortensius dixisset *Baiter*
torem *codd.*   [7] estimare *vel* extimare *codd.*: aestimare *ed. Iun.*:
existimaret *Clark*   [8] ⟨f⟩ut⟨u⟩rum *Poggius*: utrum *codd.*

[2] *add. unus cod., Poggius*:
[4] Q. *Poggius*: q *vel* que
[5] Hortensium dixisse *codd.*:
[6] quaesitorem *Manutius*: quaes-

[9] nostro *Bücheler*: non *codd.*: *del. Mommsen*
[10] divide{ret} *Baiter*: divideret *codd.*

---

[1] A request to divide up a proposed motion consisting of
several items into its parts, so that some can be approved and
others rejected (as Asconius explains just before this passage).

[2] According to Asconius, this is a verbatim quotation of Plancus' words, wherein what Hortensius is alleged to have said and

F 6 Asconius on Cicero, *Pro Milone*

But, so as to satisfy [the needs of] your age more thoroughly, I have even gone through the records of that entire period; in these I have discovered that on the day before the Kalends of March [Intercal. 27, 52 BC] a decree of the Senate was passed that the assassination of P. Clodius [P. Clodius Pulcher (**137**)], and the burning of the Senate house, and the besieging of the house of M. Lepidus [M. Aemilius Lepidus, *interrex* 52, cos. 46 BC] were done against the Republic; that nothing further was noted in the records for that day; that on the following day, that is, on the Kalends of March [March 1], < T. > Munatius explained to the People at a public meeting what had been transacted in the Senate on the previous day; at this meeting of the People he said this verbatim: "that Q. Hortensius [Q. Hortensius Hortalus (**92**), F 50] had spoken in favor of the matter being investigated by a special court before a quaesitor; that he [Hortensius] believed that it would happen that, after he had given a little bit of sweetness, they [Clodius' followers] would swallow sharpness in great quantity: against this clever man we used our own cleverness; we found Fufius [presumably Q. Fufius Calenus, cos. 47 BC] to say 'divide';[1] the remaining part of the motion was vetoed by myself and Sallust [C. Sallustius Crispus (**152**), tr. pl. 52 BC]."[2] This speech before the People, as I believe, explains what the Senate wanted to decree, and who requested the division, and who vetoed and why.

thought is reproduced in indirect speech (on text and structure, see Sumner 1965, 134–35).

171

F 7 Asc. in Cic. *Mil.*, *arg.* (pp. 35 KS = 40.21–41.1 C.)

dimisso circa horam decimam iudicio T. Munatius pro contione populum adhortatus est ut postero die frequens adesset et elabi Milonem non paterentur, iudiciumque et dolorem suum ostenderet euntibus ad tabellam ferendam. postero die, qui fuit iudicii summus a. d. VII[1] Idus Aprilis, clausae fuerunt tota urbe tabernae . . .

[1] a. d. *Graevius*: ad *codd.*   VII *Clark*: III *vel* II *codd.*: VI *Manutius*

151 C. FURNIUS

C. Furnius (tr. pl. 50 BC; RE Furnius 3) followed C. Iulius Caesar (121) in the civil war. After Caesar's assassination in 44 BC, he was a legate of L. Munatius Plancus (149) in Gaul. He then fought for M. Antonius (159) against Octavian; in 36–35 BC he administered the province of Asia for Antony. After Antony's defeat, Furnius' son (cos. 17 BC) obtained pardon for his father from Octavian (Sen. Ben.

T 1 Cic. *Fam.* 10.26.2 [ad Furnium]

o mi Furni, quam tu tuam causam non nosti, qui alienas tam facile discas!

T 2 Plut. *Ant.* 58.11

= F 5.

172

F 7 Asconius on Cicero, *Pro Milone*

After the court was adjourned around the tenth hour, T. Munatius urged the People in front of a public meeting that they should attend in large numbers on the following day and not permit Milo [T. Annius Milo (**138**)] to escape, and that they should demonstrate their own judgment and distress to those about to cast their vote. On the following day, which was the last of the trial, the seventh day before the Ides of April [April 7, 52 BC], the shops were closed throughout the city . . .

151 C. FURNIUS

2.25.1), and Octavian endowed him with the rank of an ex-consul in 29 BC, although he had not been able to serve as a consul (Cass. Dio 52.42.4).

Ancient authorities mention Furnius as a great orator (T 2, 3). Two of Cicero's letters are addressed to him (Cic. Fam. 10.25, 10.26). Furnius was active as a pleader (T 1); a speech given at a trial in the Forum is mentioned (F 5).

T 1 Cicero, *Letters to Friends* [to Furnius]

My dear Furnius, how little you know about your own case, you who so easily learn other people's!

T 2 Plutarch, *Life of Antony*

= F 5.

T 3 Hieron. *Ab Abr.* 1980 = 37 a.C. (p. 159f Helm)

Furnii pater et filius clari oratores habentur. quorum filius
consularis ante patrem moritur

T 4 Tac. *Dial.* 21.1

= **114** T 3.

At a Trial in the Forum (F 5)

F 5 Plut. *Ant.* 58.9–11

Καλουΐσιος δὲ Καίσαρος ἑταῖρος ἔτι καὶ ταῦτα τῶν
εἰς Κλεοπάτραν ἐγκλημάτων Ἀντωνίῳ προΰφερε . . .
[11] . . . Φουρνίου δὲ λέγοντος, ὃς ἦν ἀξιώματος με-
γάλου καὶ δεινότατος εἰπεῖν Ῥωμαίων, τὴν μὲν Κλεοπάτραν ἐν φορείῳ διὰ τῆς ἀγορᾶς κομίζεσθαι, τὸν
δὲ Ἀντώνιον ὡς εἶδεν ἀναπηδήσαντα τὴν μὲν δίκην
ἀπολιπεῖν, ἐκκρεμαννύμενον δὲ τοῦ φορείου παρα-
πέμπειν ἐκείνην.

152 C. SALLUSTIUS CRISPUS

*C. Sallustius Crispus (86–35 BC; tr. pl. 52, praet. 46 BC;
RE Sallustius 10) was expelled from the Senate by the cen-
sors in 50 BC but later reinstated; in 45 BC he was proconsul in the new province of Africa Nova.*

*After Caesar's assassination in 44 BC, Sallust withdrew
from politics and devoted himself to the production of his-*

T 3 Jerome, *Chronicle*

Furnius father and son are regarded as famous orators. Of these the son as an ex-consul dies before the father.

T 4 Tacitus, *Dialogue on Oratory*
= **114** T 3.

At a Trial in the Forum (F 5)

F 5 Plutarch, *Life of Antony*

Calvisius [C. Calvisius Sabinus, cos. 39 BC], a companion of Caesar [C. Iulius Caesar (**121**)], brought forward against Antony [M. Antonius (**159**)] also the following charges concerning Cleopatra . . . [11] . . . that while Furnius, who was a man of great worth and the ablest orator among the Romans was speaking, Cleopatra was carried through the Forum in a litter, and Antony, when he saw her, sprang up from the tribunal and abandoned the trial; that, hanging on to the litter, he escorted her on her way.

152 C. SALLUSTIUS CRISPUS

torical works (Sall. Cat., Iug., Hist.), which include a number of speeches put into the mouths of historical characters. Published speeches by Sallust (distinct from those in his historiographical works) seem to have existed in antiquity (Sen. Contr. 3, praef. 8).

As Tribune to the People (F 1–3)

F 1 Asc. in Cic. *Mil.* 45 (p. 43 KS = 49.6–7 C.)
= **153** F 1b.

F 2

a Cic. *Mil.* 47

deinde—non enim video cur non meum quoque agam
negotium—scitis, iudices, fuisse qui in hac rogatione sua-
denda dicerent[1] Milonis manu caedem esse factam, consilio vero maioris alicuius. me videlicet latronem ac[2] sica-
rium abiecti homines et[3] perditi describebant.

[1] dicerent *aliquot codd.*: diceret *codd. nonnulli, Asc. et
Schol.*   [2] ac *codd. Cic.*: et *Asc.*   [3] et *aliquot codd.*: ac
nonnulli codd.: om. *nonnulli codd. Asc.*

b Asc. in Cic. *Mil.* 47 (pp. 44 KS = 49.24–50.2 C.)

Q. Pompeius Rufus et C. Sallustius tribuni fuerunt quos
significat. hi enim primi de ea lege ferenda populum hor-
tati sunt et dixerunt a manu Milonis occisum esse Clodium
‹et cetera›.[1]

[1] *suppl. Clark*: consilio uero maioris alicuius *unus cod. ex Cic.*

F 3 Asc. in Cic. *Mil.*, *arg.* (pp. 33 KS = 37.18–38.3 C.)
= **150** F 2.

As Tribune to the People (F 1–3)

When Tribune of the People in 52 BC, Sallust, like his colleagues (**150** F 2, 5, 6), delivered speeches before the People (CCMR, App. A: 331, 335) against T. Annius Milo (**138**) and in vindication of P. Clodius Pulcher (**137**).

F 1 Asconius on Cicero, *Pro Milone*

= **153** F 1b.

F 2

a Cicero, *Pro Milone*

In the second place—for I do not see why I should not also carry out my business—you know, judges, that there were some who in arguing for this proposal said that the assassination was done by Milo's hand [T. Annius Milo (**138**)], but according to the plan of someone more important. It was myself, obviously, whom these despicable and reckless men described as a highwayman and cutthroat.

b Asconius on this passage

Q. Pompeius Rufus [**153**] and Sallust were the Tribunes whom he [Cicero] means. For these were the first to encourage the People over the passing of that law, and they said that Clodius [P. Clodius Pulcher (**137**)] was killed by Milo's [T. Annius Milo (**138**)] hand, ⟨and the rest⟩.

F 3 Asconius on Cicero, *Pro Milone*

= **150** F 2.

153 Q. POMPEIUS RUFUS

Q. Pompeius Rufus (tr. pl. 52 BC; RE Pompeius 41), a grandson of Q. Pompeius Rufus (83) and of L. Cornelius Sulla, prosecuted M. Valerius Messalla Rufus, a candidate for the consulship, for bribery in 54 BC, but the trial seems not have been carried through (TLRR 299; Cic. Att. 4.17.5; Q Fr. 3.2.3, 3.3.2).

As Tribune to the People (F 1–2)

*Along with his tribunician colleagues in 52 BC (**150** F 1, 2, 4, 5; **152** F 2), Pompeius delivered speeches before the People (Asc. in Cic.* Mil.*, arg. [p. 33 C.]; CCMR, App. A:*

F 1

a Cic. *Mil.* 45

dictatoris Lanuvini stata sacrificia nosse negoti nihil erat. vidit necesse esse Miloni proficisci Lanuvium illo ipso quo est profectus die: itaque antevertit. at quo die? quo, ut ante dixi, fuit insanissima contio ab ipsius mercennario tribuno plebis concitata: quem diem ille, quam contionem, quos clamores, nisi ad cogitatum facinus approperaret, numquam reliquisset.

153 Q. POMPEIUS RUFUS

As Tribune of the People in 52 BC, Pompeius was involved in the activities that led to the burning of the Senate house. Prosecuted on that account after his Tribunate by M. Caelius Rufus (162 F 32), he was found guilty (Cass. Dio 40.55.1; Val. Max. 4.2.7) and went into exile (TLRR 328).

As Tribune to the People (F 1–2)

331, 334, 335) against T. Annius Milo (138) and in vindication of P. Clodius Pulcher (137).

F 1

a Cicero, *Pro Milone*

It was no trouble to ascertain the fixed sacrifices of the Dictator of Lanuvium [Milo's role]. He [P. Clodius Pulcher (137)] saw that it would be necessary for Milo to set off for Lanuvium [place in Latium southeast of Rome] on the very day on which he set off: accordingly, he anticipated him. But on what day? On that day, as I mentioned before [Cic. *Mil.* 27], on which an extremely frenzied public meeting was roused by a Tribune of the People in his [Clodius'] pay: a day, a meeting, clamor that he would never have left, had he not hastened to a premeditated crime.

b Asc. in Cic. *Mil.* 45 (p. 43 KS = 49.5–10 C.)

hoc significat eo die quo Clodius occisus est contionatum esse mercennarium eius tribunum plebis. sunt autem contionati eo die, ut ex Actis apparet, C. Sallustius et Q. Pompeius, utrique et inimici Milonis et satis inquieti. sed videtur mihi Q. Pompeium significare; nam eius seditiosior fuit contio.

F 2 Asc. in Cic. *Mil.* 67 (pp. 45 KS = 50.26–51.7 C.)

Q. Pompeius Rufus tribunus plebis, qui fuerat familiarissimus omnium P. Clodio et sectam illam sequi se palam profitebatur, dixerat in contione paucis post diebus quam Clodius erat occisus: "Milo dedit quem in curia cremaretis: dabit quem in Capitolio sepeliatis." in eadem contione idem dixerat—habuit enim eam a. d. VIII Kal. Febr.—cum Milo pridie, id est VIIII Kal. Febr., venire ad Pompeium in hortos eius voluisset, Pompeium ei per hominem propinquum misisse nuntium ne ad se veniret.

153 Q. POMPEIUS RUFUS

b Asconius on this passage

By this he [Cicero] means that on that day on which Clodius [P. Clodius Pulcher (**137**)] was killed a Tribune of the People in his pay delivered a speech before the People. And on that day, as is clear from the records, Sallust [C. Sallustius Crispus (**152**), F 1] and Q. Pompeius delivered speeches at a public meeting, both enemies of Milo [T. Annius Milo (**138**)] and rather restless. But to me he seems to mean Q. Pompeius; for his speech to the People was more seditious.

F 2 Asconius on Cicero, *Pro Milone*

Q. Pompeius Rufus, a Tribune of the People, who had been on the friendliest terms of all with P. Clodius [P. Clodius Pulcher (**137**)] and declared openly that he was an adherent of that gang, had said at a public meeting a few days after Clodius had been killed: "Milo [T. Annius Milo (**138**)] has given you someone to cremate in the Senate house; he will give you someone to bury on the Capitol." In the same speech to the People the same man had said—for he delivered it on the eighth day before the Kalends of February [January 23, 52 BC]—that, when on the preceding day, that is the ninth day before the Kalends of February [January 22], Milo had wished to come to Pompeius in his gardens, Pompeius had sent him a message through a relative that he should not come to him.

154 Q. CAECILIUS METELLUS PIUS
SCIPIO NASICA

*Q. Caecilius Metellus Pius Scipio Nasica (interrex 53, cos. suff. 52 BC; RE Caecilius 99), a P. Scipio adopted by Q. Caecilius Metellus Pius, went through the usual political career; in the civil war he supported Cn. Pompeius Magnus (**111**) and, after the victory of C. Iulius Caesar (**121**), committed suicide near Thapsus in 46 BC (Liv. Epit. 114; App. B Civ. 2.100.417, 2.101.420; Cass. Dio 43.9.5; BAfr. 96; Cic. Fam. 9.18.2).*

*Scipio Nasica published a piece against M. Porcius Cato (**126**) (Plut. Cat. min. 57.3; Plin. HN 8.196). In Cicero he is mentioned as a good speaker (T 1).*

In 78 BC Scipio Nasica appeared as a plaintiff in a civil suit (TLRR 134; Asc. in Cic. Corn. [p. 74.13–18 C.] = Cic. Corn. I, F 38 Puccioni = 37 Crawford) and again in the

T 1 Cic. *Brut.* 212–13

"summo iste quidem dicitur ingenio fuisse," inquit [BRUTUS]; "et vero hic Scipio, conlega meus, mihi sane bene et loqui videtur et dicere." "recte," inquam [CICERO], "iudicas, Brute. etenim istius genus est ex ipsius sapientiae stirpe generatum. nam et de duobus avis iam diximus, Scipione et Crasso, et de tribus proavis, Q. Metello, cuius quattuor ⟨illi⟩ filii,[1] P. Scipione, qui ex dominatu Ti.

---

[1] quattuor ⟨illi⟩ filii *Jahn*: quattuor filii *codd.*: quattuor filii ⟨consulares⟩ *Campe*

154 Q. CAECILIUS METELLUS PIUS SCIPIO NASICA

summer of 65 BC (TLRR 208; Cic. Att. 1.1.3–4). In 70 BC Scipio Nasica was one of Verres' advocates (TLRR 177; Cic. Verr. 2.4.79–80). A Q. Metellus Pius was a witness at the trial of C. Cornelius in 66/65 BC, but he is more likely to be the ex-consul (and Scipio Nasica's adoptive father) Q. Caecilius Metellus Pius (cos. 80 BC), although Malcovati referred the remark to this Scipio Nasica (orat. I).

*In 60 BC Scipio Nasica was prosecuted by M. Favonius (**166** F 3) for misconduct in an election campaign; defended by Cicero (Cic. Pro Q. Caecilio Metello Pio Scipione [Nasica]: Crawford 1984, 115–17), he was acquitted (TLRR 238). Scipio Nasica was again taken to court for electioneering offenses, by C. Memmius in 52 BC, but the trial was abandoned (TLRR 321).*

T 1 Cicero, *Brutus*

"He [L. Licinius Crassus Scipio] is said to have been a man of extraordinary ability," he [BRUTUS] said, "and indeed this Scipio [Nasica], my colleague [as a member of the *collegium pontificum*], seems to me an excellent speaker both in private conversation and in public discourse." "You assess this rightly, Brutus," I [CICERO] said. "Indeed, his lineage comes from the stock of wisdom itself. For both about his two grandfathers, Scipio [P. Cornelius Scipio Nasica Serapio, cos. 111 BC] and Crassus [L. Licinius Crassus (**66**)], we have already spoken, and about his three great-grandfathers, Q. Metellus [Q. Caecilius Metellus Macedonicus (**18**)], who had four ‹famous› sons; P. Scipio

Gracchi privatus in libertatem rem publicam vindicavit, Q. Scaevola augure, qui peritissimus iuris idemque percomis est habitus. [213] iam duorum abavorum quam est inlustre nomen, P. Scipionis, qui bis consul fuit, qui est Corculum dictus, alterius omnium sapientissimi, C. Laeli."

On Clodius' Death in the Senate (F 2)

F 2 Asc. in Cic. *Mil.*, *arg.* (pp. 30–31 KS = 34.21–35.16 C.)

post diem tricesimum fere quam erat Clodius occisus Q. Metellus Scipio in senatu contra Q. Caepionem[1] conquestus est de hac caede P. Clodi. falsum esse dixit, quod Milo sic se defenderet, ⟨s⟩ed[2] Clodium Aricinos decuriones alloquendi gratia abisse profectum cum sex ac XX servis; Milonem subito post horam quartam, senatu misso, cum servis amplius CCC armatis obviam ei contendisse et su-

---

[1] Q. Caepionem *Manutius*: M. Caepionem *codd.*: M. Caelium *Halm*: M. Catonem *KS*   [2] ⟨s⟩ed *Clark*: et *codd.*: *lac. statuit Halm*

[P. Cornelius Scipio Nasica Serapio (**38**)], who as a private person restored the Republic to liberty from the domination of Ti. Gracchus [Ti. Sempronius Gracchus (**34**)]; and Q. Scaevola the augur [Q. Mucius Scaevola (**50**)], who was regarded as the most learned in the law and at the same time a man of most gracious bearing. [213] As to his two great-great-grandfathers, how distinguished is the name of P. Scipio, who was twice consul and who was called Corculum [P. Cornelius Scipio Nasica Corculum, cos. 162, 155, censor 159 BC], and of that other, wisest of all, C. Laelius [C. Laelius Sapiens (**20**)]!"

On Clodius' Death in the Senate (F 2)

*In 52 BC Scipio Nasica spoke in the Senate about the killing of P. Clodius Pulcher (**137**), criticizing T. Annius Milo (**138**).*

F 2 Asconius on Cicero, *Pro Milone*

About thirty days after Clodius [P. Clodius Pulcher (**137**)] had been killed, Q. Metellus Scipio, [speaking] in the Senate against Q. Caepio [name and identity uncertain], complained about this murder of P. Clodius. He said that it was wrong what Milo [T. Annius Milo (**138**)] said in his defense along these lines, but that Clodius had left in order to address the decurions in Aricia [modern Ariccia, town in the Alban Hills near Rome], having set off with twenty-six slaves; suddenly, after the fourth hour, after the Senate had been adjourned, Milo, with more than three hundred armed slaves had come against him and had attacked him unawares <on> the march beyond Bovillae

pra Bovillas inopinantem ⟨in⟩³ itinere aggressum. ibi P. Clodium tribus vulneribus acceptis Bovillas perlatum; tabernam in quam perfugerat expugnatam a Milone; semianimem Clodium extractum ⟨. . .⟩⁴ in via Appia occisum esse anulumque eius ei morienti extractum. deinde Milonem, cum sciret in Albano parvolum filium Clodi esse, venisse ad villam et, cum puer ante subtractus esset, ex servo Halicore quaestionem ita habuisse ut eum articulatim consecaret; vilicum et duos praeterea servos iugulasse. ex servis Clodi qui dominum defenderant undecim esse interfectos, Milonis duos solos saucios factos esse: ob quae Milonem postero die XII servos qui maxime operam navassent manu misisse populoque tributim singula milia aeris ad defendendos de se rumores dedisse.

³ add. Manutius   ⁴ lac. exhibent codd.: fort. iussu Milonis supplendum coni. Clark

On Pompey and Caesar in the Senate (F 3)

In the Senate in early 49 BC Scipio Nasica confirmed Cn. Pompeius Magnus' (111) intentions and encouraged the senators to follow Pompey. Scipio moved that C. Iulius

F 3 Caes. BCiv. 1.1.4–4.1

in eandem sententiam loquitur Scipio: Pompeio esse in animo rei publicae non deesse si senatus sequatur; si cunctetur atque agat lenius, nequiquam eius auxilium si postea velit senatum imploraturum. [2.1] haec Scipionis oratio,

[town on the Via Appia]. There P. Clodius, after having received three wounds, had been brought to Bovillae; the tavern in which he had taken refuge had been stormed by Milo; half-alive, Clodius had been dragged out <. . .> he had been killed on the Via Appia, and his ring had been taken off him while he was dying. Then Milo, when he learned that Clodius' young son was on the Alban estate, had come to the manor house and, since the boy had been removed beforehand, interrogated the slave Halicor so severely that he cut him up limb by limb; moreover, he had cut the throats of the caretaker and two slaves besides. Out of Clodius' slaves who had defended their master, eleven had been killed, of Milo's only two had been wounded: for this reason, on the following day, Milo had freed the twelve slaves who had worked particularly hard and had given to the People tribe by tribe a thousand sesterces to refute rumors about him.

On Pompey and Caesar in the Senate (F 3)

Caesar (121) should dismiss his army by a certain date or be regarded as a public enemy (Plut. Caes. 30.4), and he opposed proposals by others in support of Caesar.

F 3 Caesar, *Civil War*

Scipio makes the same point [as L. Cornelius Lentulus Crus (157), F 5]: that Pompey [Cn. Pompeius Magnus (111)] does not intend to fail the Republic if the Senate follows him; if it hesitates and acts too indecisively, the Senate will call for his help in vain if it wants it later. [2.1] This speech of Scipio's, because the meeting of the Senate

quod senatus in urbe habebatur Pompeiusque aberat, ex
ipsius ore Pompei mitti videbatur. . . . [6] sic vocibus consulis, terrore praesentis exercitus, minis amicorum Pompei plerique compulsi inviti et coacti Scipionis sententiam
sequuntur: uti ante certam diem Caesar exercitum dimittat; si non faciat, eum adversus rem publicam facturum
videri. . . . [4.1] omnibus his resistitur omnibusque oratio
consulis, Scipionis, Catonis opponitur.

155 M. CLAUDIUS MARCELLUS

*M. Claudius Marcellus (cos. 51 BC; RE Claudius 229) was
opposed to C. Iulius Caesar (121) and therefore went into
exile in Mytilene after the battle of Pharsalus in 48 BC; he
was later pardoned and recalled by Caesar (cf. Cic. Marc.)
but was killed near Athens on his way back to Rome in 45
BC (Cic. Fam. 4.12).*

T 1 Cic. *Brut.* 248–50

hoc loco BRUTUS: "quam vellem," inquit, "de his etiam
oratoribus qui hodie sunt tibi dicere liberet; et, si de aliis
minus, de duobus tamen quos a te scio laudari solere,
Caesare et Marcello, audirem non minus libenter quam
audivi de eis qui fuerunt." "cur tandem?" inquam [CIC-

was being held in the city [of Rome] and Pompey was
absent [as he could not cross the city boundary as *imperator*], seemed to issue from the mouth of Pompey himself
[cf. **111** F 29]. . . . [6] Thus, prompted by the consul's [L.
Cornelius Lentulus Crus (**157**)] language, fear of the
nearby army [of Pompey], and threats from Pompey's
friends, the majority, forced, unwilling, and coerced, support Scipio's proposal: that Caesar must dismiss his army
by a set date; if he does not do so, he will clearly have acted
against the Republic. . . . [4.1] All these [proposals] are
resisted, and they all are opposed by a speech from the
consul, from Scipio, and from Cato [M. Porcius Cato
(**126**)].

155 M. CLAUDIUS MARCELLUS

A letter from Marcellus to Cicero is extant (Cic. Fam.
4.11), as are letters from Cicero to him (Cic. Fam. *4.7–10,
15.9).*

*Ancient authorities mention Marcellus as a well-known
orator; in Cicero he is noted for his extensive training
and praised for commanding all the qualities of an orator
(T 1–3).*

T 1 Cicero, *Brutus*

At this point BRUTUS said: "How I wish that you felt inclined to speak also about the orators who are around today; and, if not about others, at least about two who, as I
know, tend to be praised by you, Caesar [C. Iulius Caesar
(**121**)] and Marcellus, I should like to hear no less eagerly
than I have heard about those who were around in the

ERO]; "an exspectas quid ego iudicem de istis, qui tibi sunt aeque noti ac mihi?" "mihi me hercule," inquit, "Marcellus satis est notus, Caesar autem parum; illum enim saepe audivi, hic, cum ego iudicare iam aliquid possem, afuit." [249] "quid igitur de illo iudicas," <inquam>,[1] "quem saepe audivisti?" "quid censes," inquit, "nisi id, quod habiturus es similem tui?" "ne ego," inquam, "si ita est, velim tibi eum placere quam maxime." "atqui[2] et ita est," inquit, "et vehementer placet; nec vero sine causa. nam et didicit et omissis ceteris studiis unum id egit seseque cotidianis commentationibus acerrime exercuit. [250] itaque et lectis utitur verbis et frequentibus <sententiis>[3] et splendore vocis <et>[4] dignitate motus fit speciosum et inlustre quod dicit{ur},[5] omniaque sic suppetunt, ut ei nullam deesse virtutem oratoris putem; maximeque laudandus est, qui hoc tempore ipso, quod[6] liceat in hoc communi nostro et quasi fatali malo, consoletur se cum conscientia optimae mentis tum etiam usurpatione et renovatione doctrinae. vidi enim Mytilenis nuper virum atque, ut dixi, vidi plane virum. itaque cum eum antea tui similem in dicendo viderim, tum vero nunc a doctissimo viro tibique, ut intellexi, amicissimo Cratippo instructum omni copia multo videbam similiorem."

[1] *add. Jahn*   [2] atqui *edd.*: atque *codd.*   [3] *add. Jahn*
[4] *add. edd.*   [5] dicit{ur} *Orelli*: dicitur *codd.*
[6] quod *Peter*: cum *codd.*

past." "Why, then?" I [CICERO] said. "Are you waiting for what I think about those men who are as well known to you as to me?" "Well," he said, "Marcellus is sufficiently known to me, but Caesar too little: for, the former I have heard often; in the time when I was able to form some judgment of my own, the latter was away [from Rome]." [249] "Well, what is your judgment," ⟨I said⟩, "about that man whom you have heard often?" "What do you think," he said, "other than that you will have him similar to your-self?" "Indeed," I said, "if this is the case, I should wish him to please you as much as possible." "But it is like that," he said, "and he pleases me very much, and indeed not without good reason. For he has both studied hard and, omitting all other studies, worked toward this one goal, and by daily exercises he has trained most energetically. [250] As a result of this, he uses carefully chosen words and a wealth ⟨of pointed statements⟩, and through the brilliance of his voice ⟨and⟩ the dignity of his movements what he says becomes attractive and brilliant; and all this is at his disposal to such an extent that I believe that he lacks no quality belonging to an orator. And he is to be praised most of all because at this very time, as far as pos-sible in this our general and almost fatal misfortune, he consoles himself with the consciousness of his excellent attitude and particularly with the constant attention to and renewed uptake of scholarly pursuits. For I recently saw the man at Mytilene, and, as I have said, I saw a man in-deed. Therefore, while before I have seen him compara-ble to you in speaking, so now, after he had been instructed by a very learned man and a very good friend of yours, as I learned, Cratippus [Peripatetic philosopher, 1st cent. BC], in all resources, I saw him much more comparable."

T 2 Cass. Dio 40.58.2–3

. . . καὶ τὴν ὑπατείαν ἐπ᾽ αὐτοὺς ᾔτησεν, ἐπειδήπερ
ἰδιωτεύων οὐδὲν ἰσχύσειν ἔμελλεν, ὑποπτευθεὶς δὲ
ὑπὸ τῶν τὰ ἐκείνων πραττόντων τοιοῦτόν τι δράσειν
οὐκ ἀπεδείχθη, [3] ἀλλ᾽ ὅ τε Μάρκελλος ὁ Μᾶρκος καὶ
ὁ Ῥοῦφος ὁ Σουλπίκιος, ὁ μὲν διὰ τὴν τῶν νόμων
ἐμπειρίαν ὁ δὲ διὰ τὴν τῶν λόγων δύναμιν, {δι}ῃρέθη-
σαν,[1] ἄλλως τε καὶ ὅτι αὐτοὶ μέν, εἰ καὶ μὴ χρήμασιν
ἢ βιαίῳ τινὶ ἔργῳ, ἀλλὰ τῇ γε[2] θεραπείᾳ καὶ τῇ
παρακλήσει πολλῇ πρὸς πάντας ἐχρήσαντο, ὁ δὲ δὴ
Κάτων οὐδένα αὐτῶν ἐθεράπευσε.

[1] {δι}ῃρέθησαν Xylander: διῃρέθησαν cod.   [2] γε Bekker: τε cod.

T 3 Schol. Gronov. ad Cic. *Marc.* 1 (p. 295.9–10 Stangl)

data est indulgentia Ciceroni, reversus est orator Marcellus de quo Lucanus ait [1.313]: "Marcellusque loquax."

In Support of T. Annius Milo (F 4)

F 4 Cic. *Q Fr.* 2.3.1–2
= **111** F 22.

T 2 Cassius Dio, *Roman History*

. . . and he [M. Porcius Cato (**126**)] sought the consulship against them [C. Iulius Caesar (**121**) and Cn. Pompeius Magnus (**111**)], because as a private citizen he would have no power [to intervene]; he was, however, suspected of doing something like this by their adherents and was not appointed. [3] Instead, Marcus Marcellus and Sulpicius Rufus [Ser. Sulpicius Rufus (**118**)] were chosen, the one on account of his acquaintance with the law, the other for his ability as an orator, also because, even if they did not employ money or any violent action, they yet showed great deference and exhortation to all, whereas Cato did not pay court to any of them.

T 3 Scholia Gronoviana to Cicero, *Pro Marcello*

Mildness was shown to Cicero; the orator Marcellus returned, about whom Lucan says [1.313]: "and loquacious Marcellus."

In Support of T. Annius Milo (F 4)

*In 56 BC Marcellus appeared in support of T. Annius Milo (**138**), prosecuted by P. Clodius Pulcher (**137** F 6–7) (TLRR 266).*

F 4 Cicero, *Letters to Quintus*

= **111** F 22.

On Behalf of M. Aemilius Scaurus (F 5)

F 5 Asc. in Cic. *Scaur.*, *arg.* (p. 18 KS = 20.13–18 C.)
= **92** F 48.

On Behalf of T. Annius Milo (F 6)

F 6 Asc. in Cic. *Mil.*, *arg.* (p. 30 KS = 34.15–21 C.)
= **92** F 49.

156 FAUSTUS CORNELIUS SULLA

Faustus Cornelius Sulla (quaest. 54 BC; RE Cornelius 377), the son of the dictator L. Cornelius Sulla, served in a number of junior offices and supported Cn. Pompeius

In Support of M. Aemilius Scaurus (F 1)

On Behalf of M. Aemilius Scaurus (F 5)

In 54 BC Marcellus was among those who supported M.
Aemilius Scaurus (**139**) (TLRR 295; cf. **148**).

F 5 Asconius on Cicero, *Pro Scauro*
= **92** F 48.

On Behalf of T. Annius Milo (F 6)

In 52 BC Marcellus was among those who supported T.
Annius Milo (**138**) in the court cases of that year (TLRR
306, 309), when Cicero defended Milo in the main trial
(*Cic.* Mil.).

F 6 Asconius on Cicero, *Pro Milone*
= **92** F 49.

156 FAUSTUS CORNELIUS SULLA

*Magnus (**111**), his father-in-law. After the battle of Pharsalus, Faustus fought in Africa and was killed there after
the battle of Thapsus (46 BC).*

In Support of M. Aemilius Scaurus (F 1)

In 54 BC Faustus assisted his stepbrother M. Aemilius
Scaurus (**139**) in a trial for the recovery of extorted money
by offering a testimonial for his character (TLRR 295; cf.
148).

F 1 Asc. in Cic. *Scaur.* II.46 (pp. 24–25 KS = 28.7–16 C.)

laudaverunt Scaurum consulares novem . . . unus praeterea adulescens laudavit, frater eius, Faustus Cornelius
Sullae filius. is in laudatione multa humiliter et cum lacrimis locutus non minus audientes permovit quam Scaurus
ipse permoverat.

In Support of T. Annius Milo (F 2)

F 2 Asc. in Cic. *Mil.*, *arg.* (p. 30 KS = 34.15–21 C.)
= **92** F 49.

157 L. CORNELIUS LENTULUS CRUS

*L. Cornelius Lentulus Crus (cos. 49 BC; RE Cornelius
218) supported Cn. Pompeius Magnus (**111**) and fought
for him at Pharsalus in 48 BC; after the defeat he fled to
Egypt, where he was captured and killed on the orders of
King Ptolemy XIII. When praetor in 58 BC, Lentulus had
shown support for Cicero (Cic. Q Fr. 1.2.16; Pis. 77).*

T 1 Cic. *Brut.* 268

[CICERO:] duo praeterea Lentuli consulares, quorum
Publius . . . L. autem Lentulus satis erat fortis orator, si

F 1 Asconius on Cicero, *Pro Scauro*

Nine ex-consuls commended Scaurus [M. Aemilius Scaurus (**139**)] . . . In addition, one young man commended him: his brother Faustus Cornelius, Sulla's son. In his testimonial he said many things humbly and with tears; thus he moved the listeners no less than Scaurus himself had moved them [**139** F 5].

In Support of T. Annius Milo (F 2)

*In 52 BC Faustus was among those assisting T. Annius Milo (**138**) in one of the trials of that year (TLRR 306, 309).*

F 2 Asconius on Cicero, *Pro Milone*

= **92** F 49.

157 L. CORNELIUS LENTULUS CRUS

In Cicero it is noted that Lentulus had a pleasing voice and diction, and a forceful manner of speaking; his qualities as an orator were regarded as adequate for political affairs (T 1).

T 1 Cicero, *Brutus*

[Cicero:] Besides there were the two Lentuli, ex-consuls; of whom Publius [P. Cornelius Lentulus Spinther, cos. 57 BC] . . . But L. Lentulus was an orator of considerable

modo orator, sed cogitandi non ferebat laborem; vox canora, verba non horrida sane, ut plena esset animi et terroris oratio; quaereres in iudiciis fortasse melius, in re publica quod erat esse iudicares satis.

T 2 Cic. *Har. resp.* 37

= F 4.

Against P. Clodius Pulcher (F 3–4)

F 3 Schol. Bob. ad Cic. *Clod. et Cur.* (p. 85.16–17 Stangl)

= **86** F 8.

F 4 Cic. *Har. resp.* 37

et video in haruspicum responsum haec esse subiuncta: "sacrificia vetusta occultaque minus diligenter facta pollutaque." . . . "vetusta occultaque." nego ulla verba Lentulum, gravem oratorem ac disertum, saepius, cum te accusaret, usurpasse quam haec quae nunc ex Etruscis libris in te conversa atque interpretata dicuntur.

vigor, if only an orator, but he could not bear the labor of thinking. A melodious voice, a diction certainly not too harsh, so that his speech was full of force and threat. For the courts you would perhaps look for something better; for political matters you would consider adequate what there was.

T 2 Cicero, *De Haruspicum Responsis*

= F 4.

Against P. Clodius Pulcher (F 3–4)

*In 61 BC Lentulus was the chief prosecutor of P. Clodius Pulcher (**137**) for sexual impurity in the wake of the Bona Dea scandal (cf. **137** F 9A), when Clodius was acquitted amid suspicion of bribery (TLRR 236).*

F 3 Scholia Bobiensia to Cicero, *Against Clodius and Curio*

= **86** F 8.

F 4 Cicero, *De Haruspicum Responsis*

And I see that this addition has been made to the response of the soothsayers: "Ancient and secret sacrifices have not been performed diligently enough and been desecrated." . . . "Ancient and secret." I say that, when Lentulus, that grave and eloquent orator, was accusing you [P. Clodius Pulcher (**137**)], he did not use any other words more frequently than these that are now quoted from the Etruscan books, turned against you and interpreted in that way.

On Pompey and Caesar in the Senate (F 5)

F 5 Caes. *BCiv.* 1.1.2–4.2

referunt consules de re publica infinite.[1] L. Lentulus consul senatui rei publicae se non defuturum pollicetur si audacter ac fortiter sententias dicere velint; [3] sin Caesarem respiciant atque eius gratiam sequantur, ut superioribus fecerint temporibus, se sibi consilium capturum neque senatus auctoritati obtemperaturum; habere se quoque ad Caesaris gratiam atque amicitiam receptum. . . . [2.4] hi omnes convicio L. Lentuli consulis correpti exagitabantur. [5] Lentulus sententiam Calidi pronuntiaturum se omnino negavit. Marcellus perterritus conviciis a sua sententia discessit. [6] sic vocibus consulis, terrore praesentis exercitus, minis amicorum Pompei plerique compulsi inviti et coacti Scipionis sententiam sequuntur: uti ante certam diem Caesar exercitum dimittat; si non faciat, eum adversus rem publicam facturum videri. . . . [4.1] omnibus his resistitur omnibusque oratio

---

[1] infinite *Hotoman* (cf. *Gell. NA 14.7.9*): in civitate *codd.*: {in civitate} *Faernus*: *alii alia*

157 L. CORNELIUS LENTULUS CRUS

On Pompey and Caesar in the Senate (F 5)

In January 49 BC, having just entered the consulship (along with C. Claudius Marcellus, brother of M. Claudius Marcellus [155]), Lentulus spoke in the Senate about Cn. Pompeius Magnus (111) and C. Iulius Caesar (121).

F 5 Caesar, *Civil War*

The consuls initiate a general debate about the political situation [in response to a letter received from C. Iulius Caesar (**121**)]. L. Lentulus, the consul, promises that he will not fail the Senate and the Republic if they are willing to put forward proposals boldly and forcefully; [3] but if they should look to Caesar and chase after his favor, as they have done on previous occasions, he will make a plan with himself and not comply with the Senate's authority; he too has a refuge in Caesar's favor and friendship. . . . [2.4] All these men [who had made milder proposals], rebuked with abuse from L. Lentulus, the consul, had strong feelings aroused. [5] Lentulus refused outright to ask for a vote on Calidius' proposal [M. Calidius (**140**), F 12A]. Marcellus [M. Claudius Marcellus (**155**)], thoroughly alarmed by the derision, abandoned his proposal. [6] Thus, prompted by the consul's language, fear of the nearby army [of Pompey], and threats from Pompey's [Cn. Pompeius Magnus (**111**)] friends, the majority, forced, unwilling, and coerced, support Scipio's proposal [Q. Caecilius Metellus Pius Scipio Nasica (**154**), F 3]: that Caesar must dismiss his army by a set date; if he does not do so, he will clearly have acted against the Republic. . . . [4.1] All these [proposals] are resisted, and they all are opposed

consulis, Scipionis, Catonis opponitur. . . . [2] Lentulus
aeris alieni magnitudine et spe exercitus ac provinciarum
et regum appellandorum largitionibus movetur seque alterum fore Sullam inter suos gloriatur, ad quem summa
imperi redeat.

158 M. IUNIUS BRUTUS

*M. Iunius Brutus (ca. 85–42 BC; praet. urb. 44 BC; RE
Iunius 53), officially called Q. Servilius Caepio Brutus
after adoption, initially supported Cn. Pompeius Magnus
(111) in the civil war, but later accepted C. Iulius Caesar's
(121) pardon. When he was praetor urbanus in 44 BC, he,
along with C. Cassius Longinus and others, organized
Caesar's assassination on the Ides of March. Afterward, he
went to Greece as provincial governor. After the battles at
Philippi he killed himself (42 BC) (on his life see Tempest
2017).*

*Brutus followed the Academic school of philosophy (T 2,
4, 6, 14, 15; Cic. Brut. 149). He wrote works on virtue,
duties, and patience (T 6, 8, 12; Cic. Tusc. 5.21–22; Fin.
3.6, 5.8; Att. 13.25.3), and he is said to have produced
summaries of the historical works of Polybius, Coelius An-
tipater, and Fannius (FRHist A 26). He also composed*

T 1 Cic. *Brut.* 22

[CICERO:] nam mihi, Brute, in te intuenti crebro in mentem venit vereri, ecquodnam curriculum aliquando sit

by a speech from the consul, from Scipio [Q. Caecilius
Metellus Pius Scipio Nasica (**154**)], and from Cato [M.
Porcius Cato (**126**)]. . . . [2] Lentulus is motivated by the
size of his debts, by the prospect of [the command of] an
army and provinces, and by bribes from kings to be officially recognized; and among his friends he boasts that he
will be a second Sulla [L. Cornelius Sulla], to whom supreme power shall return.

158 M. IUNIUS BRUTUS

*poetry (Plin. Ep. 5.3.5; Quint. Inst. 9.4.76). Cicero dedi-
cated several of his philosophical and rhetorical treatises
to Brutus (Cic. Fin., Nat. D., Tusc., Parad., Brut., Orat.).
Some letters by Brutus survive in Cicero's correspondence
(see also T 10, 11, 14). Brutus cultivated the Attic style of
speaking (on his oratory see Balbo 2013).*

*In Cicero, Brutus' natural abilities as an orator as well
as his great industry and studying are praised; it is mentioned that he appeared in a number of court cases, while
it is regretted that the political circumstances reduced his
options for applying his oratorical skills (T 1, 3–4). He is
said to be familiar with Demosthenic figures of thought
(T 5). Other ancient authors also highlight Brutus' oratorical skill, even though they rate his abilities as a philosopher more highly (T 7–9, 12–13; Vell. Pat. 2.36.2).*

T 1 Cicero, *Brutus*

[CICERO:] For when I look on you, Brutus, it crosses my
mind frequently to wonder apprehensively what career

habitura tua et natura admirabilis et exquisita doctrina et
singularis industria. cum enim in maximis causis versatus
esses et cum tibi aetas nostra iam cederet fascisque sum-
mitteret, subito in civitate cum alia ceciderunt tum etiam
ea ipsa, de qua disputare ordimur, eloquentia obmutuit.

T 2 Cic. *Brut.* 120

[CICERO:] quo magis tuum, Brute, iudicium probo, qui
eorum {id est ex vetere Academia}[1] philosophorum sectam
secutus es, quorum in doctrina atque praeceptis disse-
rendi ratio coniungitur cum suavitate dicendi et copia . . .

   [1] *del. Lambinus*

T 3 Cic. *Brut.* 324

[CICERO:] maxime vero perspecta est utriusque nostrum
exercitatio paulo ante quam perterritum armis hoc studium, Brute, nostrum conticuit subito et obmutuit: cum
lege Pompeia ternis horis ad dicendum datis ad causas
simillimas inter se vel potius easdem novi veniebamus
cotidie. quibus quidem causis tu etiam, Brute, praesto
fuisti complurisque et nobiscum et solus egisti . . .

your remarkable natural gifts, meticulous studying, and unique industry will one day have. For when you had been engaged in cases of the greatest significance and when our advancing age was already giving way to you and laying down the signs of office, suddenly other things in the community collapsed, and even eloquence itself, about which we are setting out to have a discussion, became mute.

T 2 Cicero, *Brutus*

[CICERO:] The more therefore I praise your judgment, Brutus, you who have followed the school [Old Academy] of those philosophers {that is, from the Old Academy} in whose teaching and precepts the method of logical discussion is joined with charm and fullness of speaking . . .

T 3 Cicero, *Brutus*

[CICERO:] The proficiency of the two of us [Cicero and Q. Hortensius Hortalus (**92**)] was made manifest most conspicuously a short time before this our common study, Brutus, greatly terrified by arms, suddenly fell silent and became mute: when according to the *Lex Pompeia* three hours each were granted for speaking,[1] we appeared daily in cases very similar to each other or rather identical, in novel ways. In these cases you also, Brutus, were involved, and you pleaded in a number of them, both with us and on your own . . .

[1] The *Lex Pompeia de vi et de ambitu* of 52 BC (*LPPR*, pp. 410–11) included limits on the length of the speeches for the prosecution and the defense (e.g., Cic. *Fin.* 4.1; Asc. in Cic. *Mil.*, *arg.* [p. 36.5–13 C.]; Tac. *Dial.* 38).

T 4 Cic. *Brut.* 331–32

[CICERO:] sed in te intuens, Brute, doleo, cuius in adulescentiam per medias laudes quasi quadrigis vehentem
transversa incurrit misera fortuna rei publicae. . . . tuum
enim forum, tuum erat illud curriculum, tu illuc veneras
unus, qui non linguam modo acuisses exercitatione dicendi sed et ipsam eloquentiam locupletavisses graviorum
artium instrumento et isdem artibus decus omne virtutis
cum summa eloquentiae laude iunxisses. [332] ex te du-
plex nos afficit sollicitudo, quod et ipse re publica careas
et illa te. tu tamen, etsi cursum ingeni tui, Brute, premit
haec importuna clades civitatis, contine te in tuis perenni-
bus studiis et effice id quod iam prope modum vel plane
potius effeceras, ut te eripias ex ea quam ego congessi in
hunc sermonem turba patronorum. nec enim decet te
ornatum uberrimis artibus, quas cum domo haurire non
posses arcessivisti ex urbe ea quae domus est semper habita doctrinae, numerari in vulgo patronorum. nam quid
te exercuit Pammenes vir longe eloquentissimus Grae-
ciae? quid illa vetus Academia atque eius heres Aristus
hospes et familiaris meus, si quidem similes maioris partis
oratorum futuri sumus?

T 5 Cic. *Orat.* 136

sed sententiarum ornamenta maiora sunt; quibus quia fre-
quentissime Demosthenes utitur, sunt qui putent idcirco

T 4 Cicero, *Brutus*

[CICERO:] But I feel sad when I look on you, Brutus, whose youth, faring as if on a four-horse chariot amid general commendation, has been hit by the bad fortune of the Republic coming in its way. . . . For yours was the Forum, yours was that racetrack, you had come there as the only one who had not only sharpened his tongue by training to speak, but had also enriched eloquence itself by the support of more serious arts and, through the same arts, had joined every ornament of virtue with the greatest renown for eloquence. [332] On your account a twofold concern touches us, that you lack the Republic and it lacks you. Yet, even though the ill-timed misfortune of the community has checked the course of your talent, Brutus, keep to your constant studies and see to it that (as you had almost, or rather quite, accomplished already) you escape from the throng of pleaders that I have crowded into this discussion. For it is not appropriate for you, having been furnished with the richest arts, which, since you could not imbibe them at home, you have brought back from that city that has always been recognized as the home of learning, to be numbered among the common group of pleaders. For to what purpose did Pammenes, by far the most eloquent man in Greece, train you? To what purpose did the famous Old Academy and its heir, my friend and guest Aristus [Academic philosopher], train you, if we are just to be similar to the greater number of orators?

T 5 Cicero, *Orator*

But the figures of thought are of greater importance; because of the fact that Demosthenes used them very fre-

eius eloquentiam maxime esse laudabilem. et vero nullus
fere ab eo locus sine quadam conformatione sententiae
dicitur. nec quicquam est aliud dicere nisi aut omnis aut
certe plerasque aliqua specie illuminare sententias. quas
cum tu optume, Brute, teneas, quid attinet nominibus uti
aut exemplis? tantummodo notetur locus.

T 6 Cic. *Acad.* 1.12

Brutus quidem noster excellens omni genere laudis sic
philosophiam Latinis litteris persequitur nihil ut isdem de
rebus Graeca desideres; et eandem quidem sententiam
sequitur quam tu, nam Aristum Athenis audivit aliquam-
diu, cuius tu fratrem Antiochum.

T 7 Columella, *Rust.* 1, *praef.* 30

nec Brutum aut Caelium Pollionemve cum Messala et
Calvo deterruere ab eloquentiae studio fulmina illa Ciceronis.

T 8 Quint. *Inst.* 10.1.123

supersunt qui de philosophia scripserint: quo in genere
paucissimos adhuc eloquentes litterae Romanae tulerunt.
idem igitur M. Tullius, qui ubique, etiam in hoc opere

quently, there are some people who therefore believe that his eloquence is particularly admirable. And indeed scarcely any topic is treated by him without some configuration of thought. And speaking is nothing other than to embellish in some fashion all or at any rate most of the ideas. Since you understand these embellishments perfectly, Brutus, what use is it to put down names or examples? The issue shall be identified only.

T 6 Cicero, *Posterior Academics*

At all events, our Brutus, eminent for every kind of distinction, sets out philosophy in Latin writing in such a way that you would not at all desire Greek writings on the same subjects. And, indeed, he is an adherent of the same doctrine as you [M. Terentius Varro]; for, for some time, he heard the lectures of Aristus [Academic philosopher] at Athens, whose brother Antiochus [of Ascalon; Academic philosopher] you [heard].

T 7 Columella, *On Agriculture*

Neither Brutus nor Caelius [M. Caelius Rufus (**162**)] or Pollio [C. Asinius Pollio (**174**)] along with Messalla [M. Valerius Messalla Corvinus (**176**)] and Calvus [C. Licinius Macer Calvus (**165**)] were deterred from the study of eloquence by those lightning bolts of Cicero [cf. Cic. *Fam.* 9.21.1].

T 8 Quintilian, *The Orator's Education*

There remain those who have written on philosophy: in this genre Roman literature has so far produced very few eloquent authors. Thus, M. Tullius [Cicero] again, as ev-

Platonis aemulus extitit. egregius vero multoque quam in orationibus praestantior Brutus suffecit ponderi rerum: scias eum sentire quae dicit.

T 9 Quint. *Inst*. 12.10.11
= **140** T 2.

T 10 Quint. *Inst*. 9.4.75–76

peius cludit[1] finis hexametri, ut Brutus in epistulis: "neque illi malunt habere tutores aut defensores, quam quos[2] sciunt placuisse Catoni." [76] iambi[3] minus sunt notabiles, quia hoc genus sermoni[4] proximum est. itaque et versus hi fere excidunt, quos Brutus[5] ipso componendi durius studio saepissime[6] facit, non raro Asinius, sed etiam Cicero nonnumquam . . .

[1] cludit *cod. rec.*: eludit *cod.*   [2] *fort.* quam quos *Winterbottom*: quamquam *cod.*: quam con *cod. suppl.*   [3] iambi *Halm*: illi *cod.*   [4] sermoni *cod. rec.*: sermonis *cod.*   [5] *corr. cod. suppl.*: brutis *cod.*   [6] studio s(a)epissime *cod. rec.*: studiosae pessim*e *cod.*

T 11 Tac. *Dial*. 18.5

[APER:] legistis utique et Calvi et Bruti ad Ciceronem missas epistulas, ex quibus facile est deprehendere Calvum quidem Ciceroni visum exsanguem et attritum, Brutum autem otiosum atque diiunctum; rursusque Ciceronem a Calvo quidem male audisse tamquam solutum et

erywhere, showed himself in this type of work too as a
rival to Plato. Brutus, excellent indeed and far more outstanding than in his speeches, had the strength to support
the weight of the subject: you would know that he feels
what he says.

T 9 Quintilian, *The Orator's Education*
= **140** T 2.

T 10 Quintilian, *The Orator's Education*

The end of a hexameter [at the end of a phrase in prose]
is a worse closure, as Brutus in his letters: "Nor do they
prefer to have guardians or defenders, other than those
whom they know have been approved by Cato." [76] Iam-
bics are less conspicuous because this meter is nearest to
ordinary speech. Thus, even whole lines of this sort usually
slip out, which Brutus, with his particular eagerness for
rather harsh composition, creates very often, Asinius [C.
Asinius Pollio (**174**)] not seldom, but even Cicero occasionally . . .

T 11 Tacitus, *Dialogue on Oratory*

[APER:] You have read, of course, the letters of Calvus [C.
Licinius Macer Calvus (**165**)] and of Brutus sent to Cicero, from which it is easy to gather that Calvus seemed to
Cicero bloodless and attenuated, Brutus, on the other
hand, leisurely and disjointed; that Cicero, in his turn, was

211

enervem, a Bruto autem, ut ipsius verbis utar, tamquam "fractum atque elumbem."

T 12 Tac. *Dial.* 21.5–6

= **121** F 46.

T 13 Tac. *Dial.* 25.3–4

= **121** T 7.

T 14 Plut. *Brut.* 2.2–8

τῶν δὲ Ἑλληνικῶν φιλοσόφων οὐδενὸς μέν ὡς ἁπλῶς εἰπεῖν ἀνήκοος ἦν οὐδ᾽ ἀλλότριος, διαφερόντως δ᾽ ἐσπουδάκει πρὸς τοὺς ἀπὸ Πλάτωνος· [3] καὶ τὴν νέαν καὶ μέσην λεγομένην Ἀκαδήμειαν οὐ πάνυ προσιέμενος, ἐξήρτητο τῆς παλαιᾶς, καὶ διετέλει θαυμάζων μὲν Ἀντίοχον τὸν Ἀσκαλωνίτην, φίλον δὲ καὶ συμβιωτὴν τὸν ἀδελφὸν αὐτοῦ πεποιημένος Ἄριστον, ἄνδρα τῇ μὲν ἐν λόγοις ἕξει πολλῶν φιλοσόφων λειπόμενον, εὐταξίᾳ δὲ καὶ πρᾳότητι τοῖς πρώτοις ἐνάμιλλον. [4] ὁ δ᾽ Ἔμπυλος, οὗ καὶ αὐτὸς ἐν ταῖς ἐπιστολαῖς καὶ οἱ φίλοι μέμνηνται πολλάκις ὡς συμβιοῦντος αὐτῷ, ῥήτωρ {μὲν}[1] ἦν, καὶ καταλέλοιπε μικρὸν μέν, οὐ φαῦλον δὲ σύγγραμμα περὶ τῆς Καίσαρος ἀναιρέσεως, ὁ Βροῦτος ἐπιγέγραπται [*FGrHist* 191 T 1]. [5] Ῥωμαϊστὶ μὲν οὖν ἤσκητο πρὸς τὰς <δι>εξόδους[2] καὶ τοὺς ἀγῶνας ἱκανῶς ὁ Βροῦτος, Ἑλληνιστὶ δὲ τὴν ἀποφθεγματικὴν καὶ Λακωνικὴν ἐπιτηδεύων βραχυλογίαν ἐν ταῖς ἐπιστολαῖς ἐνιαχοῦ παράσημός ἐστιν. [6] οἷον ἤδη καθεστηκὼς εἰς τὸν

negatively described by Calvus as languid and feeble, and
by Brutus, to use his very words, as "jerky and limping."

T 12 Tacitus, *Dialogue on Oratory*
= **121** F 46.

T 13 Tacitus, *Dialogue on Oratory*
= **121** T 7.

T 14 Plutarch, *Life of Brutus*
There was practically none of the Greek philosophers with
whom he [Brutus] was unacquainted or unfamiliar, but he
devoted himself particularly to the disciples of Plato. [3]
To the so-called New and Middle Academy he did not
wholly attach himself, but clung to the Old; and he was
always an admirer of Antiochus of Ascalon, whose brother
Aristus he had made his friend and housemate, a man who
in skill of argument was inferior to many philosophers, but
in good sense and gentleness vied with the foremost. [4]
Empylus also, whom both he himself [Brutus] in letters
and his friends often mention, as a housemate of his, was
a rhetorician, and he has left a brief and not contemptible
account of the assassination of Caesar, which is entitled
"Brutus" [*FGrHist* 191 T 1]. [5] Now in Latin, Brutus was
sufficiently trained for narrative and pleading; but in
Greek he affected the brevity of the apothegm and the
Spartan, of which he sometimes gives striking examples in
his letters. [6] For instance, when he had already em-

---

¹ *del. Coraes*   ² <δι>εξόδους *Vulcobius:* ἐξόδους *codd.*

πόλεμον γράφει Περγαμηνοῖς· "ἀκούω ὑμᾶς Δολο-
βέλλᾳ δεδωκέναι χρήματα· ἃ εἰ μὲν ἑκόντες ἔδοτε,
ὁμολογεῖτε ἀδικεῖν· εἰ δ᾽ ἄκοντες, ἀποδείξατε τῷ ἐμοὶ
ἑκόντες δοῦναι." [7] πάλιν Σαμίοις· "αἱ βουλαὶ ὑμῶν
ὀλίγωροι, αἱ ὑπουργίαι βραδεῖαι. τί τούτων τέλος ἐν-
νοεῖσθε;" [8] καὶ {περὶ Παταρέων}³ ἑτέραν· "Ξάνθιοι
τὴν ἐμὴν εὐεργεσίαν ὑπεριδόντες τάφον ἀπονοίας
ἐσχήκασι τὴν πατρίδα· Παταρεῖς δὲ πιστεύσαντες
ἑαυτοὺς ἐμοὶ οὐδὲν ἐλλείπουσι διοικοῦντες τὰ καθ᾽
ἕκαστα τῆς ἐλευθερίας. ἐξὸν οὖν καὶ ὑμῖν ἢ τὴν Πα-
ταρέων κρίσιν ἢ τὴν Ξανθίων τύχην ἑλέσθαι." τὸ μὲν
οὖν τῶν παρασήμων γένος ἐπιστολίων τοιοῦτόν ἐστιν.

³ del. Voegelin

T 15 [Aurel. Vict.] *Vir. ill.* 82.1

Marcus Brutus, avunculi Catonis imitator, Athenis philosophiam, Rhodi eloquentiam didicit.

*On the "Dictatorship" of Cn. Pompeius Magnus
(F 16–17)*

**Brutus' comments on the "dictatorship" of Cn. Pompe-
ius Magnus (111), presumably referring to his being sole
consul (52 BC), may not have been delivered, but they**

F 16 Quint. *Inst.* 9.3.95

. . . aut positis duobus vel tribus eodem ordine singulis
continua reddatur, quale apud Brutum de dictatura Cn.
Pompei: "praestat enim nemini imperare quam alicui ser-

barked upon the war [in 43 BC, after Caesar's assassination], he wrote to the Pergamenians: "I hear that you have given money to Dolabella [P. Cornelius Dolabella (**173**)]; if you gave that willingly, confess that you have wronged me; if unwillingly, prove it by giving willingly to me." [7] Again, to the Samians: "Your counsels are little-caring, your subsidies slow. What do you think will be the end of this?" [8] And {about the Patareans} in another letter: "The Xanthians, ignoring my benefactions, have made their country a grave for their madness; but the Patareans, having entrusted themselves to me, are not in want of living in freedom in all its respects. Thus it is possible for you also to choose either the decision of the Patareans or the fate of the Xanthians." Such, then, is the style of his letters conspicuous in that way.

T 15 [Aurelius Victor], *On Famous Men*

Marcus Brutus, an emulator of his uncle Cato [M. Porcius Cato (**126**)], studied philosophy at Athens and eloquence on Rhodes.

> *On the "Dictatorship" of Cn. Pompeius Magnus*
> *(F 16–17)*

may rather have been published in writing (cf. Sen. Con. *10.1.8).*

F 16 Quintilian, *The Orator's Education*

. . . or after two or three propositions have been stated, [reasons] are given continuously in the same order for each of them, as in Brutus' words about Pompey's dictatorship [Cn. Pompeius Magnus (**111**)]: "For it is better to

215

vire: sine illo enim vivere honeste licet, cum hoc vivendi nulla condicio est."

F 17 Suet. *Iul.* 49.2

missa etiam facio edicta Bibuli, quibus proscripsit colle-gam suum Bithynicam reginam, eique antea regem fuisse cordi, nunc esse regnum. quo tempore, ut Marcus Brutus refert, Octavius etiam quidam valitudine mentis liberius dicax conventu maximo, cum Pompeium regem appellas-set, ipsum reginam salutavit.

On Behalf of T. Annius Milo (F 18–21)

F 18 Quint. *Inst.* 3.6.92–93

. . . credo . . . ita hic quoque posse dici eum statum esse faciendum in quo tuendo plurimum adhibere virium pos-sit orator; [93] ideoque pro Milone aliud Ciceroni agenti placuit, aliud Bruto cum exercitationis gratia componeret orationem, cum ille iure tamquam insidiatorem occisum

rule no man than to be the slave of any: for one may live honorably without the former, while the latter is no way of living."

F 17 Suetonius, *Life of Caesar*

I take no account of the edicts of Bibulus [M. Calpurnius Bibulus (**122**), F 5], in which he marked his colleague [C. Iulius Caesar (**121**)] as the queen of Bithynia, saying that previously he was enamored of a king, now of a kingdom. At that time, as Marcus Brutus reports,[1] a certain Octavius even, a man of disordered mind and thus somewhat free in his speech, in a crowded assembly, after saluting Pompey [Cn. Pompeius Magnus (**111**)] as king, greeted him [Caesar] as queen.

[1] Because of its content, this remark is generally assigned to the same context as F 16, but the source does not identify the occasion.

On Behalf of T. Annius Milo (F 18–21)

*Brutus composed (Quint. Inst. 10.5.20) a practice speech in defense of T. Annius Milo (**138**), who was actually defended by Cicero (Cic. Mil.).*

F 18 Quintilian, *The Orator's Education*

. . . I believe . . . so, here too, it can be said that this issue [*status*] should be realized in whose development the orator can deploy his greatest powers; [93] and therefore one way of supporting Milo appealed to Cicero active in court and another to Brutus, when he composed a speech for the sake of the exercise: while the former said that he [P.

et tamen non Milonis consilio dixerit, ille etiam gloriatus sit occiso malo cive . . .

F 19 Quint. *Inst.* 10.1.23

quin etiam easdem causas ut quisque ‹egerit utile›[1] erit scire. nam de domo Ciceronis dixit Calidius, et pro Milone orationem Brutus exercitationis gratia scripsit, etiam si egisse eum Cornelius Celsus falso existimat [Cels. *Rhet.*, F 21 Marx] . . .

> [1] ut quisque egerit *ed. Col. 1527 post Regium*: utrisque *cod.*   utile *Regius (post correctores unius cod.)*: *om. cod.*

F 20 Asc. in Cic. *Mil.*, *arg.* (p. 36 KS = 41.9–14 C.)

respondit his[1] unus M. Cicero: et cum quibusdam placuisset ita defendi crimen, interfici Clodium pro re publica fuisse—quam formam M. Brutus secutus est in ea oratione quam pro Milone composuit et edidit, quasi[2] egisset—Ciceroni id non placuit ‹ut›, quisquis[3] bono publico damnari, idem etiam occidi indemnatus posset.

> [1] his *ed. Aldina 1522*: hic *codd.*   [2] quasi *Baiter*: quamuis *codd.*: quamvis non *coni. in codd. rec.*   [3] ‹ut› quisquis *Clark*: quisquis *vel* quod quis *codd.*: quod quis *Poggius*: quod qui *Manutius*: quasi qui *KS*

F 21 Schol. Bob. ad Cic. *Mil.*, *arg.* (p. 112.12–18 Stangl)

hanc orationem postea legitimo opere et maiore cura, utpote iam confirmato animo et in securitate, conscribsit. sed enim cum ratio defensionis huius ordinaretur, quonam

Clodius Pulcher (**137**)] was justifiably killed as an ambusher, though not by Milo's design, the latter positively boasted that a bad citizen had been killed . . .

F 19 Quintilian, *The Orator's Education*

Indeed, it will also be ‹useful› to know how different individuals ‹treated› the same cases: for Calidius [M. Calidius (**140**), F 7] spoke on Cicero's house, and Brutus wrote a speech on behalf of Milo for the sake of the exercise, even though Cornelius Celsus wrongly believes that he delivered it [A. Cornelius Celsus, *Rhet.*, F 21 Marx] . . .

F 20 Asconius on Cicero, *Pro Milone*

M. Cicero was the only one to reply to them [the prosecutors]: and while it would have pleased some to have the crime defended in such a way, namely that Clodius [P. Clodius Pulcher (**137**)] was killed for the sake of the Republic—a line of argument that M. Brutus followed in that speech that he composed on behalf of Milo and published, as if he had delivered it—this did not please Cicero, ‹so that›, whoever was condemned in relation to the public good, could also be killed without having been found guilty in court.

F 21 Scholia Bobiensia to Cicero, *Pro Milone*

He [Cicero] wrote up this speech later with effort according to the rules of art and greater care, when indeed he had already regained his strength of mind and was in safety. But when the plan of this defense was being ar-

modo et secundum quem potissimum statum agi pro Milone oporteret, M. Brutus existimavit κατὰ ἀντίστασιν
pro eo esse dicendum, quae a nobis nominatur qualitas
compensativa. hoc enimvero Ciceroni visum est parum
salubre, nam maluit ἀντεγκλήματος specie, id est rela ǁ
... [*desunt VIII paginae*]

On Behalf of Ap. Claudius Pulcher (F 22)

*In 50 BC Brutus, along with Q. Hortensius Hortalus (**92** F 53–54), successfully defended his father-in-law, Ap. Claudius Pulcher (**130**), when he was prosecuted by P.*

F 22 Cic. *Brut.* 324

= **92** F 54.

Eulogy of Ap. Claudius Pulcher (F 23)

F 23 Diom., *GL* I, p. 367.26–27

amicio amicui, ut Brutus laudatione Appii Claudii: "qui te[1]
toga praetexta amicuit" ...

[1] qui te *Putschius*: qui de *codd.*: quae de *edd. vet.*: quae te
Rivius

ranged, regarding the question in what manner and according to which issue [*status*] in particular one should plead on behalf of Milo, M. Brutus believed that one should speak κατὰ ἀντίστασιν ["according to a balancing counterplea"] on his behalf, which is called *qualitas compensativa* by us. Yet this seemed insufficiently salutary to Cicero, for he preferred [to speak in] the manner of ἀντέγκλημα ["countercharge"], that is . . . [text breaking off]

On Behalf of Ap. Claudius Pulcher (F 22)

*Cornelius Dolabella (**173**) for* maiestas *and* ambitus, *presumably at the second trial (TLRR 344, 345; Sumner 1973, 122–23; Cic. Fam. 3.11.1–3, 3.12.1, 8.6.1).*

F 22 Cicero, *Brutus*

= **92** F 54.

Eulogy of Ap. Claudius Pulcher (F 23)

*Brutus produced a eulogy of his father-in-law, Ap. Claudius Pulcher (**130**), when the latter died in 48 BC just before the battle of Pharsalus (Val. Max. 1.8.10).*

F 23 Diomedes

amicio, amicui ["I wrap, I wrapped"; rare form of perfect], as Brutus in the eulogy of Appius Claudius: "who wrapped you with a purple-bordered toga" . . .

On Behalf of King Deiotarus (F 24–26)

*In the settlement after the battle of Zela in 47 BC, arranged at Nicaea (in Asia Minor), C. Iulius Caesar (**121**) took away some territories from Deiotarus, king of Galatia, de-*

F 24 Cic. *Brut.* 21

[CICERO:] nempe igitur hinc tum, Pomponi, ductus est sermo, quod erat a me mentio facta causam Deiotari fidelissimi atque optimi regis ornatissime et copiosissime a Bruto me audisse defensam.

F 25 Cic. *Att.* 14.1.2

tu quaeso quicquid novi (multa autem exspecto) scribere ne pigrere, in his de Sexto satisne certum, maxime autem de Bruto nostro. de quo quidem ille ad quem deverti Caesarem solitum dicere, "magni refert hic quid velit, sed quicquid vult valde vult"; idque eum animadvertisse cum pro Deiotaro Nicaeae dixerit; valde vehementer eum visum et libere dicere . . .

Cf. Plut. *Brut.* 6.6–7.

F 26 Tac. *Dial.* 21.5–6
= **121** F 46.

On Behalf of King Deiotarus (F 24–26)

spite Brutus' intervention. A written version of the speech was apparently available in Tacitus' time (F 26).

F 24 Cicero, *Brutus*

[CICERO:] Certainly, then, from this starting point, Pomponius [T. Pomponius Atticus (**103**)], our discussion at that time arose: that I had made mention of having heard that the case of Deiotarus, that very loyal and very good king, had been defended by Brutus in the most elaborate and most copious fashion.

F 25 Cicero, *Letters to Atticus*

Please do not be slow in writing any news (and I am expecting many items), including whether the report about Sextus [Sex. Pompeius, son of Cn. Pompeius Magnus (**111**)] is sufficiently certain, but especially about our Brutus. With reference to him the one with whom I am staying [C. Matius] tells me that Caesar [C. Iulius Caesar (**121**)] used to say: "It is of great importance what he wants; but whatever he wants, he very much wants." And he had noticed this when Brutus spoke for Deiotarus at Nicaea; he had seemed to him to speak with great force and boldly . . .

F 26 Tacitus, *Dialogue on Oratory*

= **121** F 46.

Eulogy of M. Porcius Cato Uticensis (F 27–28)

*The eulogy of Brutus' uncle M. Porcius Cato (**126**), after the latter's suicide in 46 BC, seems to have been
a written version only; it was a response to Cicero's*

F 27 Cic. *Att.* 12.21.1

= **126** F 15.

F 28 Cic. *Att.* 13.46.2

legi epistulam. multa de meo Catone, quo saepissime le-
gendo se dicit copiosiorem factum, Bruti Catone lecto se
sibi visum disertum.

*On Caesar's Assassination to the People
(F 29–31A)*

*After C. Iulius Caesar's (**121**) assassination on March 15,
44 BC, Brutus delivered speeches to the People, though the
sources are not unanimous on the precise details and the*

F 29 Cic. *Att.* 15.1a.2

Brutus noster misit ad me orationem suam habitam in
contione Capitolina petivitque a me ut eam ne ambitiose
corrigerem ante quam ederet. est autem oratio scripta
elegantissime sententiis, verbis, ut nihil possit ultra. ego
tamen si illam causam habuissem, scripsissem ardentius.
ὑπόθεσις vides quae sit ‹et›[1] persona dicentis. itaque eam

---

[1] *add. Orelli*

Eulogy of M. Porcius Cato Uticensis (F 27–28)

Laus Catonis, *produced at Brutus' prompting (Cic.* Orat. *35).*

F 27 Cicero, *Letters to Atticus*
= **126** F 15.

F 28 Cicero, *Letters to Atticus*

I have read the letter [from C. Iulius Caesar (**121**) to L. Herennius Balbus (**163**)]. A good deal about my *Cato*; he [Caesar] says that by reading it very often his diction has become fuller, whereas after reading Brutus' *Cato* he seemed eloquent to himself.

On Caesar's Assassination to the People (F 29–31A)

*chronology (*CCMR, *App.* A: *349; cf., e.g., Plut.* Caes. *67.7; App.* B Civ. *2.122.512–14; Cass.* Dio *44.21.1–2).*

F 29 Cicero, *Letters to Atticus*

Our Brutus has sent me his speech delivered to a public meeting on the Capitol and asked me to correct it candidly before he publishes it. And the speech is indeed written most elegantly, with sentiments and wording so that nothing could be better. Still, if I had dealt with that matter, I would have written with more fire. You see what the nature of the theme <and> the person of the speaker is.

corrigere non potui. quo enim in genere Brutus noster
esse vult et quod iudicium habet de optimo genere dicendi, id ita consecutus in ea oratione est ut elegantius
esse nihil possit; sed ego secutus[2] aliud sum, sive hoc recte
sive non recte. tu tamen velim eam orationem legas, nisi
forte iam legisti, certioremque me facias quid iudices ipse.
quamquam vereor ne cognomine tuo lapsus ὑπεραττικὸς[3]
sis in iudicando. sed si recordabere Δημοσθένους fulmina, tum intelleges posse et ἀττικώτατα[4] ⟨et⟩[5] gravissime dici.

2 secutus *Pius*: solus *codd.*   3 ὑπεραττικὸς *ed. Cratan-*
drina: hyperatticus *lect. marg. ed. Cratandrinae adscr.*: hypar
atticus *vel sim. codd.*   4 ἀττικώτατα *unus cod. corr., Victo-*
rius: attico tota *vel sim. codd.*   5 *add. Lambinus*

F 30 Cic. *Att.* 15.3.2

Brutum omni re qua possum cupio iuvare; cuius de oratiuncula idem te quod me sentire video. sed parum intellego quid me velis scribere quasi a Bruto habita oratione, cum ille ediderit. qui tandem convenit? an sic ut in
tyrannum iure optimo caesum? multa dicentur, multa
scribentur a nobis, sed alio modo et tempore.

F 31 Plut. *Brut.* 18.7–13

οἱ δὲ περὶ Βροῦτον εἰς τὸ Καπετώλιον ἐχώρουν, ἠμα-
γμένοι ⟨τε⟩[1] τὰς χεῖρας καὶ τὰ ξίφη γυμνὰ δεικνύντες
ἐπὶ τὴν ἐλευθερίαν παρεκάλουν τοὺς πολίτας. [8] τὸ

1 *add. Ziegler*

Accordingly, I was unable to correct it. For as regards the
style that our Brutus wishes to use and the view that he
has on the best style of speaking, he has attained it in that
speech to such an extent that it could not be more elegant
in any way. But I have aimed at something different,
whether rightly or wrongly. Yet I should like you to read
that speech, if you have not already read it by any chance,
and let me know what you think. I fear, though, that you
may be led astray by your surname and be too Attic in your
judgment. But if you call to mind Demosthenes' lightning
bolts, then you will realize one can speak in both the most
Attic ‹and› the most impressive way.

F 30 Cicero, *Letters to Atticus*

I want to help Brutus in every way I can. I see that you
feel the same as I do about his little speech. But I do not
quite understand what you want me to write in a speech
purporting to have been delivered by Brutus as he has
published [his]. How on earth can this fit? Or so as, for
example, "Against the tyrant lawfully assassinated"? Much
will be said, much be written by us, but in another way and
at another time.[1]

[1] On Cicero's reaction to Atticus' suggestion, see also Cic. *Att.*
15.4.3.

F 31 Plutarch, *Life of Brutus*

The group around Brutus went up to the Capitol; smeared
with blood on their hands and displaying their naked dag-
gers, they exhorted the citizens to liberty. [8] At first, then,

227

μὲν οὖν πρῶτον ἦσαν ἀλαλαγμοί, καὶ διαδρομαὶ τῷ
πάθει κατὰ τύχην ἐπιγινόμεναι πλείονα τὸν θόρυβον
ἐποίησαν· [9] ὡς δ᾿ οὔτε φόνος ἄλλος οὔθ᾿ ἁρπαγή
τινος ἐγίνετο τῶν κειμένων, θαρροῦντες ἀνέβαινον οἵ
τε βουλευταὶ καὶ τῶν δημοτῶν πολλοὶ πρὸς τοὺς ἄνδρας εἰς τὸ Καπετώλιον. [10] ἀθροισθέντος δὲ τοῦ
πλήθους διελέχθη Βροῦτος ἐπαγωγὰ τοῦ δήμου καὶ
πρέποντα τοῖς πεπραγμένοις. [11] ἐπαινούντων δὲ καὶ
κατιέναι βοώντων, θαρροῦντες κατέβαινον εἰς ἀγοράν,
οἱ μὲν ἄλλοι συνεπόμενοι μετ᾿ ἀλλήλων, Βροῦτον δὲ
πολλοὶ τῶν ἐπιφανῶν περιέποντες ἐν μέσῳ πάνυ λαμ-
πρῶς κατῆγον ἀπὸ τῆς ἄκρας καὶ κατέστησαν ἐπὶ
τῶν ἐμβόλων. [12] πρὸς δὲ τὴν ὄψιν οἱ πολλοί, καίπερ
μιγάδες ὄντες καὶ παρεσκευασμένοι θορυβεῖν, διέτρε-
σαν καὶ τὸ μέλλον ἐδέχοντο κόσμῳ καὶ σιωπῇ· προ-
ελθόντος δ᾿ αὐτοῦ πάντες ἡσυχίαν τῷ λόγῳ παρ-
έσχον. [13] ὅτι δ᾿ οὐ πᾶσι πρὸς ἡδονὴν ἐγεγόνει τὸ
ἔργον, ἐδήλωσαν ἀρξαμένου λέγειν Κίννα καὶ κατ-
ηγορεῖν Καίσαρος ἀναρρηγνύμενοι πρὸς ὀργὴν καὶ
κακῶς τὸν Κίνναν λέγοντες, ὥστε πάλιν τοὺς ἄνδρας
εἰς τὸ Καπετώλιον ἀπελθεῖν.

F 31A App. *B Civ.* 2.137.570–142.592

*Brutus and Cassius invite the People to come up to the
Capitol. Brutus addresses them as follows: he explains that
they are not meeting the People as refugees, but rather
have to justify themselves because of the accusations of
their enemies. Looking back, Brutus points out with a*

there were cries of terror, and wild running around following the calamity increased the tumult. [9] But since neither further murders nor plundering of anyone's property happened, the senators and many of the common people took heart and went up to the men on the Capitol. [10] When the multitude was assembled, Brutus made a speech calculated to win over the People and befitting the circumstances. [11] When they applauded his words and cried out to him to come down, they [the conspirators] took heart and went down into the Forum. The others followed along in each other's company, but many eminent citizens, showing respect, escorted Brutus in their midst with great honor down from the citadel and placed him on the Rostra. [12] At the sight of him, the multitude, although it was a mixed rabble and prepared to raise a disturbance, was struck with awe and awaited in decorous silence what was going to happen. And when he came forward to speak, all remained silent for his speech. [13] But that the deed was not pleasing to all, this they showed when Cinna [L. Cornelius Cinna, praet. 44 BC, brother of Caesar's first wife, but sympathetic to the conspirators] began to speak and to denounce Caesar: they broke into a rage and reviled Cinna so bitterly that the men withdrew again to the Capitol.

F 31A Appian, *Civil Wars*

number of examples that C. Iulius Caesar [121] had not acted according to Republican principles and had assumed great power with everyone else in servitude. Brutus confirms that he and his followers, on the contrary, had a higher regard for their country than for their offices. Be-

cause of criticism with regard to colonies, Brutus calls upon the listeners to make themselves known if anyone had been settled in colonies or was about to be settled. When a large number have made themselves known, Brutus goes on to say that there will be rewards for achievements in wars against external enemies, but not by taking land from fellow citizens nor by dividing other people's property among newcomers. L. Cornelius Sulla and Caesar had not followed convention in establishing colonies to the disad-

On Octavian to the People (F 32)

F 32 Tac. *Ann.* 4.34.5

Antonii epistulae, Bruti contiones falsa quidem in Augustum probra, set multa cum acerbitate habent . . .

Unplaced Fragment (F 33)

F 33 Mar. Vict., *GL* VI, p. 9.5–6

Messalla, Brutus, Agrippa pro sumus simus ‹scripserunt›.[1]

  [1] scripserunt *om. codd., edd. vet.*

*vantage of the People. Still, Brutus assures them that they
have and will have what they have received. He promises
that he and his colleagues will remedy the single outstanding issue: they will at once pay the original possessors
out of public money the price of the land of which they
have been deprived, so that the audience will not only have
their colonies secure, but will also be free from hatred. This
speech receives praise from the populace.*

On Octavian to the People (F 32)

*Brutus' speeches to the People about Octavian, the future
emperor Augustus, seem to have been delivered in Greece
during the fighting between M. Antonius (**159**) and Octavian.*

F 32 Tacitus, *Annals*

The letters of Antony [M. Antonius (**159**)], the public
speeches of Brutus contain invectives against Augustus,
false indeed, yet with much bitterness . . .

Unplaced Fragment (F 33)

F 33 Marius Victorinus

Messalla [M. Valerius Messalla Corvinus (**176**), F 26],
Brutus, and Agrippa ⟨wrote⟩ *simus* instead of *sumus* ["we
are"].[1]

[1] This comment may refer to Brutus' speeches and/or any
other of his writings; see Suet. *Aug.* 87.2 for the same practice
attributed to Augustus.

159 M. ANTONIUS TRIUMVIR

Marc Antony (cos. 44, 34 BC; RE Antonius 30), a grand-son of M. Antonius (65), was consul in 44 BC with C. Iulius Caesar (121) and, after the latter's death, with P. Cornelius Dolabella; in 43 BC he was one of the triumviri. After the battle of Actium he killed himself at Alexandria (30 BC), upon the false rumor of Cleopatra's death (on his life, see Plut. Ant.; on his literary output, see Huzar 1982, Calboli 1997, Mahy 2013; on his career and oratory, van der Blom 2016, 248–79, on his speeches pp. 323–27).

Antony's oratorical style is defined as Asiatic by ancient sources (T 3–4). He is said to have studied with Epidius (T 1) and the Sicilian Sex. Clodius (T 2; cf. T 3), and he practiced declamation for training (T 5).

In addition to speeches, Antony wrote letters and mis-

T 1 Suet. *Gram. et rhet.* 28.1

⟨M.⟩[1] Epidius, calumnia notatus, ludum dicendi aperuit docuitque inter ceteros M. Antonium et Augustum . . .

[1] *add. Roth (ex ind.)*

T 2 Suet. *Gram. et rhet.* 29.1–2

Sextus Clodius, e Sicilia, Latinae simul Graecaeque elo-quentiae professor, male oculatus et dicax par oculorum in amicitia M. Antoni triumviri extrisse[1] se aiebat; eius-dem uxorem Fulviam, cui altera bucca inflatior erat, acu-men stili temptare dixit, nec eo minus—immo vel ma-

[1] extrisse *Status*: ex(s)tricte *codd.*

159 M. ANTONIUS TRIUMVIR

sives (Cic. Att. *10.8A, 14.13A;* Phil. *5.33, 8.25–28, 12.1, 13.22–48; Joseph.* AJ *14.12.2–6) and a work* De sua ebrietate *(Plin.* HN *14.148).*

*Moreover, in addition to the instances detailed below, Antony vetoed a proposal for a decree of the Senate against C. Iulius Caesar (**121**) in early January 49 BC (Caes.* BCiv. *1.2.7). In 45 BC Antony was forced to make a statement to a meeting of the People (Cic.* Phil. *2.78; CCMR, App. A: 344). Having entered office as consul, Antony spoke in the Senate on January 1, 44 BC (Cic.* Phil. *2.80–81). On February 15, 44 BC, at the festival of the Lupercalia, Antony delivered a speech while dressed as a Lupercus (Cic.* Phil. *2.86, 2.111, 3.12; CCMR, App. A: 345). In 40 BC he spoke in the Senate about Herod (cf.* **171** *F8).*

T 1 Suetonius, *Lives of Illustrious Men. Grammarians and Rhetoricians*

‹M.› Epidius, infamous for false accusations, opened a school of oratory and taught, among others, Marc Antony and Augustus . . .

T 2 Suetonius, *Lives of Illustrious Men. Grammarians and Rhetoricians*

Sextus Clodius, from Sicily, a teacher of both Greek and Latin oratory, a man with poor sight and a sharp tongue, used to say that he had worn out a pair of eyes during his friendship with Marc Antony, the *triumvir*. Of the latter's wife, Fulvia, one of whose cheeks was somewhat swollen, he said that she tempted the point of the pen; and because of this [comment] he was not less—on the contrary, even

gis—ob hoc Antonio gratus. [2] a quo mox consule ingens etiam congiarium accepit, ut ei in Philippicis Cicero obicit [cf. Cic. *Phil.* 2.42–43]: "adhibes[2] ioci causa magistrum, suffragio tuo et compotorum tuorum rhetorem, ⟨cui⟩[3] concessisti ut in te quae vellet diceret, salsum omnino hominem, sed materia facilis in te et in tuos ⟨dicta⟩[4] dicere.[5] at quanta merces rhetori data est! audite, audite, patres conscripti, et cognoscite rei publicae volnera. duo milia iugerum campi Leontini Sex. Clodio rhetori assignasti—et quidem immunia—ut ⟨populi Romani⟩[6] tanta mercede nihil sapere disceres."

[2] adhibes *Stephanus*: tibet *vel* tibi et *vel lac. codd.*
[3] *suppl. Beroaldus: om. codd.*   [4] *suppl. Stephanus: om. codd.*   [5] vide autem . . . dicis aliena *post* dicere *om. consulto Suet.*   [6] *suppl. Robinson: om. codd.*

T 3 Plut. *Ant.* 2.7–8

. . . ἀπῆρεν ἐκ τῆς Ἰταλίας εἰς τὴν Ἑλλάδα, καὶ διέτριβε τό τε σῶμα γυμνάζων πρὸς τοὺς στρατιωτικοὺς ἀγῶνας καὶ λέγειν μελετῶν. [8] ἐχρῆτο δὲ τῷ καλουμένῳ μὲν Ἀσιανῷ ζήλῳ τῶν λόγων, ἀνθοῦντι μάλιστα κατ' ἐκεῖνον τὸν χρόνον, ἔχοντι δὲ πολλὴν ὁμοιότητα πρὸς τὸν βίον αὐτοῦ, κομπώδη καὶ φρυαγματίαν ὄντα καὶ κενοῦ γαυριάματος καὶ φιλοτιμίας ἀνωμάλου μεστόν.

T 4 Suet. *Aug.* 86.2–3

M. quidem Antonium ut insanum increpat, quasi ea scribentem, quae mirentur potius homines quam intellegant; deinde ludens malum et inconstans in eligendo ge-

more—welcome to Antony. [2] When he [Antony] then
soon became consul, he [Clodius] even received from him
an enormous gift, as Cicero charges against him [Antony]
in the *Philippics* [cf. Cic. *Phil.* 2.42–43]: "For the sake of
jokes you employ a tutor, a rhetorician by your vote and
those of your drinking companions, and you have allowed
⟨him⟩ to say anything he likes about you; a witty fellow,
no doubt, but it is an easy matter to say ⟨clever things⟩
about you and your mates. But what a reward was given to
the rhetorician! Listen, listen, Members of the Senate,
and recognize the wounds of the Republic. You have assigned to Sex. Clodius the rhetorician two thousand *iugera*
of the Leontine territory—and free of taxes too—so that
at so great a price ⟨to the Roman People⟩ you [Antony]
might learn to have no sense."

T 3 Plutarch, *Life of Antony*

. . . he left Italy for Greece [in 58 BC], and he spent some
time training the body for military exercises and studying
to speak. [8] He adopted what was called the Asiatic style
of speaking, which was greatly flourishing at that time and
bore a strong resemblance to his own life, being boastful
and arrogant, full of empty exultation and distorted ambition.

T 4 Suetonius, *Life of Augustus*

And as for Marc Antony, he [Augustus] rebukes him for
being a madman, since he seemed to write what people
would admire rather than understand. Then, ridiculing his

nere dicendi iudicium eius, addit haec: [3] "tuque dubitas,
Cimberne Annius an Veranius Flaccus imitandi sint tibi,
ita ut verbis, quae Crispus Sallustius excerpsit ex Origini-
bus Catonis, utaris? an potius Asiaticorum oratorum
inani{bu}s[1] sententiis verborum volubilitas in nostrum
sermonem transferenda?"

[1] inani{bu}s *Gronovius*: inanibus *codd.*

T 5 Suet. *Gram. et rhet.* 25.3
= **111** T 8.

Against T. Annius Milo (F 6)

F 6 Asc. in Cic. *Mil.*, *arg.* (p. 36 KS = 41.6–9 C.)

tum intra horam secundam accusatores coeperunt dicere
Appius maior et M. Antonius et P. Valerius Nepos: usi sunt
ex lege horis duabus.

As Tribune to the People (F 7)

*When he had entered office as Tribune of the People for 49
BC, Antony gave a speech to the People (CCMR, App. A:*

perverse and inconsistent judgment in choosing a style of
speaking, he adds the following: [3] "And can you doubt
whether Annius Cimber [T. Annius Cimber, praet. prob.
43 BC] or Veranius Flaccus [identity uncertain] should be
imitated by you, so as to use the words that Sallust [C.
Sallustius Crispus (**152**)] gleaned from Cato's [M. Porcius
Cato's (**8**)] *Origines*? Or should the meaningless flow of
words in statements of the Asiatic orators rather be introduced into our language?"

T 5 Suetonius, *Lives of Illustrious Men. Grammarians
and Rhetoricians*

= **111** T 8.

Against T. Annius Milo (F 6)

*In 52 BC, at the trial of T. Annius Milo (**138**), who was
charged with the murder of P. Clodius Pulcher (**137**) and
defended by Cicero (Cic. Mil.), Antony was among the
advocates speaking against him (TLRR 309).*

F 6 Asconius on Cicero, *Pro Milone*

Then, within the second hour, the prosecutors began to
speak, the elder Appius [Ap. Claudius Pulcher (**172**), F 2],
Marc Antony, and P. Valerius Nepos: they filled two hours
according to the law.

As Tribune to the People (F 7)

*340) in December 50 BC, which included a denunciation
of Cn. Pompeius Magnus (**111**).*

F 7 Cic. *Att.* 7.8.5

habebamus autem in manibus Antoni contionem habitam
X Kal. Ian., in qua erat accusatio Pompei usque a toga
pura, querela de damnatis, terror armorum. in quibus ille
"quid censes" aiebat "facturum esse ipsum, si in posses-
sionem rei publicae venerit, cum haec quaestor eius infir-
mus et inops audeat dicere?"

*After Caesar's assassination on March 15, 44 BC, Antony
delivered speeches in the Senate (F 7B–C; Cic. Phil. 1.2,
1.31, 2.90; Plut. Cic. 42.3; Ant. 14.3; App. B Civ. 2.128.535–*

After Caesar's Assassination to the People (F 7A)

F 7A App. *B Civ.* 2.130.542–546

*In response to demands from the People after Caesar's
assassination, Antony speaks to them. He assures them
that peace is being aimed for and explains that vengeance*

After Caesar's Assassination in the Senate (F 7B)

F 7B App. *B Civ.* 2.133.555–135.564

*Appian puts a speech into Antony's mouth, given in the
Senate: Antony outlines the risk if the memory of Caesar
is not treated with respect and his arrangements are not*

F 7 Cicero, *Letters to Atticus*

Moreover, we had in our hands a speech to the People given by Antony on the tenth day before the Kalends of January [December 21, 50 BC], containing a denunciation of Pompey [Cn. Pompeius Magnus (**111**)] from the time he came of age, a protest on behalf of the people condemned [as a result of laws introduced by Pompey in 52 BC], and a threat coming from arms. In this context he [Pompey] said: "What do you expect him [C. Iulius Caesar (**121**)] to do if he gets control of the Republic, when his quaestor [Antony, quaest. 52 BC], a man without power and resources, dares to say this sort of thing?"

537) *and before the People (F 7A; CCMR, App. A: 350; cf. Cic.* Phil. *1.32; App.* B Civ. *2.142.593–94 [CCMR, App. A: 351]).*

After Caesar's Assassination to the People (F 7A)

F 7A Appian, *Civil Wars*

is not easily possible and not always advisable. Appian "reports" some of Antony's statements directly and summarizes others in indirect speech.

After Caesar's Assassination in the Senate (F 7B)

F 7B Appian, *Civil Wars*

preserved. Accordingly, a decree is passed to the effect that all of Caesar's acts and arrangements should be confirmed, while his assassins should not be prosecuted.

On Caesar's Assassins in the Senate (F 7C)

F 7C Plut. *Brut.* 19.1
= **149** F 5.

Funeral Oration for C. Iulius Caesar (F 8–12)

*Antony delivered the funeral oration for C. Iulius Caesar (**121**) in the Forum (cf. Cic. Phil. 2.89–91; Plut. Brut. 20.4); versions of the oration are provided by Appian*

F 8 Cic. *Att.* 14.10.1

at ille etiam in foro combustus laudatusque miserabiliter servique et egentes in tecta nostra cum facibus immissi.

F 9 Cic. *Att.* 14.11.1

cum[1] {equidem}[2] contionem lego de "tanto viro," de "clarissimo civi," ferre non queo. etsi ista iam ad risum. sed memento, sic alitur consuetudo perditarum contionum ut nostri illi non heroes sed di futuri quidem in gloria sempiterna sint sed non sine invidia, ne sine periculo quidem.

[1] cum *Victorius*: quin *codd.*   [2] *del. Wesenberg*: equidem *codd.*: etiam *codd. det. vel edd. vet.*: *fort.* enim *Shackleton Bailey*

159 M. ANTONIUS TRIUMVIR

On Caesar's Assassins in the Senate (F 7C)

F 7C Plutarch, *Life of Brutus*
= **149** F 5.

Funeral Oration for C. Iulius Caesar (F 8–12)

(App. B Civ. 2.143.599–146.608) and Cassius Dio (Cass. Dio 44.35.4–50.1; see Kierdorf 1980, 150–54; CCMR, App. A: 353).

F 8 Cicero, *Letters to Atticus*

Yet he [C. Iulius Caesar (**121**)] was even cremated in the Forum and praised pathetically,[1] and slaves and beggars were sent with firebrands to attack our homes.

[1] Cicero does not identify a particular speech or its author. From the context it has been assumed that this remark could refer to what Antony said about Caesar at the latter's funeral.

F 9 Cicero, *Letters to Atticus*

When I {for my part} read the speech to the People about "so great a man," about "so illustrious a citizen," I cannot stomach it.[1] Even if this sort of thing has now become a joke. But remember, that is how the habit of making pernicious public speeches is nourished, so that those men of ours, not heroes, but gods, will certainly have eternal glory, but not without ill will or even without danger.

[1] Cicero does not identify the author of the speech. From the context it has been assumed that he alludes to what Antony said about Caesar after the latter's assassination.

F 10 Cic. *Att*. 15.20.2

quod ais extrema quaedam iam homines de re publica
loqui et eos quidem viros bonos, ego quo die audivi illum
tyrannum in contione clarissimum virum appellari sub-
diffidere coepi.

F 11 Plut. *Ant*. 14.6–8

ἔτυχε μὲν οὖν ἐκκομιζομένου Καίσαρος ὥσπερ ἔθος
ἦν ἐν ἀγορᾷ διεξιὼν ἐγκώμιον. [7] ὁρῶν δὲ τὸν δῆμον
ὑπερφυῶς ἀγόμενον καὶ κηλούμενον, ἐνέμειξε[1] τοῖς
ἐπαίνοις οἶκτον ἅμα καὶ δείνωσιν ἐπὶ τῷ πάθει, καὶ
τῷ λόγῳ τελευτῶντι[2] τοὺς χιτωνίσκους τοῦ τεθνηκότος
ἡμαγμένους καὶ διακεκομμένους τοῖς ξίφεσιν ἀνα-
σείων, καὶ τοὺς εἰργασμένους ταῦτα καλῶν παλαμναί-
ους καὶ ἀνδροφόνους, τοσοῦτον ὀργῆς ἐνέβαλε τοῖς
ἀνθρώποις, [8] ὥστε τὸ μὲν σῶμα τοῦ Καίσαρος ἐν
ἀγορᾷ καθαγίσαι συνενεγκαμένους τὰ βάθρα καὶ τὰς
τραπέζας, ἁρπάζοντας δὲ τοὺς ἀπὸ τῆς πυρᾶς δαλοὺς
ἐπὶ τὰς οἰκίας θεῖν τῶν ἀπεκτονότων καὶ προσμάχε-
σθαι.

[1] ἐνέμειξε *Sintenis*: ἐπέμιξε *codd*.   [2] τελευτῶντι *Bryan*:
τελευτῶν τε *codd*.

F 12 Suet. *Iul*. 84.2

laudationis loco consul Antonius per praeconem pronuntiavit senatus consultum, quo omnia simul ei divina atque

F 10 Cicero, *Letters to Atticus*

As regards the point that you say that some people, and
loyal men at that, are now saying some very desperate
things about the political situation, I for my part on the
day on which I heard that tyrant called a very great man
in a speech to the People began to have doubts.[1]

[1] Cf. F 9 n. 1.

F 11 Plutarch, *Life of Antony*

Now it happened that when Caesar's body was carried
forth for burial, he [Antony] delivered the customary eulogy in the Forum. [7] And when he saw that the People
were mightily swayed and charmed, he mingled with the
praises also feelings of pity and indignation over the unfortunate incident, and at the close of his speech shook the
garments of the dead man, all bloody and tattered by the
swords, called those who had wrought such work villains
and murderers, and inspired the people with such rage [8]
that they burned Caesar's body in the Forum, after they
had heaped together benches and tables, and then, snatching the blazing firebrands from the pyre, ran to the houses
of the assassins and assaulted them.

F 12 Suetonius, *Life of Caesar*

Instead of a eulogy,[1] the consul Antony [44 BC] had a
herald recite a decree of the Senate in which it had voted
him [C. Iulius Caesar (**121**)] all divine and human honors

[1] Suetonius does not seem to regard Antony's speech as a
proper funeral oration. At any rate, the passage attests an utter-
ance by Antony in connection with Caesar's funeral.

humana decreverat, item ius iurandum, quo se cuncti pro salute unius astrinxerant; quibus perpauca a se verba addidit.

In the context of the political negotiations and controversies later in 44 BC, Antony voiced other attested utterances (Cic. Phil. 6.10, 7.3, 9.7), conducted various political assemblies, initiated measures that will have involved statements, delivered further speeches in the Senate, at

In Spring 44 BC to the People (F 13–13A)

F 13 Cic. *Phil.* 3.27

etenim in contione dixerat se custodem fore urbis, seque usque ad Kalendas Maias ad urbem exercitum habiturum. o praeclarum custodem ovium, ut aiunt, lupum! custosne urbis an direptor et vexator esset Antonius? et quidem se introiturum in urbem dixit exiturumque cum vellet. quid? illud nonne audiente populo sedens pro aede Castoris dixit, nisi qui vicisset, victurum neminem?

F 13A Cic. *Phil.* 5.21

M. vero Antonium quis est qui civem possit iudicare potius quam taeterrimum et crudelissimum hostem, qui pro aede Castoris sedens audiente populo Romano dixerit nisi victorem victurum neminem? num putatis, patres con-

at once, and likewise the oath with which they had all pledged themselves to watch over the welfare of that one man; to which he [Antony] added a very few words of his own.

public meetings, and to soldiers (F 13–17; cf. Cic. Phil. 1.3, 1.6, 1.11–13, 1.32, 2.91, 3.19–26, 5.19, 5.23–24, 13.19; Fam. 12.3.2, 12.22.1, 12.23.2; Att. 14.20.2, 15.2.2; App. B Civ. 3.45.186; CCMR, App. A: 354, 355, 357, 359, 361), and issued edicts (F 18–22).

In Spring 44 BC to the People (F 13–13A)

F 13 Cicero, *Philippics*

For he [Antony] had stated at a public meeting that he would be the guardian of the city [of Rome] and that he would keep an army near the city until the Kalends of May [May 1]. Ah, a fine guardian, the proverbial wolf to guard the sheep! Would Antony be the city's guardian or her plunderer and oppressor? And at any rate he further said that he would enter the city and leave it when he chose. To cap it all, did he not say in the hearing of the People, as he sat in front of the Temple of Castor, that none but the victor would live?

F 13A Cicero, *Philippics*

As for Marc Antony, who is there who can consider him a citizen rather than a most dire and most savage enemy? Sitting in front of the Temple of Castor, in the hearing of the Roman People, he said that none but the victor would live. Do you suppose, Members of the Senate, that he

scripti, dixisse eum minacius quam facturum fuisse? quid
vero quod in contione dicere ausus est, se, cum magistratu
abisset, ad urbem futurum cum exercitu, introiturum quo-
tienscumque vellet? quid erat aliud nisi denuntiare populo
Romano servitutem?

In July 44 BC to the People (F 14)

F 14 Cic. *Phil.* 1.8

cumque intempesta nox esset mansissemque in villa P.
Valeri, comitis et familiaris mei, postridieque apud eun-
dem ventum exspectans manerem, municipes Regini
complures ad me venerunt, ex eis quidam Roma recentes:
a quibus primum accipio Antoni contionem, quae mihi ita
placuit, ut ea lecta de reversione primum coeperim cogitare . . .

Against Cicero in the Senate (F 15–16)

F 15 Cic. *Phil.* 5.19–20

at ille homo vehemens et violentus, qui hanc consuetu-
dinem libere dicendi excluderet—fecerat enim hoc idem
maxima cum laude L. Piso XXX diebus ante—inimicitias

spoke more menacingly than he would have acted? Indeed, what he dared to say at a public meeting, that, after leaving office, he would stay near the city [of Rome] with an army and enter as often as he pleased, what was that but pronouncing slavery upon the Roman People?

In July 44 BC to the People (F 14)

F 14 Cicero, *Philippics*

It was the dead of night [in Sicily, on Cicero's journey to Greece], I had put up in the country house of P. Valerius [not otherwise known], my friend and companion, and on the following day [August 7] I stayed with him, waiting for a favorable wind: then a number of residents of Rhegium [modern Reggio di Calabria] came to me, among them some recently returned from Rome; from them I first received a copy of Antony's speech to the People, which pleased me so much that, after reading it, I first began to think of returning . . .

Against Cicero in the Senate (F 15–16)

With this speech delivered in the Senate on September 19, 44 BC, Antony replied to Cicero's First Philippic Oration *(Cic. Fam. 12.2.1, 12.25.4) and provoked his* Second Philippic Oration *(written as if a response given on that day).*

F 15 Cicero, *Philippics*

But that man [Antony] of vehemence and violence, who wished to ban this habit of free speech—for L. Piso [L. Calpurnius Piso Caesoninus (**127**)] had done the same

mihi denuntiavit; adesse in senatum iussit a d. XIII Kalendas Octobris. ipse interea XVII dies de me in Tiburtino Scipionis declamitavit, sitim quaerens; haec enim ei causa esse declamandi solet. [20] cum is dies quo me adesse iusserat venisset, tum vero agmine quadrato in aedem Concordiae venit atque in me absentem orationem ex ore impurissimo evomuit.

F 16 Cic. *Phil.* 2.1, 3, 4, 5, 7, 11, 15–16, 17, 18, 20, 21, 23, 25, 28, 30, 32–33, 37, 38, 39, 40, 42, 48, 49, 70, 76, 111, 112

tu ne verbo quidem violatus, ut audacior quam Catilina, furiosior quam Clodius viderere, ultro me maledictis lacessisti, tuamque a me alienationem commendationem tibi ad impios civis fore putavisti. . . . [3] cui prius quam de ceteris rebus respondeo, de amicitia quam a me violatam esse criminatus est, quod ego gravissimum crimen iudico, pauca dicam. contra rem suam me nescio quando venisse questus est. . . . at enim te in disciplinam meam tradideras—nam ita dixisti—domum meam ventitaras. . . . [4] auguratus petitionem mihi te concessisse dixisti. . . . [5] at beneficio sum tuo usus. . . . [7] . . . at etiam litteras, quas me sibi misisse diceret, recitavit homo et humanitatis expers et vitae communis ignarus. . . . [11] ut

with the utmost credit thirty days previously [on August 1, 44 BC]—declared enmity to me; he ordered me to be present in the Senate on the thirteenth day before the Kalends of October [September 19, 44 BC]. Meanwhile he spent seventeen days [September 2–19] constantly declaiming about me on Scipio's estate at Tibur, working up a thirst; for this tends to be his reason for declaiming. [20] When the day on which he had ordered me to be present had arrived, then he entered the Temple of Concord with his bodyguard in proper battle array and vomited from his utterly foul mouth a speech against me in my absence.

F 16 Cicero, *Philippics*

You [Antony], injured not even by a word, have assailed me unprovoked with abuse, as though you wished to look more reckless than Catiline [L. Sergius Catilina (**112**)] and madder than Clodius [P. Clodius Pulcher (**137**)], and you reckoned that your alienation from me would be a recommendation for you to disloyal citizens. . . . [3] Before I reply to him [Antony] concerning other matters, I shall say a few words about the friendship he charged me with having violated, which I regard as a most serious charge. He has complained that at some time or other I appeared against his interests in a civil case. . . . But you had put yourself under my direction—for so you claimed—had been a frequent visitor to my house. . . . [4] You have asserted that you conceded the candidacy for the augurate to me [ca. 53 BC]. . . . [5] But [you say] I availed myself of a kindness from you. . . . [7] . . . Then there is the letter he said I wrote to him: in his ignorance of civilized conduct and the usages of society, he even read it aloud. . . . [11]

igitur intellegeretis qualem ipse se consulem profiteretur, obiecit mihi consulatum meum. . . . [15] . . . tuus videlicet salutaris consulatus, perniciosus meus. adeone pudorem cum pudicitia perdidisti ut hoc in eo templo dicere ausus sis in quo ego senatum illum, qui quondam florens orbi terrarum praesidebat, consulebam, tu homines perditissimos cum gladiis conlocavisti? [16] at etiam ausus es—quid autem est quod tu non audeas?—clivum Capitolinum dicere me consule plenum servorum armatorum fuisse. . . . [17] . . . ad sepulturam corpus vitrici sui negat a me datum. . . . [18] qui autem tibi venit in mentem redigere in memoriam nostram te domi P. Lentuli esse educatum? . . . tam autem eras excors ut tota in oratione tua tecum ipse pugnares, non modo non cohaerentia inter se diceres, sed maxime disiuncta atque contraria, ut non tanta mecum quanta tibi tecum esset contentio. vitricum tuum fuisse in tanto scelere fatebare, poena adfectum querebare. . . . [20] at etiam quodam loco facetus esse voluisti. quam id te, di boni, non decebat! in quo est tua culpa non nulla. aliquid enim salis a mima uxore trahere potuisti. "cedant arma togae." [Cic. F 11 *FPL*[4]] quid? tum nonne cesserunt? at postea tuis armis cessit toga. . . . [21] Clodium meo consilio interfectum esse dixisti. . . . at Miloni ne favere quidem

Thus, in order to let you see what kind of consul he [44 BC] professes himself to be, he reproached me with my consulship [63 BC]. . . . [15] . . . So clearly your consulship is salutary, mine ruinous! Have you lost your sense of decency with your chastity to such an extent that you dare to say such a thing in the very temple [Temple of Concord] in which I used to consult that Senate that once flourished and ruled the world and where you have posted the most reckless men with weapons [cf. *Phil.* 2.19]? [16] But you have even dared to say—but what is there that you do not you dare?—that when I was consul, the Capitoline Hill was full of armed slaves. . . . [17] . . . He says I refused to give up his stepfather's [P. Cornelius Lentulus Sura (**100**)] body for burial. . . . [18] Yet how did it occur to you to call to our minds that you were brought up in P. Lentulus' house? . . . But you were so much out of your senses that you were fighting against yourself all through your speech; not only did you say what lacked coherence, but it was also completely out of joint and contradictory, so that your conflict was not so much with me as with yourself. You admitted that your stepfather had been involved in that enormous crime [the Catilinarian Conspiracy]; you complained that he had been punished. . . . [20] But at one point you even wanted to be witty. How unbecoming, good gods, this was for you! That is your own fault to a significant extent. For you could have picked up a little humor from your mime-actress spouse [Cytheris]. "Let arms yield to civilian garb." [Cic. F 11 *FPL*[4]] Well, didn't they at that time [in Cicero's consulship in 63 BC]? Later on, it is true, the civilian garb yielded to your arms. . . . [21] You say that Clodius [P. Clodius Pulcher (**137**)] was killed at my instigation. . . . On the other hand, I could not even

potui; prius enim rem transegit quam quisquam eum facturum id suspicaretur. at ego suasi. . . . at laetatus sum. . . .
[23] quod vero dicere ausus es idque multis verbis, opera
mea Pompeium a Caesaris amicitia esse diiunctum ob
eamque causam culpa mea bellum civile esse natum, in eo
non tu quidem tota re sed, quod maximum est, temporibus
errasti. . . . [25] sed haec vetera, illud vero recens, Caesarem meo consilio interfectum. . . . [28] at quem ad modum
me coarguerit homo acutus recordamini. "Caesare interfecto" inquit, "statim cruentum alte extollens Brutus pugionem Ciceronem nominatim exclamavit atque ei recu-
peratam libertatem est gratulatus." . . . [30] sed stuporem
hominis vel dicam pecudis attendite. sic enim dixit: "Brutus, quem ego honoris causa nomino, cruentum pugionem
tenens Ciceronem exclamavit: ex quo intellegi debet eum
conscium fuisse." . . . [32] . . . in huius me tu consili socie-
tatem tamquam in equum Troianum cum principibus in-
cludis? [33] non recuso; ago etiam gratias, quoquo animo
facis. tanta enim res est ut invidiam istam quam tu in me
vis concitare cum laude non comparem. quid enim beatius
illis quos tu expulsos a te praedicas et relegatos? . . . [37]
castra mihi Pompei atque illud omne tempus obiecisti. . . .
[38] . . . at vero Cn. Pompei voluntatem a me alienabat
oratio mea. . . . [39] . . . ne ⟨de⟩[1] iocis quidem respondebo
quibus me in castris usum esse dixisti: . . . [40] quod autem

[1] *add. Wesenberg*

lend Milo [T. Annius Milo (**138**)] encouragement, since he finished the business before anybody suspected that he was going to set about it. But I suggested it. . . . But I rejoiced. . . . [23] You further dared to say, and at great length, that through my action Pompey [Cn. Pompeius Magnus (**111**)] was detached from Caesar's [C. Iulius Caesar (**121**)] friendship and that therefore the civil war broke out through my fault: in this you were not entirely wrong, but you were wrong about the timing [59 BC], which is all-important. . . . [25] Yet all this is old news, but here is something recent, that Caesar was killed at my instigation. . . . [28] But remember how the clever fellow proved his point against me. "The moment Caesar was killed," he says, "Brutus [M. Iunius Brutus (**158**)] raised his bloodstained dagger high, called on Cicero by name, and congratulated him on the recovery of freedom." . . . [30] But observe the stupidity of the man, or of the brute, I should rather say. For he said this: "Brutus, whose name I mention with respect, called on Cicero as he held his bloodstained dagger: hence it ought to be inferred that he was in the plot." . . . [32] . . . Do you make me a partner in that enterprise, shutting me inside with the leaders as in a Trojan Horse? [33] I do not decline; I even thank you, whatever your motive in doing so. For it is so great a matter that I do not compare this odium that you want to stir up against me with the praise. For what is there happier than those men whom you boast of having driven out and banished? . . . [37] You brought up against me Pompey's camp and that whole period [ca. 49 BC]. . . . [38] . . . But certainly my speeches deprived me of Pompey' friendship. . . . [39] . . . Nor shall I make any reply ⟨about⟩ the joking you claimed I did in the camp: . . . [40] But the

idem maestitiam meam reprehendit, idem iocum, magno argumento est me in utroque fuisse moderatum. hereditates mihi negasti venire. . . . [42] . . . haec ut conligeres, homo amentissime, tot dies in aliena villa declamasti? . . . [48] intimus erat in tribunatu Clodio qui sua erga me beneficia commemorat; . . . [49] . . . in quo demiror cur Milonem impulsu meo rem illam egisse dicas, cum te ultro mihi idem illud deferentem numquam sim adhortatus. . . . [70] at quam crebro usurpat: "et consul et Antonius!" hoc est dicere, et consul et impudicissimus, et consul et homo nequissimus. quid est enim aliud Antonius? . . . [76] . . . etiam quaerebat cur ego ex ipso cursu tam subito revertissem. . . . [111] quaeris placeatne mihi pulvinar esse, fastigium, flaminem. mihi vero nihil istorum placet: sed tu, qui acta Caesaris defendis, quid potes dicere cur alia defendas, alia non cures? . . . [112] sed praeterita omittamus: hunc unum diem, unum, inquam, hodiernum diem, hoc punctum temporis, quo loquor, defende, si potes. cur armatorum corona senatus saeptus est, cur me tui satellites cum gladiis audiunt, cur valvae Concordiae non patent, cur homines omnium gentium maxime barbaros, Ituraeos, cum sagittis deducis in forum? praesidi sui causa se facere dicit.

fact that he censures my gloom as well as my jesting is a weighty argument that I was moderate in both. You said that bequests do not come my way. . . . [42] . . . Was it to gather together these points [allegations against Cicero], you madman, that you spent all these days declaiming in a country house that does not belong to you? . . . [48] He who is reminding me of the favors he has done for me was rather intimate with Clodius during the latter's tribunate [58 BC]. . . . [49] . . . I wonder why, therefore, you say that Milo committed that deed at my prompting, since, when you offered me the same service of your own accord, I never encouraged you. . . . [70] But how frequently he employs the phrase "both the consul and Antony"! This is to say "both the consul and an utterly shameless fellow," "both the consul and a completely worthless fellow." For what else is Antony? . . . [76] . . . He was even asking why I turned back so suddenly in the middle of my journey [cf. F 14]. . . . [111] You ask whether the sacred couch, the gable, the special priest [honors for Caesar; cf. Suet. *Iul.* 76] have my approval. Certainly not; none of this has my approval. But you, who defend Caesar's acts, what can you say as to why you defend some acts and do not care for others? . . . [112] But let us leave aside what is past: this one day, this single one, I say, the present day, this point of time in which I speak: defend it if you can. Why is the Senate surrounded by a circle of armed men, why do your henchmen hear me with swords, why are the doors of the Temple of Concord not open, why do you bring into the Forum the most barbarous men of all nations, Ituraeans, with arrows? He says he does it for his protection.

On Cicero's Philippics *(F 17)*

F 17 Plut. *Cic.* 41.6

Ἀντώνιος δὲ τοῦ γάμου μνησθεὶς ἐν ταῖς πρὸς τοὺς
Φιλιππικοὺς ἀντιγραφαῖς, ἐκβαλεῖν φησιν αὐτὸν γυ-
ναῖκα παρ᾽ ἣν ἐγήρασε, χαριέντως ἅμα τὴν οἰκουρίαν
ὡς ἀπράκτου καὶ ἀστρατεύτου παρασκώπτων τοῦ Κικέρωνος.

For the period of the fighting against C. Iulius Caesar's
(**121**) assassins, Appian reports addresses by Antony to
soldiers (F 17A [CCMR, App. C: 130], 17B [CCMR, App.

Addresses to Soldiers (F 17A–B)

F 17A App. *B Civ.* 4.119.499–120.507

*Appian reports that Octavian and Antony, realizing that
M. Iunius Brutus [**158**] is not willing to fight, assemble
their men; he then presents a speech by Antony to the
soldiers: Antony explains that the enemy is fearful and that
the soldiers have achieved a great victory on the preceding*

F 17B App. *B Civ.* 4.126.525–127.530

*Appian puts a speech to soldiers into the mouths of Octa-
vian and Antony: they rouse the soldiers to fight bravely
against the enemy on that very day, while mentioning the
danger of famine. The leaders present the gains to be won*

On Cicero's Philippics *(F 17)*

Whether Antony's reaction to Cicero's Philippics *was a speech or a written statement is uncertain.*

F 17 Plutarch, *Life of Cicero*

Antony, who spoke of the marriage [of Cicero] in his replies to the *Philippics* [Cicero's speeches], says that he [Cicero] cast out of doors the wife with whom he had grown old, and at the same time makes witty jibes upon the stay-at-home habits of Cicero, whom he described as unfit for business and unfit for military service.

A: 132]) and to Greeks and other inhabitants of Asia Minor (F 17C; cf. Plut. Ant. 44.3–5; Cass. Dio 50.16–22).

Addresses to Soldiers (F 17A–B)

F 17A Appian, *Civil Wars*

day and should not be worried about any plundering on the part of the enemy. Antony assures the soldiers that they will force the enemy to fight again, encourages them to engage bravely, and promises rewards and compensation.

F 17B Appian, *Civil Wars*

and illustrate the fighting technique needed to achieve that goal. The speech is said to have the desired effect on the soldiers.

To the Inhabitants of Asia (F 17C)

F 17C App. *B Civ.* 5.4.16–5.24

Appian puts a speech into Antony's mouth, given to the Greeks and all other peoples who inhabit Asia around Pergamon: Antony outlines that king Attalus left these Greeks to the Romans in his will and that the Romans immediately treated them in a better way than he had. For instance, they did not impose a tax as a fixed sum, but rather as a

From Edicts (F 18–22)

F 18 Cic. *Phil.* 3.15

at quam contumeliosus in edictis, quam barbarus, quam rudis! primum in Caesarem ut maledicta congessit depromta ex recordatione impudicitiae et stuprorum suorum! quis enim hoc adulescente castior, quis modestior, quod in iuventute habemus inlustrius exemplum veteris sanctitatis? quis autem illo qui male dicit impurior? ignobilitatem obicit C. Caesaris filio, cuius etiam natura pater, si vita suppeditasset, consul factus esset. "Aricina mater." Trallianam aut Ephesiam putes dicere.

Cf. Suet. *Aug.* 4.2.

To the Inhabitants of Asia (F 17C)

F 17C Appian, *Civil Wars*

proportion of the yearly harvest, and Caesar intervened against wrongdoings of the tax farmers. Although the Greeks supported Caesar's assassins, Antony assures them that they will not be punished; still, they will have to make a financial contribution to support the large armies.

From Edicts (F 18–22)

In the Philippics *Cicero mentions, quotes from, and comments on edicts Antony issued in late 44 BC.*

F 18 Cicero, *Philippics*

But how insolent he [Antony] is in his edicts, how uncivilized, how uneducated! First, how he heaped abuse on Caesar [Octavian], taken straight from the recollection of his own lack of chastity and debaucheries! For who is purer, who more modest than this young man, what more conspicuous example of old-time morality among the youth do we have? But what less pure person is there than he who is voicing abuse? He taunts Caesar's [C. Iulius Caesar (**121**)] son with humble birth, though even his natural father would have been elected consul if his life had continued. "A mother from Aricia [modern Ariccia, town in Latium]": you would think he was saying "from Tralles" or "from Ephesus [i.e., from Asia minor]."

F 19 Cic. *Phil.* 3.16–18

... tuae coniugis, bonae feminae, locupletis quidem certe, Bambalio quidam pater, homo nullo numero. nihil illo contemptius qui propter haesitantiam linguae stuporemque cordis cognomen ex contumelia traxerit. "at avus nobilis." Tuditanus nempe ille qui cum palla et cothurnis nummos populo de rostris spargere solebat. vellem hanc contemptionem pecuniae suis reliquisset! habetis nobilitatem generis gloriosam! [17] qui autem evenit ut tibi Iulia nata ignobilis videatur, cum tu eodem materno genere soleas gloriari? quae porro amentia est eum dicere aliquid de uxorum ignobilitate cuius pater Numitoriam Fregellanam, proditoris filiam, habuerit uxorem, ipse ex libertini filia susceperit liberos? ... idem etiam Q. Ciceronem, fratris mei filium, compellat edicto, nec sentit amens commendationem esse compellationem suam. . . . [18] at etiam gladiator ausus est scribere hunc de patris et patrui parricidio cogitasse. . . . nam me isdem edictis nescit laedat an laudet: cum idem supplicium minatur optimis civibus quod ego de sceleratissimis ac pessimis sumpserim, laudare videtur, quasi imitari velit; cum autem illam pulcherrimi facti memoriam refricat, tum a sui similibus invidiam aliquam in me commoveri putat.

F 19 Cicero, *Philippics*

... whereas of your [Antony's] wife [Fulvia], the good lady, rich at least, the father is a certain Bambalio [M. Fulvius Bambalio], a person of no consequence. There is nothing more contemptible than that man who got his name from his stammering tongue and dull wits by way of insult. "But the grandfather was a nobleman." Of course, that Tuditanus [Fulvia's maternal grandfather], who used to scatter coins from the Rostra among the People, dressed in an actor's robe and buskins. I would wish that he had passed on to his family his contempt for money! Here you have a noble family to boast of! [17] But how is it that the daughter of a Iulia [Octavian's mother] seems of humble background to you when you constantly brag of coming from the same family on your mother's side? What folly, again, this talk about lowborn wives from a man whose father [Antony's father] had as his wife Numitoria of Fregellae, the daughter of a traitor, and who himself acknowledged children by the daughter [Fadia, Antony's former partner] of a freedman? . . . He further rebukes Q. Cicero, my brother's son, in an edict and does not perceive that a rebuke coming from him is a commendation. . . . [18] But this gladiator even dared to write that he [Quintus] had contemplated the murder of his father and his uncle. . . . And in the same edicts he mentions me, without knowing whether he is praising or attacking me: when he threatens most loyal citizens with the punishment that I inflicted on the worst and the most criminal, he seems to be praising me, as though he wished to imitate me; but when he renews the memory of that most glorious act, then he thinks that he is stirring up some odium against me on the part of persons like himself.

F 20 Cic. *Phil.* 3.19

sed quid fecit ipse? cum tot edicta ⟨pro⟩posuisset,[1] edixit
ut adesset senatus frequens a.d. VIII Kalendas Decem-
bris: eo die ipse non adfuit. at quo modo edixit? haec sunt,
ut opinor, verba in extremo: "si quis non adfuerit, hunc
existimare omnes poterunt et interitus mei et perditissi-
morum consiliorum auctorem fuisse."

[1] ⟨pro⟩posuisset *Naugerius*: posuisset *codd.*

F 21 Cic. *Phil.* 3.21

quem in edictis Spartacum appellat, hunc in senatu ne
improbum quidem dicere audet.

F 22 Cic. *Phil.* 3.21–23

sententiolas edicti cuiusdam memoriae mandavi quas videtur ille peracutas putare: ego autem qui intellegeret
quid dicere vellet adhuc neminem inveni. [22] "nulla
contumelia est quam facit dignus." primum quid est dignus? nam etiam malo multi digni, sicut ipse. an quam facit
is qui cum dignitate est? quae autem potest esse maior?
quid est porro facere contumeliam? quis sic loquitur? deinde: "nec timor quem denuntiat inimicus." quid ergo? ab
amico timor denuntiari solet? horum similia deinceps.
nonne satius est mutum esse quam quod nemo intellegat
dicere? en cur magister eius ex oratore arator factus {sit},[1]
possideat in agro publico[2] campi Leontini duo milia iuge-

[1] *del. Faernus*   [2] publico p. r. *una familia codd.*

Cf. Quint. *Inst.* 9.3.13.

F 20 Cicero, *Philippics*

But what did he [Antony] do himself? After he had published so many edicts, he issued another, summoning a full Senate on the eighth day before the Kalends of December [November 24, 44 BC]: on that day he himself was absent. But how did he phrase this edict? These, I think, are its concluding words: "If anyone fails to attend, all will be able to set him down as an instigator of my destruction and of the most desperate designs."

F 21 Cicero, *Philippics*

He [Antony] calls him [Octavian] a Spartacus in his edicts, but in the Senate he dares not so much as call him a criminal.

F 22 Cicero, *Philippics*

I have committed to memory some little remarks from some edict of his [Antony's], phrases that he seems to think extremely clever: I, however, have not yet found anyone who understood what he wished to say. [22] "An insult made by the worthy is no insult." First, what is "worthy"? For many are worthy of evil, as is he himself. Or does he mean made by someone who possesses worth? But what insult can be greater? And further, what is "making an insult"? Who talks like that? Then: "nor is a threat a threat when launched by an enemy." Come now: are threats usually launched by a friend? And things like that in what follows. Isn't it better to keep silent than to say what nobody understands? Now we see why his coach [Sex. Clodius, cf. T 2], turned from an orator into a farmer, occupies two thousand *iugera* of public land in the plain of Leontini

rum immunia, ut hominem stupidum magis etiam infatuet mercede publica. [23] sed haec leviora fortasse: illud quaero cur tam mansuetus in senatu fuerit, cum in edictis tam ferus fuisset.

160 C. VIBIUS PANSA

*C. Vibius Pansa (cos. 43 BC; RE Vibius 16) was a close acquaintance of Cicero and studied oratory with him (T 1; Cic. Phil. 7.6; Quint. Inst. 8.3.54; Suet. Gram. et rhet. 25.3). Together with A. Hirtius (**161**), Pansa was consul in*

T 1 Quint. *Inst.* 12.11.6

quid porro est honestius quam docere quod optime scias? sic ad se Caelium deductum a patre Cicero profitetur, sic Pansam, Hirtium, Dolabellam <ad> morem[1] praeceptoris exercuit cotidie dicens audiensque.

> [1] <ad> morem *Winterbottom*: morem *vel* in morem *vel* more *codd.*

On Q. Ligarius (F 2)

F 2 Cic. *Lig.* 1

novum crimen, C. Caesar, et ante hunc[1] diem non auditum[2] propinquus meus ad te Q. Tubero detulit, Q. Ligarium in Africa fuisse, idque C. Pansa, praestanti vir inge-

> [1] hanc *Quint. Inst. 11.3.108, 110*   [2] non auditum *nonnulli codd. et Quint.*: inauditum *nonnulli codd. et Aquila Rom. 7, RLM, p. 24.23–24*

[on Sicily] tax free, just to make a fool more fatuous still at the public expense! [23] But these are perhaps rather trivial matters: I ask that question, why he was so gentle in the Senate when he had been so ferocious in his edicts.

160 C. VIBIUS PANSA

*43 BC during the struggle with M. Antonius (**159**); he was wounded in the battle at Forum Gallorum in spring 43 BC and died shortly afterward (Cic. Fam. 11.9.1; Phil. 14.26, 14.36; Vell. Pat. 2.61.4; App. B Civ. 3.75.305).*

T 1 Quintilian, *The Orator's Education*

And what is more honorable than teaching what you know best? Thus, Cicero reveals, Caelius [M. Caelius Rufus (**162**)] was brought to him by his father; thus he [Cicero] trained Pansa, Hirtius [A. Hirtius (**161**)], and Dolabella [P. Cornelius Dolabella (**173**)], ⟨just⟩ like a teacher, speaking and listening [to them] every day.

On Q. Ligarius (F 2)

*Alongside Cicero (Cic. Lig.), Pansa was a supporter of Q. Ligarius, prosecuted by Q. Aelius Tubero (**175** F 3–7), in the trial before C. Iulius Caesar (**121**) in 46 BC.*

F 2 Cicero, *Pro Ligario*

Strange, Caesar [C. Iulius Caesar (**121**)], and hitherto unheard of is the charge that my close friend Q. Tubero [Q. Aelius Tubero (**175**), F 3–7] has submitted to you, that Q.

nio, fretus fortasse familiaritate ea quae est ei tecum ausus
est confiteri. itaque quo me vertam nescio. paratus enim
veneram, cum tu id neque per te scires neque audire ali-
unde potuisses, ut ignoratione tua ad hominis miseri salutem abuterer. sed quoniam diligentia inimici investigatum
est quod latebat, confitendum est, opinor, praesertim cum
meus necessarius Pansa fecerit ut id integrum iam non
esset . . .

In the Senate on January 1, 43 BC (F 3)

F 3 Cic. *Phil.* 5.1

nihil umquam longius his Kalendis Ianuariis mihi visum
est, patres conscripti . . . sed querelam praeteritorum die-
rum sustulit oratio consulum, qui ita locuti sunt ut magis
exoptatae Kalendae quam serae esse videantur. atque ut
oratio consulum animum meum erexit spemque attulit
non modo salutis conservandae verum etiam dignitatis
pristinae recuperandae, sic me perturbasset eius sententia
qui primus rogatus est, nisi vestrae virtuti constantiaeque
confiderem.

Ligarius was in Africa; and C. Pansa, a man of outstanding ability, fortified possibly by that intimacy that he has with you, was bold enough to admit this. So, where I should turn I do not know. For, since you could not have known this at first hand nor heard of it from somewhere, I had come prepared to take advantage of your lack of knowledge to save an unfortunate man. But now that what was hidden has been revealed by the diligence of an opponent, one has to admit it, I suppose, especially as my friend Pansa has brought about that it is no longer a debatable question . . .

*When consul in 43 BC, Pansa gave a number of speeches (F 3–6) in the Senate and at public meetings (Cic. Phil. 12.2, 12.15; Fam. 12.7.1; CCMR, App. A: 365), in the context of the conflict with M. Antonius (**159**).*

In the Senate on January 1, 43 BC (F 3)

F 3 Cicero, *Philippics*

Nothing has ever seemed to me longer in the coming than these Kalends of January [January 1, 43 BC], Members of the Senate . . . But all complaint [about delay] of days past has been set aside by the speech of the consuls [cf. **161** F 4], who have spoken in such a manner as to make the Kalends seem eagerly awaited rather than too long delayed. And as the speech of the consuls raised my spirits and gave me hope not only of preserving safety but also of recovering former dignity, so the proposal of the gentleman first called [Q. Fufius Calenus, cos. 47 BC] would have perturbed me, if I did not have confidence in your courage and resolution.

In the Senate in Early February 43 BC (F 4)

F 4 Cic. *Phil.* 9.3

ut igitur alia, sic hoc, C. Pansa, praeclare quod et nos ad
honorandum Ser. Sulpicium cohortatus es et ipse multa
copiose de illius laude dixisti.

In the Senate in Mid-February 43 BC (F 5)

F 5 Cic. *Phil.* 10.1, 17

maximas tibi, Pansa, gratias omnes et habere et agere
debemus qui, cum hodierno die senatum te habiturum
non arbitraremur, ut M. Bruti, praestantissimi civis, litteras accepisti, ne minimam quidem moram interposuisti
quin quam primum maximo gaudio et gratulatione frue-
remur. cum factum tuum gratum omnibus debet esse, tum
vero oratio qua recitatis litteris usus es. declarasti enim
verum esse id quod ego semper sensi, neminem alterius
qui suae confideret virtuti invidere. . . . [17] . . . an vero,
si quid esset quod a M. Bruto timendum videretur, Pansa
id non videret, aut, si videret, non laboraret? quis aut sa-
pientior ad coniecturam rerum futurarum aut ad propulsandum metum diligentior? atqui huius animum erga M.
Brutum studiumque vidistis. praecepit oratione sua quid
decernere nos de Bruto, quid sentire oporteret, tantumque afuit ut periculosum rei publicae M. Bruti putaret
exercitum ut in eo firmissimum rei publicae praesidium et
gravissimum poneret.

In the Senate in Early February 43 BC (F 4)

F 4 Cicero, *Philippics*

In this as in other respects, C. Pansa, you have acted out-
standingly in that you both urged us to honor Ser. Sulpicius [Ser. Sulpicius Rufus (**118**)] and yourself said much
at length in his praise.

In the Senate in Mid-February 43 BC (F 5)

F 5 Cicero, *Philippics*

All of us, Pansa, ought to feel and express the greatest
gratitude to you; for, although we were not expecting you
to hold a meeting of the Senate today, nevertheless, after
you had received a letter from Brutus [**M**. Iunius Brutus
(**158**)], a most distinguished citizen, you did not let even
the slightest of intervals delay our immediate enjoyment
of so great a cause for happiness and congratulation. Your
action should be welcome to everybody, and particularly
the speech that you delivered after the letter had been
read. For you proved true something that I have always
observed, that a man who is confident of his own worth is
never jealous of another's. . . . [17] . . . In fact, if there were
anything that might seem to cause fear of Brutus, would
not Pansa see that; or, seeing it, would he not be concerned? Who is either wiser in forecasting the future or
more conscientious in warding off a threat? And yet you
have seen his attitude toward Brutus and his support. In
his speech he told us what we should decree concerning
Brutus, what we should feel; and he was so far from thinking Brutus' army a danger to the Republic that he placed
in it the Republic's strongest and weightiest protection.

*In March 43 BC in the Senate and
to the People (F 6)*

F 6 Cic. *Fam.* 12.7.1 [ad Cassium]

quanto studio dignitatem tuam et in senatu et ad populum
defenderim ex tuis te malo quam ex me cognoscere. quae
mea sententia in senatu facile valuisset, nisi Pansa vehementer obstitisset. ea sententia dicta productus sum in
contionem ab tribuno pl. M. Servilio. dixi de te quae potui,
tanta contentione quanta meorum ⟨laterum⟩[1] est, tanto
clamore consensuque populi ut nihil umquam simile viderim. id velim mihi ignoscas quod invita socru tua fecerim.
mulier timida verebatur ne Pansae animus offenderetur.
in contione quidem Pansa dixit matrem quoque tuam et
fratrem illam a me sententiam noluisse dici.

[1] quanta meorum ⟨laterum⟩ *Watt*: quantum forum *codd.*

161 A. HIRTIUS

*A. Hirtius (cos. 43 BC; RE Hirtius 2), like his consular
colleague C. Vibius Pansa (**160**), was a friend and pupil of
Cicero (T 1–3; Cic. Fat. 2–3; Suet. Gram. et rhet. 25.3); he
died in connection with the battle of Mutina in 43 BC.*

*In March 43 BC in the Senate and
to the People (F 6)*

F 6 Cicero, *Letters to Friends* [to Cassius]

How zealously I have defended your [C. Cassius Longinus', praet. 44 BC, one of Caesar's assassins] standing both in the Senate and before the People I prefer you to learn from your domestic correspondents rather than from myself. My motion in the Senate would have gone through with ease if Pansa had not strongly opposed it. After putting forward my views, I was presented to a public meeting by the Tribune of the People M. Servilius [tr. pl. 43 BC]. I said what I could about you, to the greatest possible power of my ⟨lungs⟩, amid such unanimous shouts of approval from the People that I have never seen anything like it. I hope you will forgive me for doing this against your mother-in-law's[1] wishes. Being a fearful lady, she was afraid that Pansa might be offended. In fact, Pansa said at a public meeting that your mother and brother[2] too had not wished me to make that motion.

[1] Servilia, the mother of M. Iunius Brutus (**158**) and of Cassius' wife, Iunia Tertia.   [2] L. Cassius Longinus (tr. pl. 44 BC). No details are known about the mother.

161 A. HIRTIUS

Hirtius was also a literary figure: in response to Cicero's Cato *he wrote a work in which he noted Cato's faults. He supplied Book 8 of Caesar's* commentarii *on the Gallic War. A letter by Hirtius to Cicero is extant (Cic. Att. 15.6) as are letters from Cicero to him. Hirtius is a speaker in*

T 1 Cic. *Fam.* 9.16.7 [ad Papirium Paetum]

Hirtium ego et Dolabellam dicendi discipulos habeo, ce-
nandi magistros; puto enim te audisse, si forte ad vos omnia perferuntur, illos apud me declamitare, me apud illos
cenitare.

T 2 Cic. *Fam.* 7.33.1–2 [ad Volumnium Eutrapelum]

quod declamationibus nostris cares, damni nihil facis.
quod Hirtio invideres nisi eum amares, non erat causa
invidendi, nisi forte ipsius eloquentiae magis quam quod
me audiret invideres. . . . [2] . . . nam et Cassius tuus et
Dolabella noster, vel potius uterque noster, studiis iisdem
tenentur et meis aequissimis utuntur auribus.

T 3 Quint. *Inst.* 12.11.6

= **160** T 1.

On January 1, 43 BC, in the Senate (F 4)

F 4 Cic. *Phil.* 5.1

= **160** F 3.

Cicero's treatise De Fato. *In 45 BC Hirtius countered criticism of Cicero that the latter's nephew was spreading (*Cic. *Att. 13.37.2).*

T 1 Cicero, *Letters to Friends* [to Papirius Paetus]

I have Hirtius and Dolabella [P. Cornelius Dolabella (**173**), T 1] as pupils in oratory, but as masters in gastronomy. For I believe you have heard, if by chance, all news is brought to you, that they practice declaiming at my house, and I practice dining at theirs.

T 2 Cicero, *Letters to Friends* [to Volumnius Eutrapelus]

In missing my declamations, you lose nothing at all. As for your envying Hirtius, if you were not so fond of him, there would be no cause for envy, unless perhaps you envied him his eloquence rather than that he listens to me. . . . [2] . . . For both your friend Cassius [C. Cassius Longinus] and our friend Dolabella [P. Cornelius Dolabella (**173**), T 2], or rather "our" in both cases, are devoted to the same pursuits and make use of my very well-disposed ears.

T 3 Quintilian, *The Orator's Education*
= **160** T 1.

On January 1, 43 BC, in the Senate (F 4)

*In his consular year (43 BC), Hirtius spoke in the Senate (F 4) until he left Rome to fight against M. Antonius (**159**).*

F 4 Cicero, *Philippics*
= **160** F 3.

162 M. CAELIUS RUFUS

M. Caelius Rufus (tr. pl. 52, praet. 48 BC; RE Caelius 35) was defended by Cicero in 56 BC (Cic. Cael.). Later, he joined the party of C. Iulius Caesar (121). As praetor, he caused an uprising in Rome, was expelled from the city, and killed in Thurii (Caes. BCiv. 3.20–22; Liv. Epit. 111; Vell. Pat. 2.68.2; Cass. Dio 42.25.3).

Caelius learned, among others, from Cicero (T 1; Quint. Inst. 12.11.6: 160 T 1). His brilliant, clever, and witty style is noted, while his later political career is regretted (T 2, 7–8; Cic. Brut. 297; Cael. 45). Other ancient authorities

T 1 Cic. *Cael.* 9

qui ut huic togam virilem dedit . . . hoc dicam, hunc a patre continuo ad me esse deductum—nemo hunc M. Caelium in illo aetatis flore vidit nisi aut cum patre aut mecum aut in M. Crassi castissima domo cum artibus honestissimis erudiretur.

T 2 Cic. *Brut.* 273

[CICERO:] nec vero M. Caelium praetereundum arbitror, quaecumque eius in exitu vel fortuna vel mens fuit; qui quamdiu auctoritati meae paruit, talis tribunus plebis fuit ut nemo contra civium perditorum popularem turbulentamque dementiam a senatu et a bonorum causa steterit

162 M. CAELIUS RUFUS

too, besides Cicero, regard Caelius as an impressive orator
(T 4, 7–9, 12; Vell. Pat. 2.36.2; Plin. Ep. 1.20.4; Sen. Dial.
5.8.6), while his style was seen as old-fashioned to a certain
extent by some in Tacitus' time (T 11).

Caelius' ability as a prosecutor and the existence of
impressive prosecution speeches by him are mentioned
(T 2–3, 6–7; for further trials in which Caelius was in-
volved, see TLRR 337, 343, 347, 348, 351). Seventeen
letters from him to Cicero are extant (Cic. Fam. 8).

T 1 Cicero, *Pro Caelio*

As soon as he [his father] had given him [Caelius] the
gown of manhood . . . I will only say this: that he was
brought to me at once by his father—nobody ever saw this
M. Caelius, while in that flower of age, except in the company of his father or myself, or in the irreproachable
household of M. Crassus [M. Licinius Crassus Dives
(**102**)], while he was being trained in the most honorable
pursuits.

T 2 Cicero, *Brutus*

[CICERO:] And indeed I believe that M. Caelius should
not be passed over, whatever his fate or his mind was like
at the end of his life. As long as he paid attention to my
authority, he was such a Tribune of the People [52 BC]
that nobody ever stood more firmly on the side of the Senate and the cause of the loyal men against the demagogic
turbulence and madness of reckless citizens. His ⟨old-⟩

constantius. ‹anti›quam[1] eius actionem multum tamen et splendida et grandis et eadem in primis faceta et perurbana commendabat oratio. graves eius contiones aliquot fuerunt, acres accusationes tres eaeque omnes ex rei publicae contentione susceptae; defensiones, etsi illa erant in eo meliora quae dixi, non contemnendae tamen saneque tolerabiles. hic cum summa voluntate bonorum aedilis curulis factus esset, nescio quo modo discessu meo discessit a sese ceciditque, postea quam eos imitari coepit quos ipse perverterat.

[1] ‹anti›quam *Stangl*: quam *codd.*

T 3 Cic. *Cael.* 78

habet a M. Caelio res publica, iudices, duas accusationes vel obsides periculi vel pignora voluntatis.

T 4 Vell. Pat. 2.68.1

. . . M. Caelius, vir eloquio animoque Curioni simillimus sed in utroque perfectior nec minus ingeniose nequam . . .

T 5 Columella, *Rust.* 1, *praef.* 30
= **158** T 7.

fashioned [?] delivery was nevertheless made very pleasant by a style brilliant and grand and at the same time
particularly clever and witty. There were some impressive
speeches of his given at public meetings and three merci-
less prosecutions, and all of these taken on as a result of
strenuous effort for the Republic. His speeches in defense, although those points that I have mentioned were
what he was better at, were still not negligible and indeed
quite tolerable. When he had been made curule aedile [50
BC] with the greatest support of the loyal men, somehow,
after my departure [to govern the province of Cilicia] he
departed from himself and came to fall after he had begun
to imitate those whom he himself had brought down.

T 3 Cicero, *Pro Caelio*

The Republic, judges, holds from M. Caelius two prosecutions, as hostages against dangerous behavior or as pledges
of goodwill.

T 4 Velleius Paterculus, *Compendium of Roman History*

. . . M. Caelius, a man closely resembling Curio [C. Scribonius Curio (**170**)] in eloquence and in spirit, although
more accomplished in both, and no less clever though a
worthless fellow . . .

T 5 Columella, *On Agriculture*

= **158** T 7.

T 6 Quint. *Inst.* 6.3.69

idem per allegorian M. Caelium, melius obicientem crimina quam defendentem, bonam dextram, malam sinistram habere dicebat.

T 7 Quint. *Inst.* 10.1.115

multum ingenii in Caelio et praecipue in accusando multa urbanitas, dignusque vir cui et mens melior et vita longior contigisset.

T 8 Quint. *Inst.* 10.2.25–26

= **121** T 5.

T 9 Quint. *Inst.* 12.10.11

= **140** T 2.

T 10 Tac. *Dial.* 18.1

= **19** T 9.

T 11 Tac. *Dial.* 21.3–4

[APER:] quid? ex Caelianis orationibus nempe eae placent, sive universae ⟨sive⟩ partes earum,[1] in quibus nitorem et altitudinem horum temporum agnoscimus. [4] sordes autem illae[2] verborum et hians compositio et inconditi sensus redolent antiquitatem; nec quemquam adeo antiquarium puto, ut Caelium ex ea parte laudet qua antiquus est.

---

[1] universae ⟨sive⟩ partes earum *Pithoeus*: universa parte serum *codd.*   [2] ill(a)e *vel* regul(a)e *codd.*

T 6 Quintilian, *The Orator's Education*

Likewise through allegory he [Cicero] said that M. Caelius, who was better at prosecuting than at defending, had a strong right hand and a weak left [cf. T 2].

T 7 Quintilian, *The Orator's Education*

Caelius had much talent and, especially in prosecuting, much wit, and he was a man who deserved that a wiser mind and a longer life had fallen to his lot.

T 8 Quintilian, *The Orator's Education*

= **121** T 5.

T 9 Quintilian, *The Orator's Education*

= **140** T 2.

T 10 Tacitus, *Dialogue on Oratory*

= **19** T 9.

T 11 Tacitus, *Dialogue on Oratory*

[APER:] Now, out of the speeches of Caelius, surely those give satisfaction, either as a whole <or> parts of them, in which we find the polish and elevation of style of the present day. [4] But that filth of words, the disjointed arrangement, and the shapeless periods savor of antiquity, and I do not believe that there is anyone so devoted to antiquity as to praise Caelius insofar as he is antiquated.

T 12 Tac. *Dial.* 25.3–4

= **121** T 7.

Against C. Antonius Hybrida (F 13–18)

*As a young man, in 59 BC, Caelius prosecuted the ex-consul C. Antonius Hybrida (**113**), who had been consul in 63 BC with Cicero, presumably for extortion or alleged involvement in the Catilinarian Conspiracy (Cic.* Cael.

F 13 Cic. *Cael.* 15

itaque a maledictis impudicitiae[1] ad coniurationis invidiam oratio est vestra delapsa. . . . nimium multa de re minime dubia loquor; hoc tamen dico. non modo si socius coniurationis, sed nisi inimicissimus istius sceleris fuisset, numquam coniurationis accusatione adulescentiam suam potissimum commendare voluisset.

---

[1] impudicitiae *unus cod., Garatoni ex Quint. Inst. 4.2.27:* pudicitiae *codd. plerique*

F 14 Cic. *Cael.* 74

accusavit C. Antonium, conlegam meum, cui misero praeclari in rem publicam benefici memoria nihil profuit, nocuit opinio malefici cogitati. postea nemini umquam concessit aequalium plus ut in foro, plus ut in negotiis

T 12 Tacitus, *Dialogue on Oratory*
= **121** T 7.

Against C. Antonius Hybrida (F 13–18)

*47); the accused was found guilty, even though defended
by Cicero (Cic.* Pro C. *Antonio collega: Crawford 1984,
124–31) (TLRR 241).*

F 13 Cicero, *Pro Caelio*

And so, from slander against immoral behavior, your
speech [of the counsel for the prosecution] has glided into
resentment regarding the conspiracy. . . . I am saying too
much on a matter that admits of not the slightest doubt;
nonetheless I say this: not only if he [Caelius] had been a
partner in the conspiracy, but even if he had not been bitterly opposed to that crime, would he ever have sought to
bring distinction to his youth particularly by a charge of
conspiracy. [continued by F 20]

F 14 Cicero, *Pro Caelio*

He [Caelius] accused my colleague [as consul in 63 BC]
C. Antonius [C. Antonius Hybrida (**113**)], that unfortunate man, to whom the recollection of an outstanding service rendered to the Republic [defeat of L. Sergius Catilina (**112**)] was of no use, while the suspicion of an
intended crime [of being involved in the conspiracy] did
him harm. From that time he [Caelius] never showed himself inferior to anyone of his own age, so that he was more

versaretur causisque amicorum, plus ut valeret inter suos gratia.

F 15 Cic. *Cael.* 78

non enim potest qui hominem consularem, cum ab eo rem publicam violatam esse[1] diceret, in iudicium vocarit ipse esse[2] in re publica civis turbulentus; non potest, qui ambitu ne absolutum quidem patiatur[3] esse absolutum ipse impune umquam esse largitor.

[1] esse *unus cod., Lambinus: om. codd. plerique*   [2] ipse ēē (*vel* e) *vel* ipse *codd.*   [3] patiatur *unus cod., Wesenberg:* patitur *vel* datur (dat) *codd. cet.*

F 16 Schol. Bob. ad Cic. *Flacc.* 5 (p. 94.27–31 Stangl)

"condemnatus est is qui Catilinam signa patriae inferentem interemit." Gaius scilicet Antonius collega Ciceronis, M. Caelio Rufo accusante non tantum pecuniarum repetundarum crimine, verum etiam ob hanc coniurationem, non ita pridem damnatus fuerat.

F 17 Quint. *Inst.* 4.2.123–24

multum confert adiecta veris credibilis rerum imago, quae velut in rem praesentem perducere audientis videtur, qualis est illa M. Caeli in Antonium descriptio: "namque ipsum offendunt temulento sopore profligatum, totis

present in the Forum, more present in lawsuits and court cases of his friends, so that his popularity among his associates was greater.

F 15 Cicero, *Pro Caelio*

For it is impossible that a man [Caelius] who has summoned to trial a man of consular rank [C. Antonius Hybrida (**113**)], because he declared that the Republic had been violated by that person, should himself be a riotous citizen in the Republic; it is impossible that a man who will not even allow one [L. Calpurnius Bestia; cf. F 19–22] who has been acquitted of bribery to be acquitted, should ever himself be a briber without any adverse consequences.

F 16 Scholia Bobiensia to Cicero, *Pro Flacco*

"He was found guilty, he who killed Catiline [L. Sergius Catilina (**112**)] waging war against his country." That is, Gaius Antonius [C. Antonius Hybrida (**113**)], Cicero's colleague [as consul in 63 BC], when M. Caelius Rufus prosecuted him, not only because of the charge of the extortion of money, but also because of this conspiracy, had been found guilty not so long ago.

F 17 Quintilian, *The Orator's Education*

A considerable contribution is made by a plausible picture of the matter added to the true facts, as this seems to bring the audience as if face to face with the matter; of this kind is that description by M. Caelius [in the speech] against Antonius [C. Antonius Hybrida (**113**)]: "And they found the man himself stretched out in a drunken stupor, snoring

praecordiis stertentem ructuosos spiritus geminare, prae-
clarasque contubernales ab omnibus spondis transversas
incubare et reliquas circum iacere passim: [124] quae tamen exanimatae terrore, hostium adventu percepto, exci-
tare Antonium conabantur, nomen inclamabant, frustra a
cervicibus tollebant, blandius alia ad aurem invocabat,
vehementius etiam nonnulla feriebat: quarum cum omnium vocem tactumque noscitaret, proximae cuiusque
collum amplexu petebat: neque dormire excitatus neque
vigilare ebrius poterat, sed semisomno sopore inter manus
centurionum concubinarumque iactabatur." nihil his neque credibilius fingi neque vehementius exprobrari neque
manifestius ostendi potest.

F 18   Quint. *Inst.* 9.3.58

at quae per detractionem fiunt figurae, brevitatis novita-
tisque maxime gratiam petunt: quarum una est ea quam
libro proximo in figuras ex συνεκδοχῇ distuli, cum sub-
tractum verbum aliquod satis ex ceteris intellegitur, ut
Caelius in Antonium: "stupere gaudio Graecus": simul
enim auditur "coepit" . . .

Against L. Calpurnius Bestia (F 19–22)

*In 56 BC Caelius launched a prosecution of L. Calpurnius
Bestia for bribery (cf. F 15), probably in connection with
the latter's candidacy for the praetorship; Bestia was de-*

with all the force of his lungs, belching repeatedly, while the distinguished ladies who shared his quarters were lying across all couches, and the other women were lying all around. [124] Half-dead with terror, having noticed the enemy's approach, they still tried to rouse up Antonius, shouted his name, and tried in vain to hoist him up by his neck; another whispered blandishments in his ear, one or two even gave him an energetic slap. When he recognized the voices and the touch of them all, he tried to put his arms round the neck of whoever was nearest. He was too much aroused to be able to sleep and too drunk to be able to stay awake; instead, in drowsy sleep, he was tossed about in the arms of the centurions and concubines." Nothing can be more plausibly invented than this, more strongly criticized, or more vividly portrayed.

F 18 Quintilian, *The Orator's Education*

But as regards figures generated by omission, they aim principally at the charm of brevity and novelty. One of these is the figure that I postponed in the last book to figures of synecdoche, when some omitted word is understood well enough from the others, as Caelius [in the speech] against Antonius [C. Antonius Hybrida (**113**)]: "the Greek to be stunned with joy": for one also hears "began" . . .

Against L. Calpurnius Bestia (F 19–22)

fended by Cicero (Cic. Pro L. Calpurnio Bestia*) and not found guilty (*TLRR 268*; Cic.* Q Fr. 2.3.6*). Soon afterward Caelius again prosecuted L. Calpurnius Bestia on the same*

285

charge (Cic. Cael. *56, 76, 78), when he was again defended by Cicero (Cic.* Pro L. Calpurnio Bestia: *Crawford 1984, 143–49 [on the various trials of Bestia and Cicero's*

F 19 Cic. *Cael.* 1

. . . sed adulescentem inlustri ingenio, industria, gratia accusari ab eius filio quem ipse in iudicium et vocet et vocarit . . .

F 20 Cic. *Cael.* 16

quod haud scio an de ambitu et de criminibus istis soda-lium ac sequestrium, quoniam huc incidi, similiter respon-dendum putem. numquam enim tam Caelius amens fuis-set ut, si sese[1] isto infinito ambitu commaculasset, ambitus alterum accusaret, neque eius facti in altero suspicionem quaereret cuius ipse sibi perpetuam licentiam optaret, nec, si sibi semel periculum ambitus subeundum putaret, ipse alterum iterum ambitus crimine arcesseret.

[1] si sese *Clark*: ses se *vel* si se *codd.*

F 21 Cic. *Cael.* 76

. . . nomen amici mei de ambitu detulit; quem absolutum insequitur, revocat; nemini nostrum obtemperat, est vio-lentior quam vellem.

speeches]); on this occasion he was found guilty (TLRR
269; Cic. Phil. *11.11*).

F 19 Cicero, *Pro Caelio*

. . . but that a young man [Caelius] of outstanding intellect,
application, and position is accused by the son [cf. F 23–
28] of a man [L. Calpurnius Bestia] whom he himself both
is prosecuting and has prosecuted . . .

F 20 Cicero, *Pro Caelio*

[continued from F 13] In this context I am inclined to
think that, since I have come upon this point, the same
kind of reply should be made about corruption and those
charges concerning political clubs and bribery agents. For
Caelius would never have been so mad that, if he had
defiled himself with that limitless bribery you allege, he
would accuse someone else of bribery, nor would he seek
to throw upon another the suspicion of such a deed for
which he might wish to enjoy a perpetual license himself,
nor, if he thought that he would have to face the risk of
being charged with bribery once, would he himself accuse
another man a second time of the offense of bribery.

F 21 Cicero, *Pro Caelio*

. . . he [Caelius] brought an action for bribery against a
friend of mine [Bestia]; him, after having been acquitted,
he prosecutes, he indicts again; he refuses to listen to any
of us; he is more violent than I could wish.

F 22 Plin. *HN* 27.4

hoc fuit venenum quo interemptas dormientis a Calpurnio
Bestia uxores M. Cae{ci}lius[1] accusator obiecit. hinc illa
atrox peroratio eius in digitum.

  [1] Cae{ci}lius *Ruhnken, Mayhoff*: Caecilius *codd., Detlefsen*

On His Own Behalf (F 23–28)

Also in 56 BC, Caelius was prosecuted under the Lex Plautia de vi *by L. Sempronius Atratinus (**171** F 1–7), a son of
L. Calpurnius Bestia, on the instigation of Clodia, seconded by L. Herennius Balbus (**163** F 1) and P. Clodius*

F 23 Cic. *Cael.* 45

audistis cum pro se diceret, audistis antea cum accusaret
. . .

F 24 Suet. *Gram. et rhet.* 26.2
= **97** F 1.

F 25 Quint. *Inst.* 11.1.51

quod mire M. Caelius in defensione causae, qua reus de
vi fuit, comprendisse videtur mihi: "ne cui vestrum atque
etiam omnium qui ad rem agendam adsunt meus aut vul-

F 22 Pliny the Elder, *Natural History*

This [aconite] was the poison that M. Caelius, the prosecutor, accused Calpurnius Bestia of using to kill the wives in their sleep.[1] Hence that damning peroration against his finger [used to apply the poison].

[1] How this allegation is linked to the charge of bribery is uncertain; or it may refer to a different trial.

On His Own Behalf (F 23–28)

(**164** *F 1); the accused, defended by himself, M. Licinius Crassus Dives (**102** F 12–13), and Cicero (Cic. Cael.), was acquitted (TLRR 275).*

F 23 Cicero, *Pro Caelio*

You have heard him [Caelius] when he pleaded for himself; you have heard him previously when he prosecuted . . .

F 24 Suetonius, *Lives of Illustrious Men. Grammarians and Rhetoricians*

= **97** F 1.

F 25 Quintilian, *The Orator's Education*

M. Caelius, in the defense in a trial in which he was charged with violence, seems to me to have understood this [the importance of the style of the defendant's speech] remarkably well: "I do not hope that to any of you and even of all those who are here to see this matter dealt with, my

289

tus molestior aut vox inmoderatior aliqua aut denique,
quod minimum est, iactantior gestus fuisse videatur."

F 26 + **27**   Quint. *Inst.* 8.6.52

sed allegoria quae est obscurior "aenigma" dicitur, vitium
meo quidem iudicio si quidem dicere dilucide virtus, quo
tamen et poetae utuntur [Verg. *Ecl.* 3.104–5]: "dic quibus
in terris, et eris mihi magnus Apollo, / tris pateat caeli
spatium non amplius ulnas?" et oratores nonnumquam, ut
Caelius "quadrantariam Clytaemestram" et "in triclinio
coam, in cubiculo nolam."[1] namque et nunc quidem sol-
vuntur et tum erant notiora cum dicerentur: aenigmata
sunt tamen . . .

[1] nolam *"revera aenigma est" Winterbottom in app.*: Nolanam
prob. Verdière

expression would seem to have been too offensive, some word too immoderate, or indeed, which is most trivial, my gestures too flamboyant."

F 26 + 27 Quintilian, *The Orator's Education*

But an allegory that is rather obscure is called *"aenigma"* ["riddle"], a fault, at least in my opinion, if speaking lucidly is a virtue; still, both the poets use it [Verg. *Ecl.* 3.104–5]: "Say in what land, and you will be the great Apollo to me, the space of heaven is not more than three cubits broad?"[1] and sometimes the orators, like Caelius: "quarter-dollar Clytemnestra" and "Coa at dinner, Nola in the bedroom."[2] To be sure, they are being solved even now and were then better known when they were uttered: still, they are *"aenigmata"* . . .

[1] For possible solutions of the riddle in Virgil, see Coleman 1977, 125–26.   [2] Clodia is compared to the mythical Clytemnestra because of her adultery and the alleged murder of her husband, Q. Metellus Celer. According to Plutarch (Plut. *Cic.* 29.5), Clodia was called *Quadrantia* since one of her lovers had sent her copper coins as if they were silver, and the smallest copper coin was called *quadrans*; Cicero alludes to the story that Clodia admitted lovers for a *quadrans* (Cic. *Cael.* 62). The "names" Coa and Nola are attested as designations for a female inhabitant of the Greek island of Kos and of a town in southern Italy, respectively. Here they are probably fictitious and may be intended to invoke associations of the fine and transparent Coan garments (e.g., Tib. 2.3.57–58; Prop. 1.2.2) and a refusal (*nolo*). Because of the allusion to Clodia, the fragments have been attributed to this speech.

291

F 28 Quint. *Inst.* 1.6.29

haec habet aliquando usum necessarium, quotiens inter-
pretatione res de qua quaeritur eget, ut cum M. Caelius
se esse hominem frugi vult probare, non quia abstinens sit
(nam id ne mentiri quidem poterat), sed quia utilis multis,
id est fructuosus, unde sit ducta frugalitas.

On T. Annius Milo to the People (F 29–30)

F 29 Asc. in Cic. *Mil.*, *arg.* (p. 29 KS = 33.21–24 C.)
= **138** F 1.

F 30 Cic. *Mil.* 91

caedi vidistis populum Romanum, contionem gladiis dis-
turbari, cum audiretur silentio M. Caelius, tribunus plebis, vir et in re publica fortissimus, in suscepta[1] causa
firmissimus, et bonorum voluntati, auctoritati[2] senatus
deditus, et in hac Milonis sive invidia sive fortuna, singulari, divina, incredibili[3] fide.

[1] in suscepta *nonnulli codd.*: et in suscepta *codd. cet.*
[2] auctoritati *duo codd.*: atque *ante* auctoritati *add. unus cod.*:
et *add. nonnulli codd.*   [3] incredibili *nonnulli codd.*: et incredibili *codd. cet.*

Cf. App. *B Civ.* 2.22.79–82.

F 28 Quintilian, *The Orator's Education*

This [i.e., etymology] is sometimes necessary to use, whenever the matter that is being dealt with needs explanation, as when M. Caelius seeks to prove that he is a *homo frugi* ["an honest, frugal man"],[1] not because he is abstemious (for he could not put that forward even as a false statement), but because he is useful to many, that is *fructuosus* ["fruitful"], whence *frugalitas* ["sober habits, self-restraint"] has been derived.[2]

[1-2] The statement has been attributed to this oration since it seems to be made in the speaker's defense.

On T. Annius Milo to the People (F 29–30)

*As Tribune of the People in 52 BC, Caelius spoke (CCMR, App. A: 329) to the People in support of T. Annius Milo (**138**), in connection with the latter's dispute with P. Clodius Pulcher (**137**).*

F 29 Asconius on Cicero, *Pro Milone*

= **138** F 1.

F 30 Cicero, *Pro Milone*

You have seen the Roman People massacred, a public meeting broken up by swords, though M. Caelius was heard in silence, a Tribune of the People, a most resolute man on behalf of the Republic, a staunch upholder of any cause taken on, a devoted champion of the aims of the loyal men and the authority of the Senate, and, in Milo's present situation, be it caused by hatred or by bad fortune, a man of unique, superhuman, and unbelievable loyalty.

On Behalf of M. Saufeius (F 31)

In 52 BC Caelius, along with Cicero (Cic. Pro M. Saufeio), successfully defended M. Saufeius, charged under the Lex Pompeia de vi in connection with the death of P. Clodius Pulcher (137) (TLRR 313). Shortly afterward, M. Sau-

F 31 Asc. in Cic. *Mil.* 95 (pp. 48 KS = 54.22–55.4 C.)

post Milonem eadem lege Pompeia primus est accusatus M. Saufeius M. f. qui dux fuerat in expugnanda taberna Bovillis et Clodio occidendo. accusaverunt eum L. Cassius, L. Fulcinius C. f., C. Valerius; defenderunt M. Cicero, M. Caelius, obtinueruntque ut una sententia absolveretur.

Against and on Behalf of Q. Pompeius Rufus (F 32)

In 51 BC, after their Tribunates, Caelius successfully prosecuted Q. Pompeius Rufus (153) under the Lex Pompeia de vi (TLRR 328; Cass. Dio 40.55.1). Later, he supported

F 32 Val. Max. 4.2.7

Caeli vero Rufi ut vita inquinata ita misericordia, quam Q. Pompeio praestitit, probanda. cui a se publica quaestione prostrato, cum mater Cornelia fidei commissa praedia non

On Behalf of M. Saufeius (F 31)

feius was again accused under the Lex Plautia de vi *and again found not guilty, defended by Cicero (Cic. Pro M. Saufeio: Crawford 1984, 219–21) and M. Terentius Varro Gibba (TLRR 314; Asc. in Cic. Mil. 95 [p. 55.10–19 C.]).*

F 31 Asconius on Cicero, *Pro Milone*

After Milo [T. Annius Milo (**138**)], under the same *Lex Pompeia*, the first to be accused was M. Saufeius, Marcus' son, who had been the leader in storming the tavern at Bovillae [town on the Via Appia] and killing Clodius [P. Clodius Pulcher (**137**)]. His prosecutors were L. Cassius [L. Cassius Longinus (**168**), F 2], L. Fulcinius, Gaius' son, and C. Valerius; the advocates for the defense were M. Cicero and M. Caelius; and they achieved that he was acquitted by a single vote [twenty-five for conviction, twenty-six for acquittal].

Against and on Behalf of Q. Pompeius Rufus (F 32)

Q. Pompeius Rufus in an inheritance case against his own mother.

F 32 Valerius Maximus, *Memorable Doings and Sayings*

As regards Caelius Rufus, just as his life was corrupt, so the pity he showed to Q. Pompeius is commendable. That man [Pompeius] had been struck down by him [Caelius] in a public trial; then, when his [Pompeius'] mother Cornelia did not hand over properties left according to the

redderet, atque iste auxilium suum litteris implorasset, pertinacissime absenti adfuit: recitavit etiam eius epistulam in iudicio, ultimae necessitatis indicem, qua impiam Corneliae avaritiam subvertit.

On Behalf of M. Tuccius (F 33)

F 33 Cael. ap. Cic. *Fam.* 8.8.1

scito C. Sempronium Rufum, mel ac delicias tuas, calumniam maximo plausu tulisse. <qua> quaeris in causa.[1] M. Tuccium, accusatorem suum, post ludos Romanos reum lege Plotia de vi fecit hoc consilio, quod videbat, si extraordinarius reus nemo accessisset, sibi hoc anno causam esse dicendam; dubium porro illi non erat quid futurum esset. nemini hoc deferre munusculum maluit quam suo accusatori. itaque sine ullo subscriptore descendit et Tuccium reum fecit. at ego, simul atque audivi, invocatus ad subsellia rei occurro; surgo, neque verbum de re facio, totum Sempronium usque eo perago ut Vestorium quoque interponam et illam fabulam narrem, quem ad modum tibi pro beneficio dederit † si quod iniuriis suis esset ut Vestorius teneret †.

---

1 <qua> quaeris in causa *C. F. Hermann*: quaeris an causa *vel* an queris causas *codd.*: quaeris qua in causa *Victorius*

---

1 When Tuccius sought to bring Sempronius Rufus to trial (*TLRR* 334), the latter responded by prosecuting Tuccius, so that Tuccius' case would be dealt with first.   2 Presumably, C. Vestorius, a businessman from Puteoli, frequently mentioned in Cicero's letters (e.g., Cic. *Att.* 14.12.3). The reason for the dispute might have been financial arrangements related to a commercial shipping venture in which all three men were involved (D'Arms

terms of a will and that man had begged his [Caelius'] help by letter, he [Caelius] supported him in his absence most staunchly: he even read out his [Pompeius'] letter in court, as a sign of his desperate need, whereby he frustrated Cornelia's irreverent avarice.

On Behalf of M. Tuccius (F 33)

In 51 BC, Caelius spoke in support of M. Tuccius (Galeo), charged under the Lex Plautia de vi *by C. Sempronius Rufus (*TLRR 335*).*

F 33 Caelius in Cicero, *Letters to Friends*

Learn that C. Sempronius Rufus, your heart's darling, has suffered a conviction for vexatious proceedings to the greatest applause. In ⟨what⟩ case, you ask. He charged his prosecutor, M. Tuccius, with assault under the *Lex Plotia* after the Roman Games, with this intention:[1] he saw that, if nobody had appeared as a defendant to be tried out of the usual order, he would have to plead his case in this year. Moreover, he had no doubt as to what would happen. He did not wish to do this little favor to anybody rather than to his accuser; therefore, without any assistant prosecutor, he went down [into the Forum] and charged Tuccius. But as soon as I heard of it, I hurry, though not summoned, up to the defense benches; I get up, and I say not a word on the matter, I finish off Sempronius up to the point that I include also Vestorius[2] and tell that story of how he did you a favor . . .[3]

1980, esp. 78–81).   [3] The final part of this sentence is corrupt and cannot be translated.

On Water Supply to the People (F 34–36)

F 34 Frontin. *Aq.* 75.3–76.1

sed et plerique possessorum, † e quorum agris aqua cir-
cumducitur †[1] {unde},[2] formas rivorum perforant. unde fit
ut ductus publici hominibus privatis † vel ad oritorum †[3]
itinera suspendant. [76.1] ac de vitiis eiusmodi nec plura
nec melius dici possunt quam a Caelio Rufo dicta sunt in
ea contione cui titulus est de aquis.

[1] e *del. Mommsen* [*an* <prop>e *legendum?*] circum-
ducitur *"vix sanum" Bücheler* [*fort.* praeterducitur, *scriba abbre-
viationem praepositionis non intelligente?*] [2] *del. Bücheler*:
inde *fons codd. rec.*: subinde *Dederich* [3] oritor(um) *vel*
ortorum *codd.*: ad hortorum <usum> *Polenus* (*vel* <usus> *Bücheler*): *fort. delendum* (*cf. Rodgers ad loc.*)

F 35 Cael. ap. Cic. *Fam.* 8.6.4

sed dici non potest quo modo hic omnia iaceant. nisi ego
cum tabernariis et aquariis pugnarem, veternus civitatem
occupasset.

F 36 *De dub. nom.*, *GL* V, p. 590.21–22

salientes aquarum generis masculini, ut Caelius: "perpe-
tuum salientem."

On Water Supply to the People (F 34–36)

As curule aedile in 50 BC, Caelius seems to have spoken to the People about the water supply (CCMR, App. A: 339).

F 34 Frontinus, *Aqueducts of Rome*

But also many owners of land close to whose fields water is led around [?] pierce through conduits of channels. Thence it happens that public pipes suspend their paths for private individuals or for the sake of their gardens [?].[1] [76.1] And about vices of this kind nothing more or better can be said than was said by Caelius Rufus in that speech to the People whose title is "about water supply."

[1] "for the sake of their gardens [?]" might be a marginal gloss that entered the text and should be deleted.

F 35 Caelius in Cicero, *Letters to Friends*

But it cannot be described how everything here stagnates. If I were not fighting with the shopkeepers and the overseers of the public water supply, torpor would have seized the whole community.

F 36 Anonymous grammarian

salientes ["fountains"] of water, of masculine gender [typically feminine], like Caelius: "a perpetual fountain" [acc.].[1]

[1] This fragment has been tentatively assigned to this Caelius and this speech because of the lemma's meaning.

Unplaced Fragments (F 37–40)

F 37 Quint. *Inst.* 1.5.61

= **176** F 22.

F 38 Quint. *Inst.* 1.6.42

nam etiamsi potest videri nihil peccare qui utitur iis verbis
quae summi auctores tradiderunt, multum tamen refert
non solum quid dixerint, sed etiam quid persuaserint. neque enim . . . iam in nobis quisquam ferat . . . nec "hos
lodices," quamquam id Pollioni placet, nec "gladiola," atqui Messala dixit, nec "parricidatum," quod in Caelio vix
tolerabile videtur, nec "collos" mihi Calvus persuaserit:
quae nec ipsi iam dicerent.

F 39 Quint. *Inst.* 6.3.39–41

narrare quae salsa sint in primis est subtile et oratorium,
ut Cicero pro Cluentio narrat de Caepasio atque Fabricio
aut M. Caelius de illa D. Laeli collegaeque eius in provinciam festinantium contentione. sed in his omnibus cum
elegans et venusta exigitur tota expositio, tum id festivis-

Unplaced Fragments (F 37–40)

F 37 Quintilian, *The Orator's Education*
= **176** F 22.

F 38 Quintilian, *The Orator's Education*

For even though anyone who uses those words that the best authors have transmitted can in no way be seen to make a mistake, it still matters a great deal not only what they said, but also what impact they had. For neither would any of us now bear . . . nor *hos lodices* ["these blankets"; masculine, usually feminine], even though Pollio [C. Asinius Pollio (**174**), F 42] approves, nor *gladiola* ["small swords"; neuter plural, normally masculine], even though Messalla [M. Valerius Messalla Corvinus (**176**), F 24] said it, nor *parricidatum* ["parricide"; rare form of *parricida*], which seems hardly bearable in Caelius, nor will Calvus [C. Licinius Macer Calvus (**165**), F 35] persuade me of *collos* ["necks"; masculine, rather than neuter as in later periods]: they would not use these words themselves nowadays.

F 39 Quintilian, *The Orator's Education*

To narrate what is humorous is particularly subtle and proper for an orator, as Cicero narrates about Caepasius and Fabricius [C. et L. Caepasii fratres (**115** + **116**), F 2] in [the speech] on behalf of Cluentius or M. Caelius about that contest between D. Laelius [tr. pl. 54 BC, quaestor in Sicily] and his colleague [probably C. Memmius] as they hurried off to their province. But in all these cases elegance and charm are required for the narrative as a whole,

301

simum est quod adicit orator. [40] . . . [41] et Caelius cum omnia venustissime finxit, tum illud ultimum: "hic subsecutus quo modo transierit, utrum rati an piscatorio navigio, nemo sciebat: Siculi quidem, ut sunt lascivi et dicaces, aiebant in delphino sedisse et sic tamquam Ariona transvectum."

F 40 Plin. *HN* 35.165

Samia testa Matris deum sacerdotes qui Galli vocantur virilitatem amputare, nec aliter citra perniciem, M. Caelio credamus, qui linguam sic amputandam obiecit gravi probro, tamquam et ipse iam tunc eidem Vitellio malediceret.

163 L. HERENNIUS BALBUS

*L. Herennius Balbus (RE Herennius 18), like P. Clodius (**164** F 1), supported the prosecutor L. Sempronius Atratinus (**171** F 1–7), in the case against M. Caelius Rufus (**162**), who was defended by himself (**162** F 23–28), M. Licinius Crassus Dives (**102** F 12–13), and Cicero (Cic. Cael.), who engages with points allegedly made by Balbus (TLRR 275).*

yet what the orator adds is wittiest. [40] . . . [41] And Caelius has fashioned everything very delightfully, but especially that passage at the very end: "He followed; but how
he crossed over, by raft or by fishing boat, nobody knew.
The Sicilians, though, as they have a naughty sense of
humor and a ready tongue, said he rode on a dolphin and
so made the crossing like Arion [cf. Hdt. 1.23–24]."

F 40 Pliny the Elder, *Natural History*

The priests of the Mother of the Gods, who are called
Galli, castrate themselves with a piece of Samian pottery,
the only way of avoiding dangerous results, if we believe
M. Caelius; he brought up in a harsh insult that the tongue
[presumably of an opponent] should be cut out in the
same way, just as if already at that point he were himself
inveighing against the same Vitellius [emperor Vitellius,
AD 69, criticized for extravagant dishes in what precedes].

163 L. HERENNIUS BALBUS

*After P. Clodius Pulcher's (**137**) death, Balbus requested
slaves of T. Annius Milo (**138**) and his wife for examination
(TLRR 306, 307; Marshall 1985, 173; Asc. in Cic. Mil., arg.
[p. 34.13–14 C.]).*

Against M. Caelius Rufus (F 1)

F 1 Cic. *Cael.* 25–26, 27, 29, 30, 35, 51, 53, 56, 57, 58, 61, 62

animadverti enim, iudices, audiri a vobis meum familiarem, L. Herennium, perattente. in quo etsi magna ex parte ingenio eius et dicendi genere quodam tenebamini, tamen non numquam verebar ne illa subtiliter ad criminandum inducta oratio ad animos vestros sensim ac leniter accederet. dixit enim multa de luxurie, multa de libidine, multa de vitiis iuventutis, multa de moribus et, qui in reliqua vita mitis esset et in hac suavitate humanitatis qua prope iam delectantur omnes versari periucunde soleret, fuit in hac causa pertristis quidam patruus, censor, magister; obiurgavit M. Caelium, sicut neminem umquam parens; multa de incontinentia intemperantiaque disseruit. quid quaeritis, iudices? ignoscebam vobis attente audientibus, propterea quod egomet tam triste illud, tam asperum genus orationis horrebam. [26] ac prima pars fuit illa quae me minus movebat, fuisse meo necessario Bestiae Caelium familiarem, cenasse apud eum, ventitasse domum, studuisse praeturae. non me haec movent quae perspicue falsa sunt; etenim eos una cenasse dixit qui aut absunt aut quibus necesse est idem dicere. neque vero illud me commovet quod sibi in Lupercis sodalem esse Caelium dixit. . . . [27] . . . deliciarum obiurgatio fuit longa, et ea lenior,[1] plusque disputationis habuit quam atrocita-

---

[1] et ea *codd.*: etiam *Clark*: et eo *Kayser*   alienior *unus cod.* (*fort.* et a causa alienior *Clark in app.*)

Against M. Caelius Rufus (F 1)

F 1 Cicero, *Pro Caelio*

Now I noticed, judges, that you listened to my friend L.
Herennius very attentively. Although in this you were influenced to a great extent by his ability and a particular
style of oratory, still at times I was afraid that his speech,
carefully presented to suggest guilt, might imperceptibly
and gently enter into your minds. For he said a lot about
profligacy, a lot about lust, a lot about the vices of youth,
a lot about morals; and, although he was gentle in the rest
of his life and was generally most pleasant in that charm
of courteous conduct that now delights almost everyone,
in this case he was some kind of very grim uncle, a censor,
a schoolmaster: he rebuked M. Caelius as nobody has ever
been by their parent; he set out much about lack of self-
restraint and want of moderation. What are you asking,
judges? I tried to excuse your careful listening, for the
reason that I myself was shuddering at such a glum, such
a bitter manner of speech. [26] And the first part of it,
which moved me less, was the claim that Caelius was intimate with my friend Bestia [L. Calpurnius Bestia], dined
with him, frequently visited him at home, helped him in
his candidacy for the praetorship. This does not trouble
me as it is evidently false; for he said that some people
dined together who are either not here or obliged to say
the same. Nor does it trouble me that he said that Caelius
was a fellow member of his in the Luperci [a college of
priests]. . . . [27] . . . The rebuking of decadent luxuries
was long, and it was rather on the quiet side; and it had
about it more of a discussion than harshness, so that it was

tis, quo etiam audita est attentius. . . . tibi autem, Balbe, respondeo primum precario, si licet, si fas est defendi a me eum qui nullum convivium renuerit, qui in hortis fuerit, qui unguenta sumpserit, qui Baias viderit. [28] . . . [29] sed tu mihi videbare ex communi infamia iuventutis aliquam invidiam Caelio velle conflare. . . . [30] . . . sunt autem duo crimina, auri et veneni; in quibus una atque eadem persona versatur. aurum sumptum a Clodia, venenum quaesitum quod Clodiae daretur, ut dicitur. omnia sunt alia non crimina, sed maledicta, iurgi petulantis magis quam publicae quaestionis. "adulter, impudicus, sequester" convicium est, non accusatio. . . . [35] . . . accusatores quidem libidines, amores, adulteria, Baias, actas, convivia, comissationes, cantus, symphonias, navigia iactant, idemque significant nihil se te invita dicere. . . . [51] . . . aurum sumpsit, ut dicitis, quod L. Luccei servis daret, per quos Alexandrinus Dio qui tum apud Lucceium habitabat necaretur. . . . [53] vidit hoc Balbus; celatam esse Clodiam dixit, atque ita Caelium ad illam attulisse, se ad ornatum ludorum aurum quaerere. . . . [56] . . . quin etiam L. Herennium dicere audistis verbo se molestum non futurum fuisse Caelio, nisi iterum eadem de re suo familiari abso-

also listened to with greater attention. . . . But it is you, Balbus, I answer first of all, with your kind permission, if it is lawful, if it is right that I should defend a man who has never refused a dinner, who has been in a park, who has used unguents, who has been to Baiae. [28] . . . [29] But you [Balbus] seemed to me to wish to trump up some prejudice against Caelius from the charges made against young men in general. . . . [30] . . . Now there are two charges [against Caelius specifically], relating to gold and to poison; in those one and the same individual is involved. The gold was taken from Clodia, the poison sought to be given to Clodia, as is alleged. All the other matters are not accusations, but slanders, matters rather of an aggressive quarrel than of a public judicial investigation. "Adulterer, lewd fellow, dealer in bribes" is abuse, not accusation. . . . [35] . . . The accusers are constantly talking about debauchery, amours, adultery, Baiae, seaside resorts, feasts, revels, concerts, musical parties, boats; and they make it clear that they say nothing against your [Clodia's] wishes. . . . [51] . . . [returning to the charges mentioned in section 30] The gold, as you [the accusers] claim, he [Caelius] took to give to the slaves of L. Lucceius [(**123**)], through whose help Dio of Alexandria [Academic philosopher], who at the time was living with Lucceius, was to be assassinated [cf. also *Cael.* 23–24]. . . . [53] Balbus had this point [potential knowledge and involvement of Clodia] in mind; he said that Clodia was not in on the secret and that Caelius told her the story that he wanted the gold for the expenses of games. . . . [56] . . . Moreover, you heard L. Herennius declare in his statement that he would not have made himself troublesome to Caelius if he [Caelius] had not a second time brought against his friend [L. Calpur-

307

luto nomen hic detulisset. . . . [57] cui denique commisit, quo adiutore usus est, quo socio, quo conscio, cui tantum facinus, cui se, cui salutem suam credidit? servisne mulieris? sic enim est obiectum. et erat tam demens is cui vos ingenium certe tribuitis, etiamsi cetera inimica oratione detrahitis, ut omnis suas fortunas alienis servis committeret? . . . [58] . . . habuisse aiunt domi vimque eius esse expertum in servo quodam ad eam rem² ipsam parato; cuius perceleri interitu esse ab hoc comprobatum venenum. . . . [61] . . . datum esse aiunt huic P. Licinio, pudenti adulescenti et bono, Caeli familiari; constitutum³ esse cum servis ut venirent ad balneas Senias; eodem Licinium esse venturum atque eis veneni pyxidem traditurum. . . . [62] "immo" inquit, "cum servi ad dominam rem totam et maleficium Caeli detulissent, mulier ingeniosa praecepit his ut omnia Caelio pollicerentur; sed ut venenum, cum a Licinio traderetur, manifesto comprehendi posset, constitui locum iussit balneas Senias, ut eo mitteret amicos, qui delitiscerent, deinde repente, cum venisset Licinius venenumque traderet, prosilirent hominemque comprenderent."

² ad eam rem *unus cod.*, *Madvig*: ad eadem rem *vel* ad rem *codd. cet.* ³ constitutum *Naugerius*: constitutum pactum *unus cod.*: constitutum factum *codd. cet.*

163 L. HERENNIUS BALBUS

nius Bestia], who had been acquitted, an action on the same charge [**162** F 19–22]. . . . [57] Finally, in whom did he [Caelius] confide, whom did he have as a supporter, whom as a partner, whom as an accomplice, to whom did he entrust such a great misdeed, entrust himself, entrust his own life? To the slaves of this woman? For thus it has been alleged. And was this man, whom you [the prosecutors] certainly credit with natural ability, although you deprive him of other qualities by your hostile language, such a fool as to entrust all his fortunes to another person's slaves? . . . [58] . . . They say that he [Caelius] had it [the poison] at home and tried its effect on some slave procured for that very purpose; that on account of his very speedy death the poison was approved by him. . . . [61] . . . They say that it was given to P. Licinius here, a decent and worthy young man, a friend of Caelius; that an arrangement was made with the slaves that they should come to the Senian Baths; there Licinius would meet them and hand over to them the box of poison. . . . [62] "No [i.e., there was no estrangement of Caelius and Clodia]," he [Balbus] says, "after the slaves had revealed to their mistress the whole affair and the villainy of Caelius, this crafty lady ordered them to promise anything to Caelius; but, so that the poison, when it was being handed over by Licinius, might be caught in the act, she ordered the Senian Baths to be arranged as a meeting place, where she might send some friends who could hide and then suddenly, when Licinius had arrived and was handing over the poison, might dart out and seize the man."

164 P. CLODIUS

P. Clodius (not in RE), like L. Herennius Balbus (163 F 1), was a supporter of the accuser L. Sempronius Atratinus (171 F 1–7) in the case against M. Caelius Rufus (162), who was defended by himself (162 F 23–28), M. Licinius

Against M. Caelius Rufus (F 1)

F 1 Cic. *Cael.* 27

nam P. Clodius, amicus meus, cum se gravissime vehe-mentissimeque iactaret et omnia inflammatus ageret tris-tissimis verbis, voce maxima, tametsi probabam eius elo-quentiam, tamen non pertimescebam; aliquot enim in causis eum videram frustra litigantem.

165 C. LICINIUS MACER CALVUS

C. Licinius Macer Calvus (RE Licinius 113), a son of C. Licinius Macer (110), is not recorded to have held any public offices and seems to have died at an early age (T 1, 5).

Calvus was a friend of the poet Catullus (Catull. 14, 50, 96; cf. Hor. Sat. 1.10.19; Ov. Am. 3.9.62) and a Neoteric poet himself (FPL[4], pp. 210–18). He may also have com-posed a work in prose about the use of cold water (Mart. 14.196). Tacitus knew of letters by him sent to Cicero and of twenty-one published speeches (T 8–9).

164 P. CLODIUS

*Crassus Dives (**102** F 12–13), and Cicero (Cic. Cael.)*
(TLRR 275). Cicero mentions that P. Clodius had ap-
peared in other court cases (F 1).

Against M. Caelius Rufus (F 1)

F 1 Cicero, *Pro Caelio*

For as for P. Clodius, a friend of mine, although he threw
himself into most impressive attitudes with the greatest
energy and went through everything full of fire with the
sternest language and a very loud voice, while I thought
well of his eloquence, still, I did not become very scared;
for in several suits I had seen him unsuccessful as a liti-
gant.

165 C. LICINIUS MACER CALVUS

The ancients praise Calvus as a great orator; he was
particularly noted for his energetic delivery, his learning,
and a carefully composed and Attic style, limited only by
*too much self-criticism (T 1–7, 10–11, 13; cf. **158** T 7).*
Cicero, focusing on Calvus' Attic style, regards his oratory
as not too effective with the public (T 1–2), while Seneca,
describing the passionate delivery, highlights its impact
(T 3). Calvus' oratory, like that of his contemporaries,
seemed old-fashioned to some in Tacitus' time (T 9).

311

T 1 Cic. *Brut.* 279–84

[CICERO:] "quamquam facienda mentio est, ut quidem mihi videtur, duorum adulescentium, qui si diutius vixissent magnam essent eloquentiae laudem consecuti." [280] "C. Curionem te," inquit BRUTUS, "et C. Licinium Calvum arbitror dicere." ". . . [283] sed ad Calvum—is enim nobis erat propositus—revertamur; qui orator fuit[1] cum litteris eruditior quam Curio tum etiam accuratius quoddam dicendi et exquisitius ạdferebat genus; quod quamquam scienter eleganterque tractabat, nimium tamen inquirens in se atque ipse sese observans metuensque ne vitiosum colligeret, etiam verum sanguinem deperdebat. itaque eius oratio nimia religione attenuata doctis et attente audientibus erat inlustris, ⟨a⟩[2] multitudine autem et a foro, cui nata eloquentia est, devorabatur." [284] tum BRUTUS: "Atticum se," inquit, "Calvus noster dici oratorem volebat; inde erat ista exilitas quam ille de industria consequebatur."

1 fuit *Corradus*: fuisset *codd.*: fuisset † *Friedrich*: cum fuisset *Schütz*: cum esset *Piderit*　　2 *add. edd.*

T 2 Cic. *Fam.* 15.21.4 [ad Trebonium]

nunc ad epistulam venio; cui copiose et suaviter scriptae nihil est quod multa respondeam. primum enim ego illas Calvo litteras misi non plus quam has quas nunc legis existimans exituras; aliter enim scribimus quod eos solos quibus mittimus, aliter quod multos lecturos putamus. de-

1 Trebonius had apparently obtained a letter sent from Cicero to Calvus in the past and criticized its contents. Calvus was probably already dead (cf. T 1) by the time of this epistolary exchange.

T 1 Cicero, *Brutus*

[CICERO:] "Yet mention ought to be made, as it seems to me at least, of two young men who, had they lived longer, would have obtained great renown for eloquence." [280] "You are referring to C. Curio [C. Scribonius Curio (**170**)] and C. Licinius Calvus, I guess," said BRUTUS. ". . . [**170** T 1] . . . [283] But let us return to Calvus—for he had been proposed by us—he was an orator more trained in scholarship than Curio, and in particular he presented a style of speaking more carefully elaborated and more recherché. Although he handled it in a knowledgeable and elegant fashion, yet examining and observing himself too much and fearing lest he might include anything faulty, he also lost true vitality. Therefore, his language, attenuated through too much scrupulousness, was great for the learned and for careful listeners, but ⟨by⟩ the multitude and by the Forum, for which eloquence is born, it was merely swallowed." [284] Here BRUTUS said: "Our friend Calvus wished to be called an Attic orator; that was the reason for that meagerness of style, which he cultivated deliberately."

T 2 Cicero, *Letters to Friends* [to Trebonius]

I come now to your letter, to which, eloquently and charmingly written, there is no need for me to say a lot in reply. For, first, I sent that letter to Calvus, not thinking that it would get into circulation any more than the one you are reading at this moment.[1] For we write in one way what we believe only the addressees will read, in another way what many will read. Secondly, I praised his talent more gener-

313

inde ingenium eius maioribus[1] extuli laudibus quam tu id
vere potuisse fieri putas primum quod ita iudicabam.
acute movebatur, genus quoddam sequebatur in quo iudicio lapsus, quo valebat, tamen adsequebatur quod probarat;[2] multae erant et reconditae litterae. vis non erat; ad
eam igitur adhortabar. in excitando autem et in acuendo
plurimum valet si laudes eum quem cohortere. habes de
Calvo iudicium et consilium meum; consilium, quod hor-
tandi causa laudavi, iudicium, quod de ingenio eius valde
existimavi bene.

[1] maioribus *Ernesti*: melioribus *codd.*: amplioribus *Orelli*
[2] probarat *Nipperdey*: probaret *codd.*

T 3 Sen. *Contr.* 7.4.6–8

CALVUS, qui diu cum Cicerone iniquissimam litem de
principatu eloquentiae habuit, usque eo violentus actor et
concitatus fuit, ut in media eius actione surgeret Vatinius
reus et exclamaret: "rogo vos, iudices: num,[1] si iste disertus est, ideo me damnari oportet?" [7] . . . solebat praeterea excedere subsellia sua et impetu latus usque in ad-
versariorum partem transcurrere. et carmina quoque eius,
quamvis iocosa si‹n›t,[2] plena sunt ingentis animi. . . . [8]
compositio quoque eius in actionibus ad exemplum De-
mosthenis viget: nihil in illa placidum, nihil lene est; omnia excitata et fluctuantia.

[1] num *edd.*: non *codd.*   [2] iocosa si‹n›t *Politianus*: iocosa
(*vel* ioca) sit *codd.*

ously than you believe could have happened truthfully;
this was first and foremost because I was of that opinion.
He was inspired by a keen intellect; he followed a certain
style [i.e., Atticism] in which, though he failed in judgment, in which he was generally strong, he still achieved
what he had approved; his reading was wide and recondite. There was no force; therefore I was urging him toward that. And in trying to rouse a man and spur him on,
it is of the greatest effect if you praise him whom you
admonish. You have my opinion of Calvus and my strategy:
the strategy that I praised in order to exhort, the opinion
that I thought very highly of his talent.

T 3 Seneca the Elder, *Controversiae*

CALVUS, who for a long time waged a most unequal contest with Cicero for the supremacy in oratory, was so violent and passionate a pleader that in the middle of a court
speech of his the defendant Vatinius [cf. F 14–28] got up
and exclaimed: "I ask you, judges: surely, just because that
man is eloquent, I should not therefore be convicted?" [7]
... [F 30] ... Moreover, he used to leave his own benches
and, carried by the impulse of the moment, would rush
right to his opponents' side. And his poetry, too, though it
is lighthearted, is full of great spirit. ... [8] Further, his
style in court speeches is vigorous on the model of Demosthenes: there is nothing sedate, nothing gentle about it,
everything excited and stormy. [continued by F 32]

T 4 Val. Max. 9.12.7

consimili impetu mortis C. Licinius Macer vir praetorius,
Calvi pater, repetundarum reus, dum sententiae diriberentur,[1] in maenianum conscendit. si quidem, cum M.
Ciceronem, qui id iudicium cogebat, praetextam ponen-
tem vidisset, misit ad eum qui diceret se non damnatum
sed reum perisse, nec sua bona hastae posse subici, ac
protinus, sudario, quod forte in manu habebat, ore et fau-
cibus suis coartatis, incluso spiritu poenam morte prae-
cucurrit. qua cognita re Cicero de eo nihil pronuntiavit.
igitur inlustris ingenii orator et ab inopia rei familiaris et
a crimine domesticae damnationis inusitato paterni fati
genere vindicatus est.

[1] diriberentur *Pighius*: diriverentur *vel* dirivarentur *vel* dicerentur *codd.*

T 5 Quint. *Inst.* 10.1.115

inveni qui Calvum praeferrent omnibus, inveni qui Ciceroni[1] crederent eum nimia contra se calumnia verum
sanguinem perdidisse; sed est et sancta et gravis oratio et
castigata et frequenter vehemens quoque. imitator autem
est Atticorum, fecitque illi properata mors iniuriam si quid
adiecturus sibi, non si quid detracturus, fuit.

[1] ciceroni *vel* ciceronem *codd.*: *del. Bonnet*

T 6 Quint. *Inst.* 10.2.25–26
= **121** T 5.

T 4 Valerius Maximus, *Memorable Doings and Sayings*

In a similar hurry to death [as Herennius Siculus, the preceding example] was C. Licinius Macer, an ex-praetor, Calvus' father; when on trial for extortion, he climbed up to a balcony while the votes were being sorted. When he had seen Cicero, who was president of that court [as praetor in 66 BC], taking off his toga praetexta [in preparation of pronouncing the verdict], he sent him someone to say that he had died, not as a man convicted, but as a defendant, and that his property could not be put to public auction. And immediately, he blocked his mouth and throat with a handkerchief that he happened to have in his hand and, having stopped his breathing, anticipated sentence by death. When Cicero learned of this, he pronounced no verdict about him. So an orator of shining talent was saved from lack of property and the reproach of a conviction in his family by his father's unusual mode of death.

T 5 Quintilian, *The Orator's Education*

I have found some who prefer Calvus to all others; I have found some who believe Cicero [T 1] that he lost true vitality by too much criticism of himself. But his oratory is solemn, serious, controlled, and often also energetic. Moreover, he is an imitator of the Attic writers, and his untimely death did him an injury, if he was on his way to add something to himself, not to take away anything.

T 6 Quintilian, *The Orator's Education*

= **121** T 5.

T 7 Quint. *Inst.* 12.10.11

= **140** T 2.

T 8 Tac. *Dial.* 18.5

= **158** T 11.

T 9 Tac. *Dial.* 21.1

[APER:] ipse mihi Calvus, cum unum et viginti, ut puto, libros reliquerit, vix in una aut[1] altera oratiuncula satis facit.

  [1] aut *Puteolanus*: et *codd.*

T 10 Tac. *Dial.* 25.3–4

= **121** T 7.

T 11 Plin. *Ep.* 1.2.2 [ad Maturum Arrianum]

temptavi enim imitari Demosthenen semper tuum, Calvum nuper meum, dumtaxat figuris orationis; nam vim tantorum virorum, "pauci quos aequus . . ." [Verg. *Aen.* 6.129] adsequi[1] possunt.

  [1] quos equos assequi *vel* quos aequus amavit qui *vel* equitius adsequi *codd.*

T 12 Fronto, *Ad M. Antoninum de eloquentia* 1.2 (p. 134.3–5 van den Hout)

. . . iam in iudiciis . . . Calvus rixatur [cf. **48** T 11].

165 C. LICINIUS MACER CALVUS

T 7 Quintilian, *The Orator's Education*
= **140** T 2.

T 8 Tacitus, *Dialogue on Oratory*
= **158** T 11.

T 9 Tacitus, *Dialogue on Oratory*

[APER:] In fact, in my view, Calvus, although he left be-
hind, I believe, twenty-one books, is satisfactory hardly in
one or two of his little speeches.

T 10 Tacitus, *Dialogue on Oratory*
= **121** T 7.

T 11 Pliny the Younger, *Letters* [to Maturus Arrianus]

For I have always tried to model myself on your Demosthenes and recently on my Calvus, though only in figures
of speech; for the force of great men like these can only
be achieved by "a few, whom kindly Jupiter . . ."[1]

> [1] Verg. *Aen.* 6.129–31: *pauci, quos aequus amavit / Iuppiter
> aut ardens evexit ad aethera virtus, / dis geniti potuere.* ("A few,
> whom kindly Jupiter has loved or shining worth has uplifted to
> heaven, sons of gods, have been able to.")

T 12 Fronto, *Correspondence*

. . . further, in the courts . . . Calvus quarrels [cf. **48** T 11].

T 13 Apul. *Apol.* 95

= **92** T 11.

Against P. Vatinius (F 14–28)

While still a fairly young man, Calvus seems to have attempted to take P. Vatinius to court three times: in 58 BC he charged him under the Lex Licinia Iunia de legum latione *of 62 BC (Cic.* Vat. *33; LPPR, pp. 383–84); the case seems to have been curtailed by the intercession of the Tribune of the People P. Clodius Pulcher (***137***) upon Vatinius' pleading (TLRR 255; Cic.* Vat. *33–34; on the political context see Gruen 1971, 62–67). In 56 BC there was a charge of* ambitus *under the* Lex Tullia de ambitu *of 63 BC (Cic.* Vat. *37; LPPR, p. 379), but the trial may have been dropped (TLRR 274). In 54 BC, Calvus prosecuted Vatin-*

F 14 Quint. *Inst.* 12.6.1

= **121** F 16.

F 15 Tac. *Dial.* 34.7

= **121** F 15.

F 16 Schol. Bob. ad Cic. *Vat.* 34 (p. 150.17–25 Stangl)

haec facta sunt cum reus esset de vi P. Vatinius accusante C. Licinio. nam cum praetor C. Memmius quaesitorem sortito facere vellet et Vatinius postularet ut ipse ⟨et⟩[1]

---

[1] *add. Osenbrueggen*

T 13 Apuleius, *Apologia*

= **92** T 11.

Against P. Vatinius (F 14–28)

ius under the Lex Licinia de sodaliciis *of 55 BC (LPPR,*
p. 407); defended by Cicero (Cic. Pro Vatinio: *Crawford*
1994, 271–80), Vatinius was acquitted (TLRR 292; Schol.
Bob. ad Cic. Planc. *40 [p. 160.22 St.]). How often Calvus*
actually prosecuted Vatinius, how many speeches there
were, and which occasion the individual testimonia (some
inaccurate) refer to is uncertain: there was certainly a trial
in 54 BC, but the notices of earlier trials may be confused
or just illustrate a hostile political atmosphere (Gruen
1967, 217–21).

F 14 Quintilian, *The Orator's Education*

= **121** F 16.

F 15 Tacitus, *Dialogue on Oratory*

= **121** F 15.

F 16 Scholia Bobiensia to Cicero, *Against Vatinius*

This [violent action against those in charge of the trial as
described by Cicero] happened when P. Vatinius was
charged with violence and C. Licinius was the prosecutor.
For when the praetor C. Memmius [**125**; praet. 58 BC]
wished to determine the president of the court by lot, and
Vatinius demanded that he himself ⟨and⟩ his prosecutor

accusator suus mutuas reiectiones de quaesitoribus facerent—ipsius etenim Vatinii lege, quam tulerat in tribunatu, non satis aperte neque distincte apparebat utrum
sorte quaesitor esset deligendus an vero mutua inter ad-
versarios facienda reiectione—conspirati quidam pro ipso
Vatinio inmissi tribunal conscenderunt et sortes quae intra
urnam continebantur dispergere adgressi sunt. atque ita
effectum est gratiose per P. Clodium ut omnia secundum
voluntatem suam Vatinius obtineret.

F 17 Schol. Bob. ad Cic. *Vat.* 10 (p. 145.7–10 Stangl)

. . . contra vero huic Vatinio et honorem quaesturae post
omnes novissimo loco datum et adhuc damnationis eius
nutare fortunam. reus postulatus erat accusatore C. Licinio Calvo.

F 18 Cic. *Q Fr.* 2.4.1

quin etiam Paullus noster, cum testis productus esset in
Sestium, confirmavit se nomen Vatini delaturum si Macer
Licinius cunctaretur, et Macer ab Sesti subselliis surrexit
ac se illi non defuturum adfirmavit.

put forward their respective rejections of presidents of the court—for according to the law of Vatinius himself [*Lex Vatinia de reiectione iudicum: LPPR*, p. 391], which he had proposed during his Tribunate [59 BC], it was not evident in a sufficiently obvious and clear fashion whether the president of the court was to be selected by lot or rather by the respective rejection among the opponents— some conspirators, sent on behalf of Vatinius himself, as-cended the tribunal and started to scatter the lots that were contained in the urn. And so it was achieved in a biased way through the agency of P. Clodius [P. Clodius Pulcher (**137**), tr. pl. 58 BC] that Vatinius obtained every-thing according to his wishes.

F 17 Scholia Bobiensia to Cicero, *Against Vatinius*

. . . but that, by contrast [to Cicero], both the honor of a quaestorship [63 BC] was given to this Vatinius after ev-eryone else in the very last place and that up to now the fortune of his conviction remained undecided. He had been summoned as a defendant with C. Licinius Calvus as prosecutor.

F 18 Cicero, *Letters to Quintus*

What is more, our friend Paullus [L. Aemilius (Lepidus?) Paullus, cos. 50 BC], when he was produced as a witness against Sestius [P. Sestius (**135**)], confirmed that he would prosecute Vatinius if Licinius Macer was hesitant, and Macer rose from Sestius' benches [cf. F 29] and affirmed that he would not fail him [Vatinius; i.e., prosecute him].

F 19 Tac. *Dial.* 21.2

[APER:] at hercule in omnium studiosorum manibus versantur accusationes quae in Vatinium inscribuntur,[1] ac praecipue secunda ex his oratio; est enim verbis ornata et sententiis, auribus iudicum accommodata, ut scias ipsum quoque Calvum intellexisse quid melius esset, nec voluntatem ei, quo ⟨minus⟩[2] sublimius et cultius diceret, sed ingenium ac vires defuisse.

> [1] inscribuntur *Lipsius*: conscribuntur *codd.*   [2] *add. Halm*

F 20 Sen. *Contr.* 7.4.6

= T 3.

F 21 Catull. 53

risi nescio quem modo e corona, / qui, cum mirifice Vatiniana / meus[1] crimina Calvos[2] explicasset, / admirans ait haec manusque tollens, / "di magni, salaputium[3] disertum!"[4]

> [1] meus *corrector unius cod.*: meos *codd.*   [2] calvus *corrector unius cod.*   [3] salaputium *unus cod. rec.*: salapantium *codd.*   [4] disertum *codd. rec.*: desertum *codd.*

F 22 Quint. *Inst.* 6.1.13

nam egregie in Vatinium Calvus "factum" inquit "ambitum scitis omnes, et hoc vos scire omnes sciunt."

Cf. Sen. *Ep.* 94.25.

F 19 Tacitus, *Dialogue on Oratory*

[APER:] But, by Hercules, the prosecution speeches that are entitled *Against Vatinius* are in the hands of all students, and especially the second oration of these; for it is elaborate in diction and pointed statements, well suited to the ears of judges, so that you may see that Calvus himself too had realized what was better and that he was not lacking will where he spoke in a ⟨less⟩ elevated and elegant fashion, but rather talent and force.

F 20 Seneca the Elder, *Controversiae*

= T 3.

F 21 Catullus

I laughed just now because of some fellow in the crowd: when my Calvus had drawn out in splendid style the accusations against Vatinius, he said, in amazement and lifting up his hands: "Great gods, what an eloquent manikin!" [cf. F 30]

F 22 Quintilian, *The Orator's Education*

For Calvus, [in the speech] against Vatinius, admirably says: "You all know that bribery took place, and everyone knows that you know this."

F 23 Quint. *Inst.* 9.2.25

paene idem fons est illius quam "permissionem" vocant
qui communicationis, cum aliqua ipsis iudicibus relinqui-
mus aestimanda, aliqua nonnumquam adversariis quoque,
ut Calvus Vatinio: "perfrica frontem et dic te digniorem
qui praetor fieres quam Catonem."

Cf. Isid. *Etym.* 2.21.30.

F 24 Quint. *Inst.* 6.3.60

sunt quaedam † vi † similia, unde Vatinius dixit hoc dictum, cum reus agente in eum Calvo frontem candido sudario tergeret idque ipsum accusator in invidiam vocaret:
"quamvis reus sum," inquit, "et panem tamen[1] candidum
edo."

  [1] panem tamen *Winterbottom*: parentem *vel* panem *codd.*:
panem item *Haupt*

F 25 Aquila Rom., *RLM*, p. 35.4–8

egregie autem et, ut mihi videtur, feliciter Licinius Calvus
in Vatinium: "non ergo pecuniarum magis repetundarum
quam maiestatis, neque maiestatis magis quam Plautiae
legis, neque Plautiae legis magis quam ambitus, neque

F 23 Quintilian, *The Orator's Education*

There is pretty much the same source for what they call "permission"[1] as there is for engaging others, when we leave some points to the judges themselves to assess and some occasionally also to the opponents, as Calvus [said] to Vatinius: "Wipe away the blushes from your face and tell us that you are worthier of becoming praetor than Cato."

[1] Greek *epitropē*: see Rutilius 2.17 (*RLM*, p. 20.12–19); *Rhet. Her.* 4.39; Lausberg 1998, §857.

F 24 Quintilian, *The Orator's Education*

There are some similarities based on the quality of things [?]: thus, when Vatinius, being a defendant with Calvus prosecuting him, wiped his forehead with a white handkerchief, and the prosecutor tried to use this very action to create resentment, he [Vatinius] made this remark: "Though I may be a defendant," he said, "I still eat also white bread."[1]

[1] The accused would be expected to be dressed in dark colors. According to Pliny the Elder, white wheat is of particular quality (Plin. *HN* 18.63–65).

F 25 Aquila Romanus

But excellently and, as it seems to me, felicitously Licinius Calvus [said] against Vatinius: "Not, then, have trials for the recovery of extorted money come to an end more than those for treason, nor those for treason more than those under the *Lex Plautia* [*Lex Plautia de vi*: *LPPR*, pp. 377–78], nor those under the *Lex Plautia* more than those for

ambitus magis quam omnium legum omnia iudicia perierunt."

Cf. Quint. *Inst.* 9.3.56; Diom., *GL* I, p. 448.21–25.

F 26 Iul. Severian. *Praec.* 19, *RLM*, p. 366.2–7

movemus . . . livorem autem simul cum odio, ut Calvus in Vatinium, cum dicit: "hominem nostrae civitatis audacissimum, de factione divitem, sordidum, maledicum accuso."[1]

---

[1] accuso *codd.*: accusatorem *ed. Lucae Fruterii*: accusato *ed. Pith. et Capp.*: accusabo *Ruhnkenius*

F 27 Charis., *GL* I, p. 224.19–20 = p. 289.13–14 B.

vehementissime pro fortissime et vere Calvus in Vatinium: "vehementissime probare."

F 28 Charis., *GL* I, p. 229.9–12 = pp. 296.21–97.1 B.

ad pro autem Licinius Calvus in P. Vatinium ambitus ⌊reum⌋:[1] "ad ita mihi Iovem deosque inmortales velim bene fecisse, iudices, ut ego pro certo habeo si parvuli ⌊pueri de ambitu iudicarent," cum certum sit⌋[2] at coniunctionem esse, ad vero praepositionem . . .

---

[1] add. *Cauchii et Putschenii ex deperdito cod. excerpta*
[2] pueri . . . sit *add. frag. cod., Cauchii et Putschenii ex deperdito cod. excerpta*: pueri *om. Cauchius, Putschen*: cum certum sit *om. Putschen*

bribery, nor those for bribery more than all those under all laws."

F 26 Iulius Severianus

And we move . . . envy together with hatred, like Calvus against Vatinius, when he says: "I prosecute a man, the most reckless in our community, rich from factions, avaricious, a slanderer."

F 27 Charisius

vehementissime ["very energetically"], instead of *fortissime* ["very forcefully"] and *vere* ["truly"], Calvus against Vatinius: "to prove very forcefully and truly."

F 28 Charisius

ad ["toward"], instead of *autem* ["but"], Licinius Calvus against P. Vatinius, accused of bribery: "But I wish that Jupiter and the immortal gods deliver well for me in such a way, judges, as I know for sure if little boys decided about bribery," although it is certain that *at* ["but"] is a conjunction and *ad* ["toward"] a preposition . . .

On Behalf of P. Sestius (F 29)

In 56 BC Calvus was among the advocates defending P. Sestius (135), including Q. Hortensius Hortalus (92 F 43–45), M. Licinius Crassus Dives (102 F 11), and Cicero

29 Schol. Bob. ad Cic. *Sest.*, arg. (p. 125.15–26 Stangl) = **92** F 45.

Against His Client C. Porcius Cato (F 30)

When C. Porcius Cato (136) had been Tribune of the People in 56 BC, he was prosecuted on two counts; the prosecutor at one or both trials was C. Asinius Pollio (174 F 15–18), and the advocate was M. Aemilius Scaurus (139 F 4). The defendant was acquitted (TLRR 283, 286; Cic. Att. 4.15.4, 4.16.5–6). Calvus, though sometimes seen as another prosecutor (TLRR 283, 286; Marshall 1985, 121),

F 30 Sen. *Contr.* 7.4.7

idem postea, cum videret a clientibus Catonis, rei sui, Pollionem Asinium circumventum in foro cae<di>,[1] imponi se supra cippum iussit—erat enim parvolus statura, propter quod etiam Catullus in hendecasyllabis vocat[2] illum "salaputium[3] disertum" [F 21]—et iuravit, si quam iniuriam Cato Pollioni Asinio accusatori suo fecisset, se in eum iuraturum calumniam; nec umquam postea Pollio a Catone advocatisque eius aut re aut verbo violatus est.

[1] foro cae<di> *Madvig*: fore cae *codd.*   [2] Catullus *codd. det.*: caturus *codd.*   hendecasyllabis vocat *codd. det.*: hendecasyllabi sucat *codd.*   [3] salapputtium *vel* salaputtium *codd.*: salapantium *codd. ad Cat. 53.5*

On Behalf of P. Sestius (F 29)

(Cic. Sest.), when P. Sestius was prosecuted by P. Albi-novanus under the Lex Plautia de vi *(TLRR 271; Alexander 2002, 206–17).*

F 29 Scholia Bobiensia to Cicero, *Pro Sestio*
= **92** F 45.

Against His Client C. Porcius Cato (F 30)

is more likely to have been Cato's defense (Gruen 1967, 223–24; 1974, 315; Linderski 1969, 296 and n. 70), as the wording of the passage below suggests. It attests an additional statement outside court: Calvus, though defending Cato, intervened when Asinius Pollio was attacked by Cato's supporters.

F 30 Seneca the Elder, *Controversiae*

[cf. T 3] The same man [Calvus], later, when he saw Asinius Pollio [C. Asinius Pollio (**174**), F 15–18] surrounded and beaten up in the Forum by clients of Cato [C. Porcius Cato (**136**)], a man defended by him [Calvus], ordered himself put up on a pillar—for he was short of stature, whence Catullus too describes him as an "eloquent manikin" in his hendecasyllables [F 21]—and swore that, if Cato had done any injury to Asinius Pollio, his [Cato's] accuser, he would initiate a justified accusation against him [Cato]. And never after that was Pollio harmed in word or deed by Cato and his supporters.

Against Asicius (F 31)

The Asicius prosecuted was probably P. Asicius, accused
of being an accomplice in the murder of Dio of Alexandria,
an Academic philosopher sent as an ambassador from

F 31 Tac. *Dial.* 21.2

[APER:] nec dissentire ceteros ab hoc meo iudicio video:
quotus enim quisque Calvi in Asicium[1] aut in Drusum
legit?

[1] Asicium *vel* Asitium *codd.*

Against Drusus (F 31A)

The defendant Drusus might have been M. Livius Drusus
Claudianus, who was prosecuted by Calvus and Q. Lucre-
tius in summer 54 BC (Cic. Att. 4.16.5). He was defended

F 31A Tac. *Dial.* 21.2

= F 31.

On Behalf of C. Messius (F 32)

F 32 Sen. *Contr.* 7.4.8

hic tamen in epilogo, quem pro Messio tunc tertio causam

165 C. LICINIUS MACER CALVUS

Against Asicius (F 31)

Alexandria to Rome in 57 BC. Asicius was defended by Cicero (Cic. Pro Asicio: Crawford 1984, 138–40) and acquitted (TLRR 267; Cic. Cael. 23–24).

F 31 Tacitus, *Dialogue on Oratory*

[APER:] And I do not see that others dissent from this assessment of mine [i.e., that the works of orators of earlier periods are not worth engaging with]. For how very few read Calvus' [speeches] against Asicius or against Drusus?

Against Drusus (F 31A)

by Cicero (Cic. Pro M. Livio Druso [Claudiano]: Crawford 1984, 182–83) and acquitted (TLRR 290; Cic. Att. 4.15.9, 4.17.5; Q Fr. 2.16.3).

F 31A Tacitus, *Dialogue on Oratory*

= F 31.

On Behalf of C. Messius (F 32)

C. Messius (tr. pl. 57, aed. 55 BC), prosecuted in summer 54 BC, was defended by Cicero (Cic. Pro C. Messio: Crawford 1984, 180–81) and Calvus; the outcome of the trial is uncertain (TLRR 289).

F 32 Seneca the Elder, *Controversiae*

[continued from T 3] Yet in the peroration, which he [Calvus] delivered for Messius, then in court for the third time,

dicente habuit, non tantum leniter[1] componit sed ‹summisse›,[2] cum dicit: "credite mihi, non est turpe misereri"; et omnia in illo epilogo fere non tantum emollitae compositionis sunt sed infractae.

[1] leniter *codd. det.*: leviter *codd.*   [2] *add. Müller*

Unplaced Fragments (F 33–37)

F 33 Plin. *HN* 33.140

vasa coquinaria ex argento fieri Calvus orator quiritat . . .

F 34 Sen. *Contr.* 1, *praef.* 12

. . . sicut ipsa "declamatio" apud nullum antiquum auctorem ante Ciceronem et Calvum inveniri potest, qui declamationem ‹a dictione›[1] distinguit; ait enim declamare iam se non mediocriter, dicere bene; alterum putat domesticae exercitationis esse, alterum verae actionis.

[1] *add. Gertz*

F 35 Quint. *Inst.* 1.6.42

= **162** F 38.

F 36 Charis., *GL* I, p. 81.24–25 = p. 102.20–22 B.

stomachus etiam in pluribus singulariter dicitur, ut ait Calvus: "quorum praedulcem cibum stomachus ferre non potest."[1]

[1] potest *Fabricius*: possunt *codd.*

he uses not only a gentle, but a ⟨submissive⟩ style of composition, when he says: "Believe me, it is not shameful to feel pity." And virtually everything in that peroration is not only of a soft, but of an effeminate composition.

Unplaced Fragments (F 33–37)

F 33 Pliny the Elder, *Natural History*

The orator Calvus cries out in protest that cooking pots are made of silver . . .

F 34 Seneca the Elder, *Controversiae*

. . . just as the term *declamatio* itself can be found in no old author before Cicero and Calvus. He [Calvus] distinguishes *declamatio* ["declamation"] ⟨from *dictio* ["speech"]⟩: for he says that by now he is declaiming not badly, speaking well; the former he regards as appropriate for exercises at home, the latter for a real speech.

F 35 Quintilian, *The Orator's Education*

= **162** F 38.

F 36 Charisius

stomachus is used in the singular even when referring to many, as Calvus says: "Their stomach cannot bear very sweet food."

F 37 Mar. Vict., *GL* VI, p. 9.1–4

Licinius Calvus q littera non est usus. consultum senati[1]
ipse scripsit, et ad C. Caesarem senatus consultum. idem
optimus maximus scripsit, non ut nos per u litteram.

  [1] consultum senati *vel* consultum senatus *codd.*: consultum
senatuis *Gaisfordius*: consultum senati idem saepe scripsit et ad
C. Caesarem senatuis consultum *maluit Keil*

166 M. FAVONIUS

*M. Favonius (praet. 49 BC [questioned by Ryan 1994]; RE
Favonius 1) fought alongside M. Iunius Brutus (**158**) and
C. Cassius Longinus at Philippi (42 BC) after the assas-
sination of C. Iulius Caesar (**121**); captured, he was pun-
ished and put to death (Suet. Aug. 13.2; Cass. Dio 47.49.4).*
  *Favonius studied oratory with Apollonius Molo at
Rhodes (F 3) and is described as having a direct and im-
petuous way of speaking, bordering on the offensive (T 1;*

T 1 Plut. *Brut.* 34.4–6

Μάρκος δὲ Φαώνιος, ἐραστὴς γεγονὼς Κάτωνος, οὐ
λόγῳ μᾶλλον ἢ φορᾷ τινι καὶ πάθει μανικῷ φιλοσο-
φῶν, ἐβάδιζεν εἴσω πρὸς αὐτοὺς κωλυόμενος ὑπὸ τῶν
οἰκετῶν. [5] ἀλλ᾽ ἔργον ἦν ἐπιλαβέσθαι Φαωνίου πρὸς
ὁτιοῦν ὁρούσαντος· σφοδρὸς γὰρ ἦν ἐν πᾶσι καὶ πρό-
χειρος. ἐπεὶ τό γε βουλευτὴν εἶναι Ῥωμαίων ἑαυτὸν

F 37 Marius Victorinus

Licinius Calvus did not use the letter *q*. He himself wrote *consultum senati* ["decree of the Senate"], and to Caesar [C. Iulius Caesar (**121**)] *senatus consultum* ["Senate's decree"; usual form of genitive for this declension]. The same man wrote *optimus maximus* ["the best, the greatest"], not, as we do, with the letter *u* [i.e., *optumus maxumus*; archaic or archaizing form].

166 M. FAVONIUS

Plut. Pomp. 60.7; Cic. Att. 4.17.4); he seems to have followed the Cynic school of philosophy (T 1).

*Favonius was among senators unhappy with the extensive powers requested for Cn. Pompeius Magnus (**111**) in autumn 57 BC (Cic. Att. 4.1.7); in early 56 BC Favonius belonged to a group of politicians confronting Cn. Pompeius Magnus (**111**) (Cic. Q Fr. 2.3.2).*

*A fragment transmitted for [Favorinus] (**52**) is sometimes attributed to M. Favonius (see **52**).*

T 1 Plutarch, *Life of Brutus*

But Marcus Favonius, who had become a devotee of Cato [M. Porcius Cato (**126**); cf. Plut. *Caes.* 21.8] and who engaged with philosophy not so much with reason as with some impetuousness and crazy passion, tried to go in to them [M. Iunius Brutus (**158**) and C. Cassius Longinus, who had withdrawn to a locked room] and was prevented by their servants. [5] It was a bit of work, however, to stop Favonius when he rushed toward anything; for he was vehement in all matters and rash. The fact that he was a

οὐδενὸς ἄξιον ἡγεῖτο, τῷ δὲ κυνικῷ τῆς παρρησίας
πολλάκις ἀφῄρει τὴν χαλεπότητα, καὶ τὸ ἄκαιρον
αὐτοῦ μετὰ παιδιᾶς δεχομένων. [6] βίᾳ δὴ τότε τῶν
παρόντων διωσάμενος τὰς θύρας εἰσῆλθε, μετὰ πλά-
σματος φωνῆς ἔπη περαίνων οἷς τὸν Νέστορα χρώ-
μενον Ὅμηρος πεποίηκεν [Hom. *Il.* 1.259]· 'ἀλλὰ πί-
θεσθ'· ἄμφω δὲ νεωτέρω ἐστὸν ἐμεῖο,' καὶ τὰ ἑξῆς.

Against the Voting on a Bill of M. Pupius
Piso Frugi Calpurnianus (F 2)

F 2 Cic. *Att.* 1.14.5
= **126** F 17.

Against Q. Caecilius Metellus Pius
Scipio Nasica (F 3)

After Favonius had been unsuccessful in his candidacy for
a political office, he prosecuted his successful competitor
Q. Caecilius Metellus Pius Scipio Nasica (154) for ambitus

F 3 Cic. *Att.* 2.1.9

Favonius meam tribum tulit honestius quam suam, Luccei
perdidit. accusavit Nasicam inhoneste ac modeste tamen;
dixit ita ut Rhodi videretur molis potius quam Moloni ope-

Roman senator he considered to be of no importance, and
from the "cynical" frankness of his speech he often took
away its offensiveness, and therefore men took his inappropriate conduct with good humor. [6] Thus, at that time,
he forced his way through the bystanders and entered the
room, reciting in an affected voice the words that Homer
had made Nestor use [Hom. *Il.* 1.259]: "But listen to me,
for both of you are younger than me," and what follows.

Against the Voting on a Bill of M. Pupius
Piso Frugi Calpurnianus (F 2)

*In 61 BC Favonius, along with others, spoke against the
proposal of a bill by the consul M. Pupius Piso Frugi Calpurnianus (104).*

F 2 Cicero, *Letters to Atticus*

= **126** F 17.

Against Q. Caecilius Metellus Pius
Scipio Nasica (F 3)

*in 60 BC; Cicero supported the defendant, who was ac-
quitted (Cic. Pro Q. Caecilio Metello Pio Scipione [Na-
sica]: Crawford 1984, 115–17) (TLRR 238).*

F 3 Cicero, *Letters to Atticus*

Favonius carried my tribe with greater credit than his
own; he lost Lucceius'. He prosecuted Nasica shamefully,
yet still in a restrained manner. He spoke in such a way
that he seemed to have spent his time at Rhodes working

ram dedisse. mihi quod defendissem leviter suscensuit.
nunc tamen petit iterum rei publicae causa.

On Ptolemy in the Senate (F 4)

F 4 Cass. Dio 39.14.1

καίτοι τὸ πρᾶγμα οὕτω περιβόητον ἐγένετο ὥστε καὶ
τὴν βουλὴν ἀγανακτῆσαι δεινῶς, ἐνάγοντός σφας ὅτι
μάλιστα Φαουωνίου τοῦ Μάρκου καθ’ ἑ‹κά›τερον,[1] ὅτι
τε πολλοὶ παρὰ τῶν συμμάχων πρέσβεις πεμφθέντες
βιαίως ἀπωλώλεσαν, καὶ ὅτι συχνοὶ καὶ τότε τῶν Ῥωμαίων ἐδεδωροδοκήκεσαν.

[1] ἑ‹κά›τερον *Reimarus:* ἕτερον *cod.*

Against Measures of C. Trebonius (F 5)

F 5 Cass. Dio 39.34.1–2

. . . ὁ δὲ δὴ Κάτων καὶ ὁ Φαουώνιος ἠναντιοῦντο μὲν
πᾶσι τοῖς πρασσομένοις ὑπ’ αὐτῶν, συνεργοὺς ἄλ-

at the mill [*molae*] rather than with Molo. He was a bit angry with me because I had appeared for the defense. Now, however, he is standing again, for the sake of the Republic.

On Ptolemy in the Senate (F 4)

In 57 BC Favonius called the Roman Senate to action against Ptolemy XII, since violence had been used, and Romans had accepted bribes.

F 4 Cassius Dio, *Roman History*

The affair [Ptolemy's activities], however, became so noised abroad that even the Senate was mightily displeased, while Marcus Favonius in particular urged them to action, on the two grounds that many envoys sent by the allies had perished by violence and that numerous Romans had again on this occasion taken bribes.

Against Measures of C. Trebonius (F 5)

In 55 BC Favonius spoke against measures of the Tribune of the People C. Trebonius, as did M. Porcius Cato (126), who also opposed a bill of Trebonius on the allocation of consular provinces (126 F 25).

F 5 Cassius Dio, *Roman History*

. . . On the other hand, Cato [M. Porcius Cato (**126**)] and Favonius resisted all their schemes, having some others

341

λους τέ τινας καὶ τοὺς δύο δημάρχους ἔχοντες, ἅτε δὲ
ὀλίγοι πρὸς πολλοὺς ἀγωνιζόμενοι μάτην ἐπαρρησι-
άζοντο. [2] καὶ ὁ μὲν Φαουώνιος μίαν ὥραν μόνην
παρὰ τοῦ Τρεβωνίου πρὸς τὴν ἀντιλογίαν λαβών,
κατέτριψεν αὐτὴν ὑπὲρ αὐτῆς τῆς τοῦ καιροῦ στενο-
χωρίας εἰκῇ βοῶν . . .

On Behalf of the People of Tenedos (F 6)

F 6 Cic. *Q Fr.* 2.10(9).2
= **122** F 7.

167 M. IUVENTIUS LATERENSIS

*M. Iuventius Laterensis (praet. 51 BC; RE Iuventius 16)
withdrew his candidacy for Tribune of the People in 59
BC, so as not to have to support Caesar's agrarian law* (Lex
Iulia agraria: LPPR, *pp.* 387–88; *Cic.* Att. 2.18.2; Planc.

Against Cn. Plancius (F 1–2)

*In 55 BC, in the competition for the curule aedileship,
Laterensis, a nobleman, was defeated by the knight Cn.
Plancius. Thereupon, he, along with L. Cassius Longinus
(***168** F 1***), prosecuted Plancius under the* Lex Licinia de

and the two Tribunes [C. Ateius Capito and P. Aquillius Gallus, tr. pl. 55 BC] as supporters; but since they were fighting as a few against many, their outspokenness was without any effect. [2] And Favonius, who obtained from Trebonius only one hour for his speech in opposition, used it up in uttering protests against this very limitation of the time in vain . . .

On Behalf of the People of Tenedos (F 6)

In 54 BC Favonius was one of the orators speaking on behalf of the liberty of the people of Tenedos.

F 6 Cicero, *Letters to Quintus*

= **122** F 7.

167 M. IUVENTIUS LATERENSIS

13, 52–53; Schol. Bob. ad Cic. Planc. *52 [pp. 161.29–62.3 St.]). In 43 BC he killed himself (Vell. Pat. 2.63.2; Cass. Dio 46.51.3).*

Against Cn. Plancius (F 1–2)

sodaliciis of 55 BC (LPPR, p. 407). Plancius was defended by Cicero (Cic. Planc.*) and acquitted (TLRR 293). In his speech Cicero engages with the arguments allegedly made by the opponent.*

F 1 Schol. Bob. ad Cic. *Planc.*, *arg.* (p. 153.9–13 Stangl)

causa pendet ex aedilitatis petitione, in qua designatus est Plancius repulsam ferente Iuventio Laterense patriciae familiae, senatore, nec minore facundia quam generis nobilitate praedito. qui nunc etiam reum de sodaliciis facit, invidioso crimine et reis metuendo propter iudices editicios de quorum condicione supra diximus.

F 2 Cic. *Planc.* 3, 4, 6, 11, 16, 18, 23, 28, 30, 31, 33, 36, 38, 43, 47, 51, 53, 54, 55, 58, 71, 72, 75, 76, 77, 83, 84, 85, 86, 90, 91, 95

equidem ad reliquos labores, quos in hac causa maiores suscipio quam in ceteris, etiam hanc molestiam adsumo, quod mihi non solum pro Cn. Plancio dicendum est, cuius ego salutem non secus ac meam tueri debeo, sed etiam pro me ipso, de quo accusatores plura paene quam de re reoque dixerunt. [4] . . . quae vero ita sunt agitata ab illis ut aut merita Cn. Planci erga me minora esse dicerent quam a me ipso praedicarentur, aut, si essent summa, negarent ea tamen ita magni ut ego putarem ponderis apud vos esse debere, haec mihi sunt tractanda, iudices, et modice, ne quid ipse offendam, et tum denique cum respondero criminibus, ne non tam innocentia reus sua, quam recordatione meorum temporum, defensus esse videatur. [5] . . . [6] quaerit enim Laterensis atque hoc uno maxime urget qua se virtute, qua laude Plancius, qua dig-

---

1 That is, Cicero's exile: Plancius, quaestor in Macedonia in 58 BC, offered shelter to Cicero (e.g., Cic. *Red. sen.* 35).

167 M. IUVENTIUS LATERENSIS

F 1 Scholia Bobiensia to Cicero, *Pro Plancio*

The case hangs on the candidacy in which Plancius became aedile-elect, while defeat was suffered by Iuventius Laterensis, a senator of patrician family, endowed with no less eloquence than nobility of descent. He [Laterensis] now even charges him with conspiracy, a crime arousing hatred and to be feared by the accused because of the proposed judges, about whose terms [of selection] we have spoken above [chosen mainly according to the preferences of the accuser; cf. p. 152.27–31 St.].

F 2 Cicero, *Pro Plancio*

In addition to the remaining labors, which I undertake in this case as greater ones than in others, I take upon myself also this burden that I have to speak not only on behalf of Cn. Plancius, whose safety I must protect no less than my own, but also on behalf of myself, about whom the prosecutors have said almost more than about the case and the defendant. [4] . . . But these points have been brought up by those men, namely that they said that the services of Cn. Plancius for me were less than they were presented as being by me myself, or that they claimed, if they were outstanding, that they still ought not to have such great weight with you as I believed: these I must deal with, judges, and in a restrained manner, so that I myself do not offend in any way, and only then when I have replied to the charges, so that the accused does not seem to be defended not so much by his own innocence as by the recollection of my sad circumstances.[1] [5] . . . [6] For Laterensis asks a question and presses hard particularly on this one matter, namely by what moral qualities, by what good reputation, by what distinction Plancius has surpassed

345

nitate superarit. . . . [11] "male iudicavit populus." at iudicavit. "non debuit." at potuit. "non fero." . . . [16] qua re noli me ad contentionem vestrum vocare, Laterensis. etenim si populo grata est tabella, quae frontis aperit hominum, mentis tegit datque eam libertatem ut quod velint faciant, promittant autem quod rogentur, cur tu id in iudicio ut fiat exprimis quod non fit in campo? "hic, quam ille, dignior" perquam grave est dictu. . . . [18] sed tamen haec tibi est prima cum Plancio generis vestri familiaeque contentio, qua abs te vincitur; cur enim non confitear quod necesse est? sed non hic magis quam ego a meis competitoribus et alias et in consulatus petitione vincebar. sed vide ne haec ipsa quae despicis huic suffragata sint. . . . [23] . . . adiungamus, si vis, id, quod tu huic obesse etiam putas, patrem publicanum . . . [28] . . . tribunus pl. fuit non fortasse tam vehemens quam isti quos tu iure laudas, sed certe talis, quales si omnes semper fuissent, numquam desideratus vehemens esset tribunus. [29] . . . [30] omnibus igitur rebus ornatum hominem tam externis quam domesticis, non nullis rebus inferiorem quam te (genere dico et nomine), superiorem aliis (municipum, vicinorum,

---

2 In Laterensis' view, by electing Plancius rather than him.

3 Both Cicero and Plancius were "defeated" for office in the sense that their competitors came from higher social classes; still, both men were elected in preference to these noblemen.

himself. . . . [11] "The People have made a bad judgment."[2] But they have made a judgment. "They should
not." But they were able to. "I do not accept it." . . . [16]
Do not, therefore [because of the actions of the People at
elections], Laterensis, challenge me to a comparison between you [Laterensis and Plancius]. For if the voting
tablet is dear to the People, as it renders visible the coun-
tenances of men and covers their minds, and provides
such liberty so that they may do what they wish, but promise what they are asked, why do you insist that what does
not happen in the Campus [Martius: venue for elections]
should happen in court? "One has greater merit than the
other" is an exceedingly offensive way of expressing it. . . .
[18] Yet, this is the first comparison you make between
yourself and Plancius, in the matter of your birth and family, where he is defeated by you. For why should I not
admit what is necessary? But he [Plancius] [was] not more
[defeated] than I was defeated by my competitors, both
on other occasions and in the candidacy for the consulship.[3] But make sure that the very things that you despise
have not supported him. . . . [23] . . . Let us add, if you
will, what you consider to be also a disadvantage to him,
that his father was a tax collector . . . [28] . . . He [Plancius]
was a Tribune of the People [in 56 BC], perhaps not so
energetic as those whom you rightly praise, but certainly
of such a kind that, if all men had always been like this, an
energetic Tribune would never have been required. [29]
. . . [30] Do you wonder, then, that this man [Plancius]—
adorned with all things, extrinsic as much as intrinsic, in
some respects inferior to yourself (in descent and reputation, I mean), superior in others (in the support from his
townsfolk, his neighbors, and his business partners, the

347

societatum studio, meorum temporum memoria, parem virtute, integritate, modestia) aedilem factum esse miraris? hunc tu vitae splendorem maculis aspergis istis? iacis adulteria, quae nemo non modo nomine sed ne suspicione quidem possit agnoscere. bimaritum[1] appellas, ut verba etiam fingas, non solum crimina. ductum esse ab eo in provinciam aliquem dicis libidinis causa, quod non crimen est, sed impunitum in maledicto mendacium; raptam esse mimulam, quod dicitur Atinae factum a iuventute vetere quodam in scaenicos iure maximeque oppidano. [31] . . . "emissus aliquis e carcere." . . . "pater vero," inquit, "etiam obesse filio debet." . . . [33] "asperius," inquit, "locutus est aliquid aliquando." immo fortasse liberius. "at id ipsum," inquit, "non est ferendum." . . . [36] sed aliquando veniamus ad causam. in qua tu nomine legis Liciniae, quae est de sodaliciis, omnis ambitus leges complexus es; neque enim quicquam aliud in hac lege nisi editicios iudices es secutus. . . . [38] tu autem, Laterensis, quas tribus edidisti? Teretinam, credo. . . . cuius tu tribus venditorem et corruptorem et sequestrem Plancium fuisse clamitas, eam tribum profecto, severissimorum praesertim hominum et gravissimorum, edere debuisti. at Voltiniam; libet enim tibi nescio quid etiam de illa tribu criminari. hanc igitur ipsam cur non edidisti? . . . [43] "Voltinia tribus ab hoc

---

[1] bimaritum *duo codd.*: maritum *codd. cet.*

recollection of my crisis, equal in virtue, incorruptibility, self-mastery)—was elected aedile? Do you taint the splendor of such a life with your blots? You cast about acts of adultery, which nobody can recognize, not only by name, but not even by suspicion. You call him bigamist, so that you also invent appellations, not only charges. You say that some man was taken to the province by him for the sake of his base passions, which is not a charge, but an unpunished and libelous falsehood; that a little mime-actress was abducted, which is said to have been done at Atina [in Latium] by some youths, on the basis of some old privilege permitted toward theater people, especially in country towns. [31] . . . "Someone was released from prison [i.e., by Plancius]." . . . "But the father [of Plancius]," he [Laterensis] says, "must also provide grounds for a charge against the son." . . . [33] "On one occasion," he says, "he [Plancius' father] said something rather acrimonious." On the contrary, perhaps rather frank. "But this very fact," he says, "is intolerable." . . . [36] But let's now pass on to the case. Therein, under the heading of the *Lex Licinia*, which deals with illegal associations, you have included all laws on corrupt practices in electioneering; for nothing else have you followed according to this law [*Lex Licinia*] other than the nomination of the judges. . . . [38] But which tribes did you nominate, Laterensis? The Teretine, I believe. . . . You were obliged to nominate that tribe whose seller, briber, and depositary you keep crying out that Plancius was, this tribe indeed, especially as it is composed of men of great austerity and conscientiousness. But at any rate the Voltinian; for you are pleased to utter some allegations against that tribe too. Why then did you not nominate this particular tribe? . . . [43] "The Voltinian tribe was

corrupta, Teretinam habuerat venalem." . . . [47] . . . itaque
haesitantem te in hoc sodaliciorum tribuario crimine ad
communem ambitus causam contulisti . . . [51] quaeris
etiam, Laterensis, quid imaginibus tuis, quid ornatissimo
atque optimo viro, patri tuo, respondeas mortuo. . . . [53]
. . . "dubitatis," inquit, "quin coitio facta sit, cum tribus
plerasque cum Plotio tulerit Plancius?" an una fieri potue-
runt, si una tribus non tulissent? "at[2] non nullas punctis
paene totidem." . . . [54] et ais prioribus comitiis Aniensem
a Plotio Pedio, Teretinam a[3] Plancio tibi esse concessam;
nunc ab utroque eas avolsas, ne in angustum venirent. . . .
[55] illud vero crimen de nummis quos in circo Flaminio
deprehensos esse dixisti caluit re recenti, nunc in causa
refrixit. neque enim qui illi nummi fuerint nec quae tribus
nec qui divisor ostendis. . . . [58] sed venio iam ad L. Cassium, familiarem meum: cuius ex oratione ne illum quidem Iuventium tecum expostulavi, quem ille omni et
humanitate et virtute ornatus adulescens primum de
plebe aedilem curulem factum esse dixit. . . . [71] at enim
nimis ego magnum beneficium Planci[4] facio et, ut ais, id

[2] at *ed. Cratandrina*: an *codd.*   [3] a *duo codd.*: *om. codd.*
cet.

[4] Planci *Lambinus*: Plancio *codd.*

bribed by him; he had purchased the vote of the Teretine."
... [47] ... Floundering, therefore, in this charge of illegal associations of tribes, you have had recourse to the
general charge of bribery ... [51] You ask, moreover, Laterensis, what answer you are to make to your ancestral
busts, what answer to that excellent and most accomplished gentleman, your late father. ... [53] ... "Do you
[judges] doubt," he [Laterensis] says, "that collusion was
employed, when Plancius, along with Plotius [A. Plotius,
aed. cur. with Plancius], carried the votes of most tribes?"
But could they have been elected together, if they had not
carried the votes of the tribes together? "But they carried
some tribes with an almost exactly equal number of
points." ... [54] You allege, moreover, that at the former
election the tribe of Anio was surrendered by Plotius to
Pedius [Q. Pedius, another candidate], the Teretine by
Plancius to yourself; that now those [tribes] have been
wrenched away by both of them, so that they would not
come to a close count. ... [55] Again, that crime concerning cash that you said was seized in the Circus Flaminius
[in the Campus Martius] was a hot topic when the matter
was fresh, now, during the trial itself, it has cooled. For
you neither show what that money was nor for what tribe
it was intended nor who the distributor was. ... [58] But
I now come to L. Cassius [L. Cassius Longinus (**168**),
F 1], a friend of mine: as a result of his speech, I have not
pressured you even as regards that Iuventius whom that
young man [Cassius], adorned with every aspect of culture
and excellence, mentioned as being the first plebeian to
be elected curule aedile [4th cent. BC]. ... [71] But I turn
Plancius' kindness into something too great and, as you [L.
Cassius Longinus (**168**), F 1] say, magnify it by my words,

verbis exaggero. quasi vero me tuo arbitratu et non meo gratum esse oporteat. "quod istius tantum meritum?" inquit; "an quia te non iugulavit?" immo vero quia iugulari passus non est. quo quidem tu loco, Cassi, etiam purgasti inimicos meos meaeque vitae nullas ab illis insidias fuisse dixisti. posuit hoc idem Laterensis. . . . [72] respondebo tibi nunc, Laterensis, minus fortasse vehementer quam abs te sum provocatus, sed profecto nec considerate minus nec minus amice. nam primum fuit illud asperius me, quae de Plancio dicerem, ‹e›mentiri[5] et temporis causa fingere. . . . [75] atque etiam clamitas, Laterensis: "quo usque ista dicis? nihil in Cispio profecisti; obsoletae iam sunt preces tuae." de Cispio mihi igitur obicies, quem ego de me bene meritum, quia te teste cognoram, te eodem auctore defendi? et ei dices, "quo usque" quem negas, quod pro Cispio contenderim, impetrare potuisse? nam istius verbi "quo usque" haec poterat esse invidia: "datus est tibi ille, condonatus ille; non facis finem; ferre non possumus." . . . [76] et mihi lacrimulam Cispiani iudici obiectas. sic enim dixisti: "vidi ego tuam lacrimulam." . . . [77] tu autem, Laterensis, qui tum lacrimas meas gratas esse dicebas, nunc easdem vis invidiosas videri. negas tribunatum Planci quicquam attulisse adiumenti dignitati meae, atque hoc loco, quod verissime facere potes, L.

---

5 ‹e›mentiri *Bake*: mentiri *codd.*

---

4 M. Cispius supported Cicero during his exile and was afterward unsuccessfully defended by Cicero in a trial for *ambitus* (*TLRR* 279; Cic. *Pro M. Cispio*: Crawford 1984, 170–72).

as though I ought to be grateful according to your decision and not mine. "What is that man's great service?" he says; "perhaps that he did not strangle you?" On the contrary, that he did not suffer me to be strangled. In this context, Cassius, you even whitewashed my enemies and denied that any plot against my life had been laid by them. Laterensis asserted the same. . . . [72] I will now reply to you, Laterensis, using less vehemence, perhaps, than I have been prompted to by you, but, indeed, with no less consideration and no less friendship. For that was, in the first place, somewhat harsh of you to suggest that what I said about Plancius I put forward as lies and inventions of opportunism. . . . [75] And you even keep crying out, Laterensis: "For how much longer are you talking about such things? As regards Cispius [M. Cispius, tr. pl. 57 BC] you have not achieved anything;[4] your style of appeal is out of date." Will you then reproach me as regards Cispius, whom I defended on your initiative, as he had done me a service, which I had found out also on your information? And you will say "for how much longer" to the person, whom you deny could have achieved what I strove for on behalf of Cispius? For the malignity of that expression "for how much longer" could be described as follows: "That man is granted to you, that man is surrendered to you; you do not stop; we cannot stand it." . . . [76] And you reproach me with the "one poor tear" I shed at the trial of Cispius. For you said this: "I saw your one poor tear." . . . [77] And you, Laterensis, who then claimed that my tears were welcome, now wish those same tears to appear as arousing hatred. You deny that the Tribunate of Plancius brought any support to my position, and at this point you call to mind, as you can do most rightly, the superhuman services

353

Racili, fortissimi et constantissimi viri, divina in me merita commemoras. . . . [83] sed haec nescio quo modo frequenter in me congessisti saneque in eo creber fuisti, te idcirco in ludos causam conicere noluisse ne ego mea consuetudine aliquid de tensis misericordiae causa dicerem, quod in aliis aedilibus ante fecissem. . . . hic etiam addidisti me idcirco mea lege exsilio ambitum sanxisse ut miserabiliores epilogos possem dicere. non vobis videtur cum aliquo declamatore, non cum laboris et fori discipulo disputare? [84] "Rhodi enim," inquit, "ego non fui"—me volt fuisse— "sed fui," inquit—putabam in Vaccaeis dicturum—"bis in Bithynia." . . . nam quod in eo me reprehendisti quod nimium multos defenderem, utinam et tu, qui potes, et ceteri, qui defugiunt, vellent me labore hoc levare! . . . [85] admonuisti etiam, quod in Creta fuisses, dictum aliquod in petitionem tuam dici potuisse; me id perdidisse. . . . te aiebas de tuis rebus gestis nullas litteras misisse, quod mihi meae quas ad aliquem misissem obfuissent. . . . [86] sed sunt haec leviora, illa vero gravia atque magna, quod meum discessum, quem saepe defleras, nunc quasi reprehendere et subaccusare voluisti. dixisti enim non auxilium mihi sed me auxilio defuisse. . . . [90] mortem me

---

5 A contrast between Cicero's training with Apollonius Molo of Rhodes and Laterensis' activities, presumably on military service.   6 *creta* also means "chalk," used for whitening garments of candidates, who appeared dressed in *toga candida*.   7 According to the scholiast (*ad loc.* [p. 167.23–30 St.]), a long letter about Cicero's consulship sent to Cn. Pompeius Magnus (**111**) in Asia (cf. Cic. *Sull.* 67); it did not find favor with Pompey and did not induce him to support Cicero against P. Clodius Pulcher (**137**).

conferred upon me by L. Racilius [tr. pl. 56 BC], a very courageous and very resolute man. . . . [83] But you have piled up these points against me incessantly in some way, and you have certainly come back to that issue rather frequently, that you did not wish the trial to coincide with the games so that I might not introduce some reference to the sacred carts for the sake of pity according to my custom, which I had previously done in the case of other aediles. . . . Here you have also added that I punished bribery with exile according to my law [*Lex Tullia de ambitu*: *LPPR*, p. 379] so that I could deliver perorations more appealing to pity. Does he not seem to you to be arguing with some practice speaker, not with a disciple of a laborious apprenticeship in the Forum? [84] "For I," he says, "have not been to Rhodes"—he implies that I have—"but," he says, "I have been"—I thought he was going to say "among the Vaccaei [a people in Hispania]"—"twice in Bithynia."[5] . . , For as regards the fact that you criticize me for defending too many, if only you, who have the ability, and others, who shirk it, would relieve me of this arduous task! . . . [85] You reminded me also that the fact that you had been to Crete provided an opportunity of making some pun upon your candidature and that I let it slip.[6] . . . You said that you had sent no memorandum about your achievements, because the one that I sent to a certain person had done me harm.[7] . . . [86] Yet these are comparatively trivial points, but those are of greater weight and moment, namely that you now wished almost to censure and criticize my withdrawal, for which you had often expressed deep sympathy. For you said that it was not helpers that failed me, but I who failed the helpers. . . . [90] You say that I was afraid of death. . . . [91] Moreover,

timuisse dicis. . . . [91] nam quod te esse in re publica libe-
rum es gloriatus, id ego et fateor et laetor et tibi etiam in
hoc gratulor; quod me autem negasti, in eo neque te neque quemquam diutius patiar errare. . . . [95] nunc venio
ad illud extremum in quo dixisti, dum Planci in me meritum verbis extollerem, me arcem facere e cloaca lapi-
demque e sepulcro venerari pro deo; neque enim mihi
insidiarum periculum ullum neque mortis fuisse.

168 L. CASSIUS LONGINUS

Against Cn. Plancius (F 1)

*In 54 BC Cassius assisted M. Iuventius Laterensis (**167**
F 1–2) in the prosecution of Cn. Plancius, who had won
the election to the curule aedileship, under the* Lex Licinia
de sodaliciis *of 55 BC (LPPR, p. 407). Cn. Plancius was*

F 1 Cic. *Planc.* 58, 59, 60, 61, 62, 63, 66, 68, 69, 71

sed venio iam ad L. Cassium, familiarem meum, cuius ex
oratione ne illum quidem Iuventium tecum expostulavi,
quem ille omni et humanitate et virtute ornatus adulescens primum de plebe aedilem curulem factum esse dixit.
in quo, Cassi, si ita tibi respondeam, nescisse id populum

you have boasted that you were free in political matters; I
grant you this, I am delighted, and I even congratulate you
on this; but when you deny this to me, I cannot allow either you or anyone else to remain under a delusion in the
matter any longer. . . . [95] I come now to that final point
when you said that, by bestowing fulsome phrases upon
Plancius' services to myself, I was making a triumphal arch
out of a sewer and honoring a piece of sepulchral masonry
like a god; for, as you allege, for me there was no danger
of either conspiracy or murder.

168 L. CASSIUS LONGINUS

*L. Cassius Longinus (tr. pl. 44 BC; RE Cassius 65) was a
brother of C. Cassius Longinus, one of Caesar's assassins.*

Against Cn. Plancius (F 1)

*acquitted, defended by Cicero (Cic. Planc.), who in his
speech comments on the points allegedly raised by the opponent (TLRR 293).*

F 1 Cicero, *Pro Plancio*

But I now come to L. Cassius, a friend of mine: as a result
of his speech, I have not pressured you [M. Iuventius
Laterensis (**167**), F 2] even as regards that Iuventius
whom that young man [Cassius], adorned with every aspect of culture and excellence, mentioned as being the
first plebeian to be elected curule aedile [4th cent. BC].
As to that, Cassius, if I was replying to you that the Roman

Romanum, neque fuisse qui id nobis narraret, praesertim
mortuo Congo, non, ut opinor, admirere, cum ego ipse
non abhorrens a studio antiquitatis me hic id ex te primum
audisse confitear. et quoniam tua fuit perelegans et per-
subtilis oratio, digna equitis Romani vel studio vel pudore,
quoniamque sic ab his es auditus ut magnus honos et ingenio et humanitati tuae tribueretur, respondebo ad ea quae
dixisti, quae pleraque de ipso me fuerunt; in quibus ipsi
aculei, si quos habuisti in me reprehendendo, tamen mihi
non ingrati acciderunt. [59] quaesisti utrum mihi putarem,
equitis Romani filio, faciliorem fuisse ad adipiscendos
honores viam an futuram esse filio meo, quia esset familia
consulari. . . . [60] quaeris quid potuerit amplius adsequi
Plancius, si Cn. Scipionis fuisset filius. . . . sed nemo umquam sic egit ut tu: "cur iste fit consul? quid potuit amplius, si L. Brutus esset, qui civitatem dominatu regio libe-
ravit?" . . . [61] profers triumphos T. Didi et C. Mari et
quaeris quid simile in Plancio. . . . rogas quae castra viderit; . . . quaeris num disertus sit. [62] . . . num iuris con-
sultus. . . . [63] iubes Plancium de vitiis Laterensis dicere. . . . idem effers Laterensem laudibus. . . . "Praeneste

---

1 Implies that getting elected is easier for men of consular
family; since Laterensis, with his higher social standing, had not
been elected, it is insinuated that Plancius had been supported
by corrupt practices.   2 These *homines novi* were elected
after celebrating triumphs, in contrast to Plancius.

People did not know this, and that there has been no one
to tell us of it, especially now that Congus [Iunius Congus,
antiquarian, late 2nd/early 1st cent. BC] is dead, you
would not, I guess, be surprised; for, though I am myself
not averse to the study of antiquity, I confess that I heard
this here from you for the first time. And since your speech
was very elegant and very adroit, worthy of both the energy and the self-restraint of a Roman knight, and since
you were listened to by these men in such a way that great
honor was paid to your talent and humane character, I will
reply to what you said, which dealt very largely with myself; within your speech even your sarcastic comments, if
you made any in criticizing me, still did not happen in an
unwelcome way for me. [59] You asked whether I thought
that the path to obtaining official positions of honor had
been easier for me, the son of a Roman knight, than it
would be for my son, since he was of consular family.[1] . . .
[60] You ask what more Plancius could have gained if he
had been Cn. Scipio's [presumably Cn. Cornelius Scipio
Calvus, cos. 222 BC, died fighting in the Second Punic
War] son [i.e., of more noble descent]. . . . Yet no one ever
argued as you [did]: "Why has that fellow become consul?
What more could he have attained if he were L. Brutus,
who freed the community from the despotism of a tyrant?"
. . . [61] You quote the triumphs of T. Didius [cos. 98 BC]
and C. Marius [seven-time consul], and you ask whether
there is anything similar in Plancius.[2] . . . You ask what active military service he has seen. . . . You inquire whether
he is eloquent. [62] . . . Whether he is a competent lawyer. . . . [63] You challenge Plancius to talk about flaws of
Laterensis. . . . At the same time you speak of Laterensis
in terms of fulsome praise. . . . "That he [Laterensis]

fecisse ludos." . . . "Cyrenis liberalem in publicanos, ius-
tum in socios fuisse." . . . [66] . . . nam quas tu commemoras, Cassi, legere te solere orationes, cum otiosus sis, has
ego scripsi ludis et feriis, ne omnino umquam essem otiosus. . . . [68] nam quod ais, Cassi, non plus me Plancio
debere quam bonis omnibus, quod eis aeque mea salus
cara fuerit, ego me debere bonis omnibus fateor. . . . [69]
quaeris a me, Cassi, quid pro fratre meo, qui mihi est caris-
simus, quid pro meis liberis, quibus nihil mihi potest esse
iucundius, amplius quam quod pro Plancio facio facere
possim . . . Opimium damnatum esse commemoras, ser-
vatorem ipsum rei publicae, Calidium adiungis, cuius lege
Q. Metellus in civitatem sit restitutus; reprehendis meas
pro Plancio preces, quod neque Opimius suo nomine libe-
ratus sit neque Metelli[1] Calidius. . . . [71] at enim nimis
ego magnum beneficium Planci[2] facio et, ut ais, id verbis
exaggero. quasi vero me tuo arbitratu et non meo gratum
esse oporteat. "quod istius tantum meritum?" inquit; "an
quia te non iugulavit?" immo vero quia iugulari passus non
est. quo quidem tu loco, Cassi, etiam purgasti inimicos
meos meaeque vitae nullas ab illis insidias fuisse dixisti.

---

[1] neque Metelli *vel* nec Q. Metelli *codd.*   [2] Planci *Lambinus*: Plancio *codd.*

exhibited games at Praeneste [modern Palestrina, near Rome]." . . . "That at Cyrene [in Africa] he [Laterensis] was generous to the tax collectors, just to the business partners." . . . [66] . . . For those speeches, Cassius, which you tell us it is your custom to read when you are at leisure, I have written during festivals and holidays, so that I would never be entirely at leisure. . . . [68] For, as to your assertion, Cassius, that I am under no deeper obligation to Plancius than to all loyal men, because to them my wellbeing was equally dear, I admit that I am in debt to all loyal men. . . . [69] You ask me, Cassius, what I could do for my brother, who is very dear to me, what for my children, compared to whom nothing can be sweeter for me, more than I am doing for Plancius . . . You remind us that even Opimius [L. Opimius, cos. 121 BC], that savior of the Republic, was condemned; you mention Calidius [Q. Calidius, tr. pl. 98, praet. 79 BC], too, by whose law [*Lex Calidia de Q. Caecilio Metello revocando: LPPR*, p. 334] Q. Metellus [Q. Caecilius Metellus Numidicus (**58**)] was restored to civil rights; you blame my intercession on behalf of Plancius, since on his own account Opimius was not acquitted, nor Calidius by that of Metellus. . . . [71] But I am turning Plancius' kindness [during Cicero's exile] into something too great and, as you say, am magnifying it by my words, as though I ought to be grateful according to your decision and not mine. "What is that man's great service?" he says; "perhaps that he did not strangle you?" On the contrary, that he did not suffer me to be strangled. In this context, Cassius, you even whitewashed my enemies and denied that any plot against my life had been laid by them.

Against M. Saufeius (F 1A)

In 52 BC Cassius was one of the prosecutors of M. Saufeius under the Lex Pompeia de vi *in connection with the death of P. Clodius Pulcher (**137**); the defendant was successfully*

F 1A Asc. in Cic. *Mil.* 95 (pp. 48 KS = 54.22–55.4 C.) = **162** F 31.

169 Q. PILIUS CELER

Against M. Servilius (F 1–2)

In autumn 51 BC Pilius prosecuted M. Servilius (RE Servilius 20) on a charge of extortion in a complex and protracted case (TLRR 338); a written version of the speech seems to have existed shortly afterward (F 2).

*The background to the case: C. Claudius Pulcher, provincial governor in Asia (55–53 BC), was charged with extortion upon his return in 53 BC (TLRR 336). He bribed M. Servilius, but was found guilty nevertheless. Apparently, the people in the province were unhappy with the money recovered: in 51 BC Pausanias attempted to prosecute Servilius (who was to be defended by M. Caelius Rufus [**162**]) under the charge "quo ea pecunia pervene-*

Against M. Saufeius (F 1A)

supported by M. Caelius Rufus (**162** F 31) and Cicero (Cic. Pro M. Saufeio: Crawford 1984, 219–21) (TLRR 313).

F 1A Asconius on Cicero, Pro Milone
= **162** F 31.

169 Q. PILIUS CELER

Q. Pilius Celer (RE Pilius 2) is often mentioned in Cicero's letters (esp. Cic. Att. 10.1.4; Ad Brut. 2.5.3–4). He fought for C. Iulius Caesar (**121**) in Gaul and was on his side in the civil war.

Against M. Servilius (F 1–2)

rit" (cf. Cic. Rab. post. 9) since he probably assumed that Servilius had received the money; his application for prosecution was not accepted by the praetor M. Iuventius Laterensis (**167**) (TLRR 337). Thereupon, Pilius proceeded to prosecute Servilius for extortion, when Ap. Claudius Pulcher (son of C. Claudius Pulcher) intervened; he asserted that Servilius had received a bribe of three million sesterces from his father. As a result of a procedural error of Laterensis, Servilius was neither acquitted nor convicted. Yet, Ap. Claudius Pulcher did not pursue the matter further; thus, Pilius was able to go ahead with the prosecution.

F 1 Cael. ap. Cic. *Fam.* 8.8.2–3

haec quoque magna nunc contentio forum tenet: M. Servilius postquam, ut coeperat, omnibus in rebus turbarat
nec quod {non}[1] venderet cuiquam[2] reliquerat maximaque
nobis traditus erat invidia,[3] neque Laterensis praetor postulante Pausania nobis patronis "quo ea pecunia pervenis-
set" recipere voluit, Q. Pilius, necessarius Attici nostri,
repetundis[4] eum postulavit. magna ilico fama surrexit et
de damnatione ferventer loqui est coeptum. quo vento
proicitur Appius minor ut indicet[5] {de} pecuniam[6] ex bonis
patris pervenisse ad Servilium praevaricationisque causa
diceret depositum HS |X̄X̄X̄|.[7] admiraris amentiam; immo,
si actionem stultissimasque de se, nefarias de patre con-
fessiones audisses. [3] mittit in consilium eosdem illos qui
lites aestimarant iudices. cum aequo numero sententiae
fuissent, Laterensis leges ignorans pronuntiavit quid sin-
guli ordines iudicassent et ad extremum, ut solent, "non
redigam." postquam discessit et pro absoluto Servilius
haberi coeptus legisque unum et centesimum caput legit,

---

[1] *del. Rubenius*   [2] quoiquam *vel* quo inquam *vel* quo-
quam *codd.*: quicquam *codd. det. sive edd. vet.*: cuipiam *Wesenberg*   [3] maximaque . . . invidia *Rutilius*: maxime qu(a)e . . .
invidi(a)e *codd.*   [4] <de> repetundis *codd. det. vel edd. vet.*

[5] indicet *Manutius*: inpicet *codd.*: indicaret *Wesenberg*

[6] {de} pecuniam *Manutius*: depecuniam *vel* de pecunia *codd.*:
D̄C̄ *Mendelssohn*   [7] |X̄X̄X̄| *Constans*: LXXXI *codd.*: LXXX
N (*pro* nummum) *Mendelssohn*

169 Q. PILIUS CELER

F 1 Caelius in Cicero, *Letters to Friends*

This great controversy too now holds sway over the Forum: M. Servilius, just as he had begun, had deranged all his affairs, and had not left anybody anything that they could sell, and had been handed over to us [as a client] amid the greatest dislike; but the praetor Laterensis [M. Iuventius Laterensis (**167**), praet. 51 BC] did not wish to accept the case when, with us as advocates, Pausanias [on behalf of the provincials] made an application for prosecution on a charge of "where that money had gone." Then Q. Pilius, a connection of our friend Atticus [T. Pomponius Atticus (**103**)], charged him [Servilius] with extortion. Much rumor immediately arose, and one began to speak vehemently of condemnation. By this wind, Appius the Younger [younger brother of Ap. Claudius Pulcher (**172**)] is tossed up so that he alleges that money out of his father's property has come to Servilius and claimed that three million sesterces had been deposited to manipulate the case by collusion. You [Cicero] are surprised at the folly, especially if you had heard his delivery and the very stupid admissions about himself and the shocking ones about his father. [3] He sends those same judges to consider the verdict who had assessed the damages. When the votes were equally divided, Laterensis, not knowing the laws, announced what each class [of judges, i.e., senators, knights and *tribuni aerarii*] had judged and, at the end, "I will not collect [i.e., the money allegedly received fraudulently]," as is the custom [assuming acquittal]. After he had left [the court] and Servilius began to be looked upon as acquitted, and he [Laterensis] read the hundred-and-first section of the law [*Lex Iulia de pecuniis repetundis*,

365

in quo ita erat: "quod eorum iudicum maior pars iudicarit id ius ratumque esto," in tabulas absolutum non rettulit, ordinum iudicia perscripsit; postulante rursus Appio cum L. Lollio † transegisset †[8] relaturum dixit. sic nunc neque absolutus neque damnatus Servilius de repetundis saucius Pilio tradetur. nam de divinatione Appius, cum calumniam iurasset, contendere ausus non est Pilioque cessit . . .

---

[8] transegisse et *C. F. Hermann*: transegisse et rem *Purser*: transegit et se *Manutius*: transegisse se et ‹rem› *Bayet*

F 2 Cic. *Att.* 6.3.10

etiam illud: orationem Q. Celeris mihi velim mittas contra M. Servilium.

170 C. SCRIBONIUS CURIO FILIUS

C. Scribonius Curio (tr. pl. 50 BC; RE Scribonius 11), the third in a series of orators of the same name and from the same family (47 + 86; cf. 47 T 4), organized magnificent games upon his father's death (Plin. HN 36.116–20). Curio first opposed C. Iulius Caesar (121) and his associates; later, he supported him and served as Caesar's legate in Africa (T 4–6, F 9; Luc. 4.819–20). After Curio had successfully fought against the Pompeians, he was killed in battle in 49 BC.

59 BC: *LPPR*, pp. 389–91], in which the following could
be found: "what the majority of those judges has decided,
this shall be lawful and binding," he did not put "acquitted" in the records, but wrote down the verdicts of the
several classes. When Appius again applied for prosecution, he [Laterensis] said that he had settled the issue with
L. Lollius [presumably a jurisconsult or one of the senior
judges] and would record the facts [?]. So now Servilius,
being neither acquitted nor convicted, with a reputation
already damaged, will be handed over to Pilius to be tried
for extortion. For Appius, although he had sworn that he
was not making a false accusation, did not have the courage to contest the right to prosecute and gave way to Pilius
. . .

F 2 Cicero, *Letters to Atticus*

And one more thing: I would like you to send me Q. Celer's speech against M. Servilius.

170 C. SCRIBONIUS CURIO FILIUS

*Letters by Cicero addressed to Curio are extant (Cic.
Fam. 2.1–7). Curio is a speaker, along with C. Vibius
Pansa (**160**), in a work by his father, which is critical of
Caesar's deeds (Cic. Brut. 218).*

*Curio is mentioned by ancient authorities as an accom-
plished orator with natural ability, characterized by elaborate diction and a wealth of thoughts, and effective with
the People, while it is regretted that he did not apply his
faculties to different purposes (T 1–7).*

T 1 Cic. *Brut.* 279–80

[CICERO:] "quamquam facienda mentio est, ut quidem mihi videtur, duorum adulescentium, qui si diutius vixissent magnam essent eloquentiae laudem consecuti." [280] "C. Curionem te," inquit BRUTUS, "et C. Licinium Calvum arbitror dicere." "recte," inquam [CICERO], "arbitraris; quorum quidem alter {quod verisimile dixisset}[1] ita facile soluteque verbis volvebat satis interdum acutas, crebras quidem certe sententias, ut nihil posset ornatius esse, nihil expeditius. atque hic parum a magistris institutus naturam habuit admirabilem ad dicendum; industriam non sum expertus, studium certe fuit. qui si me audire voluisset, ut coeperat, honores quam opes consequi maluisset."

[1] *del. Lambinus*

T 2 Vell. Pat. 2.48.3–4

bello autem civili et tot quae deinde per continuos XX annos consecuta sunt malis non alius maiorem flagrantioremque quam C. Curio tribunus pl. subiecit facem, vir nobilis eloquens audax, suae alienaeque et fortunae et pudicitiae prodigus, homo ingeniosissime nequam et facundus malo publico, [4] cuius[1] animo ‹. . .›[2] voluptatibus vel libidinibus neque opes ullae neque † cupiditates †[3] sufficere possent.

[1] cuius *Gelenius*: huius *cod.*   [2] immerso *add. Morgenstern*: obruto *add.* (*sed post* libidinibus) *Novák*   [3] dignitates *Watt*

T 1 Cicero, *Brutus*

[CICERO:] "Yet mention ought to be made, as it seems to me at least, of two young men who, had they lived longer, would have obtained great renown for eloquence." [280] "You are referring to C. Curio and C. Licinius Calvus [C. Licinius Macer Calvus (**165**), T 1], I guess," said BRUTUS. "You are guessing rightly," I [CICERO] said. "Of these the former {which he had said as something plausible} with a free and facile diction gave well rounded form to thoughts, sometimes sufficiently shrewd and at all events abundant, in such a way that nothing could be more embellished, nothing moving more easily. And he, too little trained by teachers, had a remarkable natural gift for eloquence; I have not experienced his industry, but he certainly had eagerness. If he had chosen to listen to me, as he had begun, he would have preferred to seek honors rather than power."

T 2 Velleius Paterculus, *Compendium of Roman History*

But to the civil war and the large number of evils that then followed for twenty consecutive years no other individual applied a greater and more flaming torch than C. Curio, a Tribune of the People, a man of noble birth, eloquent, reckless, prodigal alike of his own fortune and chastity and those of other people, a worthless man of the utmost cleverness, eloquent to public disadvantage; [4] neither any wealth nor pleasures [?] could satiate his mind, <overwhelmed [?]> by wishes or desires.

T 3 Suet. *Gram. et rhet.* 25.3
= **111** T 8.

T 4 Plut. *Ant.* 5.1–2

ἐπεὶ δὲ τὰ Ῥωμαίων πράγματα διέστη, τῶν μὲν ἀρι-
στοκρατικῶν Πομπηίῳ παρόντι προσθεμένων, τῶν δὲ
δημοτικῶν Καίσαρα καλούντων ἐκ Γαλατίας ἐν τοῖς
ὅπλοις ὄντα, [2] Κουρίων ὁ Ἀντωνίου φίλος ἐκ μετα-
βολῆς θεραπεύων τὰ Καίσαρος Ἀντώνιον προσηγά-
γετο, καὶ μεγάλην μὲν ἀπὸ τοῦ λέγειν ἐν τοῖς πολλοῖς
ἔχων ἰσχύν, χρώμενος δὲ καὶ δαπάναις ἀφειδῶς ἀφ᾽
ὧν Καῖσαρ ἐχορήγει, δήμαρχον ἀπέδειξε τὸν Ἀντώνιον, εἶτα τῶν ἐπ᾽ οἰωνοῖς ἱερέων οὓς Αὔγουρας[1] κα-
λοῦσιν.

[1] Αὔγουρας *Coraes*: αὐγούρας *codd.*

T 5 App. *B Civ.* 2.26.100

. . . δήμαρχός τε Κουρίων, ἐχθρὸς ὢν καὶ ὅδε τῷ
Καίσαρι καρτερὸς καὶ ἐς τὸν δῆμον εὐχαριτώτατος
καὶ εἰπεῖν ἱκανώτατος.

T 6 Cass. Dio 40.60.2–61.2

κἀν τούτῳ καὶ τὰ οἴκοι τρόπον τινά, τοῦ μὴ πάντῃ
βίᾳ ἀλλὰ καὶ πειθοῖ πράττειν δοκεῖν, προδιοικήσα-
σθαι ἐθελήσας ἔγνω συ⟨να⟩λλαγῆναι[1] τῷ Κουρίωνι·

[1] συ⟨να⟩λλαγῆναι *Reimarus*: συλλαγῆναι *cod.*

T 3 Suetonius, *Lives of Illustrious Men. Grammarians and Rhetoricians*

= **111** T 8.

T 4 Plutarch, *Life of Antony*

But when matters at Rome came to a crisis, with the aristocratic party attaching itself to Pompey [Cn. Pompeius Magnus (**111**)], who was present, and the popular party summoning Caesar [C. Iulius Caesar (**121**)] from Gaul, where he was in arms, [2] Curio, the friend of Antony [M. Antonius (**159**)], now favoring the cause of Caesar, as a result of a change of sides, brought Antony over to it. And having great influence with the masses from his eloquence and making lavish use of money that Caesar had supplied, he [Curio] got Antony appointed Tribune of the People [for 49 BC], then one of the priests who observe the birds and who are called augurs [in 50 BC].

T 5 Appian, *Civil Wars*

. . . and Curio [was elected] Tribune of the People [for 50 BC], he too a bitter enemy of Caesar [C. Iulius Caesar (**121**)], and extremely charming toward the People, and a most accomplished speaker.

T 6 Cassius Dio, *Roman History*

Meanwhile [in 50 BC], wishing to arrange matters at home beforehand in some fashion so as not to seem to be using violence indiscriminately, but also persuasion, he [C. Iulius Caesar (**121**)] decided to reconcile himself with Cu-

371

τοῦ τε γὰρ τῶν Κουριώνων γένους ἦν, καὶ τὴν γνώμην
ὀξύς, εἰπεῖν τε δεινός, τῷ τε πλήθει πιθανώτατος, καὶ
χρήματων ἐς πάντα[2] ἁπλῶς ἐξ ὧν ἢ αὐτός τι πλεονε-
κτήσειν ἢ καὶ ἑτέρῳ διαπράξειν ἤλπιζεν ἀφειδέστα-
τος. [3] καὶ αὐτὸν πολλὰ μὲν[3] ἐπελπίσας, πάντων δὲ
τῶν ὀφειλημάτων, συχνῶν διὰ τὸ πολλὰ δαπανᾶσθαι
ὄντων, ἀπαλλάξας ἀνηρτήσατο. . . . [61.2] δι' οὖν
ταῦτα ἐπὶ μακρότατόν τε ἐπεκρύψατο, καὶ ὅπως μη-
δένα τρόπον ὑποπτευθῇ μεταβεβλῆσθαί τε καὶ οὐκ
ἀνὰ πρώτους καὶ πάντα τὰ ἐναντία τῷ Καίσαρι καὶ
τότε ἔτι καὶ φρονεῖν καὶ λέγειν, καὶ ἐδημηγόρει κατ'
αὐτοῦ ἀφ' οὗ γε καὶ δημαρχεῖν ἤρξατο, καὶ ἐσηγεῖτο
πολλὰ καὶ ἄτοπα.

  [2] ἐς πάντα scripsit Boissevain e cod.: ἐς τὰ πάντα R. Stephanus
  [3] πολλὰ μὲν Bekker: μὲν πολλὰ cod. et Bekker, Anecd.

T 7 Hieron. *Ab Abr.* 1963 = 54 a.C. (p. 155d Helm)

Curio promptus et popularis orator Romae habetur insignis. qui deinceps in Africa pudore amissi exercitus mori
maluit quam evadere

Publicly Against the Political Situation (F 8)

rio. For the latter belonged to the family of the Curiones, was keen in his intellect, an accomplished speaker, greatly trusted by the masses, and most lavish of money generally for everything, by which he hoped either to gain some advantage for himself or benefit someone else. [3] So by raising many hopes for him and relieving him of all his debts, which on account of his extravagant spending were numerous, he [Caesar] attached him to himself. . . . [61.2] For these reasons [i.e., not to reveal that he had transferred his allegiances to Caesar willingly], then, he [Curio] dissembled for a very long time, and to prevent any suspicion of the fact that he had changed sides and was not still at that time among the foremost to both feel and express unqualified opposition to Caesar, he even delivered public speeches against him, as soon as he had entered upon the Tribunate, and introduced many strange measures.

T 7 Jerome, *Chronicle*

Curio is regarded as a distinguished orator at Rome, fluent and keen to win the support of the People. Later, in Africa, out of shame over the loss of the army, he preferred to die rather than to escape.

Publicly Against the Political Situation (F 8)

Curio gave public speeches in 59 BC against the political situation in the Republic (CCMR, App. A: 286).

F 8 Cic. *Att.* 2.18.1

unus loquitur et palam adversatur adulescens Curio. huic plausus maximi, consalutatio forensis perhonorifica, signa praeterea benevolentiae permulta a bonis impertiuntur.

Cf. Cic. *Att.* 2.19.3.

As Tribune of the People (F 9–11)

F 9 Liv. *Epit.* 109.2

et C. Curionis tr. pl. primum adversus Caesarem, dein pro Caesare actiones continet.

F 10 Plut. *Quaest. Rom.* 81 (283C–D)

ὁ γὰρ ὄγκος ὑπάτῳ προσήκει καὶ στρατηγῷ, τὸν δὲ δήμαρχον, ὡς Γάιος Κουρίων ἔλεγε, καταπατεῖσθαι δεῖ, καὶ μὴ σεμνὸν εἶναι τῇ ὄψει μηδὲ δυσπρόσοδον μηδὲ τοῖς πολλοῖς χαλεπόν, ἀλλ᾽ ὑπὲρ τῶν ἄλλων <. . .>¹ τοῖς δὲ πολλοῖς εὐμεταχείριστον.

¹ *lac. codd.: ἄοκνον add. Babbitt: fort. ἀπεχθανόμενον suppl. Bernardakis*

F 11 Suet. *Iul.* 50.1

= **86** F 9.

F 8 Cicero, *Letters to Atticus*

Only one person speaks and offers open opposition [against the political situation], young Curio. He gets hearty rounds of applause, a most flattering amount of general salutation in the Forum, and, moreover, a great many signs of goodwill from the loyal men.

As Tribune of the People (F 9–11)

Curio delivered a number of orations when Tribune of the People in 50 BC (cf. T 6).

F 9 Livy, *Epitome*

And it [Livy's Book 109, on 50–49 BC] includes speeches of C. Curio, a Tribune of the People, delivered first against Caesar [C. Iulius Caesar (**121**)], then on Caesar's behalf.

F 10 Plutarch, *Roman Questions*

For pride is proper for the consul and the praetor; but the Tribune, as Gaius Curio used to say, must allow himself to be trodden upon, and he must not be proud of mien, nor difficult of access, nor harsh to the multitude, but ‹indefatigable› [?] on behalf of others and easy for the multitude to deal with.[1]

[1] It is thought that Curio is most likely to have made a statement about the role of Tribunes while he held this office.

F 11 Suetonius, *Life of Caesar*

= **86** F 9.[1]

[1] Whether this speech is to be dated to the year of Curio's Tribunate is uncertain.

171 L. SEMPRONIUS ATRATINUS

L. Sempronius Atratinus (cos. suff. 34 BC; RE Sempronius 26), a biological son of L. Calpurnius Bestia and then adopted by a Sempronius, fought in Greece under M. An-

Against M. Caelius Rufus (F 1–7)

In 56 BC, as a young man, Atratinus prosecuted M. Caelius Rufus (162), who took his (biological) father L. Calpurnius Bestia to court twice (162 F 19–22); Atratinus was supported by L. Herennius Balbus (163 F 1) and P. Clodius (164 F 1). M. Caelius Rufus, charged under the Lex

F 1 Hieron. *Ab Abr.* 1996 = 21 a.C. (p. 165e Helm)

Atratinus, qui septemdecim annos natus Caelium accusaverat, clarus inter oratores habetur . . .

F 2 Quint. *Inst.* 11.1.68

aliquando etiam inferioribus praecipueque adulescentulis parcere aut videri decet. utitur hac moderatione Cicero pro Caelio contra Atratinum, ut eum non inimice corripere sed paene patrie monere videatur: nam et nobilis et iuvenis et non iniusto dolore venerat ad accusandum.

171 L. SEMPRONIUS ATRATINUS

*tonius (**159**). After his consulship, he administered the
province of Africa as proconsul and thereupon celebrated
a triumph in 21 BC.*

Against M. Caelius Rufus (F 1–7)

*Plautia de vi, was successfully defended by himself (**162**
F 23–28) as well as by M. Licinius Crassus Dives (**102**
F 12–13) and Cicero (Cic. Cael.) (TLRR 275; Alexander
2002, 218–43).*

F 1 Jerome, *Chronicle*

Atratinus, who at the age of seventeen had prosecuted
Caelius, is regarded as famous among the orators . . .

F 2 Quintilian, *The Orator's Education*

Sometimes, again, it its appropriate to spare (or to seem
to do so) our inferiors and especially the very young. Cicero uses such restraint in [the speech] on behalf of Caelius
[Cic. *Cael.*] against Atratinus, so that he seems not to be
attacking him as an enemy but admonishing him almost
like a father: for he [Atratinus] was of noble birth and a
young man and had come with not unjustified distress to
the prosecution.

F 3 Cic. *Cael.* 2, 7

sed ego Atratino, humanissimo atque optimo adulescenti
meo necessario, ignosco, qui habet excusationem vel pie-
tatis vel necessitatis vel aetatis. si voluit accusare, pietati
tribuo, si iussus est, necessitati, si speravit aliquid, pueri-
tiae. . . . [7] quam quidem partem accusationis admiratus
sum et moleste tuli potissimum esse Atratino datam. neque enim decebat neque aetas illa postulabat neque, id
quod animadvertere poteratis, pudor patiebatur optimi
adulescentis in tali illum oratione versari.

F 4 Cic. *Cael.* 8

sed istarum partium culpa est eorum, qui te agere volue-
runt; laus pudoris tui, quod ea te invitum dicere videba-
mus, ingenii, quod ornate politeque dixisti.

F 5 Cic. *Cael.* 15

posuistis enim, atque id tamen titubanter et strictim, coniurationis hunc propter amicitiam Catilinae participem
fuisse; in quo non modo crimen non haerebat sed vix di-
serti adulescentis cohaerebat oratio.

F 3 Cicero, *Pro Caelio*

But I pardon Atratinus, a very cultured and excellent young man, a friend of mine; he can plead as an excuse either filial affection or necessity or his age. If he was willing to bring the accusation, I put it down to affection; if he was under orders, to necessity; if he had any hopes, to his youth. . . . [7] I was surprised and annoyed that this part of the accusation [criticism of Caelius' life] was entrusted to Atratinus of all people. For it was not appropriate, nor did his age call for it, nor, as you could observe, did this excellent young man's sense of propriety allow him to be busy with such a speech.

F 4 Cicero, *Pro Caelio*

But the blame for the part you [Atratinus] have played rests with those who desired you to play it [cf. F 3]; the credit belongs to your scruples, because we saw that you said this against your will, and to your ability, because you spoke with grace and refinement.

F 5 Cicero, *Pro Caelio*

For you [the prosecutors] have alleged, although indeed with hesitation and hints, that he was a partner in the conspiracy on account of his friendship with Catiline [L. Sergius Catilina (**112**)]; as regards this point there was not only no crime attached, but the speech of the eloquent young man [Atratinus] hardly hung together.

F 6 Suet. *Gram. et rhet.* 26.2
= **97** F 1.

F 7 Chir. Fortun. 3.7, *RLM*, p. 124.24–26

etiam illa inter translationes ponimus, quae non verbis, sed nominibus translatis immutantur? vero,[1] cum Atratinus Caelium "pulchellum Iasonem" appellat . . .

[1] uero *vel* uerum *vel* ut *codd.*: ut *edd.*: *fort.* uero, ut cum *Halm in app.*

On Herod in the Senate (F 8)

F 8 Joseph. *BJ* 1.284

συνῆγε δὲ καὶ τὴν βουλήν, ἐν ᾗ Μεσσάλας καὶ μετ᾽ αὐτὸν Ἀτρατῖνος, παραστησάμενοι τὸν Ἡρώδην, τάς τε πατρῴας εὐεργεσίας καὶ τὴν αὐτοῦ πρὸς Ῥωμαίους εὔνοιαν διεξῇσαν, ἀποδεικνύντες ἅμα καὶ πολέμιον τὸν Ἀντίγονον ἐξ ὧν οὐ μόνον διηνέχθη τάχιον, ἀλλ᾽ ὅτι καὶ τότε διὰ Πάρθων λάβοι τὴν ἀρχήν, Ῥωμαίους ὑπεριδών. τῆς δὲ συγκλήτου πρὸς ταῦτα κεκινημένης, ὡς παρελθὼν Ἀντώνιος καὶ πρὸς τὸν κατὰ Πάρθων πόλεμον βασιλεύειν Ἡρώδην συμφέρειν ἔλεγεν, ἐπιψηφίζονται πάντες.

171 L. SEMPRONIUS ATRATINUS

F 6 Suetonius, *Lives of Illustrious Men. Grammarians and Rhetoricians*

= **97** F 1.

F 7 Chirius Fortunatianus

Do we also place among the transferences those instances that are changed by the transference not of words, but of names? Indeed, when Atratinus calls Caelius "a beautiful little Jason" . . .

On Herod in the Senate (F 8)

In 40 BC Atratinus delivered a speech in the Senate, supporting the proposal to make Herod king of the Jews (Joseph. AJ 14.381–85).

F 8 Josephus, *The Jewish War*

So he [Octavian] convened the Senate, to which Messalla [M. Valerius Messalla Corvinus (**176**), F 13A], and with him Atratinus, presented Herod and dwelt on the services rendered by this man's father and his own goodwill toward the Romans; demonstrating at the same time that Antigonus [king of Judea] was their enemy, not only from the earlier quarrel that they had had with him, but because he had also then accepted the power from the Parthians, looking down on the Romans. The Senate was moved toward this; and when Antony [M. Antonius (**159**)] came forward and said that with a view to the war against the Parthians it was expedient that Herod should be king, they all voted for it.

172 AP. CLAUDIUS PULCHER

T 1 Suet. *Gram. et rhet.* 10.3

ipse [Ateius] ad Laelium Hermam scripsit se . . . prae-
cepisse autem multis et claris iuvenibus, in quis Appio
quoque et Pulchro Claudiis fratribus, quorum etiam
comes in provincia fuerit.

Against T. Annius Milo (F 2)

F 2 Asc. in Cic. *Mil.*, *arg.* (p. 36 KS = 41.6–9 C.)
= **159** F 6.

172 AP. CLAUDIUS PULCHER

Ap. Claudius Pulcher (cos. 38 BC; RE Claudius 298) was the elder son of C. Claudius Pulcher; he and his brother studied with L. Ateius Philologus, a teacher of grammar and rhetoric (T 1).

T 1 Suetonius, *Lives of Illustrious Men. Grammarians and Rhetoricians*

He himself [Ateius] wrote to Laelius Herma(/-es) [probably another grammarian, not otherwise known] that he . . . had trained many noble young men, including also the brothers Appius and Pulcher Claudius,[1] whose companion he also was in the province.

[1] Pulcher Claudius refers to Ap. Claudius Pulcher minor, the younger brother. His *praenomen* was also Appius, probably acquired after he had been adopted by his uncle Ap. Claudius Pulcher (*RE* Claudius 297). To distinguish between the two brothers, the *cognomen* is sometimes used for the younger in place of the *praenomen* (cf. *RE* Claudius 299).

Against T. Annius Milo (F 2)

*In 52 BC Pulcher was among the prosecutors of T. Annius Milo (**138**), who was supported by Cicero (Cic. Mil.) and others (cf. **92** F 49–50) (TLRR 306, 309, 310).*

F 2 Asconius on Cicero, *Pro Milone*

= **159** F 6.

173 P. CORNELIUS DOLABELLA

*P. Cornelius Dolabella (cos. suff. 44 BC; RE Cornelius
141) supported C. Iulius Caesar (121) in the civil war. In
44 BC, after Caesar's assassination, he became* consul suf-
fectus. *Afterward, he set off for the province of Asia and
had C. Trebonius, one of Caesar's assassins, killed in early
43 BC. Thereupon, Dolabella was declared a public enemy
and, unable to defend himself in a military confrontation,
ordered one of his own soldiers to kill him.*

*Dolabella studied oratory with Cicero (T 1–4). A letter
from Dolabella to Cicero is extant (Cic.* Fam. *9.9) as are
several from Cicero to him (Cic.* Fam. *9.10–14;* Att.

T 1 Cic. *Fam.* 9.16.7

= **161** T 1.

T 2 Cic. *Fam.* 7.33.1–2

= **161** T 2.

T 3 Cic. *Fam.* 9.7.2 [ad Varronem]

. . . adventat enim Dolabella. eum puto magistrum
fore. "πολλοὶ μαθηταὶ κρείσσονες διδασκάλων." [*Anth.
Graec.* 11.176.5]

T 4 Quint. *Inst.* 12.11.6

= **160** T 1.

173 P. CORNELIUS DOLABELLA

14.17a). Dolabella was the husband of Cicero's daughter Tullia from 51 to 46 BC.

Probably in 52 BC, Dolabella was prosecuted on capital charges twice; defended by Cicero (Cic. Pro P. Cornelio Dolabella: Crawford 1984, 225–27), he was acquitted (TLRR 316, 317). As a young man in 50 BC, Dolabella prosecuted Ap. Claudius Pulcher (130) for treason and bribery; defended by Q. Hortensius Hortalus (92 F 53–54) and M. Iunius Brutus (158 F 22), the accused was acquitted (TLRR 344, 345).

T 1 Cicero, *Letters to Friends*

= **161** T 1.

T 2 Cicero, *Letters to Friends*

= **161** T 2.

T 3 Cicero, *Letters to Friends* [to Varro]

. . . for Dolabella is coming. I expect he will be the schoolmaster.[1] "Many students are better than the teachers." [*Anth. Graec.* 11.176.5]

[1] While Cicero had trained Dolabella in oratory, he here assumes that Dolabella will give instructions with reference to C. Iulius Caesar (**121**).

T 4 Quintilian, *The Orator's Education*

= **160** T 1.

As Consul to the People (F 5–7)

In 44 BC, when he was consul, Dolabella delivered several speeches to the People, especially after the assassination of C. Iulius Caesar (121) in March 44 BC (CCMR, App. A:

F 5 Cic. *Fam.* 9.14 (= *Att.* 14.17A).7–8 [ad Dolabellam]

legi enim contionem tuam: nihil illa sapientius; ita pede-temptim et gradatim tum accessus a te ad causam facti, tum recessus, ut res ipsa maturitatem tibi animadvertendi omnium concessu daret. [8] liberasti igitur et urbem peri-culo et civitatem metu, neque solum ad tempus maximam utilitatem attulisti sed etiam ad exemplum.

F 6 Cic. *Att.* 14.20.2, 4

L. Antoni horribilis contio, Dolabellae praeclara. . . . [4] . . . Dolabellae et prima illa actio et haec contra Antonium contio mihi profecisse permultum videtur.

F 7 Quint. *Inst.* 8.2.4

. . . aut, quod in oratione Dolabellae emendatum a Cic-erone adnotavi, "mortem ferre" . . .

As Consul to the People (F 5–7)

356; cf. App. B Civ. *2.122.511; Cass. Dio 44.22.1 [CCMR, App. A: 347]; App.* B Civ. *2.142.593 [CCMR, App. A: 351]; Cic.* Phil. *1.6 [CCMR, App. A: 357]).*

F 5 Cicero, *Letters to Friends* [to Dolabella]

For I have read your speech to the People: nothing wiser than that; so cautiously and gradually first an approach to the issue, then a withdrawal was made by you, so that by general consent the very facts showed the time to be ripe for your punitive action. [8] So you have rescued both the city [of Rome] from danger and the community from fear, and you have done a vast amount of good, not only for the present occasion, but also as a precedent.

F 6 Cicero, *Letters to Atticus*

L. Antonius' [brother of M. Antonius (**159**)] public speech is appalling, Dolabella's is splendid. . . . [4] . . . As for Dolabella, both that first intervention of his and this public speech against Antony seem to me to have done a lot of good.

F 7 Quintilian, *The Orator's Education*

. . . or the phrase that I noticed as having been corrected by Cicero in a speech by Dolabella, "to bear death"[1] . . .

[1] Whether this phrase comes from a *contio* speech by Dolabella is uncertain.

174 C. ASINIUS POLLIO

C. Asinius Pollio (76 BC–AD 4; cos. 40 BC; RE Asinius 25) fought on the side of C. Iulius Caesar (121) in the civil war. After Caesar's assassination, he eventually decided to support M. Antonius (159). After his consulship (mentioned in Verg. Ecl. 4), Pollio fought against the Parthians and other peoples in that area; he celebrated a triumph upon his return in 39 BC (on his life see FRHist 1:430–35).

In addition to speeches, Pollio wrote poetry (Quint. Inst. 9.4.76; Plin. Ep. 5.3.3–5; Verg. Ecl. 3.86), a historical work in Latin (Sen. Suas. 6.24–25; FRHist 56), tragedies (T 11; Hor. Carm. 2.1; Sat. 1.10.42–43; Verg. Ecl. 8.10; cf. TrRF 1:144–45), letters, literary criticism, and philosophy (Sen. Ep. 100.9). He also established a library at Rome (Plin. HN 7.115).

T 1 Hor. *Carm.* 2.1.13–14

. . . / insigne maestis praesidium reis / et consulenti, Pollio, curiae / . . .

T 2 Sen. *Contr.* 4, *praef.* 2–3

Pollio Asinius numquam admissa multitudine declamavit, nec illi ambitio in studiis defuit; primus enim omnium Romanorum advocatis hominibus scripta sua recitavit. et inde est, quod Labienus, homo ⟨tam⟩[1] mentis quam linguae amarioris, dixit:[2] "ille triumphalis senex ἀκροάσεις suas {id est declamationes suas}[3] numquam populo commisit," sive quia parum in illis habuit fiduciam

---

[1] *suppl. Håkanson*   [2] *dixit Gertz: dicit cod.*   [3] *del. ed. Romana 1585*   suas *edd. vet.*: tuas *(ex* tua*) cod.*: tuas *codd. rec.*

174 C. ASINIUS POLLIO

*Seneca the Elder reports that Pollio was the first to re-cite his writings to a select audience and that he was a declaimer, a teacher of declamation, an eloquent orator, and a historian (T 2; Sen. Contr. 3, praef. 14–15; Suas. 6.24–25). Pollio is mentioned as a great orator (T 7; **158** T 7; Vell. Pat. 2.36.2–3; Plin. HN 7.115; Sen. Dial. 9.17.7; Plin. Ep. 1.20.4) and as one of those orators who included poetic quotations in their speeches (T 8). Ancient authori-ties note his power of invention as well as his vivid and sometimes abrupt style, different from that of Cicero (T 2–6, 12; Quint. Inst. 12.10.11); Quintilian comments on Pollio's prose rhythm (**158** T 10; cf. T 3).*

T 1 Horace, *Odes*

. . . you famous bastion of piteous defendants and of the Senate in its deliberations, Pollio . . .

T 2 Seneca the Elder, *Controversiae*

ASINIUS POLLIO never declaimed with a crowd let in; nor did he lack ambition in his studies; indeed, he was the first of all Romans to recite his writings before an invited audi-ence. And hence the remark that LABIENUS, a man of a rather sharp mind as well as tongue, made: "That old man, a former triumphator, never released his recitations {that is, his declamations} to the People.": whether because he had too little confidence in them, or—what I would rather believe—so distinguished an orator regarded this occupa-tion as unworthy of his talents and wished to get exercise

sive—quod magis crediderim—tantus orator inferius id opus ingenio suo duxit et exerceri quidem illo volebat, gloriari fastidiebat. [3] audivi autem illum et viridem et postea iam senem, cum Marcello Aesernino, nepoti suo, quasi praeciperet. audiebat illum dicentem et primum disputabat de illa parte quam Marcellus dixerat: praetermissa ostendebat, tac{i}ta[4] leviter implebat, vitiosa coarguebat; deinde dicebat partem contrariam. floridior erat aliquanto in declamando quam in agendo. illud strictum eius et asperum et nimis iratum in censendo[5] iudicium adeo cessabat, ut in multis illi venia opus esset, quae ab ipso vix impetrabatur.

[4] tac{i}ta *C. F. W. Müller*: tacita *cod.*   [5] in censendo *Jahn*: incendio suo *cod.*

T 3 Sen. *Ep.* 100.7

lege Ciceronem: compositio eius una est, servat pedem, curvatur[1] lenta et sine infamia mollis. at contra Pollionis Asinii salebrosa et exiliens et ubi minime expectes relictura. denique omnia apud Ciceronem desinunt, apud Pollionem cadunt, exceptis paucissimis quae ad certum modum et ad unum exemplar adstricta sunt.

[1] servat pedem curvatur *Rossbach*: pedem curvat *unus cod.*: servat pedem curvat *codd. rel.*: pedem servat *Haase*

T 4 Quint. *Inst.* 10.1.113

multa in Asinio Pollione inventio, summa diligentia, adeo ut quibusdam etiam nimia videatur, et consilii et animi satis: a nitore et iucunditate Ciceronis ita longe abest ut videri possit saeculo prior.

from it, but scorned to make a parade of it. [3] I heard him, however, both in his prime and afterward when already an old man, when, as it were, he was instructing Marcellus Aeserninus, his grandson. He would listen to him speaking; then at first he would argue on the side Marcellus had spoken on: he showed what had been left out, filled out what had been touched lightly, and criticized faulty passages; then he would speak on the other side. He was rather more flowery in declamation than in making speeches: that stern and harsh judgment of his, rather angry in expressing opinions, was receding to such an extent that in many respects he needed allowances made for him that were hardly to be gotten from the man himself.

T 3 Seneca, *Epistles*

Read Cicero: his composition is uniform; it keeps the rhythm, undulates flexibly, and is gentle without being degenerate. But that of Asinius Pollio, by contrast, is bumpy, jerky, and drops off where you least expect it. In the end everything comes to a close in Cicero but falls flat in Pollio, except in the very few cases that are bound by a definite rhythm and a single pattern.

T 4 Quintilian, *The Orator's Education*

In Asinius Pollio there is much power of invention, the greatest carefulness, so that it even seemed too much to some, and adequate planning and spirit: from the polish and elegance of Cicero he is so far away that he could be thought a century earlier.

391

T 5 Quint. *Inst.* 10.2.17

. . . tristes ac ieiuni Pollionem aemulantur . . .

T 6 Quint. *Inst.* 10.2.25–26

= **121** T 5.

T 7 Quint. *Inst.* 12.11.28

verum ut transeundi spes non sit, magna tamen est dignitas subsequendi. an Pollio et Messala, qui iam Cicerone
arcem tenente eloquentiae agere coeperunt, parum in vita
dignitatis habuerunt, parum ad posteros gloriae tradiderunt?

T 8 Quint. *Inst.* 1.8.10–11

denique credamus summis oratoribus, qui veterum poe-
mata vel ad fidem causarum vel ad ornamentum eloquentiae adsumunt. [11] nam praecipue quidem apud Ciceronem, frequenter tamen apud Asinium etiam et ceteros qui
sunt proximi, videmus Enni Acci Pacuvi Lucili Terenti
Caecili et aliorum inseri versus, † summa † non eruditionis
modo gratia sed etiam iucunditatis, cum poeticis voluptatibus aures a forensi asperitate respirant.

T 9 Tac. *Dial.* 17.1, 6

[APER:] sed transeo ad Latinos oratores, in quibus non
Menenium, ut puto, Agrippam, qui potest videri antiquus,
nostrorum temporum disertis anteponere soletis, sed Cic-

T 5 Quintilian, *The Orator's Education*

. . . the dreary and jejune emulate Pollio . . .

T 6 Quintilian, *The Orator's Education*

= **121** T 5.

T 7 Quintilian, *The Orator's Education*

But even if there is no hope of surpassing [the best], there is still great honor in following them. Did Pollio and Messalla [M. Valerius Messalla Corvinus (**176**)], who began to be active when Cicero occupied the commanding heights of eloquence, have too little honor in their lifetime, pass on too little fame to posterity?

T 8 Quintilian, *The Orator's Education*

Finally, let us trust the greatest orators, who adduce the poems of the early writers as a support for their cases or as an adornment of their eloquence. [11] For particularly in Cicero, but frequently also in Asinius and others who are nearest [in time], we find inserted lines from Ennius, Accius, Pacuvius, Lucilius, Terence, Caecilius and others, for the sake [?] not only of the learning shown, but also of the pleasure given, when the ears can relax from the forensic asperities through poetic delights.

T 9 Tacitus, *Dialogue on Oratory*

[APER:] But I move on to the Latin orators. Among them it is not Menenius Agrippa [Agrippa Menenius Lanatus, cos. 503 BC], I take it, who may be considered ancient, that you are in the habit of putting above good speakers of

eronem et Caesarem et Caelium et Calvum et Brutum et Asinium et Messallam: quos quid antiquis temporibus potius adscribatis quam nostris, non video. . . . [6] ex quo colligi potest et Corvinum ab illis et Asinium audiri potuisse—nam Asinius in medium usque Augusti principatum, Corvinus[1] paene ad extremum duravit . . .

[1] Asinius . . . Corvinus *Borghesi*: Corvinus . . . Asinius *codd.*

T 10 Tac. *Dial.* 12.6

[CURIATIUS MATERNUS:] plures hodie reperies, qui Ciceronis gloriam quam qui Vergili detrectent; nec ullus Asini aut Messallae liber tam inlustris est quam Medea Ovidi aut Vari Thyestes.

T 11 Tac. *Dial.* 21.7

[APER:] Asinius quoque, quamquam propioribus temporibus natus sit, videtur mihi inter Menenios et Appios studuisse. Pacuvium certe et Accium non solum tragoediis sed etiam orationibus suis expressit; adeo durus et siccus est.

T 12 Tac. *Dial.* 25.3–4
= **121** T 7.

our times, but Cicero and Caesar [C. Iulius Caesar (**121**)] and Caelius [M. Caelius Rufus (**162**)] and Calvus [C. Licinius Macer Calvus (**165**)] and Brutus [M. Iunius Brutus (**158**)] and Asinius and Messalla [M. Valerius Messalla Corvinus (**176**)]; in regard to these I do not see why you should credit them to ancient times rather than to our own. . . . [6] From that it can be inferred that they [old men around now] might have listened to Corvinus and Asinius—for Asinius lasted to the middle of Augustus' reign, Corvinus almost to the end of it . . .

T 10 Tacitus, *Dialogue on Oratory*

[CURIATIUS MATERNUS:] Today you will find more people who are ready to disparage Cicero's reputation than Virgil's; nor is there any published work of Asinius or Messalla [M. Valerius Messalla Corvinus (**176**)] so celebrated as the *Medea* of Ovid or Varius' *Thyestes* [lost Augustan tragedies].

T 11 Tacitus, *Dialogue on Oratory*

[APER:] Asinius too, although he was born in a period nearer [to our own], seems to me to have pursued his studies among people like Menenius [Agrippa Menenius Lanatus, cos. 503 BC] and Appius [Ap. Claudius Caecus (**1**)]. At all events he expressed himself with Pacuvius and Accius as his models, not only in his tragedies, but also in his speeches: so stiff and dry is he.

T 12 Tacitus, *Dialogue on Oratory*

= **121** T 7.

T 13 Tac. *Ann.* 11.6.2

meminissent C. Asinii, ⟨M.⟩[1] Messalae ac recentiorum
Arruntii et Aesernini: ad summa provectos incorrupta vita
et facundia.

[1] *add. Heinsius*

T 14 Plin. *Ep.* 6.29.5 [ad Quadratum]

sed et illud, quod vel Pollionis vel tamquam Pollionis ac-
cepi, verissimum experior: "commode agendo factum est
ut saepe agerem, saepe agendo ut minus commode," quia
scilicet adsiduitate nimia facilitas magis quam facultas, nec
fiducia sed temeritas paratur.

Against C. Porcius Cato (F 15–18)

*As a young man, Pollio prosecuted C. Porcius Cato (**136**)
in one or two cases, after the latter had been Tribune of the
People in 56 BC. Cato, defended by M. Aemilius Scaurus*

F 15 Quint. *Inst.* 12.6.1

= **121** F 16.

T 13 Tacitus, *Annals* [speech of C. Silius, cos. des. in AD 48, in the Senate]

They should remember C. Asinius, ⟨M.⟩ Messalla [M. Valerius Messalla Corvinus (**176**)], and, of the more recent ones, Arruntius [L. Arruntius, cos. AD 6] and Aeserninus [M. Claudius Marcellus Aeserninus, praet. peregr. AD 19]: they had reached the summits of their profession without a stain upon their life and eloquence [i.e., since they had appeared in court cases without any monetary incentives].

T 14 Pliny the Younger, *Letters* [to C. Ummidius Quadratus Sertorius Severus]

But I have also found by experience that this saying, which I am told is Pollio's or is attributed to Pollio, is very true: "By pleading well it happened that I pleaded often; by pleading often it happened that I did it less well." For, indeed, by excessive application fluency is produced rather than ability, and not confidence, but carelessness.

Against C. Porcius Cato (F 15–18)

(**139** F 4) and presumably also by C. Licinius Macer Calvus (**165** F 30), was acquitted (TLRR 283, 286).

F 15 Quintilian, *The Orator's Education*
= **121** F 16.

F 16 Tac. *Dial.* 34.7

= **121** F 15.

F 17 Sen. *Contr.* 7.4.7

= **165** F 30.

F 18 Cic. *Att.* 4.15.4

= **92** F 47.

On Behalf of L. Aelius Lamia (F 19)

After Cicero's death Pollio wrote and published a speech on behalf of L. Aelius Lamia, a Roman knight and friend of Cicero (Cic. Red. sen. 12; Sest. 29; Pis. 64; Fam. 11.16, 11.17, 12.29.1, 13.62). There was discussion in antiquity

F 19 Sen. *Suas.* 6.14–15

quoniam in hanc suasoriam incidimus, non alienum puto indicare, quomodo quisque se ex historicis adversus memoriam Ciceronis gesserit. nam, quin[1] Cicero nec tam timidus fuerit, ut rogaret Antonium, nec tam stultus, ut exorari posse speraret, nemo dubitat excepto Asinio Pollione, qui infestissimus famae Ciceronis permansit. et is etiam occasionem scholasticis alterius suasoriae dedit. solent enim scholastici declamitare:[2] deliberat Cicero, an salutem promittente Antonio orationes suas comburat. [15] haec inepte ficta cuilibet videri potest; Pollio vult il-

---

[1] quin *Gronovius*: que *codd.*   [2] declamitare *Bursian*: declamatores *codd.*

F 16 Tacitus, *Dialogue on Oratory*

= **121** F 15.

F 17 Seneca the Elder, *Controversiae*

= **165** F 30.

F 18 Cicero, *Letters to Atticus*

= **92** F 47.

On Behalf of L. Aelius Lamia (F 19)

*about the extent to which the published speech (not in-
cluded in Pollio's Histories) reflected the delivered version
(also in GRF, F 3, p. 497: Ex oratione pro Lamia).*

F 19 Seneca the Elder, *Suasoriae*

Since we happened to come upon this *suasoria* [i.e.,
whether Cicero should beg Antony's pardon], I believe it
is not inappropriate to point out how each of the historians
conducted himself in relation to the memory of Cicero.
For nobody doubts that Cicero was neither so fearful that
he would plead with Antony [M. Antonius (**159**)] nor so
stupid that he would hope he [Antony] could be won over,
except for Asinius Pollio, who remained the most impla-
cable enemy of Cicero's reputation. And he even gave the
people in schools of rhetoric a handle for a second *suasoria*; for the people in schools of rhetoric often declaim [on
the theme]: "Cicero deliberates whether to burn his
speeches on Antony's promising him his life." [15] That
this is a crude fiction can be seen by anyone. Pollio wants

lam veram videri; ita enim dixit in ea oratione quam pro
Lamia ‹e›didit.[3] ASINI POLLIONIS. "itaque numquam per
Ciceronem mora[4] fuit, quin eiuraret {suas esse}[5] quas cu-
pidissime effuderat orationes in Antonium; multiplicesque
numero et accuratius scriptas illis contrarias edere ac
vel{ut}[6] ipse palam pro contione recitare pollicebatur."
‹ad›ieceratque[7] his alia sordidiora multo, ut ibi facile li-
queret hoc totum adeo falsum esse, ut ne ipse quidem
Pollio in historiis suis ponere ausus sit. huic certe actioni
eius pro Lamia qui interfuerunt, negant eum haec dixisse—nec enim mentiri sub triumvirorum conscientia sus-
tinebat—sed postea composuisse.

[3] ‹e›didit *Schulting*: dedit *codd.*   [4] per Ciceronem mora
Bursian: perficere nemora (*vel* nec mora) *codd.*
[5] *del. Gronovius*   [6] *del. ed. Romana 1585*
[7] ‹ad›ieceratque *C. F. W. Müller*: ceteraque *codd.*

On Behalf of M. Aemilius Scaurus (F 20–22)

F 20 Quint. *Inst.* 6.1.21

periclitantem vero commendat dignitas et studia fortia et
susceptae bello cicatrices et nobilitas et merita maiorum.
hoc quod proxime dixi Cicero atque Asinius certatim sunt
usi, pro Scauro patre hic, ille pro filio.

it to appear as the truth; for he spoke thus in that speech on behalf of Lamia that he published. [Words of] ASINIUS POLLIO: "Therefore there was never any hesitation for Cicero to disown the speeches {as his} that he had poured out very passionately against Antony; and he promised to publish many times more speeches in the opposite sense to those and more carefully written, and even to recite them personally in public at a meeting of the People." And he had added to this other things much shabbier: thus it was easily clear at once that the whole matter was false to such an extent that even Pollio himself did not dare to put it in his *Histories*. Indeed, those who were present at his speech on behalf of Lamia deny that he said these things—for he could not sustain lying within the knowledge of the *triumviri*—but composed them later.

On Behalf of M. Aemilius Scaurus (F 20–22)

*After Octavian had come to power, Pollio spoke in support of the son of M. Aemilius Scaurus (**139**).*

F 20 Quintilian, *The Orator's Education*

As for the defendant, indeed, he gets credit from his standing, brave exploits, scars received in war, noble birth, and the services of his ancestors. This theme that I mentioned last was employed by Cicero and Asinius in competition, the former defending Scaurus the father [M. Aemilius Scaurus (**139**); cf. Crawford 1984, 198–201], the latter the son.

F 21 Quint. *Inst.* 9.2.24

illis non accedo qui schema esse existimant etiam si quid nobis ipsis dicamus inexpectatum accidisse, ut Pollio: "numquam fore credidi, iudices, ut reo Scauro ne quid in eius iudicio gratia valeret precarer."

F 22 *De dub. nom.*, *GL* V, p. 592.3–4

turtur generis masculini . . . quamvis Pollio et alii dicant turturellas.

On Behalf of Moschus Apollodoreus (F 23–24)

In a September trial, Pollio, along with the lawyer Torquatus, spoke in support of the rhetor Moschus Apollodoreus, charged with poisoning. Moschus Apollodoreus was a rhetor from Pergamum; as a Roman citizen he was called

F 23

a Hor. *Epist.* 1.5.8–10

mitte levis spes et certamina divitiarum / et Moschi causam. cras nato Caesare festus / [10] dat veniam somnumque dies . . .

F 21 Quintilian, *The Orator's Education*

I do not agree with those who believe that there is a figure even when we say that something unexpected has happened to ourselves, as Pollio [says]: "I never thought it would happen, judges, that, with Scaurus as the accused, I should find myself pleading that influence should have no weight in his trial."

F 22 Anonymous grammarian

turtur ["turtledove"], of masculine gender . . . Yet Pollio and others say *turturellae* ["little turtledoves"; feminine].[1]

  [1] This fragment has been assigned by Malcovati to this speech by conjecture; since there is no information about the context, it should rather be considered an unplaced fragment.

On Behalf of Moschus Apollodoreus (F 23–24)

Vulcacius Moschus (Tac. Ann. 4.43.5). At the trial Moschus Apollodoreus was convicted and then went into exile in Massilia (modern Marseille).

F 23

a Horace, *Epistles*

Dismiss [Torquatus] airy hopes and disputes over wealth, and Moschus' case. Tomorrow, the festal day on account of Caesar's birth [Octavian's birth in September] gives an excuse for sleeping in . . .

b Porph. in Hor. *Epist.* 1.5.9

Moschus hic Pergamenus fuit rhetor notissimus. reus ve-
neficii fuit, cuius causam ex primis tunc oratores egerunt,
Torquatus hic, de quo nunc dicit, cuius exstat oratio, et
Asinius Polio.

F 24 Sen. *Contr.* 2.5.13

novi declamatores post Moschum Apollodoreum, qui reus
veneficii[1] fuit et a Pollione Asinio defensus damnatus
Massiliae docuit, et hanc quaestionem in ha{n}c contro-
versia{m}[2] fecerunt . . .

[1] veneficii *ed. Hervageniana*: beneficii *codd.* [2] ha{n}c
controversia{m} *Schulting*: hanc controversiam *codd.*

> **On M. Claudius Marcellus Aeserninus in**
> **the Senate (F 25)**

F 25 Suet. *Aug.* 43.2

mox finem fecit talia edendi Asinio Pollione oratore gravi-
ter invidioseque in curia questo A⟨e⟩sernini[1] nepotis sui
casum, qui et ipse crus fregerat.

[1] A⟨e⟩sernini *Beroaldus*: asernini vel aserni *vel* asermini *codd.*

b Porphyrio, *Commentary on Horace*

This Moschus was a very well-known Pergamene rhetor.
He was tried for poisoning, and his case was handled by
the best orators at the time, this Torquatus, about whom
he [Horace] is now speaking [addressee of the poem],
whose speech is extant, and Asinius Pollio.

F 24 Seneca the Elder, *Controversiae*

Recent declaimers, following Moschus Apollodoreus, who
was tried for poisoning and, defended by Asinius Pollio
and convicted, taught at Massilia [modern Marseille], also
made an issue of the following point in this *controversia*
. . .

*On M. Claudius Marcellus Aeserninus in
the Senate (F 25)*

*Pollio spoke about his grandson M. Claudius Marcellus
Aeserninus (praet. peregr. AD 19) in the Senate (cf. T 2).*

F 25 Suetonius, *Life of Augustus*

Soon afterward he [Augustus] put an end to exhibiting
such performances [Game of Troy] because Asinius Pollio,
the orator, complained bitterly and angrily in the Senate
of an accident to Aeserninus, his grandson, who, likewise
[as C. Nonius Asprenas had injured himself], had himself
broken his leg.

On Behalf of Liburnia (F 26–27)

F 26 Quint. *Inst.* 9.2.34–35

ut dicta autem quaedam, ita scripta quoque fingi solent, quod facit Asinius pro Liburnia: "mater mea, quae mihi cum carissima tum dulcissima fuit, quaeque mihi vixit bisque eodem die vitam dedit" et reliqua, deinde "exheres esto." haec cum per se figura est, tum duplicatur quotiens, sicut in hac causa, ad imitationem alterius scripturae componitur. [35] nam contra recitabatur testamentum: "P. Novanius Gallio, cui ego omnia meritissimo volo et debeo pro eius animi in me summa voluntate," et adiectis deinceps aliis "heres esto": incipit esse quodam modo παρῳδή
. . .

F 27 Quint. *Inst.* 9.2.6–9

quid enim tam commune quam interrogare vel percontari? . . . [7] . . . figuratum autem quotiens non sciscitandi gratia adsumitur, sed instandi . . . [9] . . . aut instandi et auferendae dissimulationis, ut Asinius: "audisne? furiosum, inquam, non inofficiosum testamentum reprendimus."

On Behalf of Liburnia (F 26–27)

*Pollio spoke on behalf of Liburnia, along with M. Valerius Messalla Corvinus (**176** F 14; cf. Quint. Inst. 10.1.23), apparently with regard to an issue of inheritance.*

F 26 Quintilian, *The Orator's Education*

And just as some words, so writings too are often made up, which Asinius does [in the speech] on behalf of Liburnia: "My mother, who was very dear and also very close to me, who lived for me and gave me life twice on the same day" and so on; then: "shall not be an heir." This is both a figure in itself and is even doubly so when, as in the present case, it is created in imitation of a second document. [35] For on the other side the will was read out: "P. Novanius Gallio, to whom, as my greatest benefactor, I will and owe everything, in recognition of his very great goodwill toward me" and then, with other matters added, "shall be the heir": it begins to be a parody of some sort . . .

F 27 Quintilian, *The Orator's Education*

For what is so common as interrogation or questioning? . . . [7] . . . But it [a question] is figured whenever it is adduced not in order to acquire information, but to drive home a point . . . [9] . . . or in order to drive home a point and take away the chance of pretending to misunderstand, as Asinius: "Do you hear me? What we impugn, I say, is a mad, not an inequitable[1] will."[2]

---

[1] A *testamentum inofficiosum* is a legally correct, but inequitable, will.   [2] This fragment has been attributed to this speech because of its content.

On Behalf of Urbinia's Heirs (F 28–34)

F 28 Tac. *Dial.* 38.2

[CURIATIUS MATERNUS:] . . . apud quos quanto maiora negotia olim exerceri solita sint, quod maius argumentum est quam quod causae centumvirales, quae nunc primum obtinent locum, adeo splendore aliorum iudiciorum obruebantur, ut neque Ciceronis neque Caesaris neque Bruti neque Caeli neque Calvi, non denique ullius magni oratoris liber apud centumviros dictus legatur, exceptis orationibus Asini, quae pro heredibus Urbiniae[1] inscribuntur, ab ipso tamen Pollione mediis divi Augusti temporibus habitae, postquam longa temporum quies et continuum populi otium et assidua senatus tranquillitas et maxime principis disciplina ipsam quoque eloquentiam sicut omnia alia pacaverat.[2]

[1] Urbiniae *Lipsius*: urbine *vel sim. codd.*   [2] o(m)nia depacauerat *vel* omnia deparauerat *vel* omnia alia (*vel* alia omnia) pacauerat *codd.*

F 29 Quint. *Inst.* 4.1.11

etiam partis adversae patronus dabit exordio materiam, interim cum honore, si eloquentiam eius et gratiam nos timere fingendo ut ea suspecta sint iudici fecerimus, inte-

174 C. ASINIUS POLLIO

On Behalf of Urbinia's Heirs (F 28–34)

Under Augustus, Pollio spoke on behalf of Urbinia's heirs against Labienus in several speeches (F 28) amid different claims to the inheritance.

F 28 Tacitus, *Dialogue on Oratory*

[CURIATIUS MATERNUS:] . . . for the fact that considerably more important cases used to be dealt with by them [the praetors] in the past, what better proof is there than that actions before the centumviral court, which now occupy the first place, used to be so much overshadowed by the prestige of other courts that not a single speech delivered before the centumviral court is being read, by Cicero or by Caesar [C. Iulius Caesar (**121**)] or by Brutus [M. Iunius Brutus (**158**)] or by Caelius [M. Caelius Rufus (**162**)] or by Calvus [C. Licinius Macer Calvus (**165**)], or in fact by any orator of rank. The only exceptions are the speeches of Asinius that are entitled "On behalf of Urbinia's heirs," yet these were delivered by Pollio himself in the middle of the reign of the divine Augustus, after a long period of peace, the continuous idleness of the People, the continued quiescence of the Senate, and particularly the imperial system had pacified even eloquence itself, just like everything else.

F 29 Quintilian, *The Orator's Education*

The other side's advocate will also provide material for the prooemium, sometimes with honor, if, by pretending to be afraid of his eloquence and influence, we make them appear suspicious to the judge, sometimes by insult, though

rim per contumeliam, sed hoc perquam raro, ut Asinius pro Urbiniae heredibus Labienum adversarii patronum inter argumenta causae malae posuit.

F 30 Quint. *Inst.* 7.2.4–5

est et illud, quod potest videri extra haec positum, coniec-turae genus, cum de aliquo homine quaeritur quis[1] sit, ut est quaesitum contra Urbiniae heredes is qui[2] tamquam filius petebat bona Figulus esset an Sosipater. [5] nam et substantia eius sub oculos venit, ut non possit quaeri an sit, quo modo an ultra oceanum, nec quid sit nec quale sit sed quis sit. verum hoc quoque genus litis ex praeterito pendet: an hic sit ex Urbinia natus Clusinius Figulus.

[1] quis *Regius*: qui *vel* quid *codd.*   [2] is qui *Spalding*: is is qui *vel* si quis *codd.*

F 31 Quint. *Inst.* 7.2.26–27

utraque enim pars suam expositionem habet atque eam tuetur, ut in lite Urbiniana petitor dicit Clusinium Figu-lum filium Urbiniae acie victa in qua steterat fugisse, iac-tatumque casibus variis, retentum etiam a rege, tandem in Italiam ac patriam suam † marginos †[1] venisse atque ibi agnosci: Pollio contra servisse eum Pisauri dominis duo-bus, medicinam factitasse, manu missum alienae se fami-liae venali inmiscuisse, a se rogantem ut ei serviret emp-

[1] Marrucinos *Cuper*: per mangones *Kiderlin*

this is rather rare, as Asinius, [in the speech] on behalf of Urbinia's heirs, put Labienus' presence as the opponent's advocate among the arguments for the wretchedness of the case.

F 30 Quintilian, *The Orator's Education*

There is also that which may seem to be placed outside these [categories], a kind of conjecture, when the question is of the identity of some individual: for example, [in the action] against Urbinia's heirs it was asked whether the man who claimed the property as a son was Figulus or Sosipater. [5] For here even his actual person comes before the eyes, so that there can be no question about the existence (as [there is if one asks] if there is [land] beyond the Ocean), nor of definition, nor of quality, but of identity. This type of dispute, however, also depends on past events: whether this man is the Clusinius Figulus who was born as a child of Urbinia.

F 31 Quintilian, *The Orator's Education*

For both parties make their own account and maintain it. Thus in the case of Urbinia the claimant says that Clusinius Figulus, Urbinia's son, escaped after the defeat of the line of battle in which he had fought, underwent various adventures, was even kept prisoner by the king, finally returned to Italy and his home among the † Margini † [?], and was recognized there. Pollio, on the other hand, said that he had served two masters as a slave at Pisaurum [modern Pesaro on the Adriatic], practiced medicine, been manumitted, joined another slave household that was for sale, and was bought as a slave, at his own request,

tum. [27] nonne tota lis constat duarum causarum comparatione et coniectura duplici atque diversa?

F 32 Quint. *Inst.* 9.3.13

nam <in>[1] receptis etiam vulgo auctore contenti sumus, ut iam[2] evaluit "rebus agentibus," quod Pollio in Labieno damnat, et . . .

> [1] *add. Halm*   [2] ut (uti *Castiglioni*) iam *Spalding*: utinam *vel* utrum nam *codd. corr. vel suppl.*

F 33 Quint. *Inst.* 8.3.32

nec a verbis modo sed ab nominibus quoque derivata sunt quaedam, ut a Cicerone [Cic. *Att.* 9.10.6] "sullaturit," Asinio "fimbriatum" et "figulatum."

F 34 Charis., *GL* I, p. 77.14–17 = p. 98.1–5 B.

clipeus masculino genere in significatione scuti ponitur, ut Labienus ait, neutro autem genere imaginem significat. sed Asinius pro Urbiniae heredibus imaginis clipeum masculine dixit: "clipeus praetextae imaginis positus."

by him [Pollio]. [27] Does not this entire case consist of a comparison between the two causes and of two different conjectures?

F 32 Quintilian, *The Orator's Education*

For ⟨as regards⟩ accepted usages, we are content even with popular parlance as authority, as *rebus agentibus* ["with things going forward/compelling"], which Pollio condemns in Labienus, and . . . have now come to prevail . . .[1]

[1] There are, however, no real examples of this phrase in extant classical Latin.

F 33 Quintilian, *The Orator's Education*

There are some derivatives not only from words for things, but also from names, like Cicero's [*Cic. Att.* 9.10.6] *sullaturit* ["wants to do a Sulla"] and Asinius' *fimbriatus* and *figulatus* [cf. F 44].[1]

[1] The coined words are based on the proper names Fimbria and Figulus as well as on the nouns *fimbriae* ("a fringe on the border of a cloth or garment") and *figulus* ("a maker of earthenware vessels, a potter"). In this speech the second term was presumably a pun on the name Clusinius Figulus (F 30, 31).

F 34 Charisius

clipeus in masculine gender is used in the sense of *scutum* ["shield"], as Labienus says; but in the neuter gender it signifies *imago* ["portrait"]. Yet Asinius, [in the speech] on behalf of Urbinia's heirs, put *clipeus imaginis* as masculine: "a shield with a portrait in front put up."

413

On Behalf of L. Nonius Asprenas (F 35–38)

Another individual defended by Pollio (cf. F 36) was L. Nonius Asprenas, probably the senator in the Augustan period and a friend of Augustus (F 37–38). L. Nonius As-

F 35 Plin. HN 35.163–64

... at, Hercules, Vitellius in principatu suo |X̄| HS condidit patinam, cui faciendae fornax in campis exaedificata erat, quoniam eo pervenit luxuria ut etiam fictilia pluris constent quam murrina. [164] propter hanc Mucianus altero consulatu suo in conquestione exprobravit patinarum paludis Vitelli memoriae, non illa foediore cuius veneno Asprenati reo Cassius Severus accusator obiciebat interisse convivas CXXX.

F 36 Quint. Inst. 10.1.22–23

= **92** F 28.

F 37 Suet. Aug. 56.3

cum Asprenas Nonius artius ei iunctus causam veneficii accusante Cassio Severo diceret, consuluit senatum, quid officii sui putaret; cunctari enim se, ne si superesset, eripere{t}[1] legibus reum, sin deesset, destituere ac praedamnare amicum existimaretur; et consentientibus uni-

---

[1] eripere{t} *Juncker*: eriperet *codd.*

On Behalf of L. Nonius Asprenas (F 35–38)

prenas was prosecuted by Cassius Severus (Quint. Inst. *11.1.57) on a charge of poisoning.*

F 35 Pliny the Elder, *Natural History*

. . . but, by Hercules, Vitellius, in his principate [AD 69] had a dish constructed worth one million sesterces; to make that, a special furnace was built in open country, as luxury has reached such a point that even earthenware costs more than vessels made of the stone murra. [164] Because of this [dish] Mucianus [C. Licinius Mucianus, cos. II AD 70], in his second consulship, in protest, upbraided the memory of Vitellius for dishes as broad as marshes, although that [dish] was not more disgraceful than the poisoned one by which the prosecutor Cassius Severus charged the defendant Asprenas with having caused the death of 130 guests.

F 36 Quintilian, *The Orator's Education*
= **92** F 28.

F 37 Suetonius, *Life of Augustus*

When Nonius Asprenas, a rather close friend of his [Augustus], was confronting a charge of poisoning with Cassius Severus as the prosecutor, he [Augustus] asked the Senate what they thought his role should be; for he hesitated, he said, for fear that, if he should support him, he might be thought to be snatching a defendant from the laws; but, if he failed to do so, to be abandoning a friend

versis sedit in subselliis per aliquot horas, verum tacitus et
ne laudatione quidem iudiciali data.

F 38 Cass. Dio 55.4.3

φίλῳ τέ τινι δίκην φεύγοντι συνεξητάσθη, προεπικοι-
νώσας αὐτὸ τοῦτο τῇ γερουσίᾳ· καὶ ἐκεῖνόν τε ἔσωσε,
καὶ τὸν κατήγορον αὐτοῦ οὐχ ὅπως δι' ὀργῆς ἔσχε
καίπερ πάνυ πολλῇ παρρησίᾳ χρησάμενον, ἀλλὰ καὶ
εὐθυνόμενον ἐπὶ τοῖς τρόποις ἀφῆκεν, εἰπὼν ἄντικρυς[1]
ὅτι ἀναγκαία σφίσιν ἡ παρρησία αὐτοῦ διὰ τὴν τῶν
πολλῶν πονηρίαν εἴη.

[1] ἄντικρυς *quod legebatur inter* τὴν *et* τῶν, *huc transposuit*
Boissevain

Against L. Munatius Plancus (F 39)

F 39 Plin. *HN, praef.* 31

nec Plancus inlepide, cum diceretur Asinius Pollio orationes in eum parare, quae ab ipso aut libertis[1] post mortem
Planci ederentur, ne respondere posset: "cum mortuis non
nisi larvas luctari." quo dicto sic repercussit illas, ut apud
eruditos nihil impudentius iudicetur.

[1] libertis *vel* liberis *codd.*

and prejudicing his case. Then, since all agreed, he sat on the benches for several hours, but in silence and without even providing a testimonial of character in court.

F 38 Cassius Dio, *Roman History*

He [Augustus] also stood by a friend who was a defendant in a suit, after having first communicated this very matter to the Senate. And he saved him, but was so far from being angry with his accuser, though this man had indulged in the utmost frankness in his speech, that later on when the same man appeared for scrutiny of his morals, he [Augustus, as censor] acquitted him, saying openly that the other's frankness was necessary for them [the Romans] on account of the baseness of the majority.

Against L. Munatius Plancus (F 39)

*Pollio wrote a letter to L. Munatius Plancus (**149**) (Gell. NA 10.26.1) and prepared speeches against him to be published after the latter's death.*

F 39 Pliny the Elder, *Natural History*

Plancus [L. Munatius Plancus (**149**)] also put it neatly, when Asinius Pollio was said to be composing orations against him, to be published by himself or his freedmen after Plancus' death, so that he would be unable to reply: "that only phantoms fight with the dead." With this remark he dealt those orations such a blow that among the educated nothing is thought to be more shameless.

Against Antony's Insults (F 40)

F 40 Charis., *GL* I, p. 79.23–80.3 = p. 100.20–25 B.

ca⌊tinus masculino⌋[1] genere dicitur, ut . . . et hinc demi-
nutive catillus fit, ut Asinius contra maledicta Antonii:
"volitantque urbe tota catilli."

[1] catinus gen. masc. ut micenas ingere et fumantes celidum
cum ferre catinos *cod. Laudunensis de gener.*

Against Valerius (F 41)

F 41 Charis., *GL* I, p. 97.10–14 = p. 124.4–10 B.

hos pugillares et masculino genere et semper pluraliter
dicas, sicut Asinius in Valer⌊ium lib. I⌋,[1] quia pugillus est
qui plures tabellas continet in seriem sutas. at tamen haec
pugillaria saepius neutraliter dicit idem Catullus in hendecasyllabis [Catull. 42.5]. item Laber⌊ius⌋[2] ⌊in Piscatore⌋[3]
[Lab. *Mim.* 71[1] R.[2–3]] singulariter hoc pugillar dicit.

[1] *suppl. ex Cauchii ex deperdito cod. excerptis Putschen*: lib. I
et in codd. posse scriptum fuisse propter Keilium monet Barwick:
Valeriam *Cauchii ex deperdito cod. excerpta*

[2] *suppl. ex Cauchii ex deperdito cod. excerptis Putschen*

[3] *add. Cauchii et Putschenii ex deperdito cod. excerpta Beda*

Against Antony's Insults (F 40)

The piece against Antony's insults may not have been a delivered oration, but rather an edited text.

F 40 Charisius

catinus ["large bowl"] is used in the masculine gender, as . . . and hence *catillus* ["small bowl"] comes about as a diminutive, as Asinius [says] against Antony's insults: "and in the entire city small bowls flit about."

Against Valerius (F 41)

Whether the piece against Valerius, apparently the poet Catullus, is an extensive speech or a grammatical work is unclear (cf. GRF, F 5, p. 499).

F 41 Charisius

hos pugillares ["this set of writing tablets"] you should say, both in the masculine gender and always in the plural, as Asinius [does] [in his work] against Valerius, in book one, since a *pugillus* ["a handful"] is what includes several tablets sewed in sequence. But still the same Catullus says *haec pugillaria* in the neuter gender rather frequently in his hendecasyllables [Catull. 42.5]. Likewise Laberius, in *Piscator* [Lab. *Mim.* 71[1] R.[2–3]], says *hoc pugillar* in the singular.

Unplaced Fragments (F 42–48)

F 42 Quint. *Inst.* 1.6.42

= **162** F 38.

F 43 Quint. *Inst.* 9.4.132–33

neque enim accesserim Celso [Cels. *Rhet.*, F 19 Marx], qui unam quandam huic parti formam dedit et optimam compositionem esse prohoemii ut est apud Asinium dixit: "si, Caesar, ex omnibus mortalibus qui sunt ac fuerunt posset huic causae disceptator legi, non quisquam te potius optandus nobis fuit": [133] non quia negem hoc † aut †[1] bene esse compositum, sed quia legem hanc esse componendi in omnibus principiis recusem.

[1] aut *codd.*: *del. correctores cod. rec.*

F 44 Quint. *Inst.* 8.3.32

= F 33.

F 45 Charis., *GL* I, p. 62.15–17 = p. 77.19–22 B.

genetivus quoque pluralis cum ratione vectigalium faciat, auctores tamen vectigaliorum dixerunt, ut Asinius: "vectigaliorum rei publicae curam esse habendam," et . . .

Cf. **176** F 19; Macrob. *Sat.* 1.4.12.

Unplaced Fragments (F 42–48)

Some of the unplaced fragments may refer to speeches or to other works by Pollio.

F 42 Quintilian, *The Orator's Education*

= **162** F 38.

F 43 Quintilian, *The Orator's Education*

Nor should I agree with Celsus [A. Cornelius Celsus], who imposed one particular form upon this part and declared the best type of composition for the prooemium to be what can be found in Asinius [Cels. *Rhet.*, F 19 Marx]: "If, Caesar, an arbitrator for this case could have been chosen out of all the human beings who exist or have existed, nobody would have been more desirable for us than you." [133] Not because I deny that this is well composed,[1] but because I do not accept that this is the regulation for the composition of all beginnings.

[1] The text is uncertain; it seems best to delete the problematic word.

F 44 Quintilian, *The Orator's Education*

= F 33.

F 45 Charisius

The genitive plural too creates *vectigalium* ["of taxes"] according to the system, yet writers have used *vectigaliorum*, like Asinius, "attention is to be paid to taxes for the Republic," and . . .

421

F 46 Prisc., *GL* II, pp. 383.14–384.1

Asinius Pollio: "sed cum ob ea, quae speraveram dolebam, consolabar ob ea quae timui," "consolabar" passive protulit.

F 47 Prisc., *GL* II, p. 513.7–8

"nanciscor" etiam "nactum" facit absque n, ut Probo et Capro et Pollioni et Plinio placet.

F 48 *De dub. nom.*, *GL* V, p. 574.6

caminus generis masculini, sicut Pollio Asinius.

175 Q. AELIUS L. F. TUBERO

Q. Aelius Tubero (RE Aelius 156) withdrew from active advocacy and turned to the study of law (T 2) after his prosecution of Q. Ligarius (F 3–7). Tubero left writings on public and private law (T 2); he also wrote a historical work about the history of Rome (FRHist 38; on his life and the identity of the historian, see FRHist 1:361–67). Dio-

T 1 Gell. *NA* 1.22.7

M. autem Cicero in libro, qui inscriptus est *de iure civili in artem redigendo*, verba haec posuit [F 1 Garbarino]: "nec vero scientia iuris maioribus suis Q. Aelius Tubero defuit, doctrina etiam superfuit." in quo loco "superfuit" significare videtur "supra fuit et praestitit superavitque

F 46 Priscian

Asinius Pollio: "but when I was sad because of the things that I had hoped for, I was consoled because of the things that I feared," *consolabar* ["I was consoled"] he has used passively [usually deponent].

F 47 Priscian

nanciscor ["I obtain"] also creates [the participle] *nactus* without *n* [instead of *nanctus*], as approved by Probus and Caper and Pollio and Pliny.

F 48 Anonymous grammarian

caminus ["furnace"], of masculine gender, as Asinius Pollio [used it].

175 Q. AELIUS L. F. TUBERO

nysius of Halicarnassus dedicated his discussion of Thucydides to him, and Varro entitled one book of his Logistorici *after him* (Tubero de origine humana). *Ancient authors describe Tubero as a very learned man, particularly in legal matters (T 1–2).*

T 1 Gellius, *Attic Nights*

And M. Cicero, in the book that is entitled *On Reducing Civil Law to a System*, wrote these words [F 1 Garbarino]: "Indeed Q. Aelius Tubero did not fall short of his predecessors in knowledge of the law, in learning he even outstripped them." In this passage *superfuit* seems to mean "he went beyond, surpassed and outdid his predecessors

maiores suos doctrina sua superfluenti tamen et nimis abundanti"; disciplinas enim Tubero stoicas dialecticas percalluerat.

T 2 Pompon. *Dig.* 1.2.2.46

post hos Quintus[1] Tubero fuit, qui Ofilio operam dedit: fuit autem patronus[2] et transiit a causis agendis ad ius civile, maxime postquam Quintum Ligarium accusavit nec optinuit apud Gaium Caesarem. . . . Tubero doctissimus quidem habitus est iuris publici et privati et complures utriusque operis libros reliquit: sermone etiam antiquo usus affectavit scribere et ideo parum libri eius grati habentur.

[1] Quintus *Mommsen*: quoque *codd.*   [2] patronus *Mommsen*: patricius *codd.*

Against Q. Ligarius (F 3–7)

Tubero prosecuted Q. Ligarius for treason before C. Iulius Caesar (121) in 46 BC. Ligarius was found not guilty, helped by Cicero's defense (Cic. Lig.*) and Caesar's clementia. The reason for the dispute was that in the civil war Tubero's father had set off to Africa with his son, and Li-*

F 3 Quint. *Inst.* 10.1.22–23

= **92** F 28.

F 4 Quint. *Inst.* 11.1.78–80

potest evenire ut in aliis reprehendenda sint quae ipsi fecerimus, ut obicit Tubero Ligario quod in Africa fuerit

175 Q. AELIUS L. F. TUBERO

in his learning, which, however, was excessive and over-abundant"; for Tubero had come to be thoroughly versed in the discipline of Stoic dialectics.

T 2 Pomponius, *Digest*

After those [other jurists] there was Quintus Tubero, who paid attention to Ofilius [Aulus Ofilius, Roman jurist]: and he was an advocate and moved from appearing in court cases to [the study of] civil law, particularly after he had accused Quintus Ligarius and had not been successful in front of Gaius Caesar [C. Iulius Caesar (**121**)]. . . . [F 7] . . . Tubero was regarded as very learned in public and private law, and he left a number of books on both areas: using also an old-fashioned style, he aspired to write, and therefore his books are regarded as little pleasing.

Against Q. Ligarius (F 3–7)

garius had not granted the two men access to the harbor or the town. They then moved to Macedonia and partici-pated in the battle of Pharsalus in 48 BC (cf. also Cic. Lig. 24–28).

F 3 Quintilian, *The Orator's Education*

= **92** F 28.

F 4 Quintilian, *The Orator's Education*

It can happen that we have to censure in others things that we have done ourselves, as Tubero charges Ligarius with

et . . . [80] Tubero iuvenem se patri haesisse, illum a senatu[1] missum non ad bellum sed ad frumentum coemen-
dum ait, ut primum licuerit a partibus recessisse: Ligarium et perseverasse et non pro Cn. Pompeio, inter quem
et Caesarem[2] dignitatis fuerit contentio, cum salvam uterque rem publicam vellet, sed pro Iuba atque Afris inimi-
cissimis populo Romano stetisse.

[1] senatu *cod. rec.*: senatum *cod.*   [2] et c(a)esarem *cod.*
rec.: cessarem *cod.*

F 5   Quint. *Inst.* 5.13.20

. . . eaque non modo in propositionibus aut rationibus, sed
in toto genere actionis intuenda: an sit . . . inhumana, ut
Tuberonis Ligarium exulem accusantis atque id agentis ne
ei Caesar ignoscat . . .

F 6   Quint. *Inst.* 5.13.31

Tubero Ligarium accusat quod is in Africa fuerit, et que-
ritur quod ab eo ipse in Africam non sit admissus.

F 7   Pompon. *Dig.* 1.2.2.46

. . . maxime postquam Quintum Ligarium accusavit nec
optinuit apud Gaium Caesarem. is est Quintus Ligarius,
qui cum Africae oram teneret, infirmum Tuberonem ap-
plicare non permisit nec aquam haurire, quo nomine eum

having been in Africa and . . . [80] Tubero says that he, as
a young man, had accompanied his father, who had been
sent by the Senate not to make war but to buy grain, and
had abandoned that side as soon as it was possible, whereas
Ligarius had both persisted and taken the side not of Pompey [Cn. Pompeius Magnus (**111**)]—between whom and
Caesar [C. Iulius Caesar (**121**)] there was a struggle for
status, while both wanted the Republic preserved—but of
Iuba [king of Numidia] and the Africans, the bitterest
enemies of the Roman People.

F 5 Quintilian, *The Orator's Education*

. . . and those points [general principles of defining cases]
are to be considered in connection not only with the statements of a case or the reasons given, but with the whole
tenor of the pleading: whether it is [**133** F 2] . . . inhu-
mane, as in Tubero's prosecuting the exiled Ligarius and
aiming to prevent Caesar [C. Iulius Caesar (**121**)] from
pardoning him . . .

F 6 Quintilian, *The Orator's Education*

Tubero accuses Ligarius of having been in Africa and com-
plains that he himself was refused permission to enter
Africa by him.

F 7 Pomponius, *Digest*

. . . [cf. T 2] . . . particularly after he had accused Quintus
Ligarius and had not been successful in front of Gaius
Caesar [C. Iulius Caesar (**121**)]. This is the Quintus Ligarius who, when he was in charge of the coast of Africa,
did not allow Tubero, deficient in resources, to land or to

accusavit et Cicero defendit: exstat eius oratio satis pulcherrima, quae inscribitur pro Quinto Ligario.

176 M. VALERIUS MESSALLA CORVINUS

M. Valerius Messalla Corvinus (cos. 31 BC; RE Valerius 261), an opponent of C. Iulius Caesar (121), first supported M. Iunius Brutus (158) and C. Cassius Longinus. After the battle of Philippi (42 BC), he transferred to M. Antonius (159) and later moved to Octavian. Messalla fought in the battle of Actium in 31 BC and later against the Aquitani, over whom he celebrated a triumph (Tib. 1.7). Messalla became the first praefectus urbis in 26 BC (Tac. Ann. 6.11.3) and the first curator aquarum in 12 BC (Frontin. Aq. 99.4); in 2 BC he was selected by the Senate to offer Augustus the title of pater patriae (F 20). Afterward, Messalla withdrew to private life and dedicated his time to literary study (on his life see FRHist 1:463–71).

T 1 Cic. *Ad Brut.* 1.15.1–2

Messallam habes. quibus igitur litteris tam accurate scriptis adsequi possum subtilius ut explicem quae gerantur quaeque sint in re publica quam tibi is exponet qui et optime omnia novit et elegantissime expedire et deferre ad te potest? cave enim existimes, Brute (quamquam non necesse est ea me ad te quae tibi nota sunt scribere; sed tamen tantam omnium laudum excellentiam non queo silentio praeterire), cave putes probitate, constantia, cura,

get water, on account of which he [Tubero] accused him
[Ligarius] and Cicero defended him: his [Cicero's] speech,
of considerable elegance, is extant; it is entitled "On behalf
of Quintus Ligarius."

176 M. VALERIUS MESSALLA CORVINUS

*Messalla was a supporter of poets, especially of Tibullus,
and produced poetry himself: bucolic poetry in Greek*
(Catalept. *9.14*) *and light amatory verses* (Plin. Ep. *5.3.5*)
*are mentioned. Further, he wrote about grammatical mat-
ters* (T *5;* GRF, *pp. 503–7*) *and produced a historical work*
(FRHist *61*).

*In ancient sources Messalla is described as an eloquent
and polished speaker, a very industrious and exact writer,
characterized by a precise use of language* (T *1–3, 7–9;*
Quint. Inst. *12.11.28;* **158** T *7;* Vell. Pat. *2.36.2–3;* Tac.
Ann. *11.6.2;* Dial. *12.6, 17.1; cf. also* Hor. Sat. *1.10.28–30;*
Ars P. *369–71;* Ov. Pont. *2.2.49–52, 2.3.75, 3.5.7*).

T 1 Cicero, *Letters to Brutus*

Messalla is with you. Therefore, with what letters, so carefully written, could I bring about that I might explain more
precisely what is going on and what the situation is in the
Republic than he will expound them to you, he who knows
everything excellently and is able to set out and report it
to you most elegantly? For do not believe, Brutus (although there is no need for me to write to you about what
is known to you; but, still, I cannot pass over such great
excellence in all virtues in silence), do not think that in

studio rei publicae quicquam illi esse simile, ut eloquentia,
qua mirabiliter excellit, vix in eo locum ad laudandum
habere videatur. quamquam in hac ipsa sapientia‹e›[1] plus
apparet; ita gravi iudicio multaque arte se exercuit in
‹se›verissimo[2] genere dicendi. tanta autem industria est
tantumque evigilat in studio ut non maxima ingenio, quod
in eo summum est, gratia habenda videatur. [2] sed pro-
vehor amore. non enim id propositum est huic epistulae
Messallam ut laudem, praesertim ad Brutum, cui et virtus
illius non minus quam mihi nota est et haec ipsa studia
quae laudo notiora.

[1] sapientia‹e› *Faernus*: sapientia *codd.*   [2] ‹se›verissimo
Clark: verissimo *codd.*

T 2 Sen. *Contr.* 2.4.8

fuit autem Messala exactissimi ingenii in omni quidem[1]
studiorum parte, Latini utique sermonis observator dili-
gentissimus. itaque, cum audisset Latronem declaman-
tem, dixit: "sua lingua disertus est." ingenium illi concessit, sermonem obiecit.

[1] quidem *post* ingenii *codd.*: *transp. Håkanson*

T 3 Sen. *Contr.* 3, *praef.* 14–15

diligentius me tibi[1] excusarem, tamquam huic rei non essem natus, nisi scirem et Pollionem Asinium et Messalam
Corvinum et Passienum, qui nunc primo loco stat, minus

[1] diligentius me tibi *Kiessling, praeeunte Bursian* (diligentis-
sime me tibi): diligentissme sibi *cod.*

uprightness, resolution, concern, and eagerness for the
Republic there is anything similar to him, so that in his
case eloquence, in which he excels to an astonishing degree, hardly seems to have a place for praise. Yet in that
very sphere more of his good sense appears, for thus has
he trained himself in the strictest type of speaking with
serious judgment and a great deal of technical skill. He is
so industrious and so indefatigable in his studying that it
does not seem that the greatest esteem should be given to
natural ability, which is extremely great in him. [2] But I
am carried away by my affection. For it is not my purpose
in this letter to praise Messalla, especially to Brutus, to
whom his worth is no less well known than to me and those
very pursuits that I praise even better known.

T 2 Seneca the Elder, *Controversiae*

And Messalla was of the most exact mode of thinking in
every branch of study; in particular he was the most careful observer of the Latin language. Thus, when he had
heard Latro [M. Porcius Latro, *declamator* and teacher of
rhetoric] declaim, he said: "In his own language he is eloquent." He granted him talent, but criticized his expression. [continued by F 15]

T 3 Seneca the Elder, *Controversiae*

I should defend myself more carefully to you [Seneca's
son(s)], pleading that I was not born for such a thing, if I
did not know that Asinius Pollio [C. Asinius Pollio (**174**)],
Messalla Corvinus, and Passienus [Augustan orator and
declaimer, d. 9 BC], who now stands in first place, are seen

bene videri ⟨dicere⟩² quam Cestium aut Latronem. [15] utrum ergo putas hoc dicentium vitium esse an audientium? non illi peius dicunt, sed hi corruptius iudicant. pueri fere aut iuvenes scholas frequentant; hi non tantum disertissimis viris, quos paulo ante rettuli, Cestium suum praeferunt, ⟨sed etiam Ciceroni praeferrent,⟩³ nisi lapides timerent. quo tamen uno modo possunt, praeferunt; huius enim declamationes ediscunt, illius orationes non legunt nisi eas quibus Cestius rescripsit.

² dicere *suppl. H. J. Müller*   minus bene audiri *Kiessling*: minus bene audire *Shackleton Bailey*   ³ *suppl. cod. excerpt.*

T 4 Sen. *Apocol.* 10.2

[AUGUSTUS:] confugiendum est itaque ad Messallae¹ Corvini, disertissimi viri, illam sententiam: "pudet imperii."

¹ admessale *vel* ad messal(a)e (ad cresalem) *vel* adme adme sale *vel* a me ad messal(a)e *codd.*

T 5 Quint. *Inst.* 1.7.35

aut ideo minus Messala nitidus quia quosdam totos libellos non verbis modo singulis sed etiam litteris dedit?

T 6 Quint. *Inst.* 4.1.8

sed ut praecipua in hoc dicentis auctoritas, si omnis in subeundo negotio suspicio sordium aut odiorum aut ambitionis afuerit, ita quaedam in his quoque commendatio

< to speak > less well than Cestius [L. Cestius Pius] or Latro [M. Porcius Latro, *declamator* and teacher of rhetoric]. [15] Do you think this the fault of the speakers or the listeners? The former do not speak in a worse way, but the latter are judging by worse standards. Boys, usually, or youths throng the schools: they prefer their Cestius not only to the highly eloquent men whom I have just mentioned, < but would also prefer him to Cicero > if they did not fear a stoning. Yet in the one way in which they can, they prefer him; for they learn off the former's [Cestius'] declamations, and they do not read the latter's [Cicero's] speeches, except the ones to which Cestius has written replies.

T 4 Seneca the Younger, *Apocolocyntosis*

[AUGUSTUS:] Thus I must have recourse to that saying of Messalla Corvinus, a most eloquent man: "I am ashamed of my power."

T 5 Quintilian, *The Orator's Education*

Or is Messalla any less elegant for the reason that he devoted certain books in their entirety not only to individual words but even to letters [*GRF*, p. 505]?

T 6 Quintilian, *The Orator's Education*

But, while a speaker's authority is most conspicuous in that case if, in taking on a job, any suspicion of sordid motive, personal enmity, or ambition is absent, there is also a certain tacit recommendation if we claim that we are feeble,

tacita, si nos infirmos, inparatos, inpares agentium contra ingeniis dixerimus, qualia sunt pleraque Messalae prohoemia.

T 7 Quint. *Inst.* 10.1.113

at Messala nitidus et candidus et quodam modo praeferens in dicendo nobilitatem suam, viribus minor.

T 8 Quint. *Inst.* 12.10.11

= **140** T 2.

T 9 Tac. *Dial.* 18.2

= **48** T 9.

T 10 Tac. *Dial.* 20.1

[APER:] quis nunc feret oratorem de infirmitate valetudinis suae praefantem, qualia sunt fere principia Corvini?

T 11 Tac. *Dial.* 21.9

[APER:] nolo Corvinum insequi, quia non per ipsum stetit, quo minus laetitiam nitoremque nostrorum temporum exprimeret; videmus enim, quam[1] iudicio eius vis aut animi aut ingenii suffecerit.

[1] videmus enim quam *Baehrens*: uiderimus (videmus *iam Acidalius*) inquam (quam *iam unus cod. corr.*) *codd.*

unprepared, and no match for the talents of the opposing party; many of Messalla's prooemia are of this kind.

T 7 Quintilian, *The Orator's Education*

Messalla, on the other hand, is polished and lucid, and somehow displaying his aristocratic qualities in his speech, inferior in strength.

T 8 Quintilian, *The Orator's Education*

= **140 T 2**.

T 9 Tacitus, *Dialogue on Oratory*

= **48 T 9**.

T 10 Tacitus, *Dialogue on Oratory*

[APER:] Who would nowadays put up with a speaker who begins by referring to the poor state of his health, a type to which almost all the openings of Corvinus belong?

T 11 Tacitus, *Dialogue on Oratory*

[APER:] I do not wish to make an attack on Corvinus, because it was not his fault that he did not exhibit the luxuriance and the polish of our time: for we see how little the strength of his mind or of his intellectual power met the demands of his discernment.

Against Aufidia (F 12–13)

F 12 Quint. *Inst.* 10.1.22–23
= **92** F 28.

F 13 Quint. *Inst.* 6.1.20

sed saepius id est accusatoris, avertere iudicem a misera-
tione qua reus sit usurus, atque ad fortiter {ad}[1] iudican-
dum concitare. cuius loci est etiam occupare quae dicturum facturumve adversarium putes. nam et cautiores ad
custodiam suae religionis iudices facit, et gratiam respon-
suris aufert cum ea ‹quae›[2] praedicta sunt ab accusatore
iam, si pro reo ‹re›petentur,[3] non sint nova, ut † Servius
Sulpicius contra Aufidiam †[4] ne signatorum, ne ipsius
discrimen obiciatur sibi praemonet.

[1] fortiter {ad} *corrector unius cod.*: fortiter ad *cod.*   [2] *add.*
ed. Vascosania 1538   [3] ‹re›petentur *Spalding*: petentur *cod.*
   [4] Servius . . . Aufidiam *"hic tamen pro Aufidia dixit: sed causa
tam obscura ut haec non audeam rescribere, ut e.g.* Servium Sulpicium ‹Messala› (*deinde* obiciat)" *Winterbottom in app.*

Against Aufidia (F 12–13)

As a young man, Messalla spoke against Aufidia, who was defended by Ser. Sulpicius Rufus (**118** F 7–10), in what seems to have been an inheritance case.

F 12 Quintilian, *The Orator's Education*
= **92** F 28.

F 13 Quintilian, *The Orator's Education*

More often, however, it is the prosecutor's business to turn the judge away from an appeal to pity that the defendant may be about to make, and incite him to give a strong verdict. This point includes also anticipating what you think the opponent will say or do. For it both strengthens the judges' scruples about observing their oath and takes away the attractiveness of those who are going to reply, because points <that> have been anticipated by the prosecutor are then not new if they are repeated on behalf of the defendant: thus [Messalla speaking] against Aufidia warns Servius Sulpicius [Ser. Sulpicius Rufus (**118**), F 7–10] not to use against him the argument of the jeopardy of the witnesses and of [Aufidia] herself.[1]

[1] The text in the final section is corrupt and uncertain, but the sense must be what the translation indicates, on the basis of suggested conjectures.

On Herod in the Senate (F 13A)

F 13A Joseph. *BJ* 1.284
= **171** F 8.

On Behalf of Liburnia (F 14)

F 14 Fest., p. 490.31–37 L.

TABEM eam, quae faceret tabescere, apud anti|quos usur-
patam Sallustius quoque frequenter | . . . et | Corvinus[1] pro
Liburnia: "propter hanc tabem[2] atque[3] | perniciem domus
totius."

  [1] coruinus *vel* curuinius *vel* coruimus *codd.*
  [2] labem *unus cod.*   [3] ac *unus cod.*

On Behalf of Pythodorus (F 15)

On Herod in the Senate (F 13A)

*Messalla argued in the Senate for Herod to be made king of the Jews, supported by L. Sempronius Atratinus (**171** F 8).*

F 13A Josephus, *The Jewish War*

= **171** F 8.

On Behalf of Liburnia (F 14)

*Together with C. Asinius Pollio (**174** F 26–27), Messalla defended Liburnia (cf. Quint. Inst. 10.1.23).*

F 14 Festus

That kind of *tabes* ["wasting disease"] that creates *tabescere* ["waste away"], used among the ancients, Sallust also [uses] frequently [i.e., *tabes* in this particular sense] . . . and Corvinus [in the speech] on behalf of Liburnia: "because of this wasting disease and the destruction of the entire house."

On Behalf of Pythodorus (F 15)

*Pythodorus, supported by Messalla, may have been the friend of Cn. Pompeius Magnus (**111**) and a wealthy Asian (Strab. 14.1.42 [p. 649 C.]).*

F 15 Sen. *Contr.* 2.4.8

non tulit hanc contumeliam Latro et pro Pythodoro Messallae orationem disertissimam recitavit {que}[1] compositamque <cum ea suam>[2] suasoriam <de>[3] Theodoto declamavit per triduum.[4]

> [1] que (*vel* quam) *del. Winterbottom*   [2] cum ea suam *add. Håkanson* (suam *add. Schulting*)   [3] *add. Faber*
> [4] per triduum *Gronovius*: patri duum (*vel* dum) *codd.*

Some of the remarks attested for Messalla, for instance the comments in relation to Antony (F 16–17, 18), may refer to written works, not to delivered speeches (F 16 = 8 HRR;

Against Antony's Letters (F 16–17)

F 16 Charis., *GL* I, p. 129.6–8 = p. 164.4–7 B.

fretus, huius fretus . . . Messalla contra Antonii litteras: "angustiae fretus."

F 17 Plin. *HN* 33.50

Messalla orator prodidit Antonium triumvirum aureis usum vasis in omnibus obscenis desideriis, pudendo crimine etiam Cleopatrae.

---

[1] Because of its content, this remark might have been made in the piece against Antony's letters, although the work it comes from is not identified.

F 15 Seneca the Elder, *Controversiae*

[continued from T 2] Latro [M. Porcius Latro, *declamator* and teacher of rhetoric] could not bear this insult [Messalla's criticism of his language; cf. T 2], and he recited Messalla's very eloquent speech on behalf of Pythodorus, and he declaimed, matched <with that, his> *suasoria* <on> Theodotus for three days.[1]

[1] Theodotus was an adviser to King Ptolemy XIII, who had Cn. Pompeius Magnus (**111**) killed. This scenario and its consequences turned into a theme for declamations (Quint. *Inst.* 3.8.55–58).

F 17 = 10 HRR; *F 18 = 7* HRR; *F 19 = 9* HRR [Commentarii de bello civili]).

Against Antony's Letters (F 16–17)

F 16 Charisius

fretus, huius fretus ["strait, of this strait"; declined as *fretus, -us* rather than the more common *fretum, -i*] . . . Messalla [in the work] against Antony's letters: "narrow spaces of a strait."

F 17 Pliny the Elder, *Natural History*

The orator Messalla revealed that Antony, the *triumvir* [M. Antonius (**159**)], used vessels of gold for all his filthy needs, offensive behavior that even Cleopatra would have been ashamed of.[1]

On Antony's Statues (F 18)

F 18 Charis., *GL* I, p. 104.18–19 = p. 133.4–6 B.

et M. Messalla de Antonii statuis: "Armenii regis spolia gausapae."

On the Settlement of Asia's Taxes (F 19)

F 19 Charis., *GL* I, p. 146.31–35 = p. 186.9–15 B.

"vectigaliorum" Cicero ad Atticum [vol. XI, p. 167 Sjö-gren]; at enim in ratione consiliorum suorum [*FRHist* 39 F 5], sed et de lege agraria "vectigalium." at vero Varro de bibliothecis II [Varro, F 53 *GRF*] "vectigaliorum," et Asinius Pollio "vectigaliorum rei publicae curam esse habendam." vectigalium Messala, "de vectigalium Asiae constitutione" . . .

To Augustus in the Senate (F 20)

On Antony's Statues (F 18)

F 18 Charisius

And M. Messalla [in the work] on Antony's statues: "spoils of the Armenian king, woolen cloaks."

On the Settlement of Asia's Taxes (F 19)

When Messalla talks about the settlement of Asia's taxes, this may, but need not, be the main or only theme of the work, probably a speech, from which the quotation derives.

F 19 Charisius

vectigaliorum ["of taxes"; rare genitive plural], Cicero [in a letter] to Atticus [vol. XI, p. 167 Sjögren]; but in the justification of his policies [*FRHist* 39 F 5] and also [in the speeches] on the agrarian law, *vectigalium* [standard plural]. But even Varro in [his work] on libraries [Book] 2, *vectigaliorum* [Varro, F 53 GRF], and Asinius Pollio [C. Asinius Pollio (**174**), F 45] "attention is to be paid to taxes [*vectigaliorum*] for the Republic." *vectigalium* Messalla, "on the settlement of Asia's taxes" . . .

To Augustus in the Senate (F 20)

In the Senate, Messalla was the spokesperson for urging Augustus to accept the title "Father of the Country" (pater patriae) in 2 BC.

443

F 20 Suet. *Aug.* 58.1–2

patris patriae cognomen universi repentino maximoque
consensu detulerunt ei: prima plebs legatione Antium
missa; dein, quia non recipiebat, ineunti Romae spectacula frequens et laureata; mox in curia senatus, neque
decreto neque adclamatione, sed per Valerium Messalam.
[2] is mandantibus cunctis: "quod bonum," inquit, "faus-
tumque sit tibi domuique tuae, Caesar Auguste! sic enim
nos perpetuam felicitatem rei p. et laeta huic[1] precari exis-
timamus: senatus te consentiens cum populo R. consalutat
patriae patrem." cui lacrimans respondit Augustus his verbis—ipsa enim, sicut Messalae, posui—: "compos factus
votorum meorum, p. c., quid habeo aliud deos immortales
precari, quam ut hunc consensum vestrum ad ultimum
finem vitae mihi perferre liceat?"

[1] ordini *post* huic *add. Torrentius,* urbi *Oudendorpius*

*Latin Version of Hyperides' Speech on
Behalf of Phryne (F 21–22)*

*Messalla is said to have translated many Greek speeches
into Latin, including Hyperides' speech on behalf of
Phryne (F 180 Jensen). Phryne, a Greek courtesan, was
defended by the orator Hyperides when she was prose-*

F 20 Suetonius, *Life of Augustus*

The entire population proffered him [Augustus] the title of Father of the Country, with a sudden and extraordinary consensus: the commons first by a deputation sent to Antium [in Latium]; then, because he did not accept it, at Rome as he came to the performances, which they attended in throngs, wearing laurel wreaths; soon afterward the Senate in the Senate house, not by a decree or by acclamation, but through Valerius Messalla. [2] He, with all commissioning him, said: "Good fortune and divine favor attend you and your house, Caesar Augustus! For thus we feel that we are praying for lasting prosperity of the Republic and happiness for this [city (?)]. The Senate in accord with the Roman People hails you Father of the Country." To this Augustus, in tears, replied in these words—for I have given his exact words, as [I have those] of Messalla—"Having attained my highest hopes, Members of the Senate, what else have I to ask of the immortal gods than that I may retain this same unanimous approval of yours to the very end of my life?"

*Latin Version of Hyperides' Speech on
Behalf of Phryne (F 21–22)*

*cuted on a capital charge (Athen. 13 [p. 590d–e]; Ps.-Plut.
X orat. 9 [p. 849E]); this speech survives only in fragments
(F 171–80 Jensen).*

F 21 Quint. *Inst.* 10.5.2

vertere Graeca in Latinum veteres nostri oratores optimum iudicabant. . . . id Messalae placuit, multaeque sunt
ab eo scriptae ad hunc modum orationes, adeo ut etiam
cum illa Hyperidis pro Phryne difficillima Romanis subti-
litate contenderet.

F 22 Quint. *Inst.* 1.5.61

ne in a quidem atque s litteras exire temere masculina
Graeca nomina recto casu patiebantur, ideoque et apud
Caelium legimus "Pelia cincinnatus" et apud Messalam
"bene fecit Euthia" et . . .

Unplaced Fragments (F 23–27)

F 23 Sen. *Suas.* 2.17

omnia grandia probanti impositum est cognomen vel, ut
Messala ait, cognomentum, et vocari coepit Seneca Grandio.[1]

[1] Grandio *ed. Veneta*: grandia *codd.*

F 24 Quint. *Inst.* 1.6.42
= **162** F 38.

F 21 Quintilian, *The Orator's Education*

Our earlier orators thought the best exercise was translating Greek material into Latin. . . . Messalla liked this practice, and there are many speeches of this sort written by him, so much so that he even vied with the well-known delicacy of Hyperides' [speech] on behalf of Phryne, a very difficult matter for Romans.

F 22 Quintilian, *The Orator's Education*

They did not even tolerate masculine Greek names ending in the letters *a* plus *s* in the nominative without good cause, and therefore we read in Caelius [M. Caelius Rufus (**162**), F 37] *Pelia cincinnatus* ["Pelia[s] with curled hair"] and in Messalla *bene fecit Euthia* ["Euthia[s] did well"][1] and . . .

[1] This fragment is assigned to this speech since Phryne's prosecutor was called Euthias (Athen. 13 [p. 590d]).

Unplaced Fragments (F 23–27)

F 23 Seneca the Elder, *Suasoriae*

As he approved everything that was big [*grandis*], he was given a *cognomen* or, as Messalla says, a *cognomentum* [mainly found in ante-classical and archaizing writers], and came to be known as Seneca Grandio [Latin rhetorician].

F 24 Quintilian, *The Orator's Education*
= **162** F 38.

F 25 Quint. *Inst.* 8.3.34

quaedam tamen perdurant. nam et quae vetera nunc sunt fuerunt olim nova, et quaedam sunt in usu perquam recentia, ut Messala primus "reatum," "munerarium"[1] Augustus primus dixerunt {reatum nemo ante Messalam, munerarium nemo ante Augustum dixerat}.[2]

[1] munerarium *utroque loco corr. duorum codd.*: numerarium *utroque loco codd.* [2] reatum . . . dixerat *del. Regius*: ut Messala . . . dixerunt *del. Gesner*

F 26 Mar. Vict., *GL* VI, p. 9.5–6

= **158** F 33.

F 27 Comm. Cruq. ad Hor. *Sat.* 1.10.28 (p. 399)

cum versus facias. eum qui versus Lucilianos laudaverat, propterea quod Graeca Latinis admixta habeant, reprehendens interrogat, utrum tunc solum hoc faciat cum versus scribit, an etiam quando causam difficillimam Petillii de furto Capitolino perorat contra Pedium Publicolam et Messallam Corvinum, qui a Graecis vocibus ita abhorruerunt, ut Messalla χοινοβάτω,[1] Latine funambulum reddiderit ex Terentio in Hecyra; ubi ait [Ter. *Hec.* 34], funambuli eodem accessit exspectatio. fuerunt hi duo Pedius Publicola et Messalla Corvinus oratores Romae valde insignes.

[1] i.e., σχοινοβάτης

---

[1] *schoenobatēs* could be used as a loan word in Latin (cf. Iuv. 3.77) and may have been the common term in Messalla's time.

F 25 Quintilian, *The Orator's Education*

Some [words], however, do stick. For even those that are now old were once new, and some are in use that are very recent, as Messalla was the first to say *reatus* ["position of being accused"] and Augustus the first to say *munerarius* ["giver of gladiatorial shows"]. {Before Messalla nobody had said *reatus*, before Augustus nobody *munerarius*.}

F 26 Marius Victorinus

= **158** F 33.[1]

[1] This fragment is also given as F 7 in *FRHist* 61.

F 27 "Commentator Cruquianus" on Horace, *Satires*

"when you make verses." The man [the interlocutor in the poem] who had praised Lucilius' verses, because they have Greek mixed into the Latin, he [Horace] asks reproachfully whether he does this only at the time when he writes verses or also when he finishes pleading the very difficult case of Petillius on the Capitoline theft against Pedius Publicola [Q. Pedius Publicola, quaest. 41 BC] and Messalla Corvinus, who were so averse to Greek words that Messalla rendered σχοινοβάτης [*schoenobatēs*, "rope dancer"][1] as *funambulus* ["tightrope walker"] in Latin, taken from Terence in the *Hecyra*, where he says [Ter. *Hec.* 34] "the expectation of a tightrope walker came in addition [to that of boxers]." These two, Pedius Publicola and Messalla Corvinus, were very eminent orators at Rome.

INDEX OF ORATORS

451

INDEX OF ORATORS

INDEX OF ORATORS